RUSSIAN LITERATURE
IN THE BALTIC
BETWEEN
THE WORLD WARS

Temira Pachmuss

Slavica Publishers, Inc.

Slavica publishes a wide variety of textbooks and scholarly books on the languages, peoples, literatures, cultures, history, etc. of the USSR and Eastern Europe. For a complete catalog of books and journals from Slavica, with prices and ordering information, write to:

Slavica Publishers, Inc.
PO Box 14388
Columbus, Ohio 43214

ISBN: 0-89357-181-4

This book was published in 1988.

q

Printed in the United States of America.

331857

IN MEMORIAM:
TO MY PARENTS

Contents

Preface

In the few books dealing with Russian literature produced in exile, the literary output of Russian authors in the Baltic is usually omitted.[1]   A possible exception is Zinaida Shakhovskaya's *Otrazheniya* (Reflections),[2] which contains a sketchy three-page outline of Russian literature in Estonia and Latvia.   Like most other publications on Russian literature in exile, *Reflections* exists only in Russian; thus even this brief reference is inaccessible to the English-speaking reader and critic.   Ludmila Foster's *Bibliografiya russkoy zarubezhnoy literatury 1918-1968* (Bibliography of Russian Emigré Literature 1918-1968),[3] as its title indicates, likewise lists names and titles only in Russian.

The purpose of this book is to rescue from oblivion Russian authors, who lived and worked in the Baltic countries in the two decades preceding World War II, and to demonstrate their great diversity as writers.   *Russian Literature in the Baltic between the World Wars* contains materials on émigré writers whose names are missing in Soviet reference works and whose literary production has been overlooked by Western scholars.   Russian writers in the Baltic have yet to find their deserved audience of appreciative readers and scholars.   My aim has been to uncover little-known but truly gifted Russian artists in exile, and to encourage exploration into this unique literary legacy.   Hence this volume is intended to fill the gap in the exposition and analysis of Russian émigré literature in Estonia, Latvia, Lithuania, and Finland.   It seeks to show the continuity of Russian literature, ensuing from the émigrés' conscious effort to maintain a viable Russian cultural tradition abroad despite difficulty doing so after many years of exile.   To the best of my knowledge, no comparable work is available in any language.

Russian Literature brings into focus various literary genres, aesthetic credos, and individual artistic methods, all of which reveal the nature and substance of Russian cultural life in that part of the world.   The major emphasis here is on the period 1920-40, considered the apogee in the literary activity of the so-called first emigration.   Important and original Russian poets and fiction

writers discussed in this book include: Yury Ivask, Igor' Chinnov,
Vera Bulich, Boris Nartsissov, Karl von Hoerschelmann, Nikolay
Belotsvetov, Leonid Zurov, Ivan Savin, and Boris Semenov. Many
other younger poets also made their debut in the Russian press
abroad at this time. Some of them will also be covered.

The selection of works included in this volume was made
largely under the tutelage of the late Professor N. E. Andreyev, an
erudite historian of Russian literature. Included are samples of
fiction, literary criticism, reminiscences, travel notes, one-act plays,
and poetry. Where biographical information is available, a concise
biblio-biographical exposition accompanies the critical discussion of
each author's work.

In presenting only samples from the much larger context of
Russian literature in the Baltic, I am aware of the necessary
limitations of my book. The subject awaits more detailed studies
and a truly comprehensive anthology. I have attempted to
accomplish merely a fraction of this immense task. Since most of
the materials provided here are almost completely unknown to
students of Russian literature, this may well be their first
introduction to the extraordinary verse of Vera Bulich, Boris
Pravdin, Ivan Belyaev, Valmar Adams-Alexandrovsky, and Karl
von Hoerschelmann, or to some of the finest writings of Boris
Semenov, Vasily Nikiforov-Volgin, Leonid Zurov, and Ivan
Savin—literary works which testify to the vital diversity of literary
genres, to active experimentation in prosody, to aesthetic rebellion
against the artistic norms prescribed and followed in their native
land, and to the literary ferment in émigré cultural life. It is my
sincere hope that, through this volume, the reader will be better
equipped to appreciate the important contribution to world
literature made by Russian poetry and fiction outside the Soviet
Union, and more able to relate it to present-day ideas, dilemmas,
and values.

This work was not undertaken for the sole benefit of students
of Russian literature; nor is it expressly geared to those who wish
to increase their understanding and broaden their view of the
European avant-garde, but lack essential facts concerning Russian
achievements in this area of modern literature. Rather, the
essentially modern character of Russian literature in exile, its
stylistic experimentation, and its philosophical and psychological

content are clearly of more far-reaching significance within the
international content of the twentieth-century avant-garde
experience. The émigré phenomenon is not merely an isolated
addendum to contemporary literature; it is organically linked to its
development. I hope that my study will help remove not only
linguistic but even some ideological barriers (at least in the eyes of
Western readers) surrounding the edifice of Russian art and
literature in exile.[4] The book may serve historians and social
scientists who deal with Russia, and would be of particular
importance to teachers and students of English and Comparative
Literature who study Russian authors in their courses. In many
instances, the literary analyses and biographical leads provided by
Russian Literature will be the only direct source of information on
the subject available to the scholar who has not mastered the
Russian language. To summarize, the volume will be the only
comprehensive English source for émigré literature and culture as
they existed in Estonia, Latvia, Lithuania, and Finland in the
1920s and 30s.

All of the English translations were made especially for this
volume. The translation of verse attempts not only to convey
literal meaning, but to illustrate poetic quality as well—particularly
striking images, individualistic use of colors and fragrances, or
sonority. The translation attempts to reflect that fragile essence of
poetry so easily distorted or lost in translation. Since in most
instances it was not possible to convey the exact nature of the
original sound instrumentation, innovative meter, rhythm, "weight"
and accent of words in relation to one another, references are
provided for the reader who wishes to have a closer look at the
artist's themes and craftsmanship and examine the original Russian
texts.

In addition to the usual difficulties encountered in the
translation process from Russian into English—due to the
emotional and semantic richness of the Russian language, its
abundance of diminutives, and its conciseness—is the "impalpable"
quality of the literary style of each writer. There is often a
certain reticence about finishing a thought or fully expressing an
idea—so that the meaning remains hidden beyond a word or an
image, a color, or a fragrance. Other works present a linguistic
challenge, for example those of Boris Semenov whose neologisms,
"word-weaving," and recreation of the medieval style—whether in
ancient, folkloristic, or modern context—were especially difficult to

translate.   The surrealistic quality of Ivan Belyaev's style is
partially lost in translation.   As a result of the difficulty in
translating, these poets, like many other Russian avant-garde
writers in exile, have failed so far to achieve notice commensurate
with their importance to modern literature.   Moreover, they suffer
from the domination of Russian literature by its great masters.   I
hope this book will make at least an initial step toward bringing
these authors well-deserved recognition.

The translation of Russian substandard, dialect, and slang
expressions also presented difficulties.   Together with broken
sentences, *Verfremdung* effects, and speech distortions, such stylistic
matters can only be approximated by foreign equivalents.
Consequently, some passages required explanation.   In some places
word or expression not present in the original was added for
clarity.

Russian names and titles are transliterated according to the
standard rules; a few exceptions allow for more common spellings.
Any italics found in the English version are in the original text.

The book consists of four parts: Russian literature in Estonia,
in Latvia, in Lithuania, and in Finland.   The works of some who
excelled in both poetry and fiction appear in the prose section of
each country.   The individual writers are presented, for the most
part, chronologically, based on their first appearance on the literary
scene.   Another ordering factor is the artistic reputation of certain
authors.

While preparing this volume, I was fortunate to have the
advice and support of many who deserve my warmest gratitude:
the late Professor N. E. Andreyev, the late Mr. P. M. Irtel von
Brenndorff, the late S. P. Jaba, the late I. E. Saburova, Mrs. M.
A. Irtel von Brenndorff, the late Mrs. E. B. von Hoerschelmann,
the late Mr. D. D. Kusmin-Karavajeff, Mr. I. V. Bazilevsky, the
late Mr. B. A. Nartsissov, the late Professor Yury Ivask, Professor
Igor' Chinnov, Dr. D. A. Levitsky, Dr. M. E. Greene, the late Dr.
Aleksis Rannit, Dr. John H. Eberstein, Mr. K. Arensky, and Dr.
M. Grossen.   They answered many of my inquiries and supplied
me with valuable information.   Mr. B. Nartsissov, Mr. I.
Bazilevsky, and Mrs. E. von Hoerschelmann presented me with
pertinent materials from their personal archives, and the Slavic
Section of the Library of the University of Helsinki enabled me to
consult the personal archives of Vera Bulich.   I thank the
University of Illinois' Graduate Research Board, its Library, its

Russian and East European Center, and the Department of Slavic Languages and Literatures for various grants given in support of research, final preparation of the manuscript, and acquisition of necessary source materials. Finally, my sincere gratitude goes to L. H. Miller, Special Language Librarian at the University of Illnois; Professor V. I. Terras; Ms. N. V. Sinaiski, and Dr. Edward Napier for their invaluable assistance.

I assume full responsibility for all factual information and interpretation.

Temira Pachmuss
Urbana, Illinois

Great care has been taken to trace the copyright holders of all works presented in this volume. Permission has been requested even in those cases where a claim could hardly be substantiated. Special gratitude is expressed to the following poets, writers, and critics (and their literary heirs) who permitted their works to be included in my English translations: Igor' Chinnov, Yury (George) Ivask (also for Ivan Savin's short story "Drol'," and for Tamara Schmelling), Meta Irtel von Brenndorff (also for her husband, P. M. Irtel von Brenndorff), Boris Nartsissov, Irina Saburova, Ivan Bazilevsky (also for Elizabeth Roos-Bazilevsky), E. B. Hoerschelmann (for K. K. Hoerschelmann), Natalie Sinaiski (for Vasily Sinaisky), and Dr. M. Greene (for Leonid Zurov). Helsinki University Library has granted permission to use the works of Vera Bulich and those of Ivan Savin (Savolainen).

Notes

1. Gleb Struve, *Russkaya literature v izgnanii* (New York: Chekhov, 1956); *Russkaya literatura v emigratsii: sbornik statey* (Pittsburgh: University of Pittsburgh Press, 1972) and *Russkaya religiozno–filosofskaya mysl' XX veka* (Pittsburgh: University of Pittsburgh Press, 1975), both edited by N. P. Poltoratzky; Nina Berberova, *The Italics Are Mine* (New York: Harcourt, Brace, 1969); *The Bitter Air of Exile: Russian Writers in the West, 1922–72* (Berkeley: University of California Press, 1977), ed. Simon Karlinsky and Alfred Appel, Jr.; and Temira Pachmuss, *A Russian Cultural Revival: A Critical Anthology of Emigré Literature Before 1939* (Knoxville: University of Tennessee, 1981).

2. Paris: YMCA Press, 1975.

3. Boston: Hall, 1970.

4.   Unfortunately, the works of these authors are virtually unknown to the Soviet reader.   The religious and mystical views of many Russian émigré writers, their individualistic attitudes, and their impressionistic or surrealistic imagery are anathema, and thus officially proscribed in the Soviet Union.

Introduction

More than sixty years have passed since the tragic exodus of many of Russia's most eminent writers, critics, philosophers, scholars, and statesmen in the wake of the October Revolution of 1917 and the ensuing Civil War. Paris soon became the émigré capital of Russian culture, art, and literature, while important émigré centers emerged throughout Europe in the early 1920s—in Berlin, Prague, Warsaw, Belgrade, Sofia, Riga, Helsingfors (Helsinki), and Revel (Tallinn). Russian authors in exile mostly practiced the genres of the short story, the tale, the novel, travel notes, memoirs, and lyrical poetry. The basic tenets were freedom and Christian optimism.

When they realized that the new government was determined to control and direct the themes, plots, and artistic techniques of all literary works, a large number of Russian writers, artists, and poets left the Soviet Union. The emergence of a rich Russian émigré literature in Finland and the Baltic countries after October 1917 was not surprising since many Russians owned estates or summer houses in the area or worked in the Baltic region as representatives of the Russian Empire. When the Bolshevik *coup d'état* took place in 1917, families fled St. Petersburg to their residences in Estonia, Latvia, Lithuania, and Finland. Other people re-established their Baltic origin and heritage, and emigrated. In 1921-23 eminent philosophers, scholars, and statesmen—like Alexey Alexandrovich Bulatov[1] (literary pseudonym Buslay) and Ivan Mikhaylovich Gorshkov—were exiled by the Soviet government and joined their compatriots in the Baltic. Other prominent public figures who went to this area were: Pyotr Alexandrovich Bogdanov, a member of the government in Estonia formed by General Yudenich; Pyotr Nikolaevich Jakobi, formerly Under-Prosecutor for the Imperial government of Russia and prominent lawyer and member of the Senate in Latvia; the financial expert Professor Leonid Moiseevich Pumpyansky; Professor Sergey Konstantinovich Bulich, Professor N. I. Misheev, and Professor Vasily I. Sinaisky. Their example was followed by several notable

artists: Nikolay Petrovich Bogdanov-Bel'sky (a member of the
Imperial Academy of Arts), Konstantin Semyonovich Vysotsky,
S. A. Vinogradov, Baron Leonid Nikolaevich Nolde, Nikolay
Fyodorovich Root (1864-1945), and Dmitry Nikiforovich
Kaygorodov.   The ballerina Sofya Vasilyevna Fyodorova-Fokina
(1879-1963) left Petersburg as did the illustrious actress Ekaterina
Nikolaevna Roshchina-Insarova (née Pashennaya, 1883-1970); the
tenor-soloist of His Majesty's Mariinsky Theatre Dmitry Alexeevich
Smirnov (1882-1944); Yury Dmitrievich Yakovlev (1888-1938), an
actor, painter, and producer; Vasily Ilyich Likhachev (1879-1965),
stage manager and later actor in the Theatre of Nezlobin in Riga;
Maria Andreevna Vedrinskaya and N. S. Barabanov, both of the
Alexandrinsky Theatre in St. Petersburg; G. M. Terekhov, I. F.
Bulatov, and Mikhail Andreevich Dudko, the choreographer of
Solovyov-Sedov's ballet *Taras Bul'ba.*   (Dudko later returned to
the Soviet Union, where he was distinguished as an Honored
Artist.)

Few are aware that the Baltic area has produced many
significant representatives of Russian literature and has served as a
backdrop for a host of literary works in the Russian language.
While the reputation of the so-called older generation of poets and
writers—authors like Igor' Severyanin or Pyotr Pil'sky—had been
established in Russia, the "younger" generation of émigré
writers—Igor' Chinnov, Yury Ivask, Boris Nartsissov, Karl von
Hoerschelmann, Boris Semenov, Victor Tretyakov, Nikolay
Belotsvetov, Ivan Savin, Vera Bulich, Leonid Zurov, Vasily
Nikiforov-Volgin, and others—developed their talents and emerged
as important writers outside their native country and far from the
influence of older Russian writers.   Viewed against the backgound
of lost dreams and nostalgic aspirations, these fresh literary
beginnings constitute one of the most remarkable and moving
chapters in modern history.

In order to sustain and further the development of Russian as
distinct from Soviet culture, the Russian intellectual community
abroad formed a sort of positive "consipiracy."   Echoes of Russian
Symbolism, Acmeism, and Futurism can be heard in works of both
older and younger generations, but there is also ample evidence of
a common striving toward innovation.   Like the Russian modernists
at the turn of the century, Russian writers in exile advocated
freedom from the prevailing norms and rebelled against the
dogmatic treatment of art made fashionable by Belinsky,

Chernyshevsky, Dobrolyubov, Pisarev, and their disciples in the Soviet Union. In protest against the nineteenth-century radicals and their twentieth-century heirs who were intent on imposing upon the arts a social and materialistic ideology, the émigré writers openly pleaded for idealism and Christian optimism or resignation, and gave expression to a highly personal, mystico-ethical *Weltanschauung.*

One salient characteristic of literature that is written in exile, especially political exile, is its orientation toward the past. Emigré literature turns to traditions and values of yesterday to provide a measure of stability within an alien and unfriendly world. A preoccupation with the past is as evident in the works of German writers who fled the Nazi regime as it is in the writings of those who left their homeland after the Bolshevik Revolution of 1917. Indeed, some of the most poignant lines written by Russian poets in exile are addressed to their native land.

A writer in exile passes through several stages which reflect his artistic progress in the host country. Initially, he feels very much an exile or refugee and he continues to write more or less in the manner he practiced at home. Sergey Mintslov, for example, held on to the style he had developed in Lithuania and Russia. Eventually the writer begins to react to his new surroundings; his homeland fades in his memory as new impressions affect him as an artist. Not only the literature of the host country, but its civilization as well may have an impact on him and his work. Finally at home in his new country, the writer develops fluency in the host lnaguage and begins to use it creatively in his own writing. The Russian poet Vladimir Adams-Alexandrovsky, for example, later often wrote in Estonian. Though love for the native soil remains strong and frequently intensifies, émigré writers gradually regain faith in life and humanity, adopt new spiritual values, and search for new literary techniques.

Various stylistic and lingistic games responsible for the unique character of Russian literature in the Baltic also play a decisive role in the history of Russian literature in exile as a whole. Lilting, deft wordplay appears in the novels and short stories of Vladimir Nabokov and Alexey Remizov, who both published in various Baltic-Russian periodicals. Russian writers, artists, musicians, and scholars in the Baltic states maintained strong bonds of communication with the other important émigré centers throughout Europe. These links fostered creativity in all areas of art and learning in the Baltic region and have contributed to the establishment there of a unique Russian émigré culture, one distinct from (though not oblivious to) its nineteenth-century progenitor and the neighboring twentieth-century Western European cultures. Russian literature in exile was neither static nor irretrievably chained to its "mother" culture in Russia, as had been incorrectly suggested by some scholars.[2]

During the nineteenth century a number of Russia's foremost authors and poets paid extended visits to the Baltic countries, especially Estonia which often provided the setting for Russian literary works. Zhukovsky, Bestuzhev-Marlinsky, Foeth, Dostoevsky, and Leskov were inspired by Estonia, as were some other turn-of-the-century writers, Sologub, Balmont, and Leonid Andreev. An important figure of nineteenth-century Russian literature, Wilhelm Küchelbecker (1797-1846), came from Estonia and identified with the oppressed Estonian people. He was born in St. Petersburg into a family of German-speaking landowners and spent his early years at his father's Avinurme estate and at a boarding school in Võru. Küchelbecker attended the Lyceum at Tsarskoe Selo with Pushkin and later became a major poet and critic, a Decembrist, and a Siberian exile. His life, one of the sad legends of Russian literature, inspired Yury Tynyanov's remarkable historical novel *Kyukhlya* (1925). Küchelbecker's poetry repeatedly refers to the country of his youth, *Estonia rodnaya*. In a poem of 1821 written for his Estonian compatriot Baron Mikhail Rosen (1796-1873), Küchelbecker speaks with strong emotion:

> Meadows of peaceful and happy Estonia,
>> Where I did not know what sorrow was,
> Whence a jealous Fate tore us away early,
> Her lovely maidens, bright-eyed shepherdesses,
>> You will see soon, my friend!
> My countryman, when the dear ones will surround you,
>> Asking you about faraway lands,
> You will be enchanted by the familiar sounds of their speech.

Here the poet nostalgically remembers the colorful, colloquial speech of Estonian peasant girls. Later, the experience of exile in Siberia reawakens memories of Estonia, as evidenced in this poem of 1832, "The Maple Tree":

> Then, from the shores of humble Avinora,
> In the forest of my native Estonia,

I first avidly extended my glances into the distance,
Tormented by confused longings.

In "Ado: An Estonian Tale" (1824), Küchelbecker once again portrays his "native" country. The poem deals with the Estonian chieftain Ado and the German invasions of the period. Ado bravely defends his fatherland and attempts to ally it with Russian Novgorod. In this work, as elsewhere in Russian literature, the Estonians emerge as a strong, honest, and simple people continually threatened with cruel oppression by overbearing conquerors. Alexander Bestuzhev-Marlinsky (1797-1837), also a Decembrist and a friend of Pushkin, likewise used Estonia as the setting for some of his stories.

Other Russian writers who sojourned in Estonia were Anton Del'vig, Valery Bryusov, Innokenty Annensky, Alexander Blok, Boris Pil'nyak, Konstantin Sluchevsky, Alexey Remizov, Ivan Bunin, Ivan Shemelyov, and the Lithuanian Ambassador to Moscow (1918-1939) Jurgis Baltrushaitis. As a national poet of Lithuana deeply involved with the Russian Symbolist movement, Baltrushaitis occupies an unusual position in Russian literature. Another Lithuanian born poet, Georgy Ivanov, lived in Latvia and in St. Petersburg, as did his wife, the poet Irina Odoevtseva. Even Pushkin was not far from the Baltic, for his estate, Mikhaylovskoe, was close to the Estonian border of later years. Pushkin's friend Nikolay Yazykov (1803-1846), a student at the University of Dorpat (Tartu), could easily visit Mikhaylovskoe and admire the countryside that later captivated the imagination of Ivask, one of the poets considered in this book.

For almost two centuries prior to their independence in 1920, the Baltic states had been provinces of the Russian Empire. Many native-born Russians lived among the indigenous population of Latvians, Estonians, Lithuanians, and Baltic Germans. Moreover, when the new states were created, they received some genuine Russian territories. To Estonia, for example, were added the regions of Pechora, Izborsk, and Ivangorod—Pechora and Izborsk settled primarily by the Setus (German Setukesen)—as well as the Prichudye area with its pious, picturesque "Old Believers." The Setus are also settlers of a border area between Balto-Finnic and Slavic cultures and strongly influenced by the Slavs, perhaps going back to the krivichi. The monasteries of Pechora and the fortresses of Izborsk and Ivangorod are monuments of Russia's feudal period and the reign of Ivan the Terrible. Latvia absorbed part of the provinces of Pskov and Vitebsk. Thus, besides the new émigrés, a considerable native Russian population lived beyond the borders of Soviet Russia. Since they were neither Soviet citizens nor émigrés, these Baltic Russians formed a peculiar historical and political group. Though they preserved their cultural independence, they fully integrated themselves into the political and economic life of the new states. The Greek Orthodox Church in the Baltic countries was independent from the Patriarch of Moscow, and Orthodox churches and monasteries pursued their activities without interference from outside. Elementary education was compulsory for Russian children, and in the larger towns there were state-supported Russian high schools and many private institutions. Russian culture was also promoted through Russian publishing houses, literary and social organizations, and a growing number of well-attended theatre and music performances by Russian artists.

On February 2, 1920, in Tartu, an armistice was signed between the Soviet government and the Estonian authorities, recognizing Estonian independence. The period of 1920-1940 was an era of intense cultural activity for all ethnic minorities in Estonia, especially for the Russians who formed the most influential group. Russian folklore traditions and the arts flourished. Russian poets and writers in Estonia had a distinct advantage over their *émigrés confrères* elsewhere in Europe because, as Gleb Struve has pointed out, in the border regions they were surrounded by Russian "countryside" and by remnants of Russian antiquity, like the Pskovo-Pechorsky Monastery and Izborsk with the grave of Truvor.

Two Russian Orthodox monasteries were located in Estonia: the cloister Puhtitsy (Kuremäe kloster), between Parde and Rakvere, for nuns; and the Uspensky Monastery founded in the fifteenth century, which sheltered monks. The picturesque Uspensky Monastery became the religious center of Moscow Orthodoxy, and because of its historical significance and singularly beautiful architecture it attracted tourists and scholars alike. It was also known as the Pskovo-Pechorsky Monastery. Kornily, the most celebrated monk of the monastry, was executed by Tsar Ivan the Terrible in 1570. Professor V. I. Sinaisky, Sergey Vinogradov, a member of the Academy of Arts, and the writer Leonid Zurov carried on extensive archeological research in the Pskovo-Pechorsky Monastery and published their findings. Fascination with the monastery's history incited Ivask and Boris Semenov to immortalize it in their poetry. Alexander Ivanovich Makarovsky was an expert on the ancient Izborsk fortress, also interesting to tourists and scholars. Ivangorod with its impressive towers was built in the fifteenth century by Ivan III on the banks of the River Narva opposite the Livonian Castle. The fortress played a glorious role in Russian history. With its beautiful setting, the famous waterfalls, and its proximity to the colorful resort Hungerburg on the Finnish Gulf (glorified by the poet Sluchevsky), it was frequented by lovers of history and beauty. The Alexandro-Nevsky Cathedral in Tallinn was another famous ancient Russian structure.

Russian schools in Tallinn included the evening Polytechnical School, founded ty the Russian Academic Group in Estonia, and the Russian National University. The Union of Russian Educational and Philanthropic Societies in Estonia published a monthly literary journal, *Vestnik* (The Herald), with reviews of the latest publications in Russian poetry and fiction. A. A. Bulatov of *The Herald* requested that Nikolay Efremovich Andreyev (1908-1982)[3] prepare a condensed version of the six-hour course, "The Paths of Russian Literature After the Revolution," which he had taught at the Russian National University of Tallinn. The shortened version was published in a collection of essays, articles, and résumés entitled *Den' Russkogo Prosveshcheniya 1934* (The Day of Russian Enlightenment 1934), assembled in commemoration of Pushkin's birthday. Thus, close ties existed between university education and cultural activities in the Russian community. Several libraries, such as the Library of the Union of Russian Educational and Philanthropic Societies and the library of "The Russian School in Estonia" (which prior to the Revolution had belonged to the Navy Society of the Imperial Baltic Fleet), had excellent collections of books and literary journals from the nineteenth and twentieth centuries and could compete with the best libraries in the Soviet Union.

There were at that time in Tallinn six Orthodox churches, four Russian and the other two Estonian. The church choirs, renowned for their members' beautiful voices, engaged celebrities like the tenor D. A. Smirnov and the "nightingale soprano" Maria Kurenko (1890-1980). Kurenko died in the United States after a successful career in Europe. Smirnov, I. Kh. Stepanov (sobriquet Zyablik [A Finch]), a young instructor of voice at the Russian High School in Tallinn, and the composer Mikhail Fyodorovich Grivsky helped maintain the quality of Russian vocal art in Estonia.

The Russian Theatre of Tallinn likewise contributed to the

vigor of Russian culture; performances were given every evening with matinees on Sundays.   Alexander Vasilyevich Pronikov, the director of the Russian Theatre in Tallinn, expertly staged both comedies and dramas and invited actors from the Soviet Union, Latvia, Paris, and Prague to perform in Tallinn.   At that time, the Moscow Art Theatre and the Third Vakhtangov Theatre staged plays by Bulgakov, Zamyatin, Strindberg, Berger, and Dickens, all under the inspiring direction of Mikhail A. Chekhov.   Stepan Leonidovich   Kuznetsov   (1899-1932)   appeared   in   D.   S. Merezhkovsky's drama *Pavel I* (Paul I); Konstantin Nikolaevich Nezlobin (1857-1930), formerly owner of an experiemental theatre in Riga, staged plays by Sumbatov, Nemirovich-Danchenko, as well as some "scenes of the heroic national past" like *Vzyatie Izmaila* (The Capture of Izmail).   I. K. Kalugin, an actor from the Alexandrinsky Theatre, appeared as Boris Godunov in A. K. Tolstoy's trilogy *Tsar Fyodor Ioannovich* and as Tsarevich Alexey in Merezhkovsky's tragedy *Tsarevich Alexey*.   Both were staged by Illarion Nikolaevich Pevtsov who later returned to the Soviet Union and was awarded the title of People's Artist for his role as Paul I. The young Estonian actor Georgy Rakhmatov, later a well-known cinema make-up artist in Paris, played the role of Peter the Great, while Andrey Nikolaevich Kuskovsky appeared as the cunning Count Pyotr Tolstoy.   The role of the lascivious Efrosinya was played by Pronikov's wife, Kotlyarevskaya.

Tragedies, comedies, farces, vaudevilles, musicals, and operas formed the repertoire of Pronikov's theatre.   The actors Nil Ivanovich Meryansky, Katenev (later of the Theatre of Russian Drama in Riga), Zvonsky, Yury Konskin, Vladimir Alexandrovich Lyubimov (1897-?), and A. K. Trakhtenberg from the National Theatre of Nicholas II in St. Petersburg performed here.   The Estonian audience was charmed by the many renowned actors and actresses residing in Estonia and Latvia: Elizaveta Timofeevna Zhikharyova (1876-?), an actress from the Maly Theatre in St. Petersburg who returned to the Soviet Union in 1927, E. N. Roshchina-Insarova, Elena Alexandrovna Polevitskaya (1881-?), M. A. Vedrinskaya, Lidiya Nikitichna Mel'nikova (1879-1955), Liliya A. Stengel, a leading actress in both the Latvian National Theatre and the Theatre of Russian Drama in Riga, E. A. Marsheva, E. O. Bunchuk, Stella Arbenina (Baroness Meierdorf), the elegant and pensive Larisa Andreevna Gatova, who later lived in Paris and now resides in New York, Pyotr Pil'sky's beautiful wife, the talented comedian Elena Sergeevna Kuznetsova, and M. A. Kryzhanovskaya. Others residing in the Baltic were Polikarp Arsenyevich Pavlov (1885-1974) and his wife Vera Mil'tiadovna Grech (1893-1974, née Kokkinaki), both from the Moscow Academy Art Theatre, and M. Margaritova. All three later lived in Paris. The charming Maria Reinhard later appeared in Paris in "society comedies." Alexey Ivanovich Kruglov interpreted Ostrovsky's plays and sang in the church choir of Tallinn. Both A. I. Grishin and M. Ya. Muratov acted and directed and were well received by the Russian and Estonian audiences. N. F. Root and Anna Petrovna Kalashnikova designed costumes and sets for Russian plays as well as for the Estonian theatre called the "Estonia." The company produced several Russian plays by Leonid Andreev whose works were much *en vogue*[4] in the 1920s. Karl Hoerschelmann painted the scenery for Lermontov's *Demon* (The Demon) and created the settings for foreign plays staged at the "Estonia" theatre.

In the 1930s the Theatre of Russian Drama in Riga occasionally visited Tallinn for guest performances of classical and modern plays. Among the members of the cast were the brilliant comedian Yury Yakovlev, the "noble father" I. F. Bulatov, and the "heroic lovers" G. M. Terekhov and Yury Ilyich Yurovsky (1894-1959). Since the early 1920's the only permanent Russian theatre outside the Soviet borders had been the one in Riga; it had an official season with daily performances. The theatre presented the stars of the Russian stage and provided training for young Russian actors. Other ethnic groups as well were encouraged to develop appreciation for the masterpieces of Russian, foreign, and Soviet drama. The plays drew large audiences of Russians, Estonians, Germans, Jews, and even Englishmen from a small group of English families in Estonia. Performances in Tallinn took place in the large, comfortable German theatre with its rich collection of costumes.

A variety of other cultural activities developed in the Baltic. In 1921 the first National Secretary of the Russian minority in Estonia, Alexey Kirillovich Yansson, called the Pechory celebrations that commemorated Pushkin's birthday the "Day of Russian Enlightenment." This name ascribed a certain "*Kulturträger*" function to the event. Sergey Mikhaylovich Schilling, his successor, coined a new name, the "Day of Russian Culture," to emphasize the enduring ties between the Russian minority in Estonia and the Russian émigrés elsewhere in the world. On June 18-19, 1938,

impressive festivities were held in the Narva Russian Social
Assembly Hall to celebrate the "Day of Russian Culture." The
ceremony was inaugurated by S. N. Dobryshevsky, Chairman of the
Committee of Russian Cultural Activities in Estonia. Professor
Mikhail Anatolyevich Kurchinsky (d. 1939), renowned scholar at
the University of Tartu and advocate of Russian cultural autonomy
and religious freedom in Estonia, delivered a long lecture on the
great Russian cultural tradition which continued to thrive in exile.
The city of Narva—famous for its "Festival of the Russian Song"
which featured a magnificent chorus of thousands from local choirs
in various parts of Estonia—was an appropriate setting for the
celebration. Soloists and string orchestras from other cities joined
the local musicians, and the concerts were broadcast throughout the
Baltic countries, Finland, and the northern parts of the Soviet
Union. The entire celebration was conducted in Russian—even the
Estonian ministers and statesmen delivered their speeches in the
Russian language—and all participants were dressed in Russian
national costumes. After a moving religious ceremony, the
Archpriest Alexander Sakharov thanked the Estonian government
for allowing the Russians to live "in peace and prosperity."

Between the two World Wars Russian literature in the Baltic
countries blossomed, unimpeded by government or party
interferences. New literary unions, groups, publishing houses,
journals, almanacs, and newspapers appeared in an enthusiastic
response to the freedom that had been denied Russians in their
native land after the Bolshevik *coup d'état* in 1917. Russian
literature prospered and witnessed energetic experimentation in
style and methods of expression.[5] One of the more vigorous groups
in Tallinn was the "Literary Circle," active since 1896, which met
every Monday in the salon of its secretary, a cultured Russian
lady, Maria Ilyinishna Padva. The meetings were attended by
Nikolay Andreyev, Ivask, Boris Vasilyevich Pravdin (1886-1950),
Pyotr Alexandrovich Bogdanov, Georgy Ivanovich Tarasov, and
other well-known representatives of Russian belles-lettres in
Estonia. The Circle was the oldest Russian literary and social
organization in exile. In addition to presenting papers and lectures
on Russian poetry and Soviet writers (a daring venture at that
time in the Baltic countries!), the members encouraged young
writers in exile to master their native language fully and to polish
their literary style.

Andreyev, in an article published in *Chisla* (Numbers; Paris,

1930–34)[6] discussed the activities of the Circle extensively. The literary season of 1931 opened in Tallinn on September 28 with a meeting devoted to the collection *Numbers* initiated by Nikolay Otsup a year earlier. Andreyev presented an informative paper, "Russian Contemporary Literature and the Journal *Numbers*," in which he explained the journal's particular appeal to readers and critics in exile and attempted to clarify its ideological and literary image. Though critical of some aspects of *Numbers*, Andreyev praised it for its attitude toward art and for its serious interest in the problems facing Russian literature at the time. Andreyev's assumptions were openly questioned by Ivask and Bogdanov and lively discussions followed. When Andreyev had answered all his opponents' questions, the guests recited poetry by Georgy Ivanov, Nikiolay Otsup, and Boris Poplavsky, and listened to a reading of Gaito Gazdanov's short story "Maître Rueil," all published in *Numbers*. At other meetings of the "Literary Circle" similar presentations about literary life in exile were followed by heated debates. At one meeting Pyotr Pil'sky told the club his recollections of Alexander Kuprin, and Andreyev discussed Kuprin's fiction. In June 1927, the Circle organized a short story competition. The committee consisted of Tarasov, Andreyev, Pyotr Moiseevich Pil'sky, Mme Padva, and the artist Root. A young writer from Narva, Nikiforov-Volgin, won the first prize while the second went to Pavel Irtel, a poet from Tallinn. In both cases the descriptive prose was of high artistic quality and resembled the style of Ivan Bunin and Lev Tolstoy with distinct outlines, intricate effects, and harmony of poetic devices. Irtel's short story entitled "Na reyde" (On the Road) was published in *Nasha gazeta* (Our Newspaper) in July 1927.

Vladimir Sergeevich Sokolov, a teacher of Russian literature and director of the Russian High School in Narva, devoted much time to the Russian "Literary Circle" in Tallinn. He collected a large Russian library and organized the "Small Literary Circle" for his own pupils. A learned man with great pedagogical talents, he inspired the young students with his lectures and challenged them to present their own papers about Symbolism, Acmeism, Futurism, and other literary trends in Russia. With the cooperation of this student group, Sokolov staged Blok's play *Roza i krest* (The Rose and the Cross), Maykov's *Dva mira* (Two Worlds), and Tagore's *Pochta* (The Post). Urged by their teacher, Andreyev and other students wrote erudite essays to be read at the meetings of the

"Small Literary Circle." Group excursions were organized to the Pechory region and other historical sites in Estonia. Sokolov never left Estonia and died in recent years at the age of eighty. He is warmly remembered by his former students.

P. A. Bogdanov, married to an Estonian from St. Petersburg, was a member of the Union of Russian Educational and Philanthropic Societies in Estonia. Once a highly respected St. Petersburg journalist, he contributed to all the Russian newspapers in Estonia and lectured at the Russian "Literary Circle." He also appeared at public gatherings with the socio-political speeches of a typical "*narodnik*," expressing neither extreme "leftist" nor extreme "rightist" views. A pleasant, civilized, and well-read man, Bogdanov was arrested and shot by the Soviets in 1940.

Following the example of Nikolay Gumilyov in St. Petersburg, the young Russian poets and writers at the University of Tartu decided to organize their own "Tsekh poetov" (The Guild of Poets). It was formed in February 1929 by Boris Pravdin, a professor at the University of Tartu, who with inspiring and informative lectures incited his students to unite local poetic talents. Members of the "Guild of Poets" included *maîtres* Nartsissov, Ivask, Dmitry Maslov,[7] Meta Roos, Boris Dikoy (Vil'de), and Elizaveta Roos-Bazilevskaya. Olga Nartsissova and Lidiya Visnapuu[8] entered the Guild as *élèves*. Boris Taggo (Novosadov) joined in the fall of 1929. Gathering in the large apartment of their mentor Pravdin, the group read, analyzed, and criticized their own poetry. Pravdin introduced members of the Guild to the "literary novelties" arriving from Russia and the West and advised them to pay close attention to the new and picturesque use of imagery in verse. The Guild focused on Acmeism and Futurism and soon manifested two predominant tendencies: a melodious and symbolist manner represented by Bazilevskaya, Maslov, and Nartsissov; and an imaginist and futurist style manifested in the verse of Taggo and Pravdin. The Guild was closely affiliated with the "Club of Poets" in Berlin and with the "Hermitage of Poets" in Prague.

The Tartu Guild ceased to exist in 1931 when *maîtres* and *élèves* graduated from the university and left. Several former members moved to Tallinn, where in 1934 they decided to form a new "Guild of Poets" in the literary salon of Pavel Irtel. Among the new members were Karl von Hoerschelmann with his interest in religion and theology, Nikolay Andreyev, and Irina Borman.

Since they had previously met at various literary, musical, or artistic soirées of the Russian "Literary Circle" in Tallinn, they were well acquainted. The new Guild continued the practice of St. Petersburg Acmeism, emphasizing unity of form and content. Not only did the poets read their own works, but also presented papers about questions of poetic form, rhythm, rhyme, image, strophe, meter, sound "orchestration," and color. Irtel's elegiac poetry delighted all.[9] Ivask, Nartsissov, and Andreyev recalled with gratitude the efforts of both Guilds to further the poetic talents and critical acumen of their members.

The Russians in Estonia also had their own literary journals, almanacs, and newspapers. The first publication established by Russian poets and fiction writers in the country was *Nov'* (The Virgin Soil, 1928-1935, Nos. 1-8). The name referred to an intention to plant a new literary foundation in virgin soil. With fresh ideas, experimental forms, and different subject matter, this fertile soil was to produce a new kind of art, rich and vigorous. The Northern Aurora was to glow brightly. With this in mind, S. M. Shilling,[10] in 1928, took advantage of Nikolay Andreyev's visit to his parents in Tallinn, to approach him about publishing a Russian newspaper there under the title *The Virgin Soil*. Shilling guaranteed a subsidy for the newspaper and appointed Andreyev as editor of the first three issues. The first issue appeared in print in October 1928 at the celebrations of the Day of Russian Culture. Andreyev wrote the leading article "Glory to the Architects of Russian Culture"; a short story "My Younger Sister"; and an article about Lev Tolstoy, "Long Live the Whole World!" Sergey Alexandrovich Levitsky,[11] who like Andreyev studied in Prague, contributed the article "Dostoevsky From a Modern Point of View." Other poems and articles came from German Khokhlov,[12] Sergey Prokhorov,[13] Irina Kaygorodova, and Roos-Bazilevskaya. Nikolay Istomin's poem "The Day of Russian Culture" was a motto for the first issue and credo for the newspaper as a whole. The objectives, as the poem implied, lay far beyond the Russian community in Estonia. The underlying idea was that all Russians were united by their national past, the present, and their cultural heritage and aspirations.

After the enthusiastic reception of the first issue of *The Virgin Soil*, Shilling and Andreyev decided to continue their work. The second issue was met with equal warmth. Editorial responsibilities fell to Sergey Prokhorov and Konstantin Ivanovich

Gavrilov,[14] the latter presently a professor of biology and zoology in Argentina. The third issue was expanded to twelve pages, and Andreyev solicited contributions from authors who had estabished literary reputations. His invitation was eagerly accepted by the "Hermitage of Poets" in Prague. The poet Alla Golovina, F. T. Lebedev, an eminent public figure in Germany today, V. F. Mansvetov, and other well-known writers from various Western European countries began to publish in The Virgin Soil. Ivask submitted his sketch "About Blok"; Victor Semenovich Frank, later internationally known for his cultural radio programs in Russian, sent from Berlin the article "Moscow in 1830"; Andreyev supplied an informative essay about V. Nabokov's artistic works and was also responsible for the leading article "Changing Generations— Cultural Unity." He linked this article with Istomin's poem "The Day of Russian Culture" and emphasized once again the common literary heritage of all Russians. The third issue of the paper contained a new section called "The Book Shelf" which consisted of Andreyev's reviews of books submitted to the editorial office. Inspired by The Virgin Soil's success, a number of young Russian writers from Riga—Istomin, Georgy Matveev, and Alexander Alexandrovich Illyukevich—founded a Russian weekly, Nasha gazeta (Our Newspaper). Unable to compete with Riga's powerful and wealthy Segodnya (Today), Our Newspaper was discontinued after a short time. However, the desire of young Russian writers in Latvia to have their own periodical bears witness to the ferment of Russian cultural and artistic life in the Baltic countries in the late 1920s and early 1930s.

Busy with studies and work at the Charles University in Prague, Andreyev had withdrawn from the editorial board by 1931. The remainder of the editorial staff dispersed: Prokhorov left for Belgium, Kaygorodova settled in England, and Gavrilov moved to Prague. Then Pavel Mikhaylovich Irtel proposed to turn the newspaper into a journal. Shilling agreed to subsidize it, and the fourth (1932) and fifth (1933) issues of The Virgin Soil were publised as thin booklets. The fifth issue contained an article by Andreyev about Prague University's Professor Alexander Kizevetter (1866-1933). It was entitled "Poslednyaya rech' A. A. Kizevettera" (The Last Speech of A. A. Kizevetter) and signed "A Student." Meta Roos and Nartsissova[15] were among the contributors; Russian painters Evgeny Benar, Hoerschelmann, N. P. Bogdanov-Bel'sky (Riga), E. Scherbina,[16] and P. Lukin provided the illustrations.

The two volumes were not particularly successful, however, and Shilling decided against further funding. Irtel then changed *The Virgin Soil* into a literary almanac printing only works of renowned authors who were paid honoraria for their poetry and fiction. Irtel became both editor and publisher. He was assisted in his work by the "Guild of Poets" in Tallinn. Andreyev continued to submit articles about literary life in Prague and about Czech poetry, and so did the Russian writers from the "Hermitage of Poets." V. Nabokov's poem "Tolstoy" was reprinted from *Rul'* (The Rudder), and a host of well-known names from France, Germany, Yugoslavia, and Czechoslovakia now adorned the pages of *The Virgin Soil.* The almanac began to draw attention abroad[17] and received largely positive reviews.

Another Russian publication of the period was *Stary Narvsky listok* (The Old Narva Leaflet). The oldest Russian newspaper in Estonia, it was founded in Narva in 1889. It produced several original writers, like Vasily Akimovich Nikiforov-Volgin who wrote in the "lyrical key." Although he considered himself a "spiritual disciple" of Boris Zaytsev, Nikiforov-Volgin published short stories in *The Old Narva Leaflet* resembling the work of Antosha Chekhonte. He also edited the journal *Polevye tsvety* (Field Flowers; Narva, 1930, Nos. 1-2). He was shot by the Bolsheviks in Tallinn in November 1940. Contributors to *Field Flowers* were Boris Vil'de, Evgeny Klever, a poet and medical student, and Leopold Aks, author of a collection of poems in the "civic note," *Ulitsa* (The Street; Tallinn, 1937). One of Aks' most remarkable poems ("Grotesquely, spiders laugh in their corners..."), about émigré squabbles and quarrels in Estonia,[18] first appeared in *Field Flowers.*

The fiction writer Vladimir E. Gushchik[19] started an illustrated literary journal, *Gamayun* (The Bird of Sadness; Tallinn, 1925). Lacking sufficient financial support from readers, only two issues came out. Similarly, only one issue of the journal *Russky magazin* (A Russian Shop; Tallinn, 1930) appeared, edited by Ivask and Sterna L'vovna Schlifstein and financed by her dentist father Lev I. Schlifstein. Contributors were Remizov, Boris Poplavsky, Hoerschelmann, Ivask, and Sterna Schifstein. The cover illustration was provided by Hoerschelmann. Other short-lived literary journals in Estonia were the almanac *Via Sacra* (Tartu, 1922) edited by V. Bergman; *Veche* (Popular Assembly; Tallinn, 1927); *Emigrant* (The Emigré; Tallinn, 1924?), an illustrated literary

journal edited and published by S. Kol'teryan; *Knut* (The Whip;
Narva, 1925?), a humoristic and satirical weekly; the almanac *Na
chuzhbine* (In a Foreign Land; Tallinn, 1921) published by I.
Belyaev; *Oblaka* (The Clouds; Tallinn, 1920), and *Otkliki* (The
Responses; Tallinn, 1921-22), an illustrated literature and art
journal edited by Z. Promisok. V. A. Peil, the only Eurasian in
Estonia, co-edited with Gushchik *Sbornik statey o Evraziystve*
(Collected Articles on Eurasianism) in Russian. Only three issues
appeared. Peil was a student of P. N. Savitsky, attended the
Russian High School in Narva, and later studied in Prague. In
1937 he successfully defended a doctoral dissertation in the College
of Commerce at Charles University. He was arrested and shot by
the Soviets in 1940.

Alexander Eduardovich Schulz, a former army officer, was the
editor of a Russian newspaper, *Vesti dnya* (The Daily News), which
presented only the Estonian viewpoint and articles on Estonian
culture. The paper reported sports and theatre news, but
concentrated on the socio-political aspects of Estonian life. A
literary section had short stories by Hoerschelmann, articles by
Andreyev (anonymously), and poems by Irtel. *The Daily News*
was a popular and informative paper, but Schulz did not allow his
contributors to express their personal opinions. To offset this lack
of perspective, Irtel, L. M. Pumpyansky, and A. S. Izgoev (literary
pseudonym of Alexander Solomonovich Lande) circulated another
Russian daily, *Tallinnsky russky golos* (The Russian Voice in
Tallinn, 1933-36). The editor was Izgoev, the former editor of the
St. Petersburg newspaper *Rech'* (The Speech); he encouraged
contributors to voice their views freely.

One of the correspondents for *The Russian Voice in Tallinn*
was Mikhail Anatolyevich Sidorov, an active member of both the
Theosophical Circle in Tallinn and the Estonian Society of Masons.
Besides journalistic work, Sidorov produced a volume of creative
writing, *Listya* (leaves; Tallinn: Kol'tso, 1920). P. A. Bogdanov,
Professor Pumpyansky, A. P. Sorokin, lawyer I. M. Gorshkov, Irtel,
and Meta Roos worked for *The Russian Voice in Tallinn*. Irtel
and Roos also worked for *Zavtra* (Tomorrow), another short-lived
Russian newspaper in the city. The daily *Poslednie izvestiya* (The
Latest News) was edited by Rostislav Sergeevich Lyakhnitsky, a
highly respected journalist before the Revolution. Contributors
were Andreyev, Arkady Averchenko, Arkady Pukhov (who later
returned to the Soviet Union), and the prominent journalist

Mikhail Artsybashev from the Russian newspaper *Za Svobodu* (For Freedom) of Warsaw. Artsybashev was considered "the Russian conscience" by many émigrés. Others that contributed were Professor V. N. Speransky (Belgium), Boris A. Lazarevsky (Paris), Alexander Alexeevich Kondratyev (Poland), Igor' Severyanin and other "bards of the White movement," as Andreyev called them. Pyotr Pil'sky, who played a leading role in Estonian journalism before his departure to Riga in 1927, was another contributor to the newspaper. *The Latest News* focused on the problems of Russians living in Estonia. This approach led to articles by A. A. Bulatov describing the specific problems of the Pechory region and pieces by G. I. Tarasov who wrote about the Russian theatre abroad. However, *The Latest News* could not compete with *Today*, which had a much larger circulation in the major cities of Estonia.

Alexey P. Sorokin (d. 1933) published the Russian newspaper *Russky golos* (The Russian Voice; Tallinn, 1931-32). It was largely a political organ for the Russian minority in Estonia, which Sorokin represented in the Estonian Parliament. After Sorokin's death in 1933 the paper ceased publication. Another Russian newspaper concerned with political and literary questions was *Svobodnaya Rossiya* (Free Russia; Tallinn, 1919-20). The paper published the announcement of Leonid Andreev's death (September 12, 1919, in Mustamiaki, Finland) and printed T. Tamanin's short story "Why?..."[20] (issue No. 84; December 25, 1919).

A number of outstanding Russian artists also settled in Estonia: N. F. Root who taught painting at the Russian High School in Tallinn and was one of Yury Ivask's teachers; D. Kuppot, Evgeny Benar, and N. Korolyov whose works appeared in Irtel's *The Virgin Soil*; Hoerschelmann, who illustrated the cover of *The Virgin Soil*, No. 5; his wife Elizaveta Berngardovna von Hoerschelmann (d. 1984), and Irtel's wife Meta Al'fredovna Roos (b. 1904). A. A. Vladovsky enjoyed great success in Estonia as an architect and artist; he designed and supervised the construction of buildings throughout the country.[21]

A Tallinn publishing house *Bibliofil* (The Bibliophile) printed the works of Russian writers living in Estonia and the novels and poetry of some pre-revolutionary writers estabished in St. Petersburg and Moscow. Albert Org,[22] an Estonain book dealer, published three books by Remizov through *The Bibliophile*. He also issued a collection of poetry, *Shatyor* (A Tent), by Gumilyov—a man greatly admired in the Baltic countries for his strong, disciplined Acmeist verse—and several works of Vasily Nemirovich-Danchenko.

After the Peace Treaty with Soviet Russia was signed on August 1, 1920, Russian life in Latvia experienced a cultural upsurge. "Na struge slov" (In the Boat of Words) was a circle of Russian poets in Riga that counted among its members Igor' Chinnov, Mikhail Klochkov,[23] Georgy Matveev,[24] Tamara Mezhak-Schmelling, and Nikolay Belotsvetov. The circle issued a monthly journal, Mansarda (The Attic; 1930, Nos. 1-6), edited by Karapetyan, Klochkov, and Matveev. Due to a lack of readership, however, "In the Boat of Words" soon vanished. Klochkov and Matveev also edited the newspaper Povorot (The Turn, 1930); only a few issues actually materialized. Among the contributors to The Turn were two pro-Bolshevik poets, Semyon Pevzner and A. Mogil'nitsky. Both were talented and skilled in the "avant-garde" manner of the Contructivists yet without the habitual futurist devices of trans-sense language or grotesque imagery. Together, Pevzner and Mogil'nitsky authored a collection, Stikhi (Poems; Berlin: Gra., 1923). Another contributor to The Turn was the poet Gerasim Alexandrovich Levin (literary pseudonym of G. Lugin), author of the collection Tridsat' dva (Thirty-two; Berlin: Petropolis, 1931). Levin called himself a disciple of the Russian Acmeists and wrote poetry in strict accordance with Acmeist aesthetics and versification. Nikolay Otsup considered Levin's work artificial and "lifeless," but Chinnov enthusiastically praised his Thirty-two in a review for The Attic. Levin's fate remains unknown.

Perezvony (Chimes, 1925-28, Nos. 1-43), a superb, richly illustrated monthly published in Riga, was edited by Sergey Alexeevich Belotsvetov and subsidized by his brother, the educated and cultured financier Nikolay Alexeevich Belotsvetov (1862-1935). V. K. Zaytsev was in charge of the literary section, while the arts and Russian antiquity sections were entrusted to the care of Professor N. I. Misheev. Contributors were Ivan Lukash and the artists Bogdanov-Bel'sky, Vinogradov, Mstislav Valeryanovich Dobuzhinsky (1875-1957). Editorial work and printing exemplified good taste. Both Chimes and the Russian newspaper Slovo (The Word, 1925-29) were issued by the publishing house Salamander. Since Chimes' goal was to serve not only the Baltic countries, it refrained from representing a specific ideological orientation. Content varied, the many illustrations were excellent; the journal enjoyed great success. It excluded political articles and only occasionally printed brief notices, with photographs, about the life of Russian émigrés in other countries. Approximately half of the material concerned art, and the remainder focused on literature. The photographic reproductions of ancient Russian churches and cathedrals were outstanding. Each issue featured a famous Russian artist whose works were represented in color photographs. In the literary section one could find the poetry of Bal'mont, Marina Tsvetaeva, Yury Galich, Olga Dalmatova, and the fiction of "Russian-Parisian" writers like Bal'mont, Bunin, Mark Aldanov, Adamovich, Teffi, Sergey Makovsky, Remizov, Khodasevich, B. Zaytsev, Shmelyov, G. Kuznetsova, Adamovich, D. Merezhkovsky, M. Osorgin, Kuprin, A. Tolstoy, Sasha Cherny, Avgusta Damanskaya (Berlin). The beautiful, stylized short stories of Ivan Savin also appeared here. Unfortunately, *Chimes*, subscribed to primarily by readers and Russian organizations abroad, did not exist for long.

L. Kormchy (literary pseudonym of Leonard Yulianovich Korol'-Perushevich) was a well-known St. Petersburg journalist and writer of adventure stories. After the revolution he moved to Riga and edited the journal *Yuny chitatel'* (The Young Reader; 1925-26, Nos. 1-16) which, like several other publications, was subsidized by N. A. Belotsvetov. Among the works Kormchy wrote in Riga were *Bratstvo chernykh sov* (The Brotherhood of Black Owls; Riga: Salamander, 1926), *Sery domik* (A Small Gray House; Riga: Salamander, 1927?), *Geny mira* (The Genius of the World; Riga: Skhola zhizni, 1930?), and *Mir luybvi* (The World of Love; Riga: Skhola zhizni, 1930?). In the 1930s he published the ultra-right newspaper *Zavtra* (Tomorrow), his outlet for thunderous articles against Marxism-Leninism and against the "Jewish masons" responsible for all the misfortunes which had befallen his beloved Russia. For these and similar accusations, Kormchy's enemies brutally attacked him twice in the street and even threatened to kill his daughter Zoya and wife Lyubov' Konstantinovna (herself a proof reader and secretary of the newspaper *Rizhsky kuryer* [The Riga Courier, 1921-24]). Shortly before World War II, in 1939, Kormchy and his family fled to Germany where he reportedly took up the pen against the insanities of Hitler. Kormchy died in West Germany.

Today (1919-1940), another newspaper in Riga, was supported by the Russian and pro-Russian Jewish minorities. Yakov

Iosifovich Brahms (1899-1982),[25] who attended the St. Michael
Artillery School in St. Petersburg and studied law in his native
Latvia, was its first publisher. Together with Dr. V. Pollak, he
founded *Today* and its evening edition *Segodnya vecherom*
(Tonight) shortly after Latvia proclaimed its independence from the
Soviet Union. *Today's* political editor was the prominent journalist
Maxim Ippolitovich Ganfman (1873-1934), while editor-in-chief was
Mikhail Semenovich Mil'rud. Another well-known journalist, B. O.
Khariton, was in charge of *Tonight.* Initially, *Today* was no more
than a local news leaflet distributed on bicycle by Brahms; but it
soon became an influential and popular newspaper in all the Baltic
countries, and eventually even in Eastern and Western Europe. It
was read with interest in France, Germany, Poland, and
Czechoslovakia. *Today's* luxurious editorial offices as well as its
printing house, established by D. Kopylevich, were located on
Mel'nichnaya ultisa, one of the more elegant streets in Riga.
Leonid Zurov was secretary until he departed for Paris in 1929.
Contributors were Pyotr Pil'sky and the majority of the leading
Russian writers in exile: Zinaida Hippius, Merezhkovsky, Bunin,
Bal'mont, Boris Zaytsev, Shmelyov, Teffi, Don Aminado, V. Sirin,
A. Tolstoy, Odoevtseva, and others. Andrey Sedykh, presently the
editor of *Novoe russkoe slovo* (The New Russian Word) in New
York, once worked as a French correspondent for *Today*. Vladimir
Nabokov's "A Matter of Chance," now included in the collection
Tyrants Destroyed and Other Stories,[26] first appeared in the June
22, 1924, issue of *Today*. With the exception of those holding
extreme "right"-or "left"-wing views, all Russian writers, poets,
and journalists in exile were welcome to submit their works. All
over the Baltic countries Russian readers bought *Today* rather than
their own local newspaper because *Today* contained more
informative articles and printed the literary works of such
illustrious writers as Zinaida Hippius, Bunin, Teffi, and
Merezhkovsky. Because of the popularity of *Today*, other Russian
newspapers, like *The Latest News*, could not compete and suffered
severe financial losses. In the spring of 1927 a new Russian
periodical, *Nasha gazeta* (Our Newspaper), appeared in Estonia. It
was published by Pavel Irtel and edited by P. Khudyakov, former
editor of a St. Petersburg newspaper, *Kopeyka* (Copec). Articles
were provided by L. M. Pumpyansky who was interested in
Russian social matters, and by Professor M. A. Kurchinsky of the
University of Tartu. *Our Newspaper* further aggravated the

financial difficulties of *The Latest News.*

Today issued two literary supplements, the journals *Dlya vsekh* (For Every Reader, 1942-44; Nos. 1-6; published by *Russky vestnik* [The Russian Herald]) and *Dlya vas* (For You); both enjoyed financial success. *For You,* an illustrated weekly that competed with the Parisian *Illyustrirovannaya Rossiya* (Russian Illustrated), appeared from December 24, 1933, until June 27, 1940 (Nos. 1-270). It was edited by R. G. Rubinstein and Anatoly Kuzmich Perov. In her reminiscences published in *Russkaya mysl'* (Russian Thought; Paris),[27] the poet Irina Odoevtseva remarked that *Today* formed the solid foundations on which Russian cultural life in Latvia rested. When the Soviet army invaded Latvia on June 17, 1940, Mil'rud and Khariton, the editors of *Today,* were arrested, deported to the Narym region with thousands of others, and executed. A third editor, Levin, allowed to stay on for a while to instruct the new editor-in-chief, soon met with the same fate as his colleagues. The Soviets appointed Rappoport, a Communist who had been imprisoned by the Latvian government, as chief of the new editorial staff. For a short time the paper was called the *Russian Gazette,* then the *Labor Gazette*; it was eventually given the name *Proletarskaya pravda* (Proletarian Truth). More than half of the original contributors were either arrested or fired.

One of *Today's* very first editors in 1919 had been the talented St. Petersburg journalist Nikolay Grigoryevich Berezhansky (Kozyrev). Not on good terms with Yakov Brahms, Berezhansky did not hold the job for long, and eventually moved to Berlin. But in 1925 Berezhansky returned to Riga and joined Ivan Lukash as editor of the other daily published by *The Salamander* and subsidized by Belotsvetov, *The Word.* Among the contributors were prominent Russian émigré writers Bunin, Artsybashev, Amfiteatrov, Zaytsev, Remizov, Kuprin, V. Sirin, Shmelyov, V. Burtsev, A. Ksyunin, S. Yablonovsky, A. Tyrkova, and S. Krechetov. *The Word* also included the contributions of Russian scientists, statesmen, and deputies of the Latvian Parliament (*Seim*) like Sergey Ivanovich Trofimov, M. A. Kallistratov, and the pedagogue E. M. Tikhonitsky. Richly illustrated with photographs, *The Word* resembled a periodical; but, like a newspaper, it had a large number of foreign correspondents throughout Western Europe, the Balkan countries, the United States, and Asia. It was popular in Russian émigré communities all over the world.

When Lukash moved to Paris to work with A. O. Gukasov
on the editorial board of *La Renaissance*, Berezhansky supervised
The Word until he returned to Berlin in 1929, signalling the end of
The Word. In Berlin Berezhansky edited three literary almanacs:
Russkaya derevnya (The Russian Village; Berlin: Dyak, 1924),
Russkaya zhenshchina (The Russian Woman; Berlin: Dyak, 1924),
and *Moskva* (Moscow; Berlin: Dyak, 1925).   He also published
several historical sketches in the journal *Istorik i sovremennik* (The
Historian and His Contemporary; Berlin, 1922, No. 1; 1923, No. 4).
In Riga his short stories appeared in *Chimes* and other Russian
periodicals.   As a member of the "Commission for Collecting and
Studying Folklore in Latvia," Berezhansky submitted essays on
folklore to the Commission, to the illustrated weekly *Russkoe ekho*
(The Russian Echo; edited by B. Orechkin, Prague, 1922? Berlin,
1925?   Lukash also wrote for it), and to the Russian weekly in
Riga *Nash ogonyok* (Our Small Light; 1923-28), edited by   V.
Vasilyev.   Irina Saburova and Alexander Perfilyev appeared in this
journal.

Other Russian journals in Riga included an illustrated weekly
of literature, politics, and art, *Novaya niva* (The New Field; Riga,
1926-27, Nos. 1-58; Paris, 1927, Nos. 6-15; Riga, 1927, Nos.
15-30); the critical and bibliographical monthly *Literatura i zhizn'*
(Literature and Life; 1928), edited by Pyotr Pil'sky and V.
Gadalin, of which only three issues appeared; and *Rodnaya Starina*
(National Antiquity), an illustrated bi-monthly journal (1928-30,
Nos. 1-9) specifically concerned with the archives of the Russian
Old Believers.   It was sponsored by the Youth Circle of the Old
Believers in Riga who called themselves "Zealots of Antiquity."   Its
goal was to engender an interest in religious ideas and religious art.
Editor-in-chief of *National Antiquity* was Anastasiy Smeils; the
editorial board consisted of Ivan N. Zavoloko, Konstantin Portnov,
Alexander Fomichev, and Konstantin Paldov.   Zavoloko, a highly
cultured and noble-minded man, was chairman of the Latvian
Society of Old Believers and at some point also secretary of *The
Word*.   He was arrested by the Soviet police in 1940 and sent to a
labor camp in the USSR.   He recently died in Latvia.

A host of other journals and newspapers, though many of
them short-lived, represented Russian thought and culture in
Latvia: the weekly *Iks* (The X; Riga, 1923) which came as a
supplement of the newspaper *Today*; the illustrated weekly *Iskry*
(Sparks; Riga, 1924, Nos. 1-5, published and edited by D.

Tsymlov); *Plyazh* (The Beach; Riga, 1923-25), a humoristic weekly, edited and published by G. Eydrigevich; *Satir* (The Satyr; Riga, 1920?), a humor-yearbook collected by the students of the Russian Polytechnic School; *Teatr i zhizn'* (Theater and Life; Riga, 1920, Nos. 1-12); the bi-monthly *Teatr i muzyka* (Theater and Music; Riga, 1922), edited by V. Vitvitskaya; the monthly *Ugolok literatury i zhizni* (The Cozy Corner of Literature and Life; Rezhitsa, 1920-22); *Mir* (The World; Riga, 1923-24, Nos. 1-3), an illustrated literary journal; the Bielorussian journal *Na chuzbine* (In a Foreign Land; Riga: Cakavik, 1920); *Novaya nedelya* (The New Week; Riga, 1925-27), another illustrated literary journal edited by N. I. Misheev; the journal *Rodina* (The Motherland), edited by Misheev and subsidized by N. A. Belotsvetov; *Dvinsky golos* (The Voice of Dvinsk; Dvinsk 1921-25?), edited by N. K. Savkov; *Gost'* (The Guest; Riga, 1923-28); *Nord-Ost* (The Northeast; Riga, 1931), a journal of literature and art. *The Riga Courier* was published and edited by the Russian journalist Donat Osipovich Zaborovsky, at one time a professor of Russian at the Military Academy in Rome. Mikhail Mironov (literary pseudonym Tsvik), a feuilleton writer, and Perfilyev contributed to *The Riga Courier* when Kormchy was in charge of the literary section. *Novy put'* (The New Direction; Riga, 1921-22), appearing daily, was edited by Grodzensky, and printed the works of P. Pertsov, A. Blok, and E. Zamaytin. In 1922, however, *The New Direction* was branded a pro-Communist publication and was closed by order of the Latvian government. *Vechernee vremya* (Evening Times; Riga, 1924-?), another daily, had great success and accepted contributions from Kormchy and Neo-Silvester (literary psuedonym of Genrikh Ivanovich Grossen). It was eventually acquired by Nikolay Belotsvetov and renamed *The Word*, the newspaper discussed earlier. Belotsvetov—a Russian patriot, idealist, and patron of the arts and literature—also generously subsidized the Russian theatre and various educational institutions in Latvia.

Amid several large Russian publishing houses in Riga, the most important by far was *The Salamander*. This powerful organization published the richly illustrated journal *Chimes*, Zurov's novel *Otchina* (Fatherland, 1928) and his collection of short stories *Kadet* (The Cadet, 1928), and the works of many other Russian authors. *Novosti illyustrirovannoy literatury* (Novelties of Illustrated Literature) was owned by the Rassen brothers. There was also the Didkovsky publishers; *Gramatu Draugs*, a large Latvian publishing house that printed Russian books; and various others.

Russian cultural life in Latvia was vigorous and fruitful because the Russian minority population enjoyed freedom and cultural autonomy. Like the Russian minority in Estonia, they had Russian churches and schools, Russian representatives in the Latvian Parliament (for example, Melenty Arkhipovich Kallistratov), Russian businesses, and movies. There was a Russian hospital, the Society of Russian Physicians, and the Russian Drama Theatre. The Theatre presented renowned Russian actors like V. I. Likhachev, N. S. Barabanov, and M. A. Vedrinskaya.[28] The Russian Drama Theatre in Riga had daily performances for some twenty years. Appearing in leading roles were: E. P. Studentsov, Elizaveta Timofeevna Zhikharyova (1875-?), Pavel Nikolaevich Orlenev (1869-1932), G. A. Gerasimov, E. A. Polevitskaya (she returned in 1955 to the Soviet Union after many years in Vienna where her husband Ivan Fyodorovich Schmidt was a producer at the Burgtheater), and Maria Nikolaevna Germanova and Elena Mavrikievna Granovskaya, both from the Moscow Academy Art Theatre. Guest performances at the Theatre were given by Vasily Ivanovich Kachalov (1875-1948), P. A. Pavlov, and V. M. Grech. Fyodor Shalyapin sang in the Latvian National Opera, while composer A. Glazunov conducted the orchestra during performances of his own ballet *Raymonda*. The Don Cossacks Choir also performed in Latvia. Riga was also the home of the People's Theatre (Elena Andrusova[28] played here), owned and directed by the beautiful actress Kirsanova-Kreisler; the Chamber Theatre, founded and directed by the celebrated actress of the Alexandrinsky Theatre in St. Petersburg Roshchina-Insarova, who later lived in Paris;[28] and the Latvian National Theatre, formerly the Theatre of Nezlobin, with its own company of Latvian actors. The National Theatre occupied a building in the center of the city complete with all the necessary technical equipment. The Artistic and Dramatic Circle in Liepāja (Libava) was directed by Elena Alexandrovna Revid. It engaged actors from various artistic groups in St. Petersburg, among them Ivan G. Eberstein, to act in plays by Ibsen and Ostrovsky.

The Russian producer Pyotr Ivanovich Mel'nikov (1870-1940), a close friend of Fyodor Shalyapin, worked in the Latvian National Opera striving to continue the cultural tradition of the Mariinsky Opera in St. Petersburg. In the same theatre, the ballerina S. V. Fyodorova-Fokina perfected the classical ballet and revived

memories of the glittering Northern Russian capital. Vera
Likhacheva (pseudonym of Vera Petrovna Jakobi), who now directs
her own ballet school in Morocco, danced in the classical repertoire
of the Russian ballet. The tenor D. A. Smirnov sang with the
Latvian National Opera periodically, appearing in the operas of
Tschaikovsky, Rimsky-Korsakov, and Moussorgsky. Producer of
the Latvian Art Theatre was Mikhail Chekhov. In 1922 M. M.
Fokin, former director of the Troitsky Theatre in St. Petersburg,
arrived in Riga and became active in the Russian theatrical life of
Latvia. Alexander A. Ritter, a well-known St. Petersburg patron
of Russian classical ballet, delivered lectures, with illustrations,
about the exquisite dancing of four stars of the Mariinsky Theatre:
Anna Pavlova, M. Kshesinskaya, O. Preobrazhenskaya, and Tamara
Karsavina.

Private music schools directed by competent Russian
musicians included: Pastukhov's Conservatory for Piano, Maevsky's
School of Music, and the Singing School directed by Professor
Iretsky-Aksern, Zherebtsova-Andreeva, and other experienced
teachers. Choral singing was taught at the musical society *Bayan*
(The Accordion), which performed Russian operas rich in choral
parts—like Rimsky-Korsakov's *Skazka o tsare Saltane* (The Fairy
Tale of Tsar Sultan). The chorus of *The Accordion* appeared in
the National Opera's production of Moussorgsky's *Boris Godunov.*
As in Estonia, Russian school choirs in Latvia participated in
celebrating the Day of Russian Culture. Lomonosov's Russian High
School had a brass band and folk orchestra chorus, and offered
classes in piano, violin, and vocal singing. All these activities
further enhanced the development of Russian cultural life in Latvia.
Guest performances by such celebrities as the pianist Professor
Nikolay Andreevich Orlov, formerly of the Moscow Conservatory;
the music director Professor N. Mal'ko; and the famous young
singers A. Cherkassky (he appeared in Tschaikovsky's *Eugene
Onegin*) and Tatyana Menotti, all helped to foster the arts.

Yury Dimtrievich Yakovlev (1888-1938), painter, actor, and
producer, worked in the Russian Drama Theatre and in the
Latvian Art Theatre. N. S. Barabanov and E. P. Studentsov, both
with the Russian Drama Theatre, contributed to the popularity of
Russian scenic art in Latvia. The architect Sergey Nikolaevich
Antinov painted scenery for the Theatre while the aesthete and
graphic art specialist Yury Georgievich Rykovsky designed
costumes. Both were talented and original designers whose work

captured the taste and style of the period. The theatre employed
as chief producer the gifted director P. A. Ungern, a specialist in
serious drama; art historian was Professor N. I. Misheev. The
Russian painters Alexey Ivanovich Yupatov and R. T. Shishko
worked in various Latvian theatres and furnished illustrations to
local publishing houses. Yupatov was the son of Professor Ivan
Feropontovich Yupatov, head of the Russian Department in the
Ministry of Education and a deputy in the Latvian Parliament.
An Old Believer, Alexey Yupatov stylized his paintings in the
ancient Russian manner "à la Steletsky and Petersburg," as
Chinnov put it. Yupatov still lives in Moscow and has designed a
number of *ex libris* for Soviet leaders and administrators. Yupatov
is also responsible for an elegant collection of articles about Nikolay
Rerikh.

The Russian painter and art historian Evgeny Evgenyevich
Klimov (b. 1901), now residing in Canada, also came from Latvia.
He was born in Mitava (renamed Elgava) into a family of lawyers
and teachers and graduated from the Academy of Arts in Riga in
1929. In addition to painting, he published several albums of
lithographs. These albums were highly praised by the Russian
painter Alexander Benois, and by the writers and critics Pyotr
Pil'sky, Shmelyov, Lukash, Zurov, and the Russian philospher I. A.
Ilyin.

In Montréal, Klimov painted the portraits of illustrious
Russian émigrés, including the four poets Ivan Elagin, Nikolay
Korzhavin, Chinnov, and Ivask, as well as Alexander Solzhenitsyn,
Andrey Sedykh, Roman Goul', and I. A. Ilyin. His style clearly
reveals the charisma of his subjects. Klimov's landscapes, genre
paintings, and still life are to be found in art museums and
galleries in Riga, Quebec, Montréal, the Russian Museum in
Leningrad, and the Museum of Fine Arts in Moscow. Exhibitions
of his works have been held in Riga, Belgrade, Den Haag, London,
Toronto, Prague, Würzburg, Quebec, Ottawa, Albany, and
Montréal.

With radiant and transparent colors Klimov creates a world
both poetic and lyrical. The calm, pensive sadness of the Russian
fields contrasts sharply with the joyous and uplifting silhouettes of
white cathedrals in Pskov framed by green branches and spacious
blue sky. Poetic stability reigns in this peaceful and beautiful
world of harmony, color, and dynamics. Klimov's paintings
—devoid of *Effekthasherei*, passion, or pressure—could be likened

on the literary level to the transparent, water color effect of Boris
Zaytsev's prose. The paintings radiate the spiritual harmony of the
world of the Russian icon—which is not suprising, for Klimov is
also an icon painter. His icons decorate the walls of Russian
cathedrals in Riga, Prague, Montréal, Ottawa, Toronto, Los
Angeles, and other cities of the Western world. They are marked
by strict compositional designs and light, joyous coloring. As an
art historian, Klimov published a great number of articles and
essays. He has appeared as a guest lecturer in the USA, Canada,
and Western Europe.

Nikolay Petrovich Bogdanov-Bel'sky, a Russian artist in
Latvia, painted mostly peasant children in the open air. He was a
friend of General Mikhail Alexandrovich Afanasyev, a member of
Yudenich's Army who was shot by the Bolsheviks in 1940, and was
a frequent guest at the General's estate Belinovo in Latgalia.
S. A. Vinogradov (from Pechory, later working in Riga) was a
genre and landscape painter whose pictures are full of light and
convey a sense of spaciousness. Other Russian painters living in
the Baltic region were Vysotsky, a specialist in the depiction of
animals, and the talented water colorist Mavriky Petrovich Jakobi.
The "Holy Trinity" of the Ioann Cathedral in Riga was from the
hand of the Russian icon painter Rykovsky. At international art
exhibitions several prizes were awarded to the wood engraver P. V.
Puzyrevsky. Shishko designed several highly original buildings and
pavilions where, occasionally, his own scene paintings were on
display. Erik Dmitrievich Pren began his artistic career as a
landscape painter, working much with oils and distemper. The
author of a novel about the White Army, *Ne rzhaveli slova* (Words
Did Not Rust), Baron L. N. Nolde also was a talented landscape
painter. He lived on his estate Zhogaty in Latvia and founded,
presumably together with Prince Anatoly Pavlovich Lieven, a
Russian patriotic organization called *Bratstvo Russkoy Pravdy*
(Brotherhood of Russian Truth). After the 1940 Soviet occupation
of Latvia, Baron Nolde immigrated to Brazil and never returned to
the Soviet Union or former Latvia.

Individual exhibitions were held of the works of
Bogdanov-Bel'sky and of M. V. Dobuzhinsky who lived in Riga for
several years. Exhibitions of contemporary Russian painting in
general were: "The Epoch of Old St. Petersburg" in 1931;
"Two-Hundred Years of Russian Painting from Personal Collections
in Riga" in 1933; and in 1937, commemorating the centennial of

Pushkin's death, "The Pushkin Exhibition." Russian artists A. P. Petrov, V. M. Alexeev, N. P. Rominsky (for many years an art instructor at Lomonosov's High School), I. K. Gorsky, P. I. Andabursky, Prince A. Massal'sky-Surin, K. Pavlov, T. V. Kossinskaya, and the two caricaturists M. K. Perts and S. A. Tsivinsky (both also widely known outside Latvia), vied successfully with artists in Estonia, Finland, and the Soviet Union.

In Riga there were many Russian social and educational institutions and organizations: *Russkoe obshchestvo v Latvii* (The Russian Society in Latvia), *Prosvetitel'noe obschestvo* (The Society of Enlightenment) chaired by E. M. Tikhonitsky, *Soyuz russkikh uchiteley* (The Union of Russian Teachers), *Grebenshchikovskaya obshchina* (The Community of Grebenshchikov), and *Obshchesvo russkikh vrachey* (The Society of Russian Physicians) headed by Professor Eduard Eduardovich Gartier. In Riga alone there were thirteen Russian elementary schools, two public high schools (state and municipal), the Commercial School for Adults, and several private Russian high schools.

Following the establishment of Finnish independence in 1917, Russian cultural and social life reached new heights in Finland as well during the 1920s and 1930s. At literary soirées, participants read poetry by Tyutchev, Apukhtin, Anna Akhmatova, Bal'mont, Maximilian Voloshin, Hippius, V. Sirin, Severyanin, Ekaterina Tauber, Khodasevich, and Bulich. On June 14, 1934, in Viipuri, A. E. Prazhkova and her literary circle organized "An Evening of Fairy Tales and Poetry by Vera Bulich." In Helsinki on March 21, 1937, Bulich gave the opening speech at "A Matinee for Children in Memory of the Great Poet A. S. Pushkin 1837-1937." On March 27, 1937, a "Literary Soirée with Vera Bulich—Selections from Finnish Lyrics" was held. Bulich read her translations of poetry by Uuno Kailas (1901-33) and Katri Vala (1901-44; pseudonym of Karin Elice Dadenström-Keikel), two contemporary Finnish poets whose verse closely resembles Bulich's. She also discussed the problems of translating poetry from Finnish into Russian and elaborated on an analytic approach to Finnish versification using examples from her own translations. An active participant in the Russian literary life of Helsinki, Bulish was one of the leading authorities on Russian belles-lettres in Scandinavia. Similarly involved in the Russian literary and cultural life in Finland was Vera Leino, a Russian language instructor at the University of Helsinki and intimate friend of Vera Bulich. Leino became a contributor to *Novy zhurnal* (The New Review; New York) in 1960.

The monthly journal *Zhurnal sodruzhestva* (The Journal of Concord, January 1933—December 1938, Nos. 1-12) was published in Viipuri and edited by F. V. Uperov, Attorney-General S. Ts. Dobrovol'sky, and Sergey Rittenberg. Among the journal's many contributors were Vera Bulich (Helsinki), Meta Roos (Tallinn), Lev Gomolitsky (Warsaw), Ekaterina Tauber (Belgrade), Victor Mamchenko (Paris), Yury Grigorkov (Helsinki), Zinaida Shakhovskaya (Paris), Yury Terapiano (Paris), Maria Widnes (Helsinki), Boris Novosadov (Tallinn), Nikolay Belotsvetov (Riga), Ilya Golenishchev-Kutuzov (Belgrade), Sergey Gorny (Berlin), Saburova (Riga), Ivask (Pechory), Hoerschelmann (Tallinn), Bazilevskaya (Tallinn), Raisa Blokh (Paris), Sofia Pregel (Paris), V. Semenov Tyan-Shansky (Helsinki), Perfilyev (Riga), Georgy Raevsky (Paris), Boris Zaytsev (Paris), Lazar' Kel'berin (Paris), Zurov (Paris), Evgeny Gessen (Prague), Alexander Kondratyev (Warsaw), Yury Mirolyubov (Brussels), A. I. Kuprin (Paris), Olga Falconette (Stockholm), and others. *The Journal of Concord* published poetry, short stories, reviews, essays, and sketches, all of high artistic merit. Particularly striking were Ivask's thought-provoking reviews of poetry and fiction in No. 5 (May 1936), a review by Kel'berin about the almanac *Krug* (The Circle; Paris) in No. 7 (July 1936), and a piece by Yury Mandel'shtam about the poetry of Terapiano in Nos. 10-11 (October-November 1938). Though *The Journal of Concord* lacked the colorful illustrations of *The Virgin Soil* and *Chimes*, it had, as the long list of contributors demonstrates, sufficient polish and variety to compete successfully with other publications. Another Russian journal in Helsinki was the monthly *Dni nashey zhizni* (The Days of Our Life; 1923, Nos. 1-2/4) with main correspondents Ivan Savin, Nikiforov-Volgin, and the young lawyer and University of St. Petersburg graduate Yury Grigorkov. K. A. Bergman was editor-in-chief.

Several Russian newspapers were printed in Finland, including *Russkaya zhizn'* (Russian Life; Helsinki, 1918-19), initiated by a group of Russian intellectuals in Finland—mostly teachers in private Russian high schools—and funded by the Special Committee for Russian Affairs in Finland which was organized in Helsinki in 1917. In the spring of 1919 *Russian Life* came under the jurisdiction of the Russian National Society in Paris. A member of the Society, N. I. Nekhoroshev (Paris), became its principal sponsor.   Professor David Davydovich Grimm, an important representative of the "right-wing" of the Cadet (Constitutional Democrats) party, and his son Ivan supervised the paper's political orientation.   By 1922 Russian politicians in Paris lost interest in a Russian national newspaper in Helsinki. Financial support was withdrawn and the sequel of *Russian Life, New Russian Life*, ceased publication.   However, one of its faithful contributors, V. I. Voutilainen, a Finn by birth but Russian in education and thought, set up a new daily paper, *Russkie vesti* (Russian News; Helsinki, 1922-23, Nos. 1-401).   It printed the works of Anna Akhmatova, Alexander Amfiteatrov, Ariadna Tyrkova, and Yury Grigorkov.   *Russian News'* successor, *Novye russkie vesti* (The New Russian News; Helsinki, 1923-25, Nos. 1-607), engaged Igor' Severyanin, Savin, Amfiteatrov, Bulich, Bal'mont, Boris Savinkov, Valentin Kataev, Evgeny Chirikov, Marina Tsvetaeva, Mark Aldanov, Arkady Averchenko, Teffi, Vladmir Burtsev, Leri (V. V. Klopotkovsky), and Grigorkov. *Novaya russkaya zhizn'* (New Russian Life; 1919-22), also published in Helsinki, featured works by Amfiteatrov, Sergy Yablonovsky, Nikolay Gorsky, Lloly L'vov, Grigorkov, and the poetry of Boris Bashkirov-Verin.   Despite its popularity, the paper was short-lived. Other short-lived Russian newspapers in Helsinki included: *Listok russkoy kolonii* (The Leaflet of the Russian Colony; March 12—April 24, 1927, edited by S. Nikolaev), *Put'* (The Path; February 1, 1921—January 8, 1922, edited by P. I. Leontyev, 1921; K. Sharin, 1921-22), and *Rassvet* (Dawn; November 14, 1919 —February 11, 1920), edited by K. Samsonov, 1919-20; Pavel Leontyev, 1920).

Under the direction of A. I. Zaytsev, E. I. Birs, I. A. Batuev, A. M. Kondyrev, and E. G. Tigerstedt, the Russian Theatre in Helsinki staged works by Russian authors and enriched the cultural life of the capital.   Russian plays—Chekhov's *The Cherry Orchard*, Merezhkovsky's *Paul I*, Sumbatov's *Betrayal*, A. Rennikov's *The Devil's Merry-Go-Round*, Vera Bulich's *Snowman Heart Cake*, to name a few—were performed in the National Theatre and in the Russian Drama Theatre.   After the October Revolution a number of leading figures of the Russian stage escaped to Finland; for example, former actress in the Moscow Art Academy Ekaterina Alexeevna Hiitonen-Ziablowa, A. M. Kondyrev, and E. G. Tigerstedt.   Vera Bulich's sister, Sofia Sergeevna Bulich-Stark, a well-known soprano of the classical repertoire, drew large audiences in Russian concerts and operas in Helsinki and Viipuri. Maria Danilovna Kamenskaya, a soloist from the Mariinsky Theatre, gave voice lessons in Viipuri and had among her students such noted singers of the Baltic region as T. A. Andreeva, Z. I. Chigaeva, V. P. Kulikova, E. I. Nikitina, V. S. Frolova-Timofeeva, M. P. Sokolova, and O. N. Trifonova. Frida Pavlovna Sergeeva, the "nightingale from Viipuri," who had studied voice in Italy and appeared at the Mariinsky Theatre, gave many successful concerts in Helsinki. Shishkina, a soloist from the St. Petersburg Gypsy Chorus, arranged for several concerts to be performed for the society "The Russian Colony in Finland." The proceeds of these popular concerts were donated to charitable organizations for poor Russians in Finland. Male singers included G. E. Heinichsen, N. A. Tyapugin, S. S. Putilin, N. S. Starostin, P. N. Selivanov, G. N. Zotov, S. A. Kulikov, and V. I. Frolov.

The largest of the three Russian amateur dramatic societies in Helsinki recruited its members from among local Russian teachers, families of officers from the former garrison Sveaborg, and the émigrés who had taken part in the amateur dramatics of St. Petersburg high society. "The Circle of Vedrinskaya" was named after a famous actress from the Alexandrinsky Theatre who had given guest performances in Finland. "The Dramatic Youth Troupe," the third Russian theatre group in Helsinki, was initiated in the mid-1930s by the Russian youth organization in Finland *Zveno* (The Link) and was chaired by F. F. Pire.[29] With enthusiasm, the three groups performed plays chosen primarily from the Russian classical repertoire, occasionally availing themselves of foreign works. For example, German playwright Vickie Baum's *The Factory of Beauty* was performed in "The Studio of the Russian Theatre" in Helsinki on April 16, 1934. On February 16, 1938, *The Link* held "A Festive Soirée in Memory of Ivan Savin (1827-1937)." Vera Bulich read some of Savin's lyrics, while Cavalry Captain D. D. Kusmin-Karavajeff presented a paper entitled "On the Eve of the Revolution."

In 1923, lovers of Russian folk music in Helsinki formed a balalaika orchestra as well as a Russian folk chorus organized by I. V. Stratov. In 1926, A. N. Hubert, the "Russian Finn," took over as director. The concerts, especially those given by the balalaika orchestra, always drew large crowds. After the death of Hubert, Vladimir Ivanovich Andreev, a graduate from the St. Petersburg Conservatory, became the new conductor; under his

superb direction the orchestra and chorus toured Estonia and other
Baltic countries with great success. Concerts of Russian opera
music were arranged by the Union of Russian Youth in Helsinki.

Every spring from 1928 until 1940 Helsinki had its Festival,
or Day, of Russian Culture. The festivities—in which all other
Russian societies, unions, and groups in Finland participated—were
organized by "The Russian Colony in Finland," founded in 1918
and chaired first by Count V. A. Buksgevden (1925-32), then by
Baron R. A. Stackelberg (1932-40). Each year the program
included a lecture on Russian history, a concert, and a special
ceremony called the "Apotheosis of Russia." During the ceremony
a young woman, dressed in the Russian national costume, would sit
on a throne or a hillock surrounded by the chorus. As the
personification of Russia's glory, she would be honored with rites
and songs. On May 27, 1934, the Day of Russian Culture had
been dedicated to the memory of Gogol. The Viipuri Russian
Chorus performed the "Apotheosis of Russia" and other important
vocal pieces. On May 19, 1935, the Day of Russian Culture
celebrated the Russian composer N. A. Rimsky-Korsakov by
playing his music in Helsinki's White Hall. In 1937, a Pushkin
celebration lasted several days. During these "Pushkin Days,"
lectures were given about Pushkin's art. Plays and concerts based
on his dramatic and lyrical compositions were performed to the
delight of huge Russian audiences. A "Lermontov Day" was
planned for 1941, but the project was thwarted by the Second
World War. In January 1944, by order of Moscow, the society
with its many so-called "collective members" was closed and the
Festival of Russian Culture forbidden. In 1952, the Helsinki Opera
Theatre took up the tradition again and celebrated a "Gogol Day."

"The Russian Colony in Finland" consisted of various
societies—like "The Circle of Russian Engineers" and the "Circle of
Russian Artists"—which were called "collective members." One of
the "collective members" of "The Russian Colony" was the literary
and philosophical society *Svetlitsa* (The Enlightened Literary Salon),
active during the second half of the 1930s. Once a week the
members of *Svetlitsa* gathered at the club of "The Russian Colony"
to discuss literary and philosophical matters. Bulich (President of
Svetlitsa), V. V. Drozdovich, Grigorkov, and the Navy officer P. F.
Svetlik, who was particularly interested in philosophy, regularly
attended these meetings. *Svetlitsa* yearly organized book exhibits,
poetry readings (Vera Bulich), and lectures on Russian

belles-lettres (Bulich, Maria Widnes, Yury Grigorkov). It also supported the activities of *Vereteno* (The Spindle), a Russian literary and artistic society in Helsinki. Igor' Severyanin and Father Ioann Shakhovskoy each honored the club of "The Russian Colony" with an appearance; Severyanin read from his poetry and Father Ioann presented a paper on Russian Orthodoxy. On each occasion every available seat in the great hall of the club was taken. Alexander Amfiteatrov, who had managed to escape from St. Petersburg in 1920, delivered a lecture on the political and economic state of affairs in Russia, which left a profound impression. The lecture took place in the offices of the newspaper *Russian Life* and attracted so many listeners that some of the audience spilled out into the wide corridors. Among the many celebrities of Russian art, theatre, and belles-lettres who visited Finland during the 1920s and 1930s were Alexander Kuprin, Boris Zaytsev, N. V. Plevitskaya, Fyodor Shalyapin, Tamara Karsavina, the famous ballet dancer and choreographer Mikhail M. Fokin and his wife, the singers Kuznetsova and Pozemkin, Dmitry A. Smirnov, and the soloist Tatyana Menotti from La Scala in Milan. The singers gave several performances at the Helsinki Opera Theatre and the Viipuri Theatre.

Biblion was a publishing house in Helsinki, its board consisting of Holger Schildt, manager Sigurd Klockars, office manager Gunnar Söderström, and the journalist Hjalmar Dahl. Fyodor Fal'kovsky, a Russian short story writer and playwright, was an important person for the publishing house throughout its existence. *Biblion* issued, among other Russian books, Leonid Andreev's novella "Dnevnik Satany" (The Satan's Diary, 1921), its sequel "Nochnoy razgovor" (The Nocturnal Conversation, 1921), and a collection of short stories by A. I. Kuprin, *Zvezda Solomona* (The Star of Solomon, 1920). *Biblion* specialized in translations from Finnish into Russian and German.[30]

In 1922, Helsinki housed a large exhibition of paintings by Professor Ilya Repin, Yury Repin, Vera Repina, and Vasily Levi. "The Circle of Russian Artists," as a "collective member" of "The Russian Colony in Finland" and a member of "The Society of Russian Artists in Finland," also arranged yearly exhibits of individual artists' works.

The president of the Society of Russian Artists in Finland was E. A. Buman-Kolomiytseva; the secretary, O. E. Kuropatova; and the treasurer, Baron M. B. Meidel. Architect L. E. Kurpatov, artist V. P. Shchepansky, sculptor M. N. Shishkin, and the very talented water color painter V. P. Semenov Tyan-Shansky all served as judges at these exhibits. A great number of other Russian artists lived in Finland: G. P. Svetlik, N. Bely, P. Päts-Blaznov, A. Blaznov, N. Blinov, M. Karpinsky, G. Pressas, N. Romanov, M. Shilkin, A. von Schulz, P. Varlechev, V. Weisner, S. Vessetov, P. Zakharov, L. Platan, and M. von Mingin. E. E. Kurpatov made sketches for the theatre, while V. I. Voutilainen worked as an artist/decorator.

In comparison with Estonia, Latvia, and Finland, Russian cultural life in Lithuania was considerably less active. The Russian population in Lithuania was sparse, and the majority of Lithuanians were Catholic and did not associate with the Russian Orthodox believers. Several Russian newspapers and journals were founded in Lithuania, but since they could not compete with Riga's *Today*, with the Russian journal *Mech* (The Sword), or with the Warsaw newspaper *Za svobodu* (For Freedom), they did not exist for long. The following Russian publications appeared in Lithuania for a short period: *Zerkalo* (Mirror; Kaunas, 1921-22), a journal of literature, art, satire, and social life, edited by I. Voronko; *Utyos* (The Rock; Vilnius, 1921-22), a literary journal edited by D. Bokham; *Zarya* (Dawn; Kaunas, 1921-22, Nos. 1-13), an illustrated weekly of literary and social satire edited by A. Bukhov; *Ekho* (The Echo), an illustrated supplement to the newspaper *Ekho Litvy* (The Echo of Lithuania; Berlin, 1923-24); the monthly magazine for literature, art, and economics *Baltiysky al'manakh* (The Baltic Almanac; Kaunas, 1932-24, Nos. 1-2), and the newspaper *Vostochnaya Evropa* (Eastern Europe) published by Aleksis Rannit in Kaunas and edited by E. L. Shklyar (1936-1940).

When Lithuania became independent, Russian actors and directors were encouraged to move there and help develop a Lithuanian national theatre and opera. Thanks to their professionalism and Stanislavskian techniques, the Russian émigrés had considerable influence on the theatrical life of the country. But Russian literary life in Lithuania was limited compared to the development of Russian belles-lettres in the rest of the Baltic area. Perhaps the most prominent author in the country was Evgeny L'vovich Shklyar, a co-editor in the Moscow "Publishing House of Writers" (1917), who translated Lithuanian poetry into Russian. Shortly before World War II, he compiled a large collection of poetry by the renowed Lithuanian poet Maironis. Shklyar also wrote poetry himself and authored a number of volumes: *Kiparisy* (The Cypresses; Kaunas: Pribaltiyskoe Iz-vo, 1922), *Karavan: vtoraya kniga liriki* (The Caravan: A Second Book of Lyrics; Berlin: Mysl', 1923), *Ogni na vershinakh: tretya kniga liriki* (Lights on the Summits: A Third Book of Lyrics; Berlin: Sever, 1923), *Vechernyaya step': chetvyortaya kniga stikhov* (The Evening Steppe: A Fourth Book of Poetry; Berlin: Kn-vo Pisateley, 1923), *Posokh: pyaty sbornik stikhov* (A Shaft: A Fifth Collection of Poems; Riga: Kul'tura, 1925), *Letuva—zolotoe imya: shestaya kniga stikhov* (Letuva—A Golden Name: A Sixth Book of Poetry; Paris: Novy Prometey, 1927), and *Poeta in Aeternum* (Riga, 1935). He also contributed to the journal *Our Little Light* in Riga. During the war Shklyar was arrested by the Gestapo and taken to a concentration camp near Kaunas where he perished. Another promising young Russian poet in Lithuania at the time was Roman Ryabinin who published in *Russkie zapiski* (Russian Annals) in 1938. His fate is unknown.

Jurgis Kazimirovich Baltrushaitis (1873-1944) was a symbolist poet who translated Ibsen, Hauptmann, and D'Annunzio into Russian. His refined but austere poetry expresses the poet's metaphysical approach to the theme of man's isolation in the universe. After the Soviet occupation in Lithuania in 1940, hoping for the victory of the Allied Forces over Hitler, Baltrushaitis moved to Paris. As is the case with the Estonian national poet Aleksis Rannit, Baltrushaitis is a Lithuanian rather than Russian poet,[31] and cannot really be included in the history of Russian literature in exile.

Russian émigré literature, while unique, must also be seen as part of a larger phenomenon, almost a tradition—that of expatriate writing in general. An international phenomenon, it involves Americans in Paris, exiled German and French intellectuals during the Nazi period, and many other émigré groups. Carson McCullers (1917-1967), the American novelist, lived in Paris (1950-55) where she wrote her novel *Clock Without Hands* (1961), a play entitled *Square Root of Wonderful* (1958), and poetry. F. Scott Fitzgerald (1896-1940) left the U. S. in search of spiritual renewal; in France (1924-30), he completed one of his most widely acclaimed novels, *The Great Gatsby* (1925), and began to write *Tender is the Night* (1934), both delineating the confusion and glitter of America in the 1920s. In protest against America's neutrality in World War I, Henry James (1843-1916), the noted American novelist and critic, became a British citizen in 1915. From 1872 to 1874 he had resided in Italy, where he wrote his first major novel *Roderick Hudson* (1876). T. S. Eliot (1888-1965), also American-born, became a British subject in 1927, and it was in England that his most celebrated works first appeared. Sylvia Plath (1932-1963), a modern American poet, went into self-imposed exile in England, where she published her novel *The Bell Jar* (1963) and several collections of poetry.

England harbored several French writers, André Maurois, for example (pseudonym of Emile Herzog, 1885-1967), a novelist, biographer, and historian. Maurois, opposed to the Nazi occupation of France, moved to England and later to the United States. *Histoire des Etats-Unis* (1943) and *Terre promise* (1946) were written during this period. The controversial English novelist and poet D. H. Lawrence (1885-1930) spent much of his life in Italy and New Mexico. He diagnosed the ills of modern civilization as resulting from the atrophy of human emotion; uninhibited passion as a revitalizing force became something of a mystical ideal for him. This philosophy, categorically rejected by most of his contemporaries, inspired *The Rainbow* (1915), *Women in Love* (1920), *The Plumed Serpent* (1926), and particularly *Lady Chatterley's Lover* (1928).

With the advent of the Nazi regime, Thomas Mann (1875-1955) went into voluntary exile first in Switzerland and later in the United States. He became an American citizen in 1944 and participated actively in the struggle against Facism. Mann did not return to Europe until 1952. During his émigré years, his thoughts about the Biblical exile were put to paper in the trilogy *Joseph und seine Brüder* (tr. *Joseph and His Brothers* [1933-45]: *The Young Joseph* [1935], *Joseph in Egypt* [1938], *Joseph the Provider* [1945]). Bertolt Brecht (1898-1956), a German poet and playwright converted to Marxism in the winter of 1928-29, left Germany in 1935 and escaped to Denmark. Via Sweden, Finland, and the Soviet Union he eventually reached the United States (1940-41). Among Brecht's anti-Nazi plays are *Der aufhaltsame Aufstieg des Arturo Ui* (The Resistible Rise of Arturo Ui, [1941]), *Furcht und Elend des Dritten Reiches* (The Private Life of the Master Race [1944]), and *Mutter Courage* (Mother Courage [1941]).

The Soviet occupation of Estonia, Latvia, and Lithuania in 1940 brought an abrupt end to all Russian cultural and literary activities in the Baltic region. Several thousand people were

imprisoned—civil servants, civic leaders, army officers, heads of
government departments, industrialists, clergy of all denominations,
publishers and editors, poets and fiction writers, artists and
actors—those of both Baltic and Russian origin. The Latvian
Commander-in-Chief, General A. Balodis, and the Estonian
Commander-in-Chief, Johan Laidener, were arrested and taken to
the Soviet Union. Laidener was formerly a colonel in the General
Staff of the Imperial Russian Army and a national hero in the
Estonian struggle for independence; he was responsible for the
suppression of a Communist uprising in Estonia on December 1,
1924. The Latvian Premier, Dr. Karl Ulmanis, and the Estonian
President, Konstantin Päts, were likewise arrested and deported to
the USSR. Antanas Smetona, the President of Lithuania, fled to
Germany with several eminent Lithuanian ministers (he later
moved, via Switzerland, to the United States).

Immediately following the invasion, Russian libraries and
bookstores were closed, and Russian books confiscated and shipped
to paper factories for reprocessing into pulp. Since there were in
Riga several private Russian libraries in addition to school libraries
and the public library with large and valuable newspaper archives,
the extent of the damage was considerable. The Ivanov library,
the oldest collection of Russian books in Riga, rich in prewar
Russian classics, was completely destroyed, as were many lending
libraries of Russian classics and Russian émigré literature. Books
that escaped the destruction were brought or confiscated by the
Soviet occupants of the Baltic countries.

The Russians of Latvia, Estonia, and Lithuania were no
longer allowed to form political parties. Of the many Russian
societies and organizations only a few charities and professional
groups remained: the athletic league "Sokol," the associations of
physicians, engineers, seamen, etc. Later on, these organizations
were also dissolved and their leaders arrested. Pyotr Pil'sky
escaped internment only because he suffered a paralytic stroke
when the secret police came to arrest him. Several months later
he died in his home. P. N. Jakobi was one of the first Baltic
victims of the Soviet regime.[32] His family was popular and
well-known in the Russian community of Riga; one of Jakobi's
sons was a journalist, the other an artist, and his daughter, Vera,
was a dancer with the Latvian National Opera. Jakobi and one of
his daughters were arrested; Pyotr Jakobi was deported to the
Soviet Union and executed. Another victim of senseless slaughter

was S. I. Trofimov, a deputy in the Latvian Parliament, whose body was found in a mass grave near Riga. With the exception of a few members of the Russian Drama Theatre, most known Russian artists, writers, and intellectuals of Riga perished. During this period the Russian writer Galich, former General Galich-Goncharenko, committed suicide under the pressure of his particular circumstances. When his daughter and her German husband had left with the first group of repatriates in 1939, Galich had remained in Riga. He was approached by the secret police and pressured to collaborate. Galich turned to the German Consulate for help, but was told that the Consul was powerless. Before the secret police could call on him again, Galich took poison.

In the Baltic region today, with its large Orthodox, Lutheran, and Catholic populations, the Church is the object of unceasing persecution. Religious holidays are forbidden and churches are no longer in use. The Soviet government has transformed the Baltic cathedrals into Communist party and Komsomol clubs, and silos, factories, dormitories, and cinemas. Beautiful churches like the Orthodox Cathedral in Riga and the Church of Christ's Resurrection in Vilnius have had a similar inglorious fate for the sake of Soviet communities. On Christmas Eve in 1952 Radio Riga announced: "God has never existed. . . . God is an invention of the capitalist. . . . " The obituary list of the clergy showed more than a thousand names from all denominations and included twenty bishops.[33]

This book is meant to be a tribute to those Russian writers in the Baltic countries whose works so graphically illustrate the divergent attitudes and philosophies prevalent among Russian intellectuals in the early 1920s and 1930s. In literature they searched for new forms of expression while they endeavored to preserve the richness of their native culture and language. In spite of personal aesthetic and philosophical differences, they were one in opposition to coercion—whether in content or in form—in artistic creation. They shared a mood of nostalgia and anguish, a longing to return to their native land, and an awareness of their role in the formation of a culture that reflected their own unique experiences in exile.

The book is also a reminder of that tragic page in the history of Russian literature and art where a culture, once rich and highly developed, was completely obliterated by a totalitarian system. The rising light of morning, which shone brightly at first, abruptly died away. The Northern Aurora ended in the murky night of Socialist Realism.

Temira Pachmuss
Urbana, Illinois

NOTES

1. A. A. Bulatov, a prominent public figure, was exiled from Russia in 1922. He settled with his family in Tallinn and opened a bookstore. In 1940 or 1941 he was arrested by the Soviet secret police and with his family deported to the Soviet Union, where they were executed.

2. See, e.g., John Glad, "The American Chapter in Russian Poetry," *Russian Language Journal*, 30, No. 106 (Spring 1976), 173–84.

3. Nikolay Efremovich Andreyev, professor emeritus at Cambridge (England), was a member of both the "Guild of Poets" in Estonia and the "Hermitage of Poets" in Czechoslovakia. A graduate in Slavic studies of the Charles University in Prague, he acted as a kind of liaison officer between the two organizations, coordinating the publications of Russian writers from the "Guild of Poets" in Prague and of those from the "Hermitage" in Tallinn. He published under the pseudonyms "K. Rem," "N. Nikolin," "A. Korsunsky," and "A–v, N." As a member of the "Hermitage of Poets," Andreyev contributed to the journal *Volya Rossii* (The Will of Russia; Prague), and the almanac *Numbers*, and served as a critic for the Russian newspaper *Russkaya mysl'* (Russian Thought; Paris). In *The Virgin Soil* Andreyev published articles about Chekhov, Leonid Andreyev, Arkady Averchenko, Igor' Severyanin, the Russian theatre, and Russian culture. He was also a theatre and art critic for *The Latest News* in Tallinn. Andreyev authored many scholarly works published in various countries. For more detail, read the special issue dedicated to N. E. Andreyev, *Canadian–American Studies*, Vol. 13, No. 1-2 (Summer–Spring 1979). Also helpful are: Nikolay Andreyev, "Ob osobennostyakh i osnovnykh etapakh razvitiya russkoy literatury za rubezhom," *Russkaya literatura v emigratsii: sbornik statey*, pod red. N. Poltoratzkogo (Pittsburgh: University of Pittsburgh, 1972), pp. 15–38, and Yury Ivask's article "Pamyati N. E. Andreyeva (1908–1982)," *Novoe russkoe slovo* dated March 14, 1982.

4. Leonid Nikolaevich Andreev (1871–1919) was a well-known and popular fiction writer in Estonia at the turn of the century. His work was praised by A. H. Tammsaare, one of the most influential Estonian men of letters, in the 1910 article "Leonid Andrejev (Tema 40. sünnipäeva puhul)", published in *Eesti Kodu*, No. 5 (1910), p. 98. Andreev's short stories, for example "Sergei Petrovich" about Friederich Nietzsche and his idea of the superman, were widely read in Estonian translation (*Postimees*, 1902, pp. 268–79). In November 1903, his short story "A Book" appeared in the newspaper *Teataja*. Subsequently, many other stories such as "The Wall" and "Silence" were translated into Estonian. Andreev's play, *Zhizn' cheloveka* (The Life of Man, 1906), was staged by

the Estonian Drama Theatre in 1921. Estonian writers were attracted
to the symbolical and allegorical aspects of the play which presented
human life as an abstraction. Among the characters are Man, His
Wife, Their Son, and Someone in Gray (representing Fate) — allegorical
figures who transcend time and space. Andreev avoids any hint of
reality by employing only black and red tones in the play. Negation
and ethical nihilism are the fundamental realities of life. There is no
purpose; all is farce. Life is but an illusion, a meaningless and dreadful
vacuum guided by the heartless figure in gray. Hence, life is fathomless
suffering and a sheer mockery of man, and not even art can beautify
the human condition. These attitudes, and especially Andreev's novel
treatment of the ideas of Dostoevsky, Nietzsche, and Schopenhauer,
appealed strongly to Estonian playwrights and their audiences in the
early 1920s. The similarities with Maeterlinck's dramatic technique also
stirred their interest. The premiere of *Dni nashey zhizni* (Days of Our
Life, 1908), directed by Yu. Rosfel'd, took place on November 1, 1909.
The Estonian producer P. Sepp staged Andreev's plays *Tsar Golod*
(Tsar Hunger, 1907) and *Okean* (The Ocean, 1911) in 1922 in the
Drama Theatre. A. Lauter was responsible for the 1922 production of
another drama by Leonid Andreev, *Tot, kto poluchaet poshchechiny* (He
Who Gets Slapped, 1916), in the Drama Theatre. The modernistic
techniques and ideas, the mysticism, antisocial orientation, and the
abstruse symbolism found in Andreev's plays influenced several Estonian
playwrights and producers, among them Friedebert Tuglas. Preoccupied
with innovative techniques, with experiments in forms and ideas, the
Estonian dramatists of the early 1920s were especially susceptible to
Andreev's "Siren of Modernism." The thirst for renewal manifested
itself somewhat later in the Estonian theatre than in other literary
genres, but the changes were equally tempestuous. Aestheticism, a
delight in refinement and an inclincation toward lyricism and fantasy
dominated the arts in Estonia during the first two decades of the
twentieth century. In Soviet Estonia all interest in Leonid Andreev and
his work ceased.

5.   "Everybody wrote poetry," Yury Ivask maintained, "even the teen-age
Victor Nekrasov" (b. 1919), a high school student he had come to know
in Pechory. According to Ivask, Nekrasov was a talented young poet.
He remembered two lines from one of Nekrasov's poems:
      "The sun in July is hot as an oven,
       The wind stealthily kisses one's shoulders..."
Nekrasov crossed the Soviet border illegally in 1938 and disappeared in
the USSR. His fate is unknown. Another youthful poet of the 1920s
was Vera Vladimirovna Schmidt, later a teacher of Russian language
and literature in a high school in Tartu. When Bunin visited Estonia
in   May 1938 and spent some time with the beautiful Maria
Karamzina, Vera Schmidt was still a student at the University of
Tartu. Her recollections of the six memorable days Bunin spent in
Tartu are printed in *Literaturnoe nasledstvo. Bunin. Kniga vtoraya*
(Literary Heritage. Bunin. Book II. Moscow: Nauka, 1973).

6.   No. 6 (1932), pp. 252–53.

7.   Dmitry Vasilyevich Maslov was a schoolmate of Boris Nartsissov. His
family originally came from Riga, but his father had a retail shop of
"peasant goods" in Tartu. Maslov was "The Number One Poet" of his
high school and wrote excellent poetry on the tragic events of the

revolution and the civil war. Upon graduation from high school in 1925, Maslov studied first commerce and then philosophy at the University of Tartu. His poetry, rich in striking imagery, was unfortunately never published. His position in the poetic universe is close to that of the two poets he most admired: Max Voloshin and Sergey Esenin. After his father's death toward the end of the 1920s, the family returned to Riga where Dmitry became involved in the "ultra-Orthodox" student movement. Fully committed to this new cause, he abandoned poetry, married a woman who had worked in his vegetable gardens, dressed as a peasant, and withdrew from former friends. This action they sincerely regretted, for Maslov's poetry had always delighted them. Here are two hitherto unpublished poems of Maslov from the album of Elizabeth Bazilevskaya-Roos (Ivan V. Bazilevsky's archives). Their original rhythmical patterns and the unique poetical expression and atmosphere are striking in the Russian language.

> God sent to Russia, as in former times to His Son,
> The Gethsemane chalice.

The girl grew tired of playing and running.
Having taken leave of her friends, she walked home.
Her stockings, high boots, and furcoat were covered with snow flakes.
And snow and ice were also on her gloves.

Her lovely face was glowing, and her cheeks
Resembled a satin, delicately scarlet and velvet.
The radiant luster of her innocent eyes
Was fearlessly meeting all passers-by...

> She was killed instantly
Under fire by an accidental bullet.
And her small corpse was left unattended on the pavement
The entire day.

Death was imprinting its marks
Deeper and deeper. The frost grew firmer.
A small spurt of blood was thickening
Amid the butts of dirty cigarettes.

Her small hands clinging to the pavement,
Her lovely mouth distorted with pain.
And the dead eyes of the child
Were gravely looking into the radiant sky.

1921

––––––––.––––––––

The crimson evening closed its eyes.
The tired wind nestled snugly to the grass.
The black forest made dark its pines.

A whiff of dampness came from the swamp.
Someone dark disappeared noiselessly,
Hiding in shaggy bushes.

The shadows float along the wild small mounds.
The sinister night weaves, like a cobweb,
The autumnal gloom among the pines.

Above the smoking stumps
The fog, like a hostile banner,
Rises in the cold air.

It is more difficult to find our path—
It gradually becomes darker
Trying to escape into the dusk.

The moon comes out like a ghost.
Two silent moonlit shadows
Accost us, uninvited.

                                                1924

8.   Lidiya Visnapuu was a Russian poet of Estonian origin. She attended
the Russian High School in Tartu and wrote poetry on religious themes,
often echoing the work of Anna Akhmatova.   In 1940, after the
occupation of Estonia by the Soviets, Visnapuu left for Germany.
Another frequent "guest" at the soirées of the "Guild of Poets" in
Tallinn was Nadezhda Arturovna Lippinger, a stately blond young
woman.   Though not a writer herself, she spoke Russian fluently and
was interested in Russian literature.   She died recently in Bavaria
(West Germany) where she had lived since the Soviet occupation of
Estonia.   Here is an example of Lidiya Visnapuu's simple lyric from the
album of Elizabeth Bazilevskaya-Roos:

Green lights whirl before my eyes,
My head is heavy and feverish.
But I feel so well—I am again with you,
I look at you and I hear your words.

Don't you agree it is frightening, isn't it—
To close one's eyes and never open them again,
Thus freeing oneself from one's reckless life
And beginning, perhaps, to live a new one?

But I won't see you in the new life—
No! I won't exchange this life for the new one.

So give me your hand, come closer,
I will tell you so much, so much...

The spring will come with its colorful flowers,
With the green leafage beginning to rustle.

A flame in my eyes, the flames before my eyes,
My head is heavy and feverish.

9.   For more details, read Yury Ivask's article in *Novoe russkoe slovo*, dated December 14, 1979.

10.   S. M. Shilling hosted the soirées of *The Virgin Soil*. He composed music for Meta Roos' poem "This Was Not Yesterday" and for Elizaveta Bazilevskaya–Roos' verse "Spring." Shilling taught sociology at the Russian High School in Tallinn. In the Estonian Parliament he spoke in favor of a strengthening of cultural ties between the Russian minority in Estonia and the Russian émigré elite in Western Europe.

11.   Sergey Levitsky was a classmate of Andreyev. A graduate of the German Karl-Universität in Prague, he received his Ph.D. in Philosophy in 1940 during the German army's occupation of Czechoslovakia. Levitsky, an erudite scholar and author of many works on philosophy, was a student of Nikolay Lossky. In the USA, he became Professor of Philosophy at Georgetown University.

12.   German Dmitrievich Khokhlov (literary pseudonym of Al. Novik) was a literary critic and a friend of Yury Ivask. He attended the Russian High School in Tallinn and enrolled at the University of Prague, but never graduated. He contributed to *Contemporary Annals* (Paris), to *The Will of Russia* (Prague), and wrote poems à la Esenin. Khokhlov was a great admirer of Alla Golovina's poetry—as well as of her beauty which resembled that of Anna Akhmatova. Khokhlov later joined the Soviet secret service and returned to the Soviet Union in 1934; there he contributed articles to *The Literary Gazette*, including works about the "Hermitage of Poets" in Prague. Eventually, he fell victim to one of the famous Soviet "purges" and disappeared in a Soviet concentration camp.

13.   Sergey Prokhorov, the youngest contributor to *The Virgin Soil*, was a gifted musician and the author of perceptive articles about music and Russian composers. He worked as conductor in Tallinn and later in Leningrad.

14.   The scientist Konstantin Gavrilov, who received his Ph.D. degree from the University of Prague, is presently a member of the Academy of Sciences in Argentina. For *The Virgin Soil*, he wrote about Pavlov, Mechnikov, and other important Russian scientists, as well as about the theories of Sigmund Freud. He became a member of the editorial staff in 1930, before the publication of the third issue in October.

15.   Olga Anatolyevna Nartsissova, Boris Nartsissov's gifted sister, was also a poet. She still lives in Estonia.

16.   Elena Vladimirovna Shcherbina (d. 1979 in Braunschweig, Germany), the wife of Baron von Korff, was an extremely beautiful woman who commanded attention and respect. A successful porcelain painter and fashion designer, Shcherbina attended the meetings of both the Tallinn "Russian Literary Circle" and the "Guild of Poets," but she came mainly to listen and never presented any papers.

17.   Read, for example, *Chisla*, No. 9 (Paris, 1933), p. 228, review "Nov'. Sbornik proizvedeny molodyozhi. Revel'. Estonia, 1933) and *Sovremennye zapiski*, Vol. LX (Paris, 1936), pp. 467–68, "Nov'. Tallinn, 1935."

18.   Read more about Aks in E. Stein, *Poeziya russkogo rasseyaniya 1920–1977* (Poetry of the Russian Diaspora 1920–1977; Toronto: Ladya, 1978), p. 11.

19.   An admirer of Kuprin, Vladimir Gushchik published several collections
       of short stories, among them *Khristovy yazychniki* (Christ's Heathens;
       Tallinn: Autori Kirjastus, 1929), *Na krayu* (On the Brink; Tallinn:
       Panorama, 1931), *Lyudi i teni* (People and Their Shadows; Tallinn:
       Russkaya kniga, 1934), *Zabytye teni* (The Forgotten Shadows; Berlin:
       Petropolis, 1937), and *Zhizn'* (Life; Brussels: Petropolis, 1938?).   He
       wrote poetry as well, and developed an interest in Eurasianism.
       Gushchik was arrested in the early 1940s, taken to the Soviet Union,
       and executed.
20.   T. Tamanin (literary pseudonym of Tatyana Ivanovna Manukhina, née
       Krundysheva, 1885–1962), was one of Zinaida Hippius' close friends. For
       more information about her, read Temira Pachmuss, *Intellect and Ideas
       in Action: Selected Correspondence of Zinaida Hippius* (Munich: Wilhelm
       Fink Verlag, 1972), pp. 461–517; and Temira Pachmuss, "A Literary
       Quarrel: Zinaida Hippius versus Tatjana Manuxina," *The Yearbook of
       the Estonian Learned Society in America*, IV (1964–67), pp. 62–83.
21.   Vladovsky published a book entitled *Vavilon* (Babylon; Tallinn, 1925),
       with his own illustrations.   The book was beautifully printed on fine
       paper, but failed to seduce the Estonian reading public at large.
22.   Albert Org owned a large book store in Tallinn and sold books
       distributed by the Russian publishing houses in Berlin — *Petropolis*, for
       example.   Yury Ivask, who loved books, bought several rare books from
       Org, including Osip Mandel'shtam's *Tristia*.
23.   The poet Mikhail Klochkov emulated the Acmeist style and rules of
       versification and was co-editor of *The Attic*.   He was not a prolific
       poet, but his verse was original, interesting, and pleasant.   His poems
       appeared in *Nash ogonyok* (Our Little Light; Riga, 1923–28).   Klochkov
       was self-educated (he was a shoemaker by profession) and held rather
       "left-wing" views.   His fate is unknown.
24.   A popular and charismatic figure, Matveev was also co-editor and
       co-publisher of *The Attic*.   He wrote poems in the "Soviet avant-
       garde" style: insipid, monotonous, quasi-modern, and completely devoid
       of any real literary value.   His short stories are written in the same
       style with similar results.   His interesting and original paintings,
       however, were admired by many.   He was adulated by women, and,
       especially after returning from Paris where he studied painting for a
       year, he became a "star."   His political views were of a "leftist"
       orientation.   Matveev died at a young age from alcohol abuse.
25.   Yakov Brahms left Latvia for the United States in 1940, lived in New
       York for a year, and then moved in 1941 to Washington, D.C.   There
       he became the owner of the Olmstead Restaurant on G Street.   A
       member of the Oveh Shalom Talmud Torah Congregation in
       Washington, he was buried in the Jewish Cemetery there.   He is
       remembered as a cultured, educated, and kind man.
26.   New York: McGraw-Hill Book Company, 1975.
27.   No. 3197, dated March 30, 1978.
28.   Read about Vedrinskaya in Elena Andrusova, "M. A.   Vedrinskaya,"
       Novoe russkoe slovo dated August 5, 1973.   About Elena Adnrusova
       herself, read her article "Russky Narodny Teatr v Rige" in *Novoe
       russkoe slovo* dated May 19, 1973.   Read about Roshchina-Insarova in
       Elena Andrusova's reminiscences "O Roshchinoy-Insarovoy" in *Novoe
       russkoe slovo* dated September 8, 1974, and in Vera Vlasova's
       "Nezabvennaya E. N. Roshchina-Insarova" in *Novoe russkoe slovo* dated

May 24, 1970. K. Arensky published a number of interesting articles
about some of the famous Russian actors and actresses working in the
Russian theatres of Riga and Tallinn at the same time. See, for
example, "Vstrechi," *Vozrozhdenie*, No. 211 (Paris, 1969), pp. 51–69;
"Zhizn' otdannaya teatru" in *Novoe russko slovo* dated September 2,
1979; and "Russky teatr v emigratsii" in *Russkaya zhizn'* (San
Francisco) dated August 28–31, 1979.

29.   Various Russian youth societies and unions were also very active in
Estonia: the Svyatogor Society in Narva, the Russian Student Society
in Tartu (primarily concerned with public education among the Russians
in Tartu), and the Union of the Russian Christian Student Movement
(mainly engaged in charitable work) in Tallinn, Tartu, Narva, and
Pechory. These youth organizations were involved in philanthropic
activities throughout Estonia, especially among the Russian population.

30   Ref. Ben Hellman, "Biblion. A Russian Publishing House in Finland,"
Studia Slavica Finlandensia, Tomus II (Helsinki, 1945).

31.   Similarly, Tito Colliander (b. 1904), a Finnish writer who witnessed the
1917 October Revolution in St. Petersburg and has written a great deal
about it in his memoirs and novels (all in Swedish), cannot be
considered a Russian writer. I am grateful to Poeten Bo Setterlind of
Sweden and to Professor Irina Masing–Delic of Johannesburg (South
Africa), for the information concerning Tito Colliander's life and work.
For the newspaper *Today*, in the late 1930s, Aleksis Rannit wrote about
Peter Linzbach, the Estonian stage designer of the French film *Under
the Roofs of Paris*; about the Estonian poet Henrik Visnapuu; the writer
A. H. Tammsaare, and about modern Estonian graphic art.

32.   Jakobi loved poetry, wrote poems himself, and published a book,
Pushkin o russkikh poetakh v perepiske s druzyami (Pushkin about
Russian Poets in Correspondence with Friends: Riga: Filin, 1937), and
a journal in Riga, *Zakon i sud* (Law and Court). A collection of his
poems appeared under the title *Pesenki Mefistofelya* (Mephistopheles'
Songs). For more information, read D. A. Levitsky's article about
Jakobi and his family in *Posev* (March, 1981), p. 46.

33.   For more detail, read Irina Saburova, "The Soviet Occupation of the
Baltic States," *The Russian Review*, Vol. 14, No. 1 (January 1955), pp.
36–49.

ESTONIA

SEVERYANIN, IGOR'
(1887-1941; pseudonym of Lotarev, Igor' Vasilyevich)

Born in St. Petersburg, the son of an officer, Severyanin was the most important Russian poet living in Estonia before the Revolution and between the two World Wars. His first verse, published in 1904, was impressionistic and neoromantic. But by 1909 he had developed his own quasi-modernistic style characterized by Bohemianism, a penchant for decadent elegance, modern philosophical pseudo-profundities, a pursuit of synaesthetic effect, neologisms, an emphasis on modern (especially foreign) vocabulary, and ingenious word play, which influenced Mayakovsky and Bryusov, among others. In 1911 Severyanin published a brochure, *Prolog Ego-Futurizma* (Prologue of Ego-Futurism), and an "Ego-Futurist" group of poets was formed. Its manifesto in 1912 proclaimed supreme individualism and radical modern poetic form. Late in 1912 Severyanin broke with the Ego-Futurists and joined the Cubo-Futurists for a brief period. His volume, *Gromokipyashchy kubok* (Thunder-seething Goblet, 1913), was an unqualified success and several more collections were equally well received.

After the 1917 Revolution Severyanin continually lived in Estonia and visited Berlin, Brussels, Paris, Zurich, Prague, Bucharest, Sofia, and Belgrade. The resident of Estonia is a different poet. Some of his poems in this period are connected with his stay in the idyllic fishing village of Toila on the Gulf of Finland. He produced water imagery of remarkable freshness and originality and dealt with the simple pleasures of country life. His poetry became more conventional, yet it often stated moral and social points with dignity and expressed personal emotions with grace and simplicity. Consistent with the poet's return to nature is a Tolstoyan pacifism and humanist mentality, expressed in poems full of outrage, indignation, and sorrow at war, man's inhumanity to man, and social injustice. Severyanin's former flippancy and aestheticism disappeared almost completely. Instead, somber notes of self-recrimination and loneliness are in the foreground. An interesting and original feature of Severyanin's poetry is the Estonian motifs which occur everywhere in his compositions: the sounds, landscape descriptions (Estonian), and a great fondness for Estonian people.

A prolific translator of Estonian poets—Henrik Visnapuu, Marie Under, Aleksis Rannit—Severyanin also translated from French, German, Serbian, Bulgarian, and other languages. He was an ideal, metrically exact translator with his versifying skills and excellent ear for sound effects. These qualities did not escape the attention of some Estonian poets, who took him as a model and even subsidized the publication of his Russian verse in Estonia. Under the influence of Russian modernist poetry the young Henrik Visnapuu, who called Severyanin "a new Pushkin," turned from epigonic Romanticism to rhythmical experiments of a phoneticist and later of an Ego-Futurist. In addition to the structural principles he borrowed, Visnapuu tried to achieve the same musicality that characterized the Russian modernists, especially Bal'mont and Severyanin, with whom young Visnapuu was on good terms.

As a northern bard, Serveryanin did not strike any artificial poses. He came to Estonia as an Ego-Futurist, but then a change took place in his artistic and personal posture. His poetry became easy-flowing, with a melodiousness lending itself to music, and at times even religious. N. E. Andreyev, who was at one of Severyanin's poetry readings in Estonia, recalls: "He recited his poems simply, quietly stressing their rhythm, and in a slightly singing voice. The poems were overflowing with optimism and youthful power: 'What beautiful days are now, oh, what beauty is everywhere: The garden blossoms, rings, smells sweet—God save it...' Severyanin recited many other poems; his success was tremendous. When he finished with the poem 'At her resurrection Russia pardons all guilty!' a thunderous applause engraved Severyanin in my memory as 'the Bard of the Baltic and Scandinavia.' I was commissioned by R. S. Lyakhnitsky, editor of the newspaper *The Latest News*, to write a report about this concert in verse for *The Latest News*." Andreyev's parents remembered Igor' Severyanin as an earnest, sincere person, pleasant and simple in manner, and always polite and attentive. Aleksis Rannit, an intimate friend of Severyanin, shared N. Andreyev's opinion.

In her reminiscences, "On the Shores of the Seine River," Irina Odoevtseva also remembers Severyanin's soirée. "Lofty,

genuine poetry," is what she calls his verse. "Severyanin is a
genuine poet—I don't doubt it now. Fyodor Sologub, who glorified
him as a 'great Russian poet,' was right. Deeper and deeper, I
yielded to the spell of his unusual way of reciting—his singing
which 'hypnotically' affected me. I closed my eyes, I sank to the
bottom of this sparkling, thunder-seething whirl of poetry. . . .
That day I was captivated, I was charmed, I was 'Severyaninized!'
'Oh, if only to hear more and more of his poems!' I thought."[1]

It may appear surprising that the younger Russian poets in
Estonia, except Yury Shumakov, remained free of Igor' Severyanin's
influence, whereas some of the Estonian, Finnish, and Polish poets
did experience it. The Russian poets still saw Igor' Severyanin as
the Ego–Futurist, author of the following collections of poetry
published in Moscow in 1915: *Siren' moey vesny* (The Lilac of My
Youth), *Morozhenoe iz sireni* (Ice Cream from Lilac), *Za strunnoy
izgorodyu liry* (Beyond the String Fence of the Lyre), and
Egofuturizm. He was still the "classic" of Ego–Futurism, a literary
movement the Russian poets rejected in the 1920s and 1930s. His
lyricism, combined with parody, irony, and humor,[2] appeared
old-fashioned to poets leaning toward the "Parisian note." They
did not see in Severyanin the "Bard of the Baltic and
Scandinavia," whose image so strongly appealed to the Estonian
poets and especially to the Siuru group (Expressionists).[3] However,
Boris Pravdin, Valmar Adams, and other Russian writers of the
early 1920s, enchanted with Severyanin's pre-revolutionary poetry,
continued writing in his former fashion.

Severyanin, who insisted his poems be called *poezy*, published
many volumes in exile, including *Vervena.   Poezy 1918-1922*
(Vervain: Poezy of 1918-1922; Tartu: Odamees, n.d.), *Ministrel'.
Noveyshie poezy* (Minstrel: The Latest Poezy; Berlin-Moskva, 1921),
Mirreliya.   Noveyshie poezy (Mirrellia: The Latest Poezy,
Berlin-Moskva, 1922), *Feya Eiole.   Poezy (1920-1921)* (The Fairy
Eiole, Poezy 1920-1921; Berlin: Otto Kircher & Co., 1922),
Paduchaya stremnina.   Roman v 2-kh chastyakh, v stikhakh (A
Falling Rapid: A Novel in Two Parts, in Verse; Berlin: Otto
Kircher & Co., 1922), *Solovey.   Novye poezy* (The Nightingale:
New Poezy; Berlin: Nakanune, 1923), *Tragediya Titana.* Kosmos,
izbornik I (The Tragedy of Titan: The Cosmos, First Collection;
Tartu: Bergman, 1923), *Roza oranzhevogo chasa.   Poema detstva v
3-kh chastyakh* (The Dew of the Orange Hour: A Poem of
Childhood In Three Parts; Tartu: Bergman, 1925), *Kolokola sobora*

chuvstv. Avtobiografichesky roman v 3-kh chastyakh (The Bells of the Cathedral of Emotions: An Autobiographical Novel in Three Parts; Tartu: Bergman, 1925), *Klassicheskie rozy. Stikhi 1922-1930 g.g.* (The Classical Roses: Poems 1922-1930; Belgrade: Russkaya biblioteka, 1931), *Adriatika. Lirika* (The Adriatic: Lyrics; Narva: Severyanin, 1932), *Medalyony. Sonety i variatsii o poetakh, pisatelyakh i kompozitorakh* (Medallions: Sonnets and Variations about Poets, Fiction Writers, and Composers; Belgrade: Severyanin, 1934), and *Royal' Leandra. Roman v strofakh* (Leander's Piano: A Novel in Stanzas; Bucharest: Severyanin, 1935). Severyanin's last book of poetry, *Ocharovatel'nye razocharovaniya* (Charming Disenchantments), was never published. The manuscript may be found in the Central Literary Archieves in Moscow.

The last Soviet ambassador to Estonia in 1940 pressured Severyanin to write a long poem to honor Stalin, but did not succeed. Severyanin died in 1941.

NOTES

1. Irina Odoevtseva, *Russkaya mysl'* dated March 16, 1978.
2. Cf. "Nelly" which influenced the poetry of Sasha Cherny and Nikolay Agnivtsev.
3. Read "Estonian Literature," from *The Virgin Soil*, No. 6 (1934): " . . . Coming into existence in 1905, the literary group 'Young Estonia' developed the slogan: 'We will be Estonians, but we shall also become Europeans.' The group's most prominent representatives were Gustav Suits and the novelist and critic Friedebert Tuglas. 'Young Estonia' was the first organized movement in the history of Estonian culture. It preferred the romantic and purely artistic in literature. Though the movement's influence continues today, primarily in matters of form, subsequent literature moved closer toward depicting real life. In the last decade Aestheticism, as a cult of form, a delight in refinement, and an inclination toward lyricism and fantasy, has given way to concern with the urgent problems of modern existence.

    There are no longer any staunch defenders of the Aestheticism favored by 'Young Estonia' during the years of reaction after 1905. It does not occur to anyone to defend its positions; instead, it is increasingly subject to attack. These assaults have led to an almost complete rejection of lyric poetry, even though it was of higher quality than narrative prose. The development of prose writing, on the other hand, continues. Among the best representatives of this type of literature were Anton Hansen Tammsaare, Mait Metsanurk, Albert Kivikas, Oskar Luts, and others. Readers demanded novels and the genre quickly advanced to the forefront. Estonian authors were remarkably prolific, but the quality unfortunately did not keep pace with the quantity of literary material put on the market. Yearly competitions held by various publishers had a somewhat harmful effect, since the prize books were occasionally of questionable artistic merit. Gradually, refined literature—lyric poetry, the short story, and drama—yielded to popular tastes and abandoned the realm of the imaginative, the fantastic, and the purely poetic, to focus on everyday reality.

At the same time, a conflict developed between the principles of internationalism and nationalism, but it was not felt too acutely. Estonian national poetry, possessing its own character, remains archival material that arouses the curiosity of those who study folklore, but fails to tempt the poet. Nevertheless, national and folk elements penetrate contemporary Estonian literature. Authors have turned their attention to the airplane, but they likewise glorify the swallow (Henrik Visnapuu, Marie Under, Artur Adson); they record the new rhythms of the city (Johannes Semper and Johannes Barbarus, who is very close to the French 'Unanimists'), and describe their native fields. In short story and novel, drama and comedy (Hugo Raudsepp), local, unadorned everyday life is portrayed in an attempt to develop a 'small' theme proposing a solution to the predicaments common to mankind.

Estonia, as a country at the crossroads, must be politically alert; stagnation is unthinkable. Thus the Estonian writer is always a critic as well, and a criticial spirit reigns at literary soirées and discussions. As a result, the writing fraternity is composed of fiercely competitive groups with contradictory slogans. This attitude enlivens literary life on the one hand, but the inclination toward criticism dampens enthusiasm on the other. This is why numerous examples of heroism and self-sacrifice are found in the history of the Estonians. Their struggle for independence, for example, is not satisfactorily reflected in their writings. . . . "

(Actually, the Arbujad group of the 1930s and its principal critics Ants Oras and Aleksander Aspel were staunch fighters for the Aestheticism and Western–European formalism. The significant poets of this movement, Heiti Talvik and Betti Alver, together with Aleksis Rannit, are the true formalists of Estonia. —Temira Pachmuss)

Chtets–deklamator: sbornik statey (The Reader–narrator: A Collection of Articles). Berlin: Ladyzhnikov, 1922

Her Monologue

It cannot be! Dreams, you are lying to me!
You cannot have forgotten me in parting...
I remember how, when in the flood of passion,
You wanted to burn my letters...to burn them...you!...

I know that priceless gifts are burned:
Lightning burns the arrogant heights,
The poet kindles violent bonfires of pearls,
And the manufacturer—oak groves for his machines;

Insensitive people burn the hearts,
Which for their sake have forgotten everything in the world;
The brigand burns the sanctuary of the palace
That prides itself on the revelry of centuries;

And geniuses burn their vigor
In alcohol—the symbol of weaknesses...
But to burn the letters, where I sing of you,
My love! Where I unfurl my wings!

One cannot burn them—like eternal beauty!
One cannot burn them—like the sunny sky!
In them are echoes of Eden and Erebus...
It cannot be! Dreams, you are lying to me!

———————·———————

The Thirteenth

I have a twelve-story palace,
I have a princess on each floor.
A wailing whirlwind somehow spied and eavesdropped—
And the whole world already knows.

It knows—and I don't care. I don't cheat with my heart!
I love all twelve of them—even to the scaffold!
I shall tune my harp, my golden harp,
I shall hide nothing, I shall tell everything...Here it is:

All my princesses are loving wives,
I am their sovereign, their loving husband.
By my searing kiss their breasts are burned,
The streams of their souls flow together in cascades.

Each one subtly complements another,
Each one is beautiful, each one has her charm:
One noiselessly laments, one loudly laughs—
My every heart rejoices!

I love each princess equally,
I give myself to each magnanimously...
Day and night I tread the stairs,
Drawing the curtain from bed after bed...

Day and night I walk, day and night I do not sleep,
In rapture, there is no time to grieve over a single moment.
My life begins with kisses and flows from kiss to kiss;
Eternal oblivion does not let me live.

But there are nights: I climb into the tower,
Alone I ascend to the thirteenth floor,
And I watch the sea, and I watch the field,
And one and the same vision charms me.

It would be nice in this glass room
To drink the black grape of golden dreams
With the eternally nameless, so strangely desired,
One whom I know not and am glad not to know.

The cliffs entreat the stars, the stars entreat the cliffs,
I vaguely understand the secret of cliffs and stars—
I fill the goblets with wine and soul
And propose an unrequited toast!...

———·———

July Noon

An elegant carriage, in electric pulsation,
Elastically rustled on the highway sand;
In it two virgin ladies, in quick-tempoed ecstasies,
In scarlet-meeting aspirations—like petal-seeking bees.

And pines flitted round, ideals of equality,
The sky floated, the sun sang, a little breeze somersaulted;
And under the tires of the motor, dust smoked, gravel
    jumped,
A little bird concurred with the wind on the road without
    roads...

At the monastery fence a monk froze like a pillar, ominously,
Hearing in the carriage's hoarseness sounds of "moral
    dissipation"...
And in fright shaking off the awakened grains of sand,
He cursed, with innocuous gaze, the frolicsome carriage.

Laughter, fresh as the sea, laughter, hot as a crater,
Flowed like lava from the carriage, cooling off in the heights
    of the spheres,
A path of water rustled quick as lightning under the wheels,
And the chauffeur, urged on, became drunk on the wine of
    ectasy.

————————·————————

The Rocking Chair of a Daydreaming Lady

To L. D. Ryndina

How nice it is for you to dream
Rocking in a cane hammock
Above a mystical eye—above a scumless pond!
Like visions, lady surprisers
Above the rocking chair of the daydreaming lady
Shine languorously in the moonlight: now Verlaine, now
    Proudhon.

What a miracle and wonder!
Lady Godiva are you now,
In an instant Iolanthe, in another Sappho...
You only have to spin around—
And your heart begins to dream:
Everything on earth is possible, you can do anything!

You rock to the left—
Queen of Queens,
Lady sovereign of the planet of blue antelopes—
Where, from deep sighs of gillyflowers,
There is such rapture
That an ordinary serf dreams in purple!
You rock to the right—
Glory smiles on you,
And your name breathes a fragrance like the flowers in the
gardens of paradise.

———————·———————

Violet Trance

Oh, Lily of liqueurs—oh, Crême de Violette!
I drank a violaceous vial of violet visions...
I immediately ordered a cabriolet
And sat on the gray maple in a satiny interval.

Clad in black velvet, my chauffeur—and minion—
Turned the crank, and the motor, shuddering,
Rushed forward like a neighing stallion,
And the rapturous wind tore off my beret.

I ordered him to go full speed. I impudently ordered him
To cast a spell on nature and lose his way!
When the chauffeur refused, I threw him out;
The car roared and whizzed through nature—full speed and
recklessly!

Did I drive through a village? Neither voices nor huts!
Did I cut into deciduous woods? Neither tree nor stump!
If the motor had exploded, I would have gnawed my hands!...
I became thunderously drunk, intoxicating everything along
my way...

And suddenly, with a frenzied jerk, my maplemobile froze.
I noticed a lily on a slope by a waterfall.
I bent down before her, hunchbacked with joy,
Thanking her for the meeting, for the blessed outcome...

I am inebriated. I am spring. I am calm. I'm a dreamer.
And am I really to blame that the flight of the lily
Can be seen so seldom, that the lilyless path is gray...
Oh, poison of violet visions—oh, Crème de Violette!

———————.———————

It was by the sea, where the foam is lacy,
Where a city carriage is rarely seen,
The queen played Chopin in the tower of her castle,
And, listening, the page fell in love with her.
It was all very simple, it was all very sweet;
The queen gave order to cut the pomegranate,
And she gave him half—and later made love
To the tune of sonatas, and exhausted the page.
But then she surrendered—surrendered thunderously;
Till dawn the lady slept as his slave.
It was by the sea, where the waves are turquoise,
Where the foam is lacy and sonatas are heard.

———————.———————

In a rustling moire dress, in a rustling moire dress,
Along the moonlit path, you pass like a mirage!...
Your dress is refined, your cape azure,
And the sandy path has leaves ornately patterned.
Like spider legs, like jaguar fur.
For a refined woman the night is always bridal,
Amorous ecstasies destined for you by fate,
In a rustling moire dress, in a rustling moire dress,
You are so aesthetic, you are so elegant!...
But whom will you take for your lover?   And will you find one
    good enough?
Wrap your tiny feet in an expensive jaguar plaid,
And sitting comfortably in a small motorized landau,
Entrust your life to a boy in a rubber mackintosh...
And close your eyes with your jasmine dress,
With your rustling moire dress, your rustling moire dress...

———————.———————

Champagne poured into a lily, champagne into a lily!
The sparkling champagne become sacred!
Mignon with Escamilio, Mignon with Escamilio!
Champagne in a lily is a sacred wine,
Ecstatically I sing Reichstag and Bastilio,
The dove and the hawk, the courtesan and the monk, impetuosity
　　　and sleep,
The disharmony of seas, lighthouse-unison.

———————·———————

The spring day is hot and young,
The entire city is sunlit!
I am myself again, again I am young,
I am young and in love again.
What scope, what freedom,
What songs and flowers!
My soul sings and yearns for the field.
I address all strangers like friends.
I'd love to fly in a carriage over pits and bumps,
I'd like to speed over fresh green meadows,
Look rosy-cheeked peasant woman in the face,
Kiss my enemy as a friend!
Rustle, leafy spring oak forests;
Grow, grass; bloom, lilac;
No one is guilty; all people are right
On such a blessed day!

———————·———————

In the morning the forest turns pink and lacy;
A tiny spider climbs up its fine-spun web;
The cheery dew glistens like diamonds;
What air, what light, what beauty!
Oh, I love to stroll through early morning oats,
To see a bird, a little frog or wasp,
To hear the sleepy crowing of the rooster
Swap with the distant echo: ha, ha, ha!...
Oh, I love to shout purposelessly in the morning!
Oh, I love to meet a wench in the trees.

Meet and, leaning against the fence,
Chase from her face the shadow of daybreak.
And embrace her trembling breast,
Arouse her somehow from slumber to life!

————·————

Yakor': antologiya zarubezhnoy poezii
(The Anchor: An Anthology of *Emigré*
Poetry; Berlin: Petropolis, 1938)
compiled by G. V. Adamovich and M.
L. Kantor

Only You Alone!

Not a single flower, not a single leaf.
My garden has turned autumnal. My garden is in pain.

I walk back and forth, I look from side to side.
What I am thinking, I will tell you now.

Only you alone are always, always, tender.
Always vital to my soul in mournful autumn.

I have only to gaze into your eyes
And spring has come again, and nightingales begin to warble.

And on my lips youthful verse begins to gleam
From the touch of your life-giving lips.

And though there may be in the garden not a single blossom,
And though there may be in the goblet not a single sip,

And though there may be in my desk not a single verse—
I await your beckoning benevolent hand!

————·————

In the Monastery Sunset

If the sunset is golden,
It is stifling in the holy tower.

How can I accept mortification
Of the flesh, of my own flesh?

I fling my spirit into heaven...
My feeble entreaties are in vain:
Whoever has partaken of the bread
Is forever a slave of the flesh.

These blossoms, these birds,
Odors, and the strip of sky
Gilded with warmth
Simply drive one mad...

Even in our labor we are idle—
Have mercy, take pity!
You, yourself, scattered temptations
Throughout your wondrous creation...

Where, then, will I find in my weak spirit
The strength for mortification of the flesh?
If the sunset is golden—
It is unbearable in the garden...

———————·———————

The nightingales of the monastery garden,
Like all other nightingales on earth,
Say that there is but one delight,
And that this delight is love...

And the flowers of the monastery meadow
With a caress only flowers can give
Say that there is only one virtue:
To touch your beloved's lips..

The lakes of the monastery forest,
Filled to overflowing with blue,
Say that no gaze is more azure
Than the gaze of those in love and beloved.

———————·———————

En Route

I go, and with each step more zealously
Adding mile to mile—link to link.
Who am I? I am Igor' Severyanin,
Whose name is as daring as wine.

In my throat are spasms of ecstasy,
And the hair on my head
Flies into wondrous motion,
As in olden days in Moscow...

There were gold-domed churches
And souls more fragile than glass.
There my life was in the flower of its glory,
My life flowed in the flower of its glory.

Glory, foaming and golden!
They are bitter, your turbid dregs.
And reciting myself to myself,
I swallow mile after mile.

————·————

The One Called Sadness

Like a woman no longer young, but still
Captivating in her langour,
She fluffed up a bed of red maple leaves,
She, whom people call sadness...

And she reclined, attracting both sinfully and slyly
With the sadness of fading passion.
Necessary to my soul as glory
The curve of her autumnal shoulder...

With the passing years we cease to sing of spring:
The closer we come to old age, the more clearly we see
That the empty desolation of autumn
Is nearer the heart than the gardens of spring.

Via Sacra: Almanac (Tartu: Izd. Vadim Bergman, 1922)

The Bacchante from Kalyari
A One-Act Mignonette

Livorno Station.   Train car, partitioned lengthwise.   Doors of all the compartments are open.

PORTER.	Follow me, please. Number five.
	Here's your seat—in the third compartment.
PASSENGER.	An empty car! What bliss!
	Will the train be stopping here long?
PORTER.	It leaves at three—according to schedule.
	Thank you, sir. Good day.
PASSENGER.	So, Africa, farewell! Next to Italy
	Your beauty seems nasty to me.
	And so, after this transfer,
	I will be home within two hours.
	Beloved! A two-month separation!
	Let me kiss your elegant hands,
	Let me utter heartfelt words!
	My wife! Desired one! How painful!
	My soul is devoutly attracted to you.
	Forgive me: I'm barely alive myself...
	Can it be I'm to blame that you
	Could not go on tour with me?
	So on Doctor Verne's advice
	You remained at home, half-ill.
	But how could I ever have left you? That
	Is the question that needs to be answered.
	Let singing be my only income,
	And Marcella—my only friend in the world!
	But without an income one cannot surround
	One's darling with considerate attention,
	And so I am doomed to wanderings,
	Sliding forever from stage to stage,
	Portraying some kind of automaton...
CONDUCTOR.	Your ticket, please. Number six.
	Please sit here in this compartment.

WOMAN
PASSENGER.   Thank you. Put the basket here.
              That's right.
PASSENGER.   Will you allow me to smoke?
SHE.   But this is the smoking section.
HE.   I know. It's for smokers and...mourners.
SHE.   Please speak more clearly.
HE.   Madam, don't ask. I'm too
              Depressed.
SHE.   But I am fine.
              And so we'll drink [Veuve] Clicquot
              And abandon ourselves to all sorts of excesses...
HE.   Who will—we?
SHE.   Of course, I, and you,
              Maestro Leggiere, first tenor.
HE.   But who are you?
SHE.   For your head, I
              Am a puzzle, for your soul—betrayal...
              Uncork the champagne more quickly:
              I want to drink the flowing needles—
              In me streams the blood of a true Creole,
              In my brain are the patterned whims of fairies...
              I love you, Maestro Leggiere...
              You will be mine, if not—here's the cure!
HE.   I will be yours? You say, "yours,"
              When my wife may be dying,
              When, when...
SHE.   His blood is already stirring...
              Come to me, my beloved, faithful page.
HE.   You are a prostitute! You are a filthy fiend!
              You are a monster! Stop using that tone.
SHE.   ...Look through the web of my *dessous*
              At the rose of my flesh in ecstasy...
              Look more boldly, feast your eyes, don't be shy—
              I will give you my flaming body.
              For a whole year I have wanted to possess you,
              And finally! Oh, awaited hour, break forth!
              Take me—lest I boldly take poison.
              Why are you hesitating? Come close—and possess
                  me!

HE.   But wait a bit, hear me out, evil one,
          You are beautiful, to be sure, but have mercy—
          I feel the battle within my chest,
          I am all inflamed...

SHE.   Take me: I am a funnel,
          In an instant I will cool your tormenting heat.
          I am awaiting you. Taste ecstasy with me.

HE.   I can't. I shouldn't. Leave me.
          My wife is ill.

SHE.   But I am well,
          And I want you. Only I am reality,
          Whereas she is delirim, grimly torturing.

HE.   But I love her.

SHE.   Love her, why not?
          I am not interfering with your love. Kiss me,
          Caress me, and afterwards throw me aside.
          What does it matter that you will take me?
          Think about it a little. Is there really
          A transgression hidden in this—to be before the
             world
          Free from conventions and the paths
          Of daily prejudices? Two minutes
          Are enough for a brief betrayal,
          Giving me such great ecstasy!
          Oh, can it be possible that you reject me?
          Oh, can it be possible? Hurry, there is only half
             an hour
          Left to Ravenna, you know.
          So from passion let us create miracles!
          Look how you are suffering. In an hour
          You'll walk in to your sick—perhaps dead—wife.
          In me is the well of your future strength.
          You, overwhelmed by my passion,
          Will find in me the source of new strength,
          And, in the unhappy event, oblivion as well...(She
             cries).

HE.   What? Did I not ask you to be mine?
          Did I not understand? Did I reject you? Did I
             not moisten
          With tears, your gaze, full of inspiration?

Forgive me, forgive.   I will be yours, believe me,
Yes, yours forever!

SHE.   Close the door tighter
And take back the ages—give an instant...

CURTAIN

———————·———————

Aero-farce

A Farce in Three Scenes

Scene One

The Apartment of a Married Couple

HUSBAND.   (Folding a telegram)
                I must go to Geneva for about three days.
                The Commercial Bank is calling me...
                I must abandon my queen.
WIFE.   Tell them to uncork my drink immediately.
                I want to drink to your success.
HUSBAND.   (Rings. A servant appears.)
                Get my wife her favorite drink.
WIFE.   And also candy, halvah, and nuts...
HUSBAND.   Bring everything she has ordered.
WIFE.   So when does your train leave?
HUSBAND.   At ten after three.
                In twenty-four hours I'll be in Geneva.
WIFE.   And so,
                Will you forsake me?   Don't take it into your
                    head
                To play tricks on me in Geneva.
HUSBAND.   You're a funny one!
WIFE.   So are you!
HUSBAND.   Good-bye, my dear!
WIFE.   Good-bye, my beloved!
HUSBAND.   Take care of yourself, and so forth.
WIFE.   Stop
                The banalities.

HUSBAND.   Well, may you be guarded
By the seraphim.
(Drops the telegram and walks away)
WIFE.   I only hope I see him again!
(Picking up the telegram)
Pleasant news!   Could I have imagined anything
        like this?
So, you wanted to make a fool of your wife?
"The Commercial Bank" is named Juliet?
I am declaring war on you without delay!
Out of your holiday I'll make a workday, and
Cruelly disrupt your devilish plan.
(Rings and speaks to the servant)
Order me a special plane from Blerio
For five this afternoon!

                         *

                    Scene Two

                 Aboard the Plane

WIFE.   When will we get to Geneva?
PILOT.   At seven exactly.
It's a two-hour flight from here.
WIFE.   Do you fly cool-headedly enough?
PILOT.   Only your beauty could distract me.
WIFE.   Be frank, I'm not really that pretty, am I?
PILOT.   You are simply beautiful, madam.
WIFE.   What a pleasant suprise!   I'll answer you
                truthfully:
I'm glad you're a model pilot!
PILOT.   I'm moved, madam, by your praise...
WIFE.   Just as I am moved by your compliment to me...
Tell me: Are we high above the ground?
PILOT.   More than two thousand feet in all.
WIFE.   In the magic
Of the flight, I completely forgot the purpose
Of my trip to Geneva.
PILOT.   What is your purpose?

WIFE.	I'm going to get even with my spouse, find him in his lover's
	Bed—those whom the sight of me will scarcely intoxicate...
PILOT.	Would it not be better to gaze on one in whom
	You are able to stir an excess of amorous desires?
WIFE.	Are you offering me an intoxicating drink?...
PILOT.	Oh, rather let me draw you to my heart!

*

Scene Three

Juliet's Apartment

WIFE.	(Lies in Juliet's bed)
HUSBAND.	(Entering)
	Juliet! I hope I'm not dreaming! I am with you again!
	My soul is scorched with mad passion!
	Yesterday, I finally got away from my wife!
WIFE.	But I am not Juliet. I am your wife!
HUSBAND.	My wife?! Not Juliet?! I must be insane! Oh, God!
	When did I lose my mind?!
	This is all like a fairy tale, a miracle!
	But how did you get here? Trains from home
	Come to Geneva only once a day?
	What do your crazy jokes mean?
	But no, I am insane! I must be ill! Yes! Yes!
WIFE.	Yes, yes! You belong in a dungeon
	Or in a madhouse. Shame and disgrace on you!
	I came by plane,
	And made love to the pilot on the way!
HUSBAND.	She, unfaithful to me! But where is Juliet?
WIFE.	She set off for N. on an airplane,
	Lost her heart to the pilot, blacked out...
HUSBAND.	Oh, these infidelities drive me made!
WIFE.	But that's not all. He's taking her for his bride
	And asks you as witness at the wedding.

HUSBAND.   (Giving in)
                What can I do! All right. I was already thinking
                    myself
                That it's time for me to stop being...being...
                                            ...A scoundrel!

                        CURTAIN

                                    Completed in March, 1922.
                                        Toila, Estonia.

————————·————————

The poems of Severyanin that appeared in *The Reader-Narrator* represent a variety of styles: There is an imaginative verse, stylized and humorous love poetry, a serious love poem, and two poems extolling the joys of nature.   Throughout, Severyanin's poetry abounds in striking, concrete imagery—colorful, lush, and sensuous.   His lexicon, frequently supplemented with eccentric neologisms, is unusual, particularly in his earlier poems.

Four poems in the collection are typical of Severyanin's earlier period as an Ego-Futurist before World War I. Often bizarre and ambiguous in style and imagery, they provide the best examples of the neologisms (usually untranslatable, unfortunately) for which he was famous. In his playful "The Rocking Chair of a Daydreaming Lady," Severyanin imitates the motion of the rocking chair by doubling the length of every line and extending these longer lines to the left of the margin.   One stanza in particular shows the exoticism of Severyanin's imagery:

        You rock to the left—
        Queen of Queens,
    Lady sovereign of the planet of blue antelopes,
        Where, from deep sighs of gillyflowers,
        There is such rapture
    That an ordinary serf dreams in purple!

"July Noon" and "Violent Trance" are delightfully preposterous poems centering on early motorcars.   In the first poem, a monk is scandalized by "two virgin ladies" in a motorized "carriage," while the car's amazing speed puts the ladies in "quick-tempoed ecstasies" and inebriates the chauffeur.   The poem's rhythm mimics the car's "electric pulsation." Each line is composed of eight trochees with a caesura in the middle, but in effect only every other foot has a strong stress. Thus, the result is: x́ x x́ x x́ x x́ x / x́ x x́ x x́ x x́ x. The weaker stresses create pulsation.

In "Violent Trance" speed again brings about a kind of ecstasy—the *persona*, whizzing recklessly through nature, becomes "thunderously drunk, intoxicating everything along my way..." But his drunkenness is also caused by dreams and flowers. It is the "Crème de Violette, a violaceous vial of violet visions..." that starts him on his wild ride, but "a lily on a slope by a waterfall" immediately subdues him and leads to the beautiful meditation at the end of the poem: "And am I really to blame that the flight of the lily/Can be seen so seldom, that the lilyless path is gray..."

The vignette "Champagne poured into a lily..." is among Severyanin's most famous poems, still often recited in Russia by the younger generation. It is composed in a four-foot amphibrachic meter and contains much repetition and internal rhyme which make for a unique rich sound. Its apparent lack of meaning also contributed to its popularity. The entire content of the poem is based on unlikely combinations of diverse elements, frequently opposites, of which "champagne into a lily" is the quintessence. The synthesis of these radically different elements leads to a heightened synaesthetic experience and transforms the champagne into "a sacred wine."

"The Thirteenth" is quite different in style but it probably also dates from Severyanin's earlier period. Written in a humorous vein, it seems somewhat like a parody of the serious metaphysical poetry of the Symbolists. It begins like a playful love poem but, instead of one beloved, the poet has twelve. He loves them all equally; he writes: "Each one subtly complements another." He portrays himself as "their sovereign," who gives himself "to each one magnanimously"; the "eternal oblivion" of kisses and rapture "does not let me live." "But there are nights" when the poet ascends to the "thirteenth floor" of his "twelve-story palace," hoping to catch a glimpse of yet another lady, "the eternally nameless, so stangely desired,/One whom I know not and," Severyanin adds whimsically, "am glad not to know." For the Symbolists a female figure like Vladimir Solovyov's Sophia or Blok's "Beautiful Lady" represented the spiritual embodiment of the divine wisdom of the universe, but she is subject to

Severyanin's mocking irony here.   Divine wisdom is summed up and dismissed neatly in the last stanza: "The cliffs entreat the stars, the stars entreat the cliffs,/I vaguely understand the secret of cliffs and stars." He ends with another image characteristic of the Symbolists: "I fill the goblets with wine and soul/And propose an unrequited toast!..."   Thus, by juxtaposing the unresponsive and ill-fated dream lady with his twelve real and loving princesses, Severyanin lightly dismisses the ideal in favor of the sensual and the concrete.   The irresistible attraction exerted by the "thirteenth" is negative and disturbing and is resented.

"Her Monologue" stands out from the rest because of its serious nature.   It is a love poem composed from a woman's point of view and built around the idea of burning, which becomes a leitmotif.   "The poet kindles violent bonfires of pearls," to which the *persona* contrasts her lover's burning of her letters.

"It was at the sea, where the foam is lacy" is a beautiful stylized poem, simple, controlled, and symmetrical like a Chopin sonata.   The sensuous detail and the neologism "thunderously" reveal Severyanin's touch.   Each line is divided by a caesura into two musical phrases, each consisting of two trochees followed by an amphibrach.   Repetition and internal rhyme also contribute to the poem's musical nature.

The poem "In a rustling moire dress" requires some observations on Severayanin's artistic method, his mastery of sound and imagery tricks.   The poem consists of fifteen lines; the first, eighth, and fifteenth are practically identical: "In a rustling moire dress, in a rustling moire dress."   These lines are shorter than the other lines, forcing the reader to dwell on them longer, to pronounce the words more slowly and emphatically.   Metrically, the poem is an ususual combination of trochee and amphibrach, with dactylic endings before the caesuras and at the end of the lines.   These dactylic endings produce a rich melodiousness, languorously drawn out.   In addition, the hissing consonant sounds, *sh*, *zh*, *ch*, *s* and *z*, are used repeatedly to imitate the rustling sound of the dress.   The imagery is sensuous and unusual.   For example, the pattern of the leaves on the sandy path is "Like spider legs, like jaguar fur."   The thoughts expressed are original: "For a refined woman the night is always bridal."   This line has become a favorite aphorism among sophisticated Russian teen-agers. The lady with her rich refined elegance is contrasted sharply with her escort: "Wrap your tiny feet in an expensive jaguar plaid,/And sitting comfortably in a small motorized landau,/Entrust your life to a boy in a rubber mackintosh..." Severyanin's vocabulary, his use of Western words like "aesthetic" and "comfortable," produce quite a strange effect in the original Russian.

"In the morning the forest turns pink and lacy" and "The spring day is hot and young" are more conservative and uncharacteristic of the early Severyanin. Full of life and sensuous enjoyment of love and nature, they contain a wealth of concrete, but rather conventional details. The two poems indicate Severyanin's life in Estonia, which led to a considerable shift in the basic tenor of his poetry. Several of his later poems, included in Adamovich's and Kantor's anthology of émigré poetry, *The Anchor*, are more subdued and reveal a mood of meditation and notalgia. The themes of these poems range from the bittersweet pleasures of love and the sadness of aging to questions of religious faith and the decline of poetic creativity.

"The One Called Sadness" opens with the image of "a woman, no longer young, but still/Captivating in her languor . . . whom people call sadness." The paradoxical impulses of passion and sadness intermingle in the second stanza to produce a rich texture of lyrical ambiguity. The disparate themes converge in the strikingly beautiful epithet of her "autumnal shoulder," which becomes a pivotal image enabling the shift to a discussion of the inexorable passage of time.

"In the Monastery Sunset" is striking for the way in which Severyanin uses physical details—"These blossoms, these birds,/ Odors, and the strip of sky/Guilded with warmth"—to emphasize, by contrast, the poet's metaphysical anguish. Particularly effective are the beginning and ending lines of the poem: "If the sunset is golden,/It is stifling in the holy tower"; "If the sunset is golden—/It is unbearable in the garden." A golden sunset could scarcely cause physical pain; instead, this beautiful image serves to stress the spiritual torment experienced. The world around is so beautiful that it is impossible to renounce it.

The loss of poetic inspiration and public recognition is the subject of two poems in this group. In "Only You Alone" Severyanin writes: "My garden has turned autumnal. My garden is in pain." The garden, of course, is his poetry. The poet addresses his Muse, with the hope that she will again visit him: "I have only to gaze into your eyes—/And spring has come again, and

nightingales begin to warble./And on my lips youthful verse begins
to gleam/From the touch of your life-giving lips." Still optimistic
that inspiration eventually will come, the poet concludes: "I await
the beckoning of your benevolent hand."

In "En Route" Severyanin regains, at least for the moment,
the bravado and energy of his earlier Ego-Futurist days when he
states, "Who am I? I am Igor' Severyanin,/Whose name is as
daring as wine." He makes it clear that he has not yet lost his
poetic inspiration or ability to write. "In my throat are spasms of
ecstasy,/And the hair on my head/Flies into wondrous motion,/As
in olden days in Moscow..." Nonetheless, the tone of the poem is
sad, as Severyanin yearns for the recognition and glory of his
Moscow days. Now he is merely "reciting myself to myself" and
swallowing the "bitter," "turbid dregs" of his glory. Particularly
effective in this poem is the delicate image evoking the "olden
days" destroyed by the Revolution: "There were gold-domed
churches/And souls more fragile than glass."

The rollicking one-act plays "Aero-farce" and "Bacchante
from Kalyari" both date from Severyanin's earlier period. Written
in 1922 in Estonia, the plays treat the themes of adultery and
sexual promiscuity—shockingly unconventional to Russian audiences
—in a humorous, ironic vein and make fun of romantic traditions.
The language of the plays is stylized and artificial; the dramatic
situation is bizarre and incongruous. In "Aero-farce," a wife, on
the way to Geneva to prevent her husband from committing
infidelities, ends up being unfaithful herself. In "Bacchante from
Kalyari," a passenger's gushy protestations of love for his wife soon
become ludicrous when a "bacchante" attempts to seduce him and
he, protesting wildly ("you are a filthy fiend!"), wavers and
succumbs! Thus, in both plays the woman triumphs and the man
is seen as weak and insincere. Much of the humor of the plays
can be attributed to the clever dialogue. Both women speak and
act with amazing frankness, while the men are simply
dumbfounded. In "Bacchante from Kalyari," for example, when he,
bemoaning his fate, says "Madam, don't ask: I'm too/Depressed,"
she answers, "But I am fine./And so we'll drink *Clicquot*/And
abandon ourselves to all sorts of excesses..." to which he can reply
only "Who will—we?" And later when he protests that his wife is
ill, she retorts, "But I am well,/And I want you." When the wife
in "Aero-farce" finds out that her husband has an affair with
Juliet, she immediately orders a plane, flies to Geneva, and awaits

him in his mistress' bed!   But when the husband arrives, he doesn't even notice the difference at first.   The plays are clever in conception and poetic finish and are enjoyable reading.   They are both written in verse.   "Aero-farce" is in a four-foot iambic. Various rhyme schemes are used to create the impression of a frivolous, but natural and illogical conversation highlighting the characters' idiosyncracies.

ALEXANDROVSKY, VLADIMIR
(VALMAR ADAMS; b. Jan. 30, 1899)

Adams-Alexandrovsky was born in St. Petersburg.   Russian by birth but a resident of Estonia, he signed his creative works with both names.   He studied in Tartu and Prague.   An assistant professor at the University of Tartu in the 1930s, Adams is the author of several publications, including *Peyzazh u Gogolya* (Landscape in Gogol); articles and poems in the literary almanacs *Via Sacra, In a Foreign Land,* and *Staroe i novoe* (The Old and the New; Tallinn: N. E. Bagrov, Nos. 1-4, 1931-33), and a collection of poems *Zhitie* (Live; n.p., n.d.).[1]

Adams still writes poetry in Estonian, and is considered an Estonian poet and scholar interested in Russian literature and culture.   One of his latest publications is *Ob umenii govorit' publichno* (About the Art of Speaking in Public; Tartu: Tartu University, 1965; 59 pp.).

Via Sacra (from the cycle "Early Spring")

Via Sacra

I have grown all shining and serene.
God has sent us spring again.
I no longer want to sleep
On the painfully clear-cut road.
Art has become a young maiden to me again,
And again I believe in popular legends,
And again the ailing Firebird
Molts its fiery feathers.

Silence forms lakes in my mind.
Only a few thoughts have crowded together like children...
And at night—a large moon
Shines on the puddles.

_____._____

Leidale

Our white meeting has died,
And the meteors' flares have burned out;
One uncaressing evening you wrote:
"In this world there is nothing, nothing.

The sun no longer serves the liturgy
And the gusts do not weave a minuet;
There is no king and no crown prince,
And no emerald palace."

Sleek clouds, like handkerchiefs,
Swelled up with light, like tears...
I so clearly saw the trap,
And confirmed: There is nothing in the world.

1922

_____._____

Revelation

Else-dem Profil ihrer Seele.

In my crystalline intoxication
I don't need the joy of happiness.
The Mother of God, in Her evil struggle,
Like a little girl, is friendly with me.
All white, distant, immovable,
My cold God is terrible.
I love Him and I hate Him.
I want to be like Him, serene.
On my solitary road
I don't need strangers' shadows:

Oh, happiness—it is so *little*;
The pulse of life so monotonous.
I pray to God that I may be able to complete my path,
But let it remain a *mystery*:
I cannot allow you
To understand my path!

————.————

The lyrics of Adams-Alexandrovsky are tightly compressed, emotionally and thematically complex experiments in verse. The themes range from meditations on love and its loss, to a religious search for the meaning of life and comprehension of man's relationship to God.

In "Via Sacra" these motifs are presented indirectly, while the main body of the poem reveals the poet's internal reactions to the fact that "God has sent us spring again." With its delicate warmth, the return of spring seems to open the poet's consciousness the way it opens the buds of flowers long clenched by cold winter's hand. The abysses of doubt, disbelief, and confusion become resolved, not through an individual effort of will, but by the inevitable processes of enigmatic nature. These processes, it seems, are intimately bound with the image of God and raise question of a spiritual order.

"Leidale," on the other hand, deals in romantic terms with the death of romance. The *persona's* naïve lover describes the terminated love affair as the end of an age of romance: "There is no king and no crown prince." The description by the narrator, conversely, is still and unemotional: "Our white meeting has died." His apparent restraint lends force to the last line of the poem: "I . . . confirmed: There is nothing in the world." Adams-Alexandrovsky's use of rich, dazzling imagery and new, unusual similes—such as "sleek clouds, like handkerchiefs,/Swelled up with light, like tears..."—energizes the theme and adds a fresh perspective.

"Revelation" is a brief, but dense and ambivalent poem about the *persona's* uneasy recognition of his own mortality, smallness, and ignorance in the face of an omniscient, all-powerful God. This realization leads him to cry out "I love Him and I hate Him," not only accentuating the nature of this relationship, but revealing the poet's duality. This duality of irreconcilable tendencies within him

is manifest in other places.   It is to Adams–Alexandrovsky's credit
that he is able to place such antithetical considerations within a
single poem and, by their synthesis, lead his readers to new visions
of reality and of God.

Formally, these poems are not as experimental as the works
of some of the other Imaginist poets.   "Revelation" is written in
iambic tetrameters, common in Russian verse.   "Leidale" and "Via
Sacra," however, are both written in ternary meters—"Leidale" in
anapestic trimeter and "Via Sacra" in amphibrachic trimeter.   In
both of these poems an occasional syllable is omitted, resulting in
slight metric variations.   In "Via Sacra" the pattern is modified
further: Lines one to four and nine to twelve have alternating
feminine and masculine rhymes, but the rhymes in lines five to
eight are all feminine, making this section (in which the poet
amplifies his conception of art, his "Via Sacra," with its somewhat
"decadent" characteristics) stand out in contrast to the rest of the
poem.

NOTE

1. Adams–Alexandrovsky's first collections of poetry *Suudius lumme* (The Kiss
    into the Snow, 1921) and *Valguse valust* (About the Pains of Light, 1926)
    provoked a spirited discussion in Estonia.   Adams–Alexandrovsky appeared
    here as a modernist poet, artificial and even at times obscure, yet highly
    cultured and revealing profound feeling and thought.   See also his third
    collection of poems, *Maise matka poolel teel* (In the Middle of My Path on
    Earth, 1932).

PRAVDIN, BORIS VASILYEVICH (1886–1950?)

Pravdin was a professor at the University of Tartu, where he
taught Russian language and literature in the School of Law.
Lawyers in Estonia at that time were still using the Special Baltic
Book of Laws of the Russian Empire.   It was Pravdin who created
the Tartu "Guild of Poets," a friendly, semi–serious group
consisting of several beginning poets and their older colleague,
Professor Pravdin.   He was about forty, a passionate chess player,
and a close friend of Russian poets Igor' Severyanin and Ivan
Belyaev.   Because he spent his summers in Paris, he knew many
Russian writers and artists there, in particular Goncharova and

Larionov who always visited his home in Tartu on the way from
Paris to Russia and back.   Larionov presented him with a mosaic
portrait, "Man with Moustache," in which Pravdin merrily
recognized himself.

Pravdin was on intimate terms with "Parisian note" poets
like Georgy Adamovich and his adherents, but was a modernist
himself.   One of his miniatures in verse began in this way:

> Moy poyas stoit dva talanta
> > serebra.
> Ya doch' verkhovnogo ierofanta
> > Ammona-Ra.
> (My belt costs two silver talers.
> I am the daughter of Supreme Hierophant Ammon-Ra.)

———————·———————

Via Sacra

> So cold were the pillars,
> The ancient, stern, white hall,
> When your mysteriously moaning voice
> First flared up, then died away!
>
> You angrily sang about Gomorrah
> And wove myrtles in honor of Beauty;
> And in a Verlainified version of "Amores"
> You prayed to Reality and to Dream.
>
> But neither your regular sestets
> Nor the maidenly hymns of Visnapuu
> Uplifted the crowd from the drowsy mire,
> Or enveloped it in azure.
>
> Let us be blind and wretched;
> Carry your selfless cross.
> Your unexpected arrival was
> For a few a "goblet of Hebe."

7.II.1920

———————·———————

Perka

Not to that one.

I like the stormy Perka
With her carnival spirit.
She undoubtedly is a daydreamer,
And I—not exactly a stranger.

Her impetuosity is near and dear to me,
The rapturously whirling tone,
Her flaming aggressiveness
And boundless effusiveness.

Sobbing fireworks
Of clear, refined poems
Are nothing before the screeches of Perka,
Bacchante of Estonian forests.

If excesses against a background
Of shop windows and cinemas are naïve,
Are the transports of a woman satirist to blame
For the wine splashing in them?

A special yardstick is needed here,
An approach by a non-banal path.
Long live the stormy Perka
With her carnival spirit!

                                                    1920

———————·———————

V. M.

Let's go off to the century of the Duchesse de la Vallière,
To the age of Boileau, shepherdsesses, and Molière,
Of grand refined manners,
Haughty curls, and artificial beauty marks.

Put on a garment in the style of Louis Quatorze
Of a pinkish opal shade,
And drink icy, green fruit juice
From a slender crystal goblet.

Let violinists play a minuet
In the mysterious, invisible pavilion.
Let a powdered poet read to you
A trite madrigal in a minor key.

How pathetic he is! How dull his gaze has grown!
How cruel you are!...And in the darkness of the garden,
With a rain of rubies, splendid fireworks
Will announce to you the beginning of the masquerade.

———————·———————

The poems of Boris Pravdin are exquisitely crafted pieces which attain a moving, emotional tenor through the intermingling of many different lyrical elements. Like Osip Mandelshtam's, Pravdin's modernism largely consists of the careful allusions which, in Pravdin's poetry, range from myths of ancient Greece to the style and manners of seventeenth-century Neoclassical France.

This aspect of his verse is especially evident in "So cold were the pillars," where a Biblical allusion to Gomorrah, references to "a Verlainified version of 'Amores,'" and the "maidenly hymns of Visnapuu," as well as "a goblet of Hebe," all amplify Pravdin's lyric in praise of a fellow poet. These allusions enhance the lyrical quality of the poetry by widening and deepening its emotional tone.

The poet and the value of poetry are central in "V. M." as well. Here Pravdin evokes a stylized scene of seventeenth-century France with its "grand, refined manners" and its "style of Louis Quatorze." The superimposition of these details sets off the figure of the pitiful "powdered poet" with his "trite madrigal in a minor key." This poet is an ambivalent figure, perhaps he signifies no more than a pleasant, though ineffective, diversion before the masquerade. Perhaps his voice is drowned out by "the rain of rubies, splendid fireworks . . . " Pravdin may be implying that the clamor of the world overcomes the poet and that the truth he hopes to convey is lost amid the fashions of the day.

In "V. M.," Pravdin hints at an affectation and artificiality characteristic of Russian decadent literature of the *fin-de-siècle*. Pravdin sees this literature as trite and pretentious, an escape to seventeenth-century Neoclassical France with its "grand, refined manners" and the strict aesthetic rules of Boileau. The "powdered poet" reading his "trite madrigal in a minor key" is pathetic. The imagery is striking and colorful—"a rain of rubies," "icy, green fruit juice." Pravdin's intent seems serious. There may be some critical allusions to Symbolism, as in the lines "in the mysterious, invisible pavilion" or "in the darkness of the garden."

The bizarre and ambiguous poem "Perka" is clearly a jest at the expense of Igor' Severyanin, whose language and style are imitated here. In fact, Severyanin's neologism *"grezerka,"* a rapturous, daydreaming lady, appears in the first stanza in the original rhyming with "perka." "The stormy Perka/With her carnival spirit" seems to be an Estonian version of Severyanin's *grezerka*, whose "boundless effusiveness" and "sobbing fireworks/Of clear, refined poems/Are nothing before the screeches of Perka,/Bacchante of Estonian forests." Perhaps Perka can also be a personification of Pravdin's own style of writing. At least, by pointing out Perka's affinities with the *grezerka*, Pravdin suggests that his style shares some of Severyanin's characteristics. But Pravdin remains original and more excessive than Severyanin. The amphibrachic meter also contributes to the poem's intoxicating tone.

Here is an unpublished poem of Boris Pravdin from the album of Elizabeth Bazilevskaya-Roos. "Philidor" reveals Pravdin as a passionate chess player, who used striking images in his poems.

From the cycle "Kaissa's Delights"

Philidor

Philidor (François–André–Dunican), compositeur français et célèbre joueur d'échec, né à Dreux, 1726–95.)
Petit Larousse illustré.

You are akin to me, the majestic maestro
Of the famous epoch of white wigs.
The Copernicus of the chess! For whom in deathless glory
The fanfares of three centuries resound.

And isn't it for you that the recollections blossom
In the elegant Café de la Régence—
Where you were the first—so the sayings go—
To give à l'aveugle a brilliant séance?

The creator of the chess opening—this date remains
    immortal.
The father of chess expertise! O how keen
Your positional game!

How wise are the words of Your Treatise!
Outside of the path made by your efforts alone
Lasker and Réti are quite impossible!

1926

BELYAEV, IVAN (literary pseudonym INNO VASK)

Belyaev, a close friend of Boris Pravdin and a very talented Russian poet in Estonia, was the author of a collection of poetry, *Prokazhenny perst* (A Leprous Finger; Tartu: Bergman, 1924). He contributed to the almanacs *Via Sacra, In a Foreign Land,* and *The Old and the New.* He wrote ultramodernistic poetry, wanted to have nothing in common with the "Parisian note," and practiced free verse. His modern style is evident in the following lines: "With my leprous finger, I piously furrow my brow/The incense of my stench [rises] to a mysterious God..." "Can one's soul flow into paper?..." In answer to this question, the letters forming the title of the volume stretched themselves viscously over the cover. Each page had its own semantic definition, such as "A Sounding Shaft-Bow," "The Sounding Shaft-Bows," and "The Unfolded Sounding Shaft-Bows."

Accompanied by his wife Zizi Albrecht, Belyaev left Estonia for the Soviet Union in 1926. He died in a Soviet labor camp, and she returned to Estonia and told their friends of her husband's fate.

Via Sacra

I wrapped my holey heart in cotton
It's sort of cold. I huddle up. Life is so bumpy.
The past sneaks up from behind like a shadow, absurdly
     emaciated.
I shudder at the thought. In general, everything is absurd.
                              It would be easier to die.

My life is a running sore, with ragged skin.
For what?   To whom will I show my pain?   It's rather
     stupid.
But life gets insolent, sticks out its tongue, and makes faces,
And you jolt along on its bumps, so disoriented, out
                         of step...

I withdraw into myself—I leave the main road and hide in
     the bushes.
The tiniest breeze gets on my nerves.   Deeper into the
     cotton!
I see how the sun cuts flowers with golden scissors.
I glance indifferently at the path, gnawed and trampled
                         by mankind's boot...
And spit at everything. I am calm. I do not envy my
     bustling fellow man...

                 —————·—————

Starry vomit is spread out above me like a peacock's tail.
I see a bull in the sky,
Kneeling,
Kicking up the black earth with his legs,
Prayerfully bellowing about something.
And I myself—so
Small,
Hurt,
I also want to drop down on my hands
And quietly start barking
About eternity
Straight into the jaws of the sky,

Toothless,
So it would know me,
The little one,
Who knows how to bark.

—————·—————

Ex libro amoris

Love again?   And again, falls into marshy holes
And the step, hollow, heavy, on the swampy paths
Of love?...
Yes, yes, I realize, again it has overtaken me,
Again it shoots at me the pitiless needles
Of love...
And covered with a hazy crimson shroud,
In blissful, slavelike spinelessness I abandon myself to the
      sting
Of love...
Pierce me then! Yawn like the toothy abyss!
Weave from blood and magnet a web
Of love!...

—————·—————

To M. Denisova

Such a tiny little fellow—
                  —yet how he wept
—Alone on the square.
But behind him—
                  loathsome like a rag—
The street language, calico-red, fluttered.
And all around floated grimaces,
                                    obscene,
Furrowing the square.
And laughter bared its rotten teeth
Then I approached
                  and said quietly:
"Ladies and gentlemen! I demand absolute silence!"
I said quietly.

And all the nasty little Philistines tumbled out of their
    windows,
Out of their little potbellied houses,
          their little mugs against the stones.

———————·———————

Belyaev's verse is noteworthy for its verbal experimentation,
its Dostoevskian intensity, and its lyrical compactness.   Images,
themes, and concepts are interwoven to produce a volatile mixture
of ambivalent, subjective perspectives.   With startling metaphors,
unusual epithets, and lyrical dexterity, Belyaev asserts a unique
vision of man, his relations with the world, and his significance
within the universe.

The imagery is heightened by the often feverish pitch of the
persona's sensations and reactions to the world.   This Dostoevskian
aspect of Belyaev's verse not only points to his metaphysical
preoccupations, but also to his physical perceptions.   "The tiniest
breeze gets on my nerves," he notes in the poem, and "I wrapped
my holey heart with cotton."   Indeed, this poem may serve as an
example of Belyaev's poetic style.   Similes like "The past sneaks
up from behind like a shadow, absurdly emaciated" and metaphors
like "My life is a running sore" are effectively combined with a
personification of the sun cutting "flowers with golden scissors,"
and the epithet of "mankind's boots," which gnaw and trample the
path of life.   All these images underscore Belyaev's unexpectedly
romantic notions about man and the universe.

Some of these romantic concepts are expanded and developed
in his other lyrics.   For example, in "Ex libro amoris," the poet
speaks of the "swampy paths" of love whose "pitiless needles"
shoot and sting him.   It is significant that although the imagery
used is far from traditional romantic imagery, the *persona* of the
poem embodies the romantic view of love—he is the "victim" of
an inexplicable emotion beyond his control.   In other words,
Belyaev seeks new forms of expression for the eternal romantic
theme   through   the   intense   internalization   of   his   *persona's*
experiences.

The same technique is salient in "Starry vomit is spread out
above me like a peacock's tail," where a resplendent night sky is
perceived as "starry vomit."   But here too the *persona* reinforces
his romantic view by stating that, despite the awareness of his

mortal smallness in the face of the eternal "jaws of the sky," he would nevertheless "quietly start barking . . . /So it would know me . . . " By assertion of the self in light of the universe, Belyaev emphasizes his romantic disposition which is, however, continually distorted through the "antiromantic" imagery.

The poem "Such a tiny little fellow—" centers on the poet's isolation and sense of uselessness in a world of vulgarity and Philistinism. At the beginning of the poem he weeps at the loathsome street language, the obscene grimaces, and rotten laughter that characterize the bourgeois life around him. Then the imagination takes over. Instead of remaining passive, the poet steps forward and quietly takes charge, "And all the nasty little Philistines tumbled out of their windows..." The poem once again reveals Belyaev's predilection for the shocking, the incongruous, and the sharp contrasts. The street language is "calico red," laughter "bared its rotten teeth," and the little houses of the Philistines are "potbellied." In addition to intense emotions and metaphysics, there is a touch of humor. For example, the *persona* says: "'Ladies and gentlemen! I demand absolute silence!' / I said quietly."

Belyaev's methods of versification are as avant-garde as his imagery. Some of the poems are written in blank verse with no noticeable meter or rhyme patterns. One, "I wrapped my holey heart in cotton," is accented verse, rhymed, with six or seven stressed syllables per line. The poem "Ex libro amoris," though lacking a definite meter, is rich in sound. The poem can be divided into four three-line sections, each ending in the emphatic line "of love." The first two lines of each stanza rhyme; they are inexact but rich-sounding rhymes typical of the avant-garde. There are also frequent repetitions of certain consonants, especially the labials and sibilants, to convey the paradox of love with its inherent delirium, passion, and pain.

———————·———————

Via Sacra

Instant Photos of an Imaginist

I

Frivilous stars probably think
That I am taking bites of you—piece after piece—
Others watch sullenly, with enmity,
And it seems one is about to jump down.

It will approach, wrapped in a spotless dinner jacket,
Involuntarily squinting through a mother-of-pearl lorgnette;
It will understand what is going on and mutter: "Shocking"
And, turning red, will amputate the upturned branch.

More ridiculous than Kant, it will wander up to the sky,
Tripping with embarrassment on the transcendental stairs...
And on the morrow the constellations will be arranged trans-
    parently:
    It is strictly forbidden
        to be in love
            in a public place.

————·————

IV

Your lips are saturated with the most powerful narcotics,
They anesthetize me to everything but you,
With greedy, little gulps I would like
To drink all of you, all—and become effusively keyed up.

Your lips inject millions of bacteria,
Which animate and hasten my thoughts,
The tocsins of thunderous five-act mystery plays
Bombard my nerves, turned sour from languor.

Your lips pump up my jaded heart,
Like Venus' old motorcycle tire;
It straightens itself out and rapturously spins,
And my nerves playfully sparkle in it like spokes.

Your lips are marinated in enticing love potions,
Your lips are more alluring than precious stones:
I would set them in platinum and wear them like a
     necklace...
My darling, my beauty...give them to me!...

———————·———————

The anonymous lyrics, entitled "Instant Photos of an
Imaginist," were probably written by Ivan Belyaev. Their
surrealistic presentation and associative leaps of thought are among
the more extreme examples of avant-garde Imaginist poems.
Russian poetry and all the arts in Russia underwent a thorough
re-examination in the early decades of the twentieth century and
led to bold experimentation of style and expression. In his poetry,
Velemir Khlebnikov investigated the various possibilities of a
"trans-sense" language, or *zaum*, which could be universally
transmitted and understood. Igor' Severyanin, like Khlebnikov, was
a member of the Futurist school of Russian literature, and sought
in his early poetry and plays new, often revolutionary modes of
expression. In fact, the *Via Sacra* poets were all, to a certain
extent, attached to the Imaginist group of writers and were
experimental to a degree.

"Instant Photos of an Imaginist" consists of four poems, but
only the first and last are presented here. The poems, "Frivolous
stars probably think" and "Your lips are saturated with the most
powerful narcotics," illustrate many of the features typical of the
Via Sacra poets: metaphors, similes, and epithets. "Your lips
pump up my jaded heart,/Like Venus' old motorcycle tire," and
"frivolous stars," "Tripping with embarrassment on the
transcendental stairs," are based on a successful coalescence of
incongruous elements. Like his *Via Sacra* contemporaries, the poet
prefers the short lyric and the theme of delirious love. In "Your
lips are saturated with the most powerful narcotics," the poet
imaginatively explores the motif through the concept of beloved's
lips from which he develops a rich array of hyperbolic and

energetic comparisons to express his ardor.

The playful tone which animates and enhances this poem also is found in "Frivolous stars probably think," although in this case the poet eschews the cataloguing technique to engage in a surrealistic play of images and intonations. The personification of stars in the first stanza is developed in the second into an impressionistic depiction of one star as a narrow-minded and straight-laced society matron. The two realms—the celestical and the earthly—merge in the third stanza where the star-matron, "more ridiculous than Kant," "will wander up to the sky." In the unexpected addendum the star contrives with the heavens to stop the behavior of the *persona* and his beloved, and the poem leaps into a realm of experimental expression.

The poems are refreshing in their energy, in their joyous intonations, and in their bracing strength and vitality. Thanks to the unique imagery and modes of awareness that underlie the lyrics, the anonymous poet succeeds, like the other *Via Sacra* writers, in creating novel perspectives for the eternal themes of poetry.

SEMENOV, BORIS KONSTANTINOVICH (1874-1940?)

A highly original writer, Semenov was one of the favorite poets of Alfred Bem in Prague, where Semenov studied at the university. Semenov was a close friend of Yury Ivask. After serving as an officer in the White Army during the Revolution of 1917, Semenov settled in Pechory (Estonia), where he was Secretary of the Union of the Russian Education Societies. Later he went to Prague and became a member of the Prague "Hermitage of Poets" and of "The Peasants' Will" party, headed by Sergey Semenovich Maslov. After returning to Estonia he was arrested by the Soviets in 1940 and disappeared in labor camps, never to return.

Semenov wrote simple melodious poems, dignified thematically and stylistically. His works appeared in various literary journals and almanacs, including *The Virgin Soil, Volya Rossii* (The Will of Russia), *Svoimi putyami* (Walking to the Beat of One's Own Drum), and *Contemporary Annals.*

The Virgin Soil, No. 8 (1935)

A Halter

High on the hill above the plowed fields—it is not a gathering of hoary sorcerers, but mossy boulders praying to the golden eve above the sea.

Revealed are ages primeval; towers tower across half the sky, while over the sea drunken quiverings flee; ships set sail into open space, hoary monarchs reflect scarlet at the tower chamber threshold.

Crimson carpets are rolled out, radiant feasts are summoned forth.

And—it is not moons casting their anchors into the sloping tiles of the balcony, but princes in silver brocade ascending into pearled tower chambers.

*

Churning
sea,
sky,
mountains,
the rudders turn, the heavy-laden vessels inch along.
—With scalding resins meat is cured.
Iron clangs.
Horses nicker.
Roaring thunder, lightening encircled, pursue the boats, ruffle the waves.
Squeak,
creak,
crash
dashes
splash—

hey, don't fail—
overtake the trail
into the sunset vale...

*

A hundred flames flare—multi-resonant feasts, forged sorceries thunder and drop to earth amber.   And clear light wine streams across velvet; firebirds cry through a gem-encrusted window; raging branches sway
to and fro, to and fro...
Dancers wind and unwind in the ritual augural dance.   Sunset wreaths begin to sound their bells.

Sunset's wreaths writhe into rings, and rings into new rings, and all the plant wreaths ring their bells.

Who will catch, who will seize the undulating border?

—Only the firebirds know, but they tell no one.

The firebirds alone know; telling no one, they wait for the scorching sunset to turn to ashes...while the princess sleeps
and dreams—
of golden anchors, sinking one by one into the sea.

*

Beyond the marsh above the pine forest, an aurochs is pierced by an evil spruce.   Its belly gapes open; the trees have turned crimson.   The bleeding wounds pour forth ichor; the aurochs' eye has grown dim.   The ruddy beast has banished beyond the mountain, licking its wounds with the mead of saliva.

In the sunset aloes wither, in the marshland buds grow fat, in the bog a bittern puffs, an old owl bristles—and beneath the moss, slowly writhing, a tremor rolls.

     The land becomes hilly.   A stump exposes a root.

     Its shadow turns grainy with dust, and disintergrates...

Rat-faced hags in the prickly thicket squint from behind a fir tree.

Like a gray haze they slip by and ripple, ripple past.   One by one, sliding, gliding.

     bounding,

     round and round.

Into the thicket they toss the yarn, hook it, tie it here and there...

The gray flax fibers swell—binding fir to fir.

Mice scurry in the mire, pounce higher, higher, higher; catch their little claws in the threads; their elbows moving chug-a-lug, they grab at thread after thread;

     the spindles turn, drowsy grass snakes dance; loops are

     plaited, dusty fancywork stitched; neither fir nor

     birch can be seen, neither forest nor glade...

A fog has descended...

                         a fog has descended...

White flax entangles everything...Dreams weave, wind, flow.   A distant silver peal.   The stump shines forth, unwinking.   A stirring

                             of idleness.

*

Faded are the tsarevna's gold-set pearls; the moons grow horns; frogs croak in the bog.   Frenzied snakes writhe like bright copper in milk; emeralds glow on slag-wood in the distance, and mysterious grasses

                           blossom and nod...

Sorceries rumble.   Intoxicating poisons pour forth all around,

     velvet, velvet

     bright and radiant

     afflicts the eyes.

Sleep.

     A dream—of a drunkard, evil and raucous, hunting

a firebird;   he falls down and laughs...he plucks it...

The birds begin to croak and moan, they whirl in fever, hurling flame.

In the scarlet fray they tear the banner through and through.

Someone's anvil shoulders break through the ceiling...

                 Help!

            In cruel strife the foe is fearful.

A blunt fist rips the cloth

          on the table.

The gold grows dim.   Their snouts become vicious in the poison fumes;
with snarling and snorting, paws convulse...Scuffling rib-smashers lash out
from a heap, the bowlegged shadows fall head over heels.   Heads ram heads
                              (bone-splintering).
                              Crunch,
                              snap,
                              (a tooth
                              cracks)
Fists mash and knead in an evil fever, the devil's hopak dance flies on.
                              You won't escape
                                        the savage grin—
     The stinger flings an angled light...a knife—into blood...walls—into
cries...

                                             shadows spring
                                             apart...
     in the corners they cross themselves briskly; the young moon will not
rise again from the azure carpets...

                                   *

     Oh, my homeland,
                    tinkling—silver...
                    the golden-horned
                    deer has fallen.
Dogs gather in dark packs, cats pluck at the curved horn.
The mist withdraws its bears from the lakes,
a horse snorts.
     The bonfire is out.

                    _____·_____

     The difficulties presented by the translation of the poem are
great; yet one is tempted to try to convey, if only partially, its
charm and mood.   It is written in the peculiar rhythm and syntax
of the Russian fairy tale, as any child will recognize when hearing
half a line.   In this respect, the poem reminds one of some of
Pushkin's fairy tales.   Sounds and phrases are repeated with an
energetic, almost chanting or songlike meter:
          drug za drugom shmygom, shmygom, pereprygom...
          tkyotsya, vyotsya, lyotsya son...
There is play with sounds: skrip, skrep, khlip, v khlyab' vlip.
Images and sounds merge into one another and fade away as in a
dream.   The writer describes ordinary scenes of country life—
nature, the weaving of linen, drunken brawls—strangely entwining
them with fantastic scenes from fairy tales—princes, ships, jewels,
firebirds—and with a fantastic interpretation of the ordinary—the
old women seem to be mice, nature seems enchanted.
     The poem—clearly a poem, though not written in the

expected verse form—encompasses the time just before the sunset
until the darkness of night. Sound and mood change dramatically
while the light gradually diminishes, and the process is conveyed in
a magic fairy world and in an eventful, glorious past. The rising
new moon, seen from this magical perspective, turns into several
moon princes clamoring up to the balconies of their princesses. A
storm arises and is perceived as an enchanted feast of sound and
light. The horizon at sunset becomes a writhing line of dancers.
The sun is an aurochs, whose blood tinges the forest as his eye
grows dimmer and finally vanishes. Then fog arises and drapes all
the trees, as if they had been hung with strands of flax by busy
weavers. There is a vicious drunken brawl in the darkness and
someone is killed, perhaps the young moon. Is it only a dream, or
an evil omen? It is now deep night, the bonfire is out, darkness
surrounds. With the cry "O my homeland" the allegorical
significance of the apocalyptic vision becomes clear: During an
intoxicating nightly celebration, enticing as well a horrifying,
Russia, the golden deer, is killed by wild dogs, and darkness
prevails.

  Thus Semenov uses the traditional ending of the Russian
bylina to express his despair over Russia's fate after the Revolution
of 1917 and to give the poem another meaning. The poem is not
merely a fairy tale, a *bylina*, or a dream, but the author's chaotic
vision, uttered in consecutive moments of attraction and revulsion,
of a doomed fatherland. Though the title of the poem is enigmatic
and much of the symbolism too personal to allow for a ready
interpretation, Semenov's skillful use of rich Russian vocabulary,
the way he selects and arranges extremely unusual words—
archaisms, dialectal forms, neologisms—makes for a powerful,
unforgettable impression of the passion and terror provoked by
radical political upheavals. The Russian text reads like music,
music as modern as the text of the poem.

———————·———————

NOTE

1. (*Terem*) the women's quarters in medieval Russia.

NOVOSADOV, BORIS
(1907-1945; literary pseudonym of Boris Taggo)

Novosadov's father, owner of an orthopedic shoe store in St. Petersburg, was Estonian while his mother was Russian. From early childhood Boris suffered from severe myopia and, though he graduated from the University of Tartu, he was disqualified as a teacher. He had first enrolled in the Department of Philology and then in the School of Law. He also took a number of correspondence courses in chemistry, but failed to find a position in this field as well. A nervous stutterer, but very lively and sociable, Boris Taggo affected cynicism and bravado while indulging in writing poetry. His poems were more to the "left" than the works of even the most "leftist" Futurists, including Vladimir Mayakovsky. Because of his radical attitude toward images and themes, Novosadov was never accepted as a member of the "Guild of Poets."

Some memorable, witty, and aphoristic lines can be found in Novosadov's verse. For example, "I am a promissory note. Bank is my Fate. God is my cosigner," taken from his first collection (*Shershavye virshi: stikhi* [Rough Doggerel Rhymes; Tallinn, 1936]). A profound dissatisfaction with life produces the main themes of Novosadov's strange poetry. Bitterness, protest, and irony are his favorite poetic moods. Love is mentioned rarely. Although futurist in content and tone, his poems have a classic structure and are written in traditional iambs and quatrains. They were published in Pavel Irtel's almanac, *The Virgin Soil*.

During the German occupation of Estonia, Novosadov came up with the ingenious aphorism "Vozhdey-vozhzhami" ("The reigning—with reins!"), which meant "whip Hitler and Stalin with reins." Ivask, who admired Novosadov's poetry, urged him to incorporate this Tsvetaevaesque expression in his verse.[1] Novosadov replied: "I tried, but have failed," whereupon Ivask allegedly exclaimed: "What a pity! Such an apt aphorism!" Novosadov contributed to a Russian newspaper financed by the Germans and published in Estonia during the German occupation. When the Red Army returned to Estonia in 1940, he was arrested and sent to a labor camp in the Soviet Union where he perished in 1945. He was survived by his wife, who belonged to the famous Estonian Poska family. Jan Poska signed the Tartu Peace with the Soviets, which granted Estonia its independence. A prominent pianist and also poetically inclined, Mme Novosadov supported her husband in his innovative poetic efforts.

Novosadov's second volume of verse is entitled *Po sledam bezdomnykh Aonid* (Following in the Steps of the Homeless Muses; Tallinn: Russkaya kniga, 1938).

NOTE

1. Ref. Yury Ivask, *Homo Ludens, Vozrozhdenie*, No. 240 (1973), pp. 22–23.

The Virgin Soil, No. 7 (1934)

From the Cycle *Summer 1934*

Dedicated to M. L.

A dim light enters the window.
Still I manage to breathe.
Black cats are forever
Crossing my path.

I have no faith in happiness,
Mirage of Kitezh.
And you can see that too,
Yet you curse me not for my coldness.

I cannot love at all
As one should—ardently,
And autumn awaits me,
A candle extinguished beforehand.

—————·—————

The Virgin Soil, No. 6 (1934)

Immortality

Immortality is measured in centuries
And in layers of dead earth;
Rocks disintegrate in the wind,
Suns are extinguished in the world's dust.

The slaves have forgotten the sounds of their ringing songs,
Have forgotten their gods;
Mold lays waste to parchments
In the quiet depths of temples and tombs.

Only someone's unpretentious little fairy tale
To this day still wanders among the crowd,
And Chinese children often mumble
Sheaves of words by the sot Li-Tai-Pe.

———————·———————

A deeply religious and cultured poet, Novosadov seems to have been preoccupied with the eternal themes. Since little of his poetry is available, not much is known of its general nature. But the two disparate poems selected here, "Immortality" and "From the Cycle *Summer 1934*," clearly share the same voice of a highly personal, erudite, and often anguished poet.

In "Immortality," the poet ironically contrasts the eternal theme of time's passage with the sacred notion of art's immortality. The first two stanzas represent the passage of time in untouched or uncultivated matter on earth and in the universe, then time's passage in human emotions and beliefs—civilizations change as gods are forgotten and perhaps replaced by others—and finally, time's passage in human knowledge, history, and science, codified in documents. These parchments, even when carefully hidden, cannot escape the mold and rotting process of time. However, the introductory line of the poem, "Eternity is measured in centuries," sets the tone for a curious ambiguity because eternity by definition cannot be measured. The poet sheds an ironical, questioning light on all human efforts to grasp the notion of eternity. Consequently, the third stanza, diametrically opposed to the preceding two stanzas, contains examples illustrating the possibility of a certain form of immortality—the survival of a fairy tale in the minds of men, or of age-old Chinese verses in the mouths of children—and should be read ironically. With mild cynicism, the poet questions the validity of the immortal art ideal: If man knows nothing of eternity and can conceive of the idea only in terms of temporality, the notion of immortal art is necessarily dubious. Indeed, the miraculous survival of the "unpretentious little fairy tale" and of

Li–Tai–Pe's words murmured many centuries after their creation is not presented as major achievement. Yet Li–Tai–Pe is one of China's foremost poets. Though seduced by its charms, Novosadov seems to question carefully the ultimate importance of art.

Less complex than "Immortality," the poem "From the Cycle *Summer 1934*" centers on a single, personal thought, the poet's incapacity for passion or love. A melancholy, morose mood, not unlike the mood of "Immortality," pervades the poem and poignantly enhances the final impression of mental and physical fatique, senselessness, and hopelessness. Resignation characterizes both poems, but in the last one the reader senses a mute despair carefully held in check by the technical control of the poet.

SHUMAKOV, YURY DMITRIEVICH (b. 1914)

The son of a physics and mathematics teacher at the Russian High School in Tartu, Yury Shumakov published three volumes of poetry: *Tretya vstrecha: stikhi* (A Third Meeting: Poems; Bratislava: Al'tair, 1934), *Vne: stikhi* (Outside: Poems; Belgrade–Tartu: Orsa, 1935), and *Okolo: stikhi* (Nearby: Poems; Tartu, 1936). He belonged to the Russo–Estonian circles preoccupied with Futurism and translated the works of several Estonian poets into Russian. His Russian rendering of *Marie Under: Izbrannye stikhi 1900–1930* (Marie Under: Selected Poems 1900–1930; Tartu, 1935), as well as his other translations, are very meritorious. Shumakov's own poetry appeared in *The Virgin Soil* and in *Anchor: An Anthology of Emigré Poetry*.

Shumakov still lives in Tartu and teaches at the university there.

Anchor: An Anthology of Emigré Poetry

The word became transparent,
Like a flowing ribbon of light.
The melodious moan of the waves
Spilled like blue weeping.
How much tenderness,
How much sadness—

In uncertainty,
In blue verbiage.
The nights are becoming longer,
Ever shorter the days;
I feel lonelier with every instant,
Akin to those who weep.

————————·————————

From the Walls of the Monastery

The dark brow of local forests,
The hazel trees, the early dew,
The beauty of awakened fields,
The pillows of green hills.

The heartfelt lament of oak trees
About dreams age-old,
Below the chasuble of the glowing clouds—
The icon of the blue sky.

Both time and space are extinguished.
With the severe smile of permanence
Into my soul looks Silence—
Dispassionate guard of holy slumber.

————————·————————

There is a definite tendency toward eccentric and even pretentious imagery in the first poem. Shumakov's predilection for Futurism with its "trans-sence" language is obvious, but his images are sometimes incorrect, for example "siny plach" or "sineustnost'." These and similar expressions obscure the meaning of the poem. Hoever, Shumakov was less inclined toward experimentation in meter than his famous futurist predecessors.

His use of colors, esecially blue and red, seems to link his poetry with that of the symbolist writers. He uses many other colors: black, green, turqoise, yellow, orange, and violet. Along with futurist devices, Shumakov uses symbolist images such as "the icon of the blue sky," "the chasuble of the glowing clouds," and "holy slumber." The symbols have religious and mystical implications.

The Virgin Soil, No. 5 (1933)

Along a heap of rocks, decayed to dusty gray
—I wander out on the jagged pier
—Inhale the fresh scent on the lake,
And the astringent resin of the pine forest.

How pleasant for a youth to stand here
In the bright blossoming of the will to live,
When a wave and a gust of wind
Submissively whisper to me, "As you wish!"

Tartu-Yuryev, Estonia

———————·———————

"Along a heap of rocks, decayed to dusty gray" paints a picture of a youth standing out on a pier in a lake, full of the joy of life. In striking contrast are the decayed rocks of the pier. Shumakov appeals to the reader's sense of smell: The "fresh scent of the lake" and "the astringent resin of the pine forest" are both symbols of youth and life. The youth is so full of vitality and so convinced of his power that even "a wave and a gust of wind" seem willing to submit to his will. Sound orchestration is an important aspect of the poem. Shumakov uses repetition of sounds within each line to help create the desired effect. In the first stanza, the repetition of strong consonant sounds such as "zh," "r," velars "k," "g" and "kh," and the vowel "u," creates the impression of a wide expanse and imitates the sound of breaking waves. In the second stanza, the hissing consonant sounds "sh," "s," and the fricative "v" predominate, mimicking the whispering of the wind and the waves. The rhymes are also quite rich. The poem is written in iambic tetrameter with alternating dactylic and in masculine rhymes, all amplifying the sound of the gusting wind and the breaking waves.

IRTEL, PAVEL MIKHAYLOVICH (1896-1979)

Pavel Irtel, Freiherr von Brenndorff, of Hungarian descent, was born in St. Petersburg. He attended a school in Moscow for two years, then went to Simbirsk when his father, General Irtel, was appointed a professor of mathematics and physics and Inspector of the Simbirsk Cadet Corps. Pavel and his brother graduated from this Corps in 1913 and continued their studies for two more years in the Artillery Academy in St. Petersburg. During World War I, Irtel was an officer in the Household Guard of Heavy Artillery. He received various military orders and distinctions. When the Revolution occurred in 1917, he was a captain in the Imperial Army. Toward the end of 1917 he found himself in Odessa, where he joined the White Army and fought against the Red Army in the Crimea. On the ship that took him from Odessa to Constantinople he met his father and brother. General Irtel died in Constantinople; Pavel remained there working as an electrician in an American School for adults. When he heard two years later that his mother had managed to leave the Soviet Union for Estonia, Pavel Irtel joined her in Tallinn and found employment with the Foreign Correspondence Department of the Scheel Bank. Irtel's wife, Elena Pavlovna Solovskaya (daughter of the director of a high school in Belgrade), whom he had married in Odessa, came to Tallinn from Belgrade. A theosophist, Elena arranged meetings in their home and later, when the Tallinn Society of Theosophy was formed, she became an active member. In 1931, however, she divorced Pavel Irtel and left for Geneva. Four years later Irtel married Meta Al'fredovna Roos.

Irtel was well known in Russian circles in Estonia. He became editor and publisher of the almanac *The Virgin Soil* and was active in the Estonian "Guild of Poets." Meetings of the Guild often took place in Irtel's home. Karl von Hoerschelmann, Boris Nartsissov, Yury Ivask, Irina Borman, Meta Roos, and her sister Elizabeth Roos participated in these literary soirées. Lidiya Leppinger, Mme Roslavleva, and Mikhail Sidorov, devoted "lovers of Russian poetry," also attended the meetings. All of them took part in the Russian "Literary Circle" chaired by Mme Padva. But by 1938 Russian literary life in Tallinn began to decline, and in 1939 the members of the "Guild of Poets" as well as the participants of the Russian Circle left for Germany. Pavel Irtel first worked in a bank in Bromberg, Poland, and then acted as an interpreter of Slavic languages in the German Army, where he was a captain. After the war, he joined his family in Göttingen and took a job in the foreign correspondence section of a bank in that city.

"My poetic credo is to be sincere and truthful," said Pavel Irtel in an interview, referring especially to his short story "V syrykh polyakh" (In the Wet Fields; *The Virgin Soil*, No. 6). He liked neither Vladimir Nabokov's works nor Igor' Stravinsky's music. "Their works are artificial, not flowing freely from their hearts. Not noticing any other human being, they are always everywhere preoccupied with themselves. In *Dar* [The Gift], Nabokov busied himself with verbal games—there is no plot in this novel. Even Nabokov's and Stravinsky's faces are unpleasant to look at—fleshy and almost carnivorous, expressing no concern for anybody else," Irtel said.

In his poetry, Irtel followed the style of *Numbers* but with a certain spiritual, Dostoevskian nuance. His poetic mode resembles the "Parisian note," for in his poetry there is always an elegiac evocation of a past gone forever, or a personal meditation stemming from the poet's intimate contact with nature. In both cases, the *persona's* voice is solemn, resonant, and often nostalgic. He seldom gives way to wild flights of poetic fancy, preferring instead to convey his themes, emotions, and ideas through a rich impressionistic atmosphere (as in "Moscow" and "Autumn"), created through a simple style using only a few metaphors and similes. Often his editorial intonations are enhanced by the poetic apostrophe when he addresses the friends and lovers of his past in an effort to make sense of the chaos of war and exile that threatens to engulf him, and to elucidate his inner turmoil. Thus, "On the Volga" is addressed to a childhood friend or brother and accentuates the poet's regret and loss. "A cool, timorous, early morning" moves from natural scenery to the anguish of lost love, merging the two only in the last line of the image of the wind "mixed in thoughts of our experience."

These themes as well as those touching on war, national and personal history, the tribulations caused by exile, and the passage of time are all mingled in a single, distinctive voice. The spiritual dimension of Irtel's work is especially noticeable in "On Easter Night" where "the wilderness gives voice and . . . stealthily arrays itself in green chasubles." In "Moscow," religious feelings—

particularly for the joyful Easter holiday—merge with an acute
sense of nostalgia to create a striking and original impression. A
remarkable feature of Irtel's work is consistency of theme and voice
for more than forty years.

In other lyrics Irtel achieves an almost dreamlike ambiance
through impressionistic images derived from the *persona's* internal
landscape. Images, like "The dream of the white night envelops
the towers" and "In the white twilight of deserts," suggest a
surrealistic world. The images convey almost a nightmare haunted
by spectral activities of the elements: "The gusty wind blows and
tells fortunes" and "the plants which weave nets . . . resembling
maidenly arms." In poems like these, with their predilection for
shades of light and dark and for objects changing form before the
persona's eyes, Irtel explores layers of reality and creates a richly
ambiguous poetic texture.

He published extensively in *The Virgin Soil* and in *Anchor:
An Anthology of Emigré Poetry.*

Autumn

With the first light frost of early autumn,
The leaves became covered and wrinkled;
They tremble, plucked and scattered by the wind,
Skim along paths, quiver on puddles,
And the night casts strange, playful shadows
On the pines, the heather, and the sand.
The disk of the moon, growing pale, scowls,
And the shrill, penetrating whistle of a train is heard.
An irrepressible wave of new anxiety
Beats timidly and sweetly in my heart,
And the wooded silence takes my breath away
In the blissful harmony of ethereal, autumnal reflections.

16.9.29, Tallinn

On Easter Night

Incorporeal night of Easter Spring.
Lilac cupola over a misty grove.
Easter night, tender, sensitive,
And a first tiny sprout, abashedly scrawny.

Above a little reddish bog
A figdety spring bird peers into the dark hollow of a tree,
And the wilderness gives voice and in a distant corner
Stealthily arrays itself in green chasubles.

Over the city the clang of Easter bells;
Bell towers magically melodious at night...
And amid the clamor of the people, my involuntary
Sigh of regret about something was absurdly drowned out.

2.4.33, Tallinn

————·————

The Virgin Soil, No. 7 (1934)

The dream of a white night envelops towers;
The footstep of a white night resounds on the flagstones.
The sky, lusterless and not terrifying,
Sedately follows the orbits.

Walls and boulevards are somnolent.
The bush on the slope glistens like silver.
The silhouette of a timid couple
Hides in a niche and drowns.

It is the reeds weaving nets,
Beckoning to illusory lands.
Maidenly arms, like lashes,
Will entwine one and not let go.

————·————

The Virgin Soil, No. 4 (1932)

The Nemme Suburb

Small dark alleys, long fences everywhere,
    Among the fragrant pines cottages sleep.
        It's so quiet beneath the window...

The lights are snuffed out. Naïve, innocent
    Shadows fall, dreams fly,
        Dreams about the distant, the otherworldly.

And the bright stars, serenely and ceremoniously moving
    In a silent circle, speak
        About the mysterious, your own.

                                Nemme, Estonia

———————·———————

The Virgin Soil, No. 7 (1934)

Dense mists hung low
Over the pine's fragile twig.
But thoughts, poor thoughts...
And such strange dreams
Tell fortunes, mislead, and deceive...
    A pine forest in ashen chasubles;
There birds sing the glory of the Trinity,
And tears fall onto the carpet
From bilberries, mosses, and mold,
Not tears, but rain from God...
    You didn't search for the words,
But asked, timidly and severely,
In a respectful whisper:

"Tell me about what is most important."

———————·———————

The Wanderer

Morning—familiar, quiet, early...
Roosters asleep in the yards.
The misty field...like a silver flame
Extends to the distant hillocks.
Embarrassed by the night wind's caresses,
The grasses are covered with dew;
Beyond the marshy hummocks glows a small swamp;
The moss is like a carpet...I, barefoot,
Step gently, hair tousled,
Drink in the air, like honey;
I hear in my memory echoes of a voice,
The image stands out in my mind;
All that I have perceived, that I have greedily
      traversed.
All that makes the earth rich,
Is mixed by the wind with thoughts of my past,
Faint like the wake of a ship.

————·————

In the white twilight of deserts
The gusty wind blows and tells fortunes.
A distant monastery.
My fading memory.

Bilingual harmony of a Psalm—
Captivity and murmur of ancient sorrow.
From a hill near the shore
A soaring flight, proud and solemn.

Amid the sad ringing of cliffs and glaciers
Amid the plaintive cries of the birds
At the icon-lamp, alone,
I turn the pages.

————·————

The Virgin Soil, No. 8 (1935)

In the mournful nights of winter
On skis in snow to the hilltops...

In storms and fogs and harsh weather—
The poor deception of verse.

In an anxious doubling instant,
The laws of divine books.

And during twilight's affectionate hour
A peaceful tale about you...

—————·—————

To Ant. Ladinsky

Beneath wind and dust,
Along the white stones,
Following the song and the distant past
—to the names!

Oh, the sober numbers!
And the inscription: museum...
From the words of Gostomysl
And the glory of princes

There remained for us tombstones,
And dust on the burial wreath,
And the willow's shadow,
And the fragile bark...

The raven and gerfalcon
Are put into archives.
And in speech
We have become so cold.

We do not dream of
Gonfalons and helmets,
As powerful themes
For worthy verse.

We ask a beggar woman
To foretell our path;
Without a roof, without food,
Somehow we will get by.

_____._____

In a Foreign Land

Stubborn...exact...the march of time;
Year after year...in an even row they file past.
Across the stones of public squares,
Into the same distance and twilight they descend,
Whither idle fate, as always
Inexorable, speeds helpless people.
The days flash by in hurried, uneven succession,
Not brightening with any rapture the misery
In the, alas, proud fate of the exile.
Neither sun nor flowers, nor the hearty kiss of a pretty
girl
Can bring one happiness.
It is painful for me to hear the hum of the crowd;
Stealthily, I hurry along the walls...
Oh, how naïve and blind
Are my good neighbors, in their honest simplicity,
When I gaze, humiliated and humble,
Taken unawares in a morbid dream...
Oh, how alien are they to me,
When tired and pale
I return home, to my poor corner,
And greedily greet the heap of old books...
What a happy moment amid my suffering!
Exhausted by physical labor,
I find the strength to light the fire, I fall prone

On the disheveled bed, and all night long
I rave over *The Devils*; I recite "Poltava" as if it were the Lord's
    Prayer,
      And there is no weariness! Lofty transport
      Quickens my consciousness, my blood races; with pride
        I read the glory of my native land...!
Oh no, I shall not vanish, nor dissolve into a strange country—
Behind me is tradition, devotion to sanctity;
All the pain of the tormented earth is in my past—
        I am the son of my fatherland!
      Oh, if I could only prove, realize my dreams...
    But, Russia of the future, do not let me darken
        Your brow with the seal of reproach.

                        Tallinn-Revel, Estonia

On the Volga

We used to live in the countryside around Simbirsk,
Where the Volga flowed about a mile wide,
Where the nights often sheltered fugitives,
Where brown resin smelled like honey.

As soon as the snow had melted and the beasts of the forest woke
    up,
Thawing ice would wash up on sand bars,
Like the sea, bursting the banks of the Volga,
And the first raft would float to the surface past Kostroma.

The water would seethe, glittering under the timber,
Bearing out trunks on the Volga's deep flow—
Pines and firs of the north country
From the Ural Mountains, from an unknown cliff.

Here Svyatoslav carried out his campaigns,
Here villages were sacked by the wild Pugachov,
Here into the turbulent waters Sten'ka Razin
Flung the beauty, to the songs of his bold retinue...

Here our childhood flowed by, the years
Till the terrible outbreak of ominous war,
When suffering and the drafting of soldiers
Touched the Volga and her waves.

We used to fish and angle on rafts;
When lucky, we would catch sturgeons
And kindle nightly fires in the field,
And, lying by the bonfire, cook our soup.

Above us occasional stars would flicker.
Noiselessly the mighty river flowed.
Beckoning us to distances unknown,
Beyond field, pine forest, and the Volga's shores.

Göttingen, 1979

Moscow

I learned to read at my nanny's knee,
And read not the primer, but newspapers,
Spread out on the floor like a cardboard snake kite;
I was not washed and still undressed.

We lived in Moscow then, where a string of carts
Stretched past the house at Kamenny Brod;
There factory people hurried to work
In the spring warmth and in the frost.

As soon as April sun had melted the snow
And kiosks had enlivened the sidewalks,
Friendly rattling carts would announce the spring,
And children would run to the boulevards.

There they would roll Easter eggs, and the shouts
Of young people would resound along the paths;
An old man, sitting on a bench, would smile
And every passer-by would slacken his pace.

Over the Kremlin and over all of gold-domed Moscow
Chimes would drift and drone,
Like the echo and weeping of antiquity,
Moans of Russians in distant Tatar camps.

In shirts and scarves of rich red calico,
The capital would celebrate Holy Easter.
By the flow of all these feelings, all these sounds and words,
Even a stone would be moved.

Göttingen, 1979

----------·----------

Petersburg

I dream in rosy pastels
Of Peter's spire reflected in the wide expanse of the Neva,
Rastrelli's ethereal façades,
And the changing of the guard at noon.

On the Nevsky rushing, ringing trams,
Bustling crowds,
Sudden regimental music.
Glittering shop windows, and splashing of colors

Of clothes, uniforms, women's fashions,
And foreign languages,
And the poverty of northern nature
On the beach of Finnish sand.

I dream of the buzzing of lecture halls,
The noisy family of students,
Arguments over basic principles;
I dream of my youth.

Days pass and with them years
While we go our separate ways
And share the adversities of exile
In an alien land, by alien waters.

I dream of a view of the former capital,
A gray sky above.
There in the heights stretch the memories
Of my happy youth.

Göttingen, 1979

—————·—————

Irtel von Brenndorff often begins a poem with a description of nature and ends with a personal meditation. "Autumn" is constructed in this manner. The poet uses a few carefully chosen details—leaves, shadows, the moon, and a train whistle—and portrays them so graphically and beautifully that he makes the reader feel the emotion that he must have felt that autumn night. Nature here provides the impetus for his personal feelings and reflections: "An irrepressible wave of new anxiety/Beats timidly and sweetly in my heart,/And the wooded silence takes my breath away/In the blissful harmony of ethereal, autumnal reflections." The meter, with alternating masculine endings, gives the poem a lyrical, lilting quality. In "On Easter Night" the poet becomes aware of the insignificance of his personal thoughts compared to the solemnity of Easter. The "first tiny sprout, abashedly scrawny" and the "fidgety spring bird" are dwarfed by the vastness and beauty of surrounding nature, represented by the sky—"Lilac cupola over a misty grove"—which transforms the whole earth into a church. The wilderness, like a priest, "gives voice and in a distant corner/Stealthily arrays itself in green chasubles." Irtel, a religious man, imbues some of his poems with elements of Russian Orthodox ritual. In the last stanza the poet's "sigh of regret" is about something so insignificant that it should be "absurdly drowned out" by the "clamor of the people" and "magically melodious" Easter bells. The meter of the poem is amphibrachic tetrameter, which heightens the musical effect. "The dream of a white night envelops the towers" and "Dense mists hung low" contain impressionistic images used to achieve an ethereal, almost surrealistic quality. Objects change shape before the *persona's* eyes as he explores various perceptions of the world. There seem to be two levels of reality in "The dream of a white night envelops the towers." The poem is ambiguous and can be interpreted in a number of ways. The haunting final lines, "Maidenly arms, like lashes,/Will entwine one and not let go," produce a sinister effect. Do these lines represent the dream, seen against the more real background of the first two stanzas, or are those stanzas the dream and the last stanza reality? "Dense mists hung low" is somewhat more straightforward, but again instead of connecting his thoughts logically to express an idea, Irtel arranges images to create an emotional impression. "Dense mists," "poor thoughts," and "strange dreams" that "tell fortunes, mislead, and deceive" characterize the pine forest. As in the poem "On Easter Night," nature has religious connotations. The pine forest is arrayed "in ashen chasubles," "birds sing the glory of the Trinity," and the tears that fall are "not tears, but rain from God." Thus, although the poem's religious theme is not stated, the last line of the poem, "'Tell me about what is most important,'" could be a prayer.

"The Wanderer," which seems to be a revision of a poem Irtel wrote in 1929, presents a strikingly beautiful picture of early morning when the roosters were still asleep. The details are delicate and obviously chosen with great care. The similes and metaphors are especially successful: "The misty field...like a silver flame/Extends to the distant hillocks"; the grasses are "embarrassed by the night wind's caresses"; the poet "drinks in the air, like honey," and his past is "faint like the wake of a ship." The poem's dactylic meter, alternating between four-foot lines with dactyl rhymes and three-foot lines with masculine rhymes, adds to its beauty.

"In the White Twilight of Deserts" has an ancient, Biblical aura about it. It presents stark, solitary landscape, or perhaps two landscapes, since the "sad ringing of cliffs and glaciers" in the last stanza seems to conflict with the "white twilight of deserts" at the beginning. The poet sees himself as a monk who, "at the icon-lamp, alone," turns the pages and mentally relives the old Biblical heritage. But this Biblical heritage, the "Bilingual harmony of a Psalm—/Captivity and murmur of ancient sorrow," seems a metaphor for Irtel's personal memories and the monk-like solitude, a metaphor for the loneliness of his life in exile.

"Beneath the wind and dust" provides an interesting example of how Irtel attempts to rediscover the past. As he searches for meaning in the distant past, the *persona* finds only "tombstones, /And dust on the burial wreath" and cold, uninspiring numbers and inscriptions in museums and archives. All the excitement and pageantry of the past—"the glory of the princess" and "gonfalons and helmets"—have been forgotten, "And in speech/We have become so cold." Irtel relates the past to the present, focusing on the reader's personal perception of the past rather than on the "objective" past itself. The last stanza ("We ask a beggar woman/To foretell our path") suggests that the reader's own time too will someday seem as distant as the past in this poem.

"In a Foreign Land" describes Irtel's exile; he is weary from poverty and physical labor, and is depressed because of separation from his homeland. The poem begins with a portrayal of "the march of time," which is seen by an exile as a meaningless, inexorable succession of days and years. Then the poet dwells on his unhappiness, his isolation from the crowd and from his "good neighbors." But he finds "a happy moment amid my suffering" in a "heap of old books." The weariness disappears and he vows to be loyal to the traditions of his homeland and not to "dissolve into a strange country," for he feels that he himself has a part to play in Russia's destiny.

The meter of the poem is iambic, with line lengths varying from three to eight feet. The vast majority of the lines contain five or six feet, and these long and ponderous lines produce an effect of solemnity, a tone also supported by the occasional use of Old Church Slavic expressions, such as "chelo" and "Rus' gryadushchaya." To heighten the poetic effect, long lines are followed by shorter ones throughout the poem. The rhyme pattern is quite irregular; the unevenness in both rhyme and meter perhaps mimics the "unhurried, uneven succession" of days in exile.

Three poems included here are much more recent. Written in Göttingen in 1979, the year of the poet's death, they form a trilogy encompassing Irtel's early childhood ("On the Volga"), boyhood ("Moscow"), and adolescence ("Petersburg"). There is no ambiguity here; Irtel writes in a more direct, descriptive style, employing only a few figures of speech. The *persona's* voice is solemn, resonant, and nostalgic. In all three poems we keenly feel the poet's sense of loss, his appreciation for the places of his youth, and his regret that he was unable to return. In "On the Volga," as in many of the other poems discussed above, there are vivid descriptions of nature—the "brown resin" that "smelled like honey," the Volga whose banks burst "like the sea," and the water "glittering beneath the timber." History plays a role here too. Irtel recalls the violent times of Svyatoslav, Pugachov, and Sten'ka Razin, and more recently the First World War, when "suffering

and the drafting of soldiers/Touched the Volga and her waves."
But he remembers his childhood as a peaceful interlude and evokes
the quiet nights when he and his friends went fishing, and the
river "beckoned us to distances unknown,/Beyond field, pine forest,
and the Volga's shores." These last lines should perhaps be read
ironically, in view of the long exile Irtel was to face later in life,
when he was unable to return to Russia.

In "Moscow" and "Petersburg" we again find vivid
descriptions and minute details, but this time they are in the
context of city life where there are "newspapers/Spread out on the
floor like a cardboard snake kite," an old man smiling on a bench,
"rushing, ringing trams," and "the buzzing of lecture halls." Both
poems begin with happy, bustling activity, but then a sudden
change occurs. In "Moscow" Easter chimes "drift and drone,/Like
the echo and weeping of antiquity,/Moans of Russians and distant
Tartar camps." The poem ends with a sudden burst of intense,
religious feeling: "By the flow of all the feeling, and all these
sounds and words,/Even a stone would be moved." At the end of
"Petersburg," Irtel's mind turns to "the adversities of exile/In an
alien land, by alien waters." Now Petersburg is only a distant
dream. He imagines "A gray sky above," which is perhaps a
political reference, or an expression of the poet's sadness at being
unable to return. Memories "there in the heights" are all that is
left "of my happy youth."

Meta Roos published a volume of Irtel's poems entitled *P.
Irtel. Stikhi 1919-1935* (P. Irtel: Poems 1929-1935; Paris: YMCA
Press, 1981), 76 pp.

Irtel also won fame as a short-story writer.

IVASK, YURY PAVLOVICH
(1910-1986; literary pseudonyms B. Afanasyevsky,
G. Issako, B. A., and Yu. I.)

Yury Ivask, poet, critic, and scholar, was born in Moscow.
After the Revolution his family moved to Estonia where he studied
law at the University of Tartu. He also studied philology at the
University of Hamburg. He fled to Germany during the war,
immigrated to the United States in 1949, and embarked on an

academic career. In 1954 he received his Ph.D. from Harvard University. His dissertation was "Vyazemsky as a Literary Critic." He taught Russian literature at the University of Kansas, the University of Washington in Seattle, Vanderbilt University, and the University of Massachusetts in Amherst. His publications include *Severny bereg: stikhi 1933-1936* (The Northern Shore: Poems 1933-1936; Warsaw: Svyashchennaya lira, 1938), *Tsarskaya osen': vtoryaya kniga stikhov* (Regal Autumn: A Second Book of Poetry; Paris: Rifma, 1953), *Khvala* (Praise; Washington, DC: Kamkin, 1967), *Zolushka* (Cinderella; New York: Mosty, 1970), *Konstantin Leontyev: zhizn' i tvorchestvo* (Konstantin Leontyev: Life and Works; Bern, 1974), the long autobiographical poem *Homo Ludens* (Paris: *La Renaissance*, Nos. 240-242, 1973), *Zavoevanie Meksiki: skaz raeshnika* (Conquest of Mexico: The Tale of a Rhymester; New England Publishing Co., 1984), *Ya—Meshchanin* (I—a Petty Bourgeois; New England Publishing Co., 1986), and many others. He also wrote introductions to the works of other authors, for example, "V. Rozanov. *Izbrannoe*" (V. Rozanov. *Selected Works;* New York: Chekhov, 1950), and "O. Mandel'shtam. *Sobranie sochineny*" (O. Mandel'shtam. *Collected Works*; Washington, DC, 1968, Vol. III). He published many perceptive, erudite essays on various Russian poets, including Batyushkov, Boratynsky, Foeth, Sluchevsky, Marina Tsvetaeva, Boris Pasternak, Andrey Bely, Georgy Ivanov, Mikhail Kuzmin, Alexander Blok, Anna Akhmatova, and Velemir Khlebnikov. Ivask contributed poetry and essays to numerous Russian newspapers, journals, almanacs, and anthologies. He was editor of *Na Zapade: antologiya zarubezhnoy poezii* (In the West: An Anthology of Russian Emigré Poetry; New York: Chekhov, 1953), and he edited the literary journal *Opyty* (Experiments; New York: M. Tsetlin, 1953-58). Ivask also published extensively in American and Western European periodicals, including *The Slavic Review, The Russian Review, The Slavic and East European Journal,* and *Die Zeitschrift für Slavische Philologie.* His favorite contemporary Russian poets were Osip Mandel'shtam, Marina Tsvetaeva, Igor' Chinnov, Valery Pereleshin, and Dmitry Bobyshev. Ivask also admired the Anglo-Welsh poet Dylan Thomas, known for his rich assonance, alliterations, and rare words, and the French poet Guillaume Apollinaire, who opposed traditional structure in poetry and advocated artistic experiementation in the first two decades of the twentieth century.

Ivask's poetry is close to Acmeism, featuring colorful images from a mythical landscape of Byzantino-Muscovite and occidental culture. The poems echo other cultures as well. Ivask's early poetry is written in a classical manner. Its basic tenor is quiet. The style evinces simplicity and clarity. The language is restrained, elegant, and stylized; its archaic expressions are in perfect harmony with its philosophical content. Ivask writes about the meaning of life and death, and reflects upon the concepts of valor, heroic deeds, glory, friendship, and loneliness. These qualities, as well as the classical simplicity and transparency of his style and the so-called "disconnected associations" that the reader has to recreate, link his early poetry with the "Parisian note." But his impressionistic technique, together with a deep interest in the sound of words, intentional infractions of syntax rules, such as the absence of punctuation marks and occasional elements of *zaum* or trans-sense language, mark Ivask's poetry with originality even in its early stage. Gleb Struve described this mode of poetic creation as Ivask's "Aspiration to combine in one line the Russian 'Empire style' of the nineteenth century with the Russian 'Renaissance' of the twentieth century, or Pushkin and Boratynsky with Annensky and Mandel'shtam."[1]

Recently Ivask's poetry has taken a turn toward freer rhythms, surrealist imagery, and a Khelbnikovian surrender to the myth-making power of language. It is a radically new manner of writing. It is intimate; highly personal associations fuse with modulated sound patterns, inner rhymes, neologisms, and elliptical imagery. Ivask asserts that his mature style was formed partially under the unfluence of Derzhavin; the English metaphysical and intensely religious poets John Donne, Richard Crashaw, and George Herbert; and the Spanish poet Luis de Góngora, who delighted in philosophical arguments. Thus Ivask's Neo-Baroque style is quite different from that of the "Parisian note." It is addressed to the ear rather than to the eye.

Ivask's almost Dantesque poem *Homo Ludens*—actually a cycle of lyrical septa—is the Odyssey of a poetic spirit. It is Ivask's magnum opus, *poème* with a unique genre in the history of Russian literature. Laszlo Dienes, a recent critic, calls *Homo Ludens* "A smaller poet's *Divina Commedia*, a spiritual panorama of a religious poet."[2] There are recondite philosopical and literary references, trains of associations and images, and "sound-chains"—all of which create the strong impression of a game, aesthetic pleasure, poetic imagination, enjoyment of nature, sports, and Russian peasant food. Ivask's imagery is vivid, and his rhymes are strong, varied, and original. The fanciful Neo-Baroque manner is sustained throughout the poem. Ivask's later poetry is fresh, joyous, carefee, and serene. Its basic moods embrace the love of God's creation, firm faith in the world's fundamental goodness, and curiosity about the sensory world.[3] Such poetry is not easy to translate because the sound texture is lost in another language, and the cement which bonds the content—the stream of personal associations, playful and discordant sound instrumentation, teasing half-rhymes, extravagant images, and frequent enjambements—is impaired in the process. Yury Ivask is a gifted, highly cultured, and original poet.

Professor N. E. Andreyev (Cambridge, England) remembered Yury Ivask as a member of the "Guild of Poets" in Tallinn. At one of the meetings of the Tallinn Russian Circle, Ivask gave a talk entitled "A Word About Gogol." Andreyev published the lecture in *The Virgin Soil* (No. 2, 1929). In 1926-27, fascinated with Marina Tsvetaeva's poetry, Ivask wrote "strange, precious verse devoid of poetic transports," Andreyev recalled. He further maintained that Ivask was influenced by Karl von Hoerschelmann's philosophy as is reflected in *Homo Ludens*.[4]

After graduation from the School of Law in Tartu, Ivask worked as a tax inspector's secretary in the Pechory region. Together with Sterna L'vovna Schliffstein, he founded the literary journal *A Russian Shop*. Only one issue appeared, but it served as a prototype for Pavel Irtel's almanac *The Virgin Soil*. Ivask and Schliffstein published the fiction of Alexey Remizov and Boris Poplavsky, as well as their own poetry. Later Ivask went to Latvia to see Igor' Chinnov; from there he proceeded to Germany and Paris where he visited Marina Tsvetaeva, Z. N. Hippius, D. S. Merezhkovsky, and other renowned Russian writers living in France.

NOTES

1. Gleb Struve, *Russkaya literatura v izgnanii* (New York: Chekhov, 1956), p. 36.
2. Laszlo Dienes, "On the Poetry of Yuri Ivask," *World Literature Today*, Spring 1979, Vol. 53, No. 2, pp. 234-37.
3. Georgy Adamovich, "Igor' Chinnov. *Partitura. Stikhi.* Izd. *Novogo zhurnala*, 1970. Yu. Ivask. *Zolushka. Stikhi.* Izd. zhurnala *Mosty*, 1970." *Novy zhurnal*, Book 102, 1971, pp. 382-86.

4.   *Vozrozhdenie*, No. 240 (1973), p. 18.

Contemporary Annals, LVI (Paris, 1934)

Boratynsky[1]

Northern shore of despondency,
The deep pontus slumbers.
A straight line of death—
Sorrowful horizon.

The mournful prophecy of a seagull.
The white twilight is lusterless.
God of his own solitude—
The pallid poet is motionless.

As if half-awake, like a drowsy Finn,
A wave flows languidly.
It is his, Boratynsky's,
Gloomy country.

"Happiness," he whispers, "there is no happiness..."
Then smiling—"So be it!"
Light stupor of voluptuousness—
Melancholy solitude.

———·———

The Virgin Soil, No. 6 (1934)

Pontus

Dead snow frames
The black heavy sea.
What is this open space to you?
What is it to you, meaningless man?

*

Sprinkle into it
Densely golden salt—emptiness—
Near the hot, black mouth
Twisted in pain...

These large, moist salt shakers
Are stars—more and more of them—and blood...
The bold, salty waves, eternal,
Collide, join in battle—again...

Glory, where do you come from, majestic glory,
You, who all my life drove me mad?
Aren't you yourself from the salty bosom of the sea?
The mist rises, and takes out of the darkness
My fatal, inglorious soul,
And the salty darkness, white and smooth,
(I listen to the voice of inspiration in the distance;
Somewhere it repeats glory in a dream.)
Melts in this glistening silence.

From the ancient darkness, I died, the Assumption,
From a light in the darkness, I arose, the Ascension.
What then is happening inside me now?

*

On the very horizon,
Where the fury of the stars is lessening,
You hear the rumbling of Pontus,
Roaring—breathing out, roaring—breathing in?

———————.———————

The Virgin Soil, No. 7 (1934)

An Epitaph

I obeyed the commandment,
And autumn is radiant with golden glory.
Pale blue are my thoughts.

I obeyed the commandment,
And death's silvery light streams down.
Quiet delirium of snowflakes.

———————·———————

In these poems Yury Ivask achieves lyrical restraint and
solemnity.   His concern is with the traditional themes of poetry,
the meaning of life and death, as well as the " . . . poet's
languishing desire to 'resolve all enigmas' and to attain a
reconciliation of consciousness with reality," as Pyotr Bicilli notes.
(P. Bicilli, "Yury Ivask.   *Severny bereg.*   Warsaw, 1938,"
Sovremennye Zapiski, LXVI [1938], p. 476.)   This tension between
consciousness and reality permeates "The Pontus," where disparate
conceptions are juxtaposed—death and resurrection, light and dark,
and "majestic glory" and the "ignoble soul."   On the surface, the
poem is a stylized representation of the Pontus, but it can also
represent the poet's psyche.   Consciousness and reality mingle.
The poet becomes part of the Pontus, and vice versa.   Thus, when
Ivask asks "What is happening inside me now?" the response is a
"rumbling of the Pontus."
      Like "The Pontus," "An Epitaph" achieves this dual
perspective of inner thoughts and outer reality.   Which law the
persona has obeyed remains unmentioned and is irrelevant.   The
fulfillment and its consquences of winter's approach likened to
"death's silvery light" culminates in a rich and ambivalent
texture—unusually striking in such a short lyric.

The Northern Shore

An evening of glory and grandeur,
Solemn are passionate words.

Rising tide of the sea's despair.
A hopeless surge of wind.

Full of superstitious fears,
Burst the heart of lightning.

And I beg, amid waves and crowds,
Transform me, *Abba*, into a pillar.

_____._____

The Second Death

1.

A corpse emerging from the grave,
I will make up for my loss,
My eyes are open, at last,
I'll see the long forgotten.

And with a stranger's voice,
Wrapped in an infamous shroud,
I will shout to the dead and to the living,
Not I, but He is great and glorious.

A large throng of youths
Shall raise me like a banner
To the heights, and dim slumber—
Fog—will dissolve over us.

Bright day will strike the eyes,
The crowd will enter the abode of glory,
And the beloved canopy
Of wide, dense oaks shall murmur...

Smile, my unseen friend,
Call the hero by his name!
Hearkening to the welcome sound,
We shall exit from this earthly order.

2.

Sad is your story, O heart,
Of the first death, of the fall,
But now the hour
Of willing oblivion enraptures...

There, I glide unknowing,
Into the blue of the sky,
So high, and still higher...
Earthly sounds are hushed, hushed.

Farewell, glorious oak trees,
I part forever with the earth.
Blue ice caresses my brow,
Brushes my closed lids.

———————·———————

Regal Autumn: A Second Book of Poems

Even in November they happen sometimes,
These sunlit days do occur;
They shine briefly
But fail to conceal the bitter truth.

The dwelling of late autumn
Seems even more empty and melancholy;
And you, my soul, are worse off
Than this poor cemetery.

All the same, the earth is proud
Of its sun-filled radiance,
Of its meager otherworldly glory,
And the invalid is at peace with pain and grief.

———————·———————

Homo Ludens (*La Renaissance*, No. 240, 1973), pp. 17-18

. . . .

The hyperborean land of Izborsk
On the border of Livonia.
Andreyev smiles broadly.
He generously ladles the past
From a bowl...Sullen, keen-eyed Zurov:
No *kurgan* can hide from his sharp vision.
Oh, how narrow is his skull![2]
Like one of the tribe of Vseslav:
He is a changling, an emaciated wolf.
But the ancient oak grove is sparse now.
Where is the magic retinue of the Prince of Polotsk?[3]
Both pressed on for glory,
Their roundup scarcely finished,
And the distant voice did not fall silent.

. . . .

I went to see the poet [Igor' Chinnov]. In Riga.
The Dvina stretched out wide as the Neva.
Poetry of the arrested moment;
It shows no grace towards me...
Dressed for five o'clock tea. A cup of tea.
A snob's mien. I sense, I suspect:
Chinnov has the winning point.

Those poems of twilight, shimmering
With pearls in half-sleep,
Delicate, otherworldly, poems we love:
Ethereal creations, they whisper among themselves...
Green tweed and flame of Moses.
His necktie (or banner) is the burning bush.
Friends of thirty years.

To all appearances a cheerful lad:
Is he not a clown from Khlebnikov?
At night the Lamenter (from Annensky)
Would urge him: "Cry more often!"

He would comfort himself with Pushkin's Frisky Muse:[4]
Truly, she can do with him what she will!
He is her cuckoo of melancholy: coo-coo, coo-coo.
. . . .

And who was it long ago that first
Suggested to me *Homo Ludens* and the Paradise game
Of this and a future age?
I will unlock the precious casket,
Which harbors the manuscripts of Karl Hoerschelmann,
And the vernal chestnuts of old friendship
In decades past

Will amaze us now again
With mignonette candles...Oh, there's no news
From you, but I know: You are alive
Beyond the mountains of Bavaria...Not Karl, but Pierre
        Bezukhov:
An overgrown child and a dweller of paradise.
You do not construct quiet cloisters,
But carousels, circuses, casinos

By the genial power of imagination...
How I would like to sit again, the three of us,
From Saturday, remember, until almost
Sunday, in times long past, at the table.
Snowstorms howled beyond the double panes
And Mandel'shtam's Walhalla raved about Italy:
If only we could go there, too!

Mushrooms, evangelical fishes, vodka
And a blissfully multicolored painted paradise.[5]
What unexpected joy, a real find.
Was it colors or sounds?   Could it be Time, the monster?
It's all past now; and, dressed in white,
Elizaveta[6] smiles at us;
Greetings to her from America

I send...
. . . .

———————·———————

Ivask's poetry is often melancholic. Although he portrays nature's beauties, they are always qualified by the poet's state of mind. Bitterness, despair, and hopelessness are the predominant moods. Nothing in these poems indicates a vision of anything beyond the material world, nothing beyond the "willing oblivion" of death: "Blue ice caresses my brow,/Brushes my closed lids." ("The Second Death")

His outlook is autumnal and it is not suprising to find an entire volume of his work devoted to autumn—*Regal Autumn*. There is little light in this work, except for the brief, wan light of fall days. He holds no great aspirations for the fate of his soul: "Transforms me, *Abba*, into a pillar," from "Evening of Glory...," or "And you, my poor soul, are worse off/Than this poor cemetery," from "Even in November..."

While the content and tone of Ivask's poetry are not especially uplifting, the intensity of the semantics and sounds commands the admiring attention of the reader. Naturally, much of this is forfeited in translation. The imagery is frequently obscure and subjective. "The Second Death" illustrates Ivask's vision of life. He sees life as a brief transition from one death to another. Man is born into death through the Fall and goes on to the second—final death—oblivion. Ivask himself views his lyrical hero in "The Second Death" as being resurrected after his first death, experiencing true enrapture, and greeting his second death as happiness. Ivask's later poems, including *Homo Ludens*, are "grateful hymns," as he himself described them.

Homo Ludens, a unique genre in modern Russian poetry, is autobiographical, humorous, and literary in its allusions.   The section chosen for translation here describes Ivask's visit to Latvia and his friendship there with Igor' Chinnov, and with Karl Hoerschelmann in Tallinn. In translation, the force, apt wit, and colorful mosaic of images are diminished, but the nature of the poet's mind and the role of literature and literary relationships in his personal life are clearly suggested.

NOTES

1.   E. A. Boratynsky (1800–1844), a Russian poet, lived for a short time in exile on the shores of the Baltic Sea in Finland.
2.   At the end of the 1930s, historian Nikolay Andreyev and writer Leonid Zurov visited the Pechora region for archeological research. A *kurgan* is an ancient Varangian burial mound. The narrow skull may refer to Zurov's Varangian ancestry.

3. Prince Vselav of Polotsk was believed to be a werewolf.
4. From "Little House in Kolomna" by Pushkin.
5. A reference to Hoershelmann's painting called *Paradise*, which he made to illustrate his theory of the "Paradise game" that greatly influenced Ivask.
6. Elizaveta Berngardovna von Hoerschelmann, wife of Karl. Read more about Ivask's *Homo Ludens* in Valentin Evdokimov's article "Igra pera i podvig vdokhneveniya," *Vestnik RKhD*, No. 4 (978), pp. 131-4.

NARTSISSOV, BORIS ANATOLYEVICH (1906-1982)

Nartsissov was born in the Mordvinian village of Noskaftym in the Saratov province, where his father worked as a physician. Nartsissov's mother, née Valentina Jansson, was an Estonian of Swedish descent. Later the family moved to Yamburg, Petersburg province, where Boris attended the Commercial School. In 1919, after the retreat of General Yudenich's army, the Nartsissovs found themselves in Estonia. Boris graduated from the Russian High School in Tartu (1921-24) and entered the Department of Chemistry at the University there. He completed his master's degree in chemistry in 1936. In 1937, he became a lieutenant in the Estonian Army. He was in charge of a chemical warfare defense laboratory. After the occupation of Estonia by the Red Army in 1940, Nartsissov was appointed lecturer in chemical warfare at a Soviet infantry school. He and the students were evacuated from the school and sent to Siberia during the early part of the Second World War. Ordered to the front lines, Nartsissov became ill. Lost and unconscious, he was found in the woods by the Germans. Because he was an Estonian officer, he was sent back to Tallinn. He worked there as a chemical engineer at an oil-shale mill until he was evacuated and dispatched to Germany in 1944. After the war, he worked as a chemist in American military laboratories near Munich (Bavaria) until he immigrated to Australia in 1949. Nartsissov came to the United States in 1953, where he was later appointed to a scientific research post in Columbus, Ohio, and later he worked in the Library of Congress, Washington, D.C. He resigned in 1971 and lived near the capital.

As a poet Nartsissov started out very early, publishing in *The Virgin Soil* and *Contemporary Annals* and reciting his poetry for the Russian literary circles in Tartu and Tallinn. He acknowledged

Gumilyov, Bal'mont, Blok, and Bunin as his great predecessors and models in poetry. Their works revealed to him the beauty of the world and written word. From Bunin stems Nartsissov's preoccupation with the eye and the unspoiled eager vision in primordial man; from Blok stems Nartsissov's sonorous and often melodious vocabulary. But Nartsissov is more modern than Bunin and Blok. Akin to the Surrealists, he sees and hears the music of the universe differently, more like Zabolotsky and in the vein of the innovative, archaic, and rhythmical prose of Remizov. However, Nartsissov's poetry is influenced more by the surrealistic character of contemporary life rather than by the works of his literary predecessors. His fancy word patterns in the poem "From a Monastery Chronicle" (*Memory*, 1965, p. 26), for example, resemble that of Remizov. Slavianisms and Church Slavianisms, regional words and folk images occur frequently and are curiously juxtaposed with scientific terms and colloquialisms. In addition to this hybrid and seemingly incongruous mixture, he uses neologisms and experiments with syntax. Nartsissov's dreams echo the endless chain of hallucinations in Remizov's prose poems. The witchcraft and devilry presented in everyday situations reflect Zabolotsky ("Columns"), Remizov ("Posoloni"), E. T. A. Hoffmann, and Edgar Allan Poe, whose works Nartsissov translated with pleasure. He denied his dependence on Severyanin, whose poetry he rejected as "not serious." Nartsissov listed his favorite prose writers as Gogol, whose "bold visual relief" he admired; Dostoevsky with his "impressive novelistic technique"; Mark Aldanov and his subtle psychological analysis; and Mikhail Bulgakov with his "strikingly original mode of narration." Nartsissov disliked Osip Mandle'shtam, an "incomprehensible poet," and found Vasily Rozanov a mere "cloyingly sweet writer."

    With his own profile and his own technique Nartsissov had a very personal conception of the world, which consists of two entities. One is the world as we know it; the other is the world of miracles. Wood goblins, house spirits, and moon sprites populate the latter. In craftmanship and artistic taste, Nartsissov was an Acmeist, but he had also written excellent grotesque poems, historical sketches (of Cromwell, for example), and poetic landscape descriptions. His forte lies in the portrayal of lyrical scenery. His memories of the pale beauty of the Baltic countries resulted in an evocative cycle of poems *Estonica*. These Estonian landscapes, colored by nostalgia, are precise and harmonious. Like Serveryanin,

Nartsissov expressed a deep respect for the Estonian national character: tenacity, strength in the face of adversity, and a penchant for hard work. Besides poetry dealing with the Estonian countryside and cities, Nartsissov also produced impressive verses about the "timeless land" of Australia, as well as some poems about America. His poetic credo dictated that all of the *persona's* impressions be rendered in visual and colorful images. Following Bunin's aritistic method, Nartsissov generally adhered to the classical forms of verse using rhymes and meter, but occasionally he used blank verse with great skills, as in "The Head," "The Unicorn," and "A Conversation."

Several of Nartsissov's most fascinating and original poems are poetic fragments from a modern scientific view. In fact, some of his poetry represents a scientific and mythological *Weltanschauung.* His scientific background is responsible for some of the bolder and more fantastic concepts. One cycle of poems focuses on the human brain illuminated from various perspectives, including the physiological. The poems are a splendid demonstration that every aspect of modern life can be treated poetically. Nartsissov is equally gifted at fusing the old mythology with new mythological images—the Biblical Apocalypse with its modern representation. A personal prophetic note is always present through the poet's vision of the last judgement. Surrealistic *Angstträume*, sometimes simple and realistic, sometimes eerily imaginative, are always psychologically convincing. In spite of deeply atavistic features in some of his poems, such as "The House Spirit" and "The Mire," the bulk of his verse is very contemporary, even "Kafkaesque." Nartsissov's ghosts are not merely terrifying, they are also very real, as in "The Ghost" and "The Witness."

In spite of its overall modern character, Nartsissov's poetry displays a strong affinity with Romanticism in its preoccupation with the mirror theme, fascination with the moon, and the concern with the supernatural, metaphysics, and *Naturphilosophie.* The romantic theme of the double that is developed in his poetry reaches intricate complexities. It is personified in the double of mortal daylight and the double of moonlight, who survives the death of his "master." As in romantic works, the moon and the stars figure prominently in Nartsissov's poetry. Quite frequent also are Apocalyptic visions, explosions, the collapse of the earth, and the imminence of doomsday.

With regard to the "instrumentation" of his poetry, Nartsissov

followed Pushkin's sober and austere sense of rhythm and rejected
the pursuit of melodious patterns of euphony and sound symbolism
for their own sake.   In this respect, Nartsissov was the antipode of
Severyanin as well as Ivask, both poets of the "melodic" type.   His
poems are visual; his images are almost tangible and frequently
arranged in contrasting sound patterns; the sounds change into
patterns which, as in "A Fairy Tale" (*Poems*, 1958, p. 37), can be
both heard and seen.   Imagery derived from the romantic or
classical legacy is happily combined with bright folk images of daily
life.   Even attic dust and wood lice are poeticized.   Although
ordinary words are used, Nartsissov's images are unusual in their
suggested power, for example:

> "A candle, like a golden flower,
> Blossoms in the gray twilight."
>
> (*Memory*, 1965, p. 14)

Both in the images and use of Russian language, Nartsissov's
landscape lyrics reflect his extensive travels and the range of his
interests.   These   interests   include   chemical   technology   and
linguistics, gardening and mysticism, anthropology and philosophy,
the theme of the double, legends, and an enlightened, pacified,
spiritual attitude toward the world.   Original and innovative, his
works radiate a sense of pensive, Pushkin-like sadness.   Nartsissov's
metrics, however, differ from Pushkin's.   The rhythmic structure of
Pushkin's verse is predominantly iambic, the meter characteristic of
Russian   versification   until   the   end   of   the   nineteenth   century.
Nartsissov used the two-and three-syllabic metric feet common in
the   Silver   age   of   Russian   poetry   (1890-1920).   Furthermore,
Pushkin's   style   is   clear   and   serene;   his   verse   symbolizes   the
"sun-path," Nartsissov's, the "moon-path."
Nartsissov   translated   into   Russian   the   poetry   and   prose   of
Aleksis Rannit and A. H. Tammsaare.   Some of these excellent
translations were published even in the Soviet Union.   In 1939, the
Tallinn "Guild of Poets" recommended Nartsissov to the Union of
Estonian Poets who wanted to have their works published in the
USSR and had approached the Russian "Guild" in search of a
suitable translator.   Nartsissov authored six volumes of poetry:
Stikhi (Poems; New York: Litfund, 1958), *Golosa* (Voices;
Frankfurt/Main: Posev, 1961), *Pamyat'* (Memory; Washington, DC:
Russkaya kniga, 1965), *Podyom* (Ascent; Leuven, Belgium: A.

Rosseels, 1969), *Shakhmaty* (Chess; Washington, DC: Nartsissov, 1974), and *Zvoyzdnaya ptitsa* (A Star Bird; Annandale, VA: Charles Baptie Studios, 1978).

Some of Nartsissov's poems were translated into English by Robert M. Morrison in *Australia's Russian Poets* (1975) and by John Glad in *Russian Poetry: The Modern Period* (1978). The Canadian poet Meery Devergnas translated several of Nartsissov's verses into French. His poetry is represented in various anthologies, such as *Muza Diaspory* (The Muse of Diaspora), *The Journal of Concord*, *Perekryostok* (Crossroads), and others. Nartsissov is the author of several surrealistic short stories and novellas, for example "Pis'mo samomu sebe" (A Letter to Myself), published in *Vozrozhdenie* (La Renaissance; Paris, 1967), No. 188.

A Star Bird

Antiquity

He built a bonfire at the foot of the temple,
And adorned it.
The smoke billowed up and headed straight for heaven,
And nourished the Deity on high.

In a ponderous, still non-Aryan dialect
He said the words.
He was dressed in sheepskins
And had a receding forehead.

The transparent flame trembled beneath the sun.
The bonfire began to die out.
He looked at the sooty, sacrificial stone,
And was powerless to understand something.

But above, rising upward amid rough stones,
Above shrubs in bloom,
An unpolished, marble god, smiling,
Peered tensely into the void.

————·————

I don't know now if it was a dream or not,
But the vision remains welcome:
A joyless, ashen world I was shown,
A tranquil world, strange and mute.

Above the stinging, cold, shifting sand
Withered grass leaves swayed,
And on this red, dry sand
No one, except the wind, has left a trace.

The surf, dashing against the shores,
Phosphorized from the twilight into a white arc.
And in the green sky, one after the other,
Enormous moons arose.

And then I understood that I was wholly
Alone on this distant planet.
And all around I saw only bloody sand
And lifeless, raceme grass.

―――――――・―――――――

The Wind

All day it strained recklessly, madly,
And toward nightfall completely broke loose;
With a roar it rolled across the roofs,
And then pounced and grew brutal.

It moved through the room in currents,
And the candle's flame wavered.
And shadows crept stealthily up on me,
Like lemurs from a dark hall.

I was entirely alone,
Abandoned by all other people,
I kept watch into the deep of night
Over the fire and the melted wax.

And when it howled and reverberated,
Grating like iron sheets,
The flame turned blue and almost died out,
Drawing painfully near to the ground.

And I saw myself as this flame,
Encircled by a dismal darkness which,
In drunken currents, together with the lemurs,
Hastened to blow it out.

———————·———————

The Spider

Electricity gleamed over the table
With a stubborn, dry, lifeless light.
The rain fell steadily. Outside, the night
With its tear-stained face clung to the black windows.

Calculations lay side by side.
Ink drops shimmered quiescently.
All of sudden my mind sensed something—
I saw something drawing near me.

I hear a rustling sound, quick and squeaking;
I looked, and over the table on the wall,
I saw springy spider legs
With angular, broken joints.

It was here yesterday. And now again today.
It crawled up and stiffened. And the sickening
Horror of nocturnal loneliness
Struck me with a stinging tremor.

I can't kill it. I don't dare.
And it knows this. In predaceous silence
I must watch, as its crooked legs
Show gray against the wall.

———————·———————

Memory

I recall, down a narrow little path
Amid elder trees, through a marshy hollow,
I would go home from the forest.
Fingers, press my eyes shut! Frame the picture!
Gather scraps of painful memories,
I don't have many left.

Just as if it were yesterday. With warm clover
And resin, like the sunny north,
The fragrances of this yesterday waft in my memory.
I walk along the border and run my hand
Along the ears of grain, as I would stroke billowy hair.
How white the birch bark glistens!

This little path interwove club moss with cobwebs,
Clustered with prickly raspberry,
Became overgrown with roadside leaves
Through the twilight of alder thickets—
Across flashes of injured memory—
To an abandoned, desolate home.

———————·———————

In the poetic world of Boris Nartsissov, disparate elements
merge to attain a unique lyrical tenor. Nartsissov tends to blur
the boundaries between dream and reality, between objective
descriptions and subjective vision, between the distant, almost
prehistoric past and the technologically colored present. Within
this magical universe the wind may be anthropomorphized as easily
as shadows turn into lemurs; spiders crawl silently over a wall and
take on monstrous proportions in the poet's imagination.
Nartsissov has a predilection for the primeval elements— earth,
wind, fire, and water. An atmosphere of anxiety and isolation
achieved through Kafkaesque symbolism and combined with
realistic, sensual nature descriptions make for a fascinating mixture
representing the poet's views and indicating his unceasing efforts to
investigate the primal impulses which alternately haunt and propel
man.
Characteristic of this kaleidoscopic poetic universe is an

essentially existential outlook which stresses man's sense of isolation and alienation. By presenting the theme in different poems Nartsissov offers many perspectives. Thus, in "Antiquity" the problem of man's existence is dealt with in a careful portrayal of an ancient ritual to "the Deity on high." The poem achieves an ironic resonance when it is revealed in the last stanza that the sheepskin-clad figure worships "an unpolished, marble god, smiling," as it "tensely peered into the void," perhaps sensing, as the world "void" signals, its own finite and isolated existence.

Man's fundamental loneliness also forms the subject of the lyric "I don't know now whether it was a dream or not." The depiction of a chilling internalized dream landscape of "stinging, cold, shifting sand," "green sky," and enormous moons," is carried by a somber undertone which converges in the last stanza with the musings of the *persona* and accentuates his awareness that " . . . I'm wholly/Alone, on this distant planet."

"The Spider" has a curiously unsettling effect by juxtaposing the calm, depressing picture of a man working on "calculations" in the "lifeless light" of an electric bulb, with an accumulation of images emphasizing the primal terror felt by the man at the sight of the spider. The text takes on additional meaning when the poet observes that the man noticed the insect's presence through a sensation of the mind. Hence the fundamental ambiguity of the symbol; the reader has to decide whether the spider is an internal manifestation, an external phenomenon, or both. Nartsissov's description of "predaceous silence" and of the spider whose "stiffened" limbs offer a sickening sight because of its angular, broken joints leads the reader from implications of a sinister, bestial, irrational existence to the logical calculations on the table. The "nocturnal loneliness" points again to the poet's existential frame of reference. Reason and irrationality frequently form an uneasy alliance in Nartsissov's poetry. As a whole, the combinations arising from successful juxtapositions of opposing elements are rich, multi-faceted, resonant, and unique in both scope and presentation.

The following two unpublished poems from the album of Elizabeth Bazilevskaya-Roos illustrate Boris Nartsissov's early Muse:

The amber dreams of clouds float hurriedly,
Melting away on the blue sky.
The yellow leaves tear off the willow,
Falling down like a swarm of dying butterflies.

The gusty fresh wind walks resiliently
On the rustling, droning branches of trees,
Bending the blood-red maples toward one another
And brushing my cheeks with its cold caress.

The autumnal pale shadow
Streams along the grey, washed-out but dry narrow path.
The honey colored mushroom, on its thin, crooked leg,
Climbed onto the black, birch tree stump.

The evening sun with its cold radiance
Glows in the thin and dry leafage.
With its resilent, cold breathing the wind chases
My golden dreams into the blue sky.

September 21, 1928

—————·—————

When they destroyed my sacred possessions
And drove me out like a beggarly slave,
The barren deserts gave me a shelter
Their stones as sharp as ancient coffins.

I cursed and wept over my loss.
My sorrow was stinging like a bitter wormwood.
In the revelation which came to me from on high
The great desert soon became my truth.

Then I understood what I had found in exile
A world given and comprehensible to me alone,
The nameless countries revealed themselves to me.
In an opposite silence the murmur of lyres resounded.

I created mirages of savage beauty.
My seconds became transformed into years.
I ordered the chains of mountains to guard me.
And severed forever my ties with the past.

1927

HOERSCHELMANN, KARL KARLOVICH (1899-1951)

Karl Karlovich von Hoerschelmann, poet, artist, writer, critic, and essayist, belonged to the Tallinn Guild of Poets (1933-38). Son of a general in the medical corps, Hoerchelmann was born to a prominent Baltic family in Sebastopol. He received his education in the Cadet Corps (1906-16) and in the Mikhaylovsky Artillery Academy in Petersburg. Tall and slender, with a fine military bearing, he served as a captain of the Bodyguards in the Third Artillery Brigade. Later he entered the Philosophy Department at the University of Odessa, but was soon called by the White Army. He fought in Southern Russia in the armies of Wrangel and Denikin; later he was interned for more than a year in Gallipoli (Dardanelles). By way of Rumania, Bulgaria, and Poland, Hoerschelmann reached Riga, and in 1922 he settled in Tallinn, where he worked as a draftsman in the Ministry of Agriculture. He was also involved in painting and graphics and held exhibits of his graphic art in Estonia. Yury Ivask regarded the painting "Paradise" as Hoerschelmann's best work.[1]

When the Baltic countries were occupied by Soviet forces in the fall of 1940, Hoerschelmann and his family escaped to Poland and then to Germany. There, in Eichstätt, he illustrated a Catholic children's magazine and painted the Crucifixion for a local monastery. Hoerschelmann and his wife, Elizaveta Berngardovna (née von Rosendorf), were both outstanding artists and worked mainly in water color, which under their brushes takes on the appearance of enamel. In the paintings of Elizaveta Berngardovna, immobile, seemingly frozen objects (often flowers of the field) entice the observer with peaceful lines and colors. Their eloquent silence corresponds with some of the quiet scenes full of inner expressiveness in the works of Turgenev and Tolstoy. Hoerschelmann's paintings, on the other hand, often portray the fantastic.   Pavel Irtel, editor and publisher of the almanac *The Virgin Soil*, asked Hoerschelmann to illustrate this publication, and the cover of the fifth issue of *The Virgin Soil* (April 1933) was done by him.   It is a stylized and modernistic treatment of Russian folklore motifs, similar to the early paintings of Kandinsky.

The Virgin Soil, No. 6 (1934)

For some reason I have to tell you
That outside my window the weather is fine,
That today outside my window the arching dome
Of the heavens is bright gray,

That a slanting ray lights the neighboring house,
And a yellow cat has perched on the roof.
For some reason I have to tell you
That I am alive and see this roof.

———·———

Proud am I of a trust beyond measure:
Someone's creating love
Has entrusted to me a scrap of the universe—
These stars and this blood.

I was given to myself unconditionally,
Only one commandment I observe:
With the entrusted stars and blood
To do the best I can.

To do the best I know how,
At my own risk.   And again
Into the former hands, as I grow cold,
Return both stars and blood.

———·———

The Virgin Soil, No. 7 (1934)

I once had the good fortune to be born.
They promised: Life is ahead.
My head whirls with hopes,
So much strength in my shoulders and chest!

And here is youth. Already the end is in sight.
Here is old age. But where? When?
Beyond the window—a lattice fence,
Telephone wires.

Is that all? Of course, to the grave.
Is this life? What else? That's it.
That means this one is just a trial run,
That means there will be yet another.

———·———

Hoerschelmann's poems, very precise and expressive in intonation, are fequently written as unexpected aphorisms. In style they are akin to the formal aspects of the "Parisian note" poetry: puzzling, inquiring intonations, intentional simplicity of vocabulary, unfinished sentences, an abundance of parenthetic clauses, and a distinct tendency toward simplified, diary-like entries. They are, however, concrete and forceful, and we do not have the painful sensation that the poet had been severed from his Russian roots. Like all other members of the "Guild of Poets" in Estonia, Hoershelmann was tied to his new country by his Baltic descent and family relations. Furthermore, since the Estonian landscape resembles that of the Russian North, there is less pessimism and hardly any feeling of isolation and alienation in the poetry of Russian writers in Estonia compared with the literary works of the Russian "Parisians." Also different are Hoerschelmann's impetuous rhythms, his sense of the spaciousness of the universe in which planets and constellations speed from one place to another, and the inimitable metaphoric games as seen, for example, in his poem "Perseus."

Hoerschelmann's literary work may be viewed as an ongoing philosophical inquiry into the nature of life and death, the significance of earthly existence, and man's unique place within the huge universe.   Such considerations find expression in both his prose and verse through a variety of perspectives which range from the most prosaic observations of empirical reality to fantastic vignettes in the genre of science fiction.   Thoughts on love and the meaning of death form a central motif.   "I once had the good fortune to be born" is a good example of his aesthetic technique and its execution.   The poem, in fact, is constructed much like a mathematical problem or a scientific hypothesis.   Proceeding from the known—I was born; I possess a brain and a body; I will die—he moves gradually away from this empirical framework into the realm of metaphysical speculation on what lies beyond death in the form of questions: "Here is old age.   But where?   When?" Yet in the center of the poem Hoerschelmann unexpectedly interrupts this train of thought to remark "Beyond the window—a lattice fence, telephone wires."   The abrupt semantic and emotional shift that this description evokes as well as its snapshot-like quality enhance the emotional depth of the poem and save the abstract reflections from wandering off in an obscure and meaningless direction.

The poem "For some reason I have to tell you" is constructed symmetrically.   The meter is iambic, with lines varying from four to six feet in length.   In both content and formal structure the lines are arranged so that the last two lines of the second stanza echo the first two lines of the first stanza and the middle four lines form a syntactic unit.   Repetition is an important device here.   Two lines ("For some reason I have to tell you") are nearly identical, and half the lines in the poem begin with the word "that."   The rhyme scheme is not remarkable; it is abab, with alternating masculine and feminine rhymes.   Laconic and deceptively simple, the poem is nevertheless full of thematic content, emphasizing the personal and the essential as Hoerschelmann advocated in one of his critical essays.   In formal structure the two poems "Proud am I of a trust beyond measure" and "I once had the good fortune to be born" are similar.   Both combine binary and ternary meters for a musical effect.   The rhyme schemes are abab, with feminine and masculine rhymes alternating throughout, and both poems use repetition of entire lines or parts of lines to accentuate certain sounds and themes.

The observations of everyday reality prevalent in Hoerschelmann's lyrics are often replaced in his prose by fantastic and exotic texture.   Significantly, the underlying philosophical examination of the world still remains intact. A good example of his prose technique is found in the vignette "In One of the Neighboring Worlds." Hoerschelmann again probes considerations of life and death by juxtaposing earthly existence with life on "one of the neighboring worlds, a world with eleven suns, and consequently no shade at all..." From this unique perspective, life on earth, with its "unprecedented quantity of darkness," its "primeval, savage people," and its "barbaric language," is approached with a tone akin to an anthropological study of the coarse rituals of an uncivilized tribe. The narrator's ironic conclusion about our planet is that "the process of its (the earth's) creation has hardly even begun...."

The Virgin Soil, No. 6 (1934)

In One of the Neighboring Worlds

In one of the neighboring worlds, a world with eleven suns and consequently no shade at all, occurred the following event: Uncle Pete returned from his travels. The children flitted out into the anteroom, joyfully clapping little wings. Even Mama flew out to meet him. Uncle was quite a sight—he wore striped trousers and stood under an umbrella. It was obvious from first glance that he really had been to some outlandish places.

They all gathered around a table in the dining room, but there was no light. Lamps are unnecessary in a world with eleven suns.

"I have been to a distant and terrible universe," Uncle Pete began while eating his favorite salad of violet petals. "In that astonishing world there are shadows. Not only shadows; you might say that this entire world is nothing but shade, complete darkness. Only very rarely do you catch sight of a bright spot; they call these spots stars in the barbaric language of that world. Just imagine: There's as much darkness as the size of the room, but only as much light, say, as the size of a pinhead....

"Sister, wouldn't it be better to send the youngsters out? They are too young to be hearing this kind of thing...

"Completely black worlds orbit around these stars. The natives living on them are primeval, savage people. They live only on the very surface, at the shore of the void which surrounds them. They move around their little islands, hanging their heads down over the abyss. In the majority of cases they have only one sun. At night the sun sets, and the natives drop off to sleep because they have nothing better to do..."

Uncle Pete took a gulp of early morning dew from the glass and continued:

"These people don't live all the time, as one would expect, but only a short time. They live a while, and then they die. This is a very strange custom; I didn't quite understand why it was introduced.

"In this world they depend primarily on each other, their neighbors, for nourishment. For this purpose they breed the savages of a special tribe whom they call animals for their comparative lack of culture.

"Sister, put on your sweater. Are you feverish?

"In general, I must say, these are crude, but courageous and determined people. Like bold pioneers, they wander around in raincoats and galoshes through rain, snow, and wind, among houses built from little pieces of earth. There aren't even any roofs over their streets for getting in out of the bad weather.

"I have a hypothesis with regard to this remote world as a whole. It seems to me that in contrast to other worlds, it is not yet completely created. Judging from the unprecedented quantity of darkness, the process of its creation has hardly even begun..."

The children pressed close to one another. The tips of Mama's wings trembled nervously. Even farther looked aside and sniffed the large violet rose for its soothing effect.

In order to distract and comfort them, Uncle Pete started to hand out the presents he had bought from the distant world. For father—a snapshot of the Milky Way taken in profile. It was clearly visible how much darkness there really was in that world. For Mama—a bottle of perfume with five drops of liquid, the same liquid which flows from the eyes of the natives—why, it is not clear! For the nephews, a few little things—shoe laces; a pair of teeth on a round pink plate, separate from the man; a white sheet speckled with black dots—Uncle called it a scrap of newspaper; and other obscure knickknacks. The corpse of a special species of native which Uncle had brought back provoked the greatest interest; it was small, black, with a tiny proboscis, transparent wings, and a very amusing name: "Fly."

———————·———————

By showing life on earth as seen through the eyes of a visitor from outer space, Hoerschelmann points to the absurdity of the human condition and makes us laugh at things that are usually thought of as normal. This piece is a good example of the device of *ostranenie* (making something strange). Serious and humorous details are interwoven. Among the serious are the strange human "custom" of dying, the breeding of animals ("savages") for food, and the vial of human tears ("a bottle of perfume"). More humorous aspects include the description of the natives' habit of sleeping "because they have nothing better to do," the courage of "bold pioneers" who "wander around in raincoats and galoshes," and the presents of the false teeth and the dead fly. Hoerschelmann's creativity is manifest also of his portrayal of the world with eleven suns. In a matter-of-fact tone he mentions the children "joyfully clapping their little wings" and Uncle Pete taking a gulp of dew and eating "his favorite salad of violet petals." It is a delightful and touching vignette, conveyed in simple and colloquial language.

In all of Hoerschelmann's stories we find meditations on the nature of human existence and its spiritual reality and on death and other metaphysical questions. The confrontation of the fantastic with empirical reality in these stories creates a startling, lively effect. The fantastic world is described in simple, concrete terms. Unfortunately, many of his stories on fantastic or exotic subjects were lost with the archives of Nikolay Otsup in Paris.

Questions of a spiritual nature, a salient feature of his entire literary legacy, are especially prominent in Hoerschelmann's religious writings. In the essay "On the Kingdom of God,"[2] he reveals the possibility of the transfiguration on earth of man's inner world and the creation of the Kingdom of God, which is love. Like Dostoevsky's elder Zosima and like Zinaida Hippius, Hoerschelmann believed that the Kingdom of God is within the individual's soul. Dostoevsky, Hippius, and Hoerschelmann maintained that love is able to transform the entire world. This world is closely connected with the "other world"; they coexist.[3] Death, the only real enemy of life, is "an exit from it." Only by conquering the fear of death can one earn the right to speak of the meaning and significance of human existence. Man's task on earth is "to sift out from life the paradise contained within it and affix it in its pure form. . . . Every evil can be rectified except for death. We must make death also rectifiable—and this is the resurrection," Hoerschelmann asserts in the article "On Play."[4] Hoerschelmann has written other stories on the theme of death and suicide. They are saturated with irony and "play,"[5] for example, the miniature tale "Suicide and the Stars,"[6] "Story Without a Title,"[7] and others.

His "teachings" about paradise and play made a powerful impression on Yury Ivask: If the best thing in life is play, then surely it must continue in the other world. In Ivask's opinion, the following discoveries by Hoerschelmann are particularly important:

"In order to transform life completely into play, life itself must be regarded somewhat as a toy; this is resurrection.

"In order to transform life into paradise, two things must be overcome: boredom and death. Play is able to conquer both of these.

"Life is eternally childlike in creativity. Only death is truly serious.

"Death will be conquered only when life is saturated with laughter, laughter without reason, like a child's.

"We cannot create eternal bliss by our own power, but we can create 'a decent eternity' by our own power. This is play."[8]

Hoerschelmann's teaching about play found its way into Ivask's poem "Playing Man. *Homo Ludens*":

>"And who was it that long ago first
>Suggested to me *Homo Ludens* and the Paradise game
>Of this and a future age?"[9]

Ivask reminisces about the evenings spent with Karl and Elizaveta von Hoerschelmann when the three of them would sit and discuss the philosophy of Berdyaev, and Fyodorov, and the poetry of Blok, Osip Mandel'shtam, and others of the Symbolist–Acmeist epoch. Hoerschelmann loved the works of Dostoevsky, Blok, Georgy Ivanov, Vyacheslav Ivanov, and Khodasevich. He wrote several articles on Dostoevsky and illustrated several of Blok's poems. Among Hoerschelmann's philosophical works, close to Dostoevsky's novels in concept and metaphysical theme, is the remarkable work "The Fallen Angel. Extracts from a Diary."[10]

As in Dostoevsky's fantastic story "Dream of a Ridiculous Man," sin arises in paradise as a result of the intellect, the rational reflections of an angel. The angel subjects paradise to a critical appraisal and then desires to "avoid this company (the Creator and His cohorts) and leave." He justifies his rebellion against God thus: "He gave me reason and will. And what is my reason? It is the judge. Is His world indeed good if it needs to be reformed? And will? This is the armament of reason." In the new world created by the angel everything is to be "whirled topsy-turvy" because it is "fun." A white, mother-of-pearl angle brings him the Creator's message that freedom is given to be used only for love and not for anger. But the "black angel" is determined to use the freedom granted him by the Creator for his own purposes—for the destruction of the world of harmony and perfection. His rebellion takes place in several stages. He tempts Eve with the apple of knowledge and she puts on the fig leaf as the first gesture of denial of His perfection. "The universe was turned about. Paradise was ended and world history began," the "black angel" triumphs. Next, the first blood is spilled when Cain murders Abel. Then follows the creation of time, space, movement, and longing for the future. In this manner the basis is laid for a new world, which has "turned away from Him, forgotten Him." Like Dostoevsky's "Ridiculous Man," "the black angel" strives not only to assert his individuality, to satisfy his ego. In accordance with the allegory of the Fall in the Old Testament, both Dostoevsky and Hoerschelmann describe the rise of evil through the awakened consicousness of Adam and Eve, who until this time had lived in peace, contentment, and harmony with the universe. Intellect, which gives rise to vanity, ambition, sensuality, desire for revenge, and striving for evil, presents man with a choice between good and evil. At the age of eighteen Dostoevsky wrote to his brother Mikhail (in a letter of October 31, 1838) that the beauties of nature, the soul, love, and God can be apprehended only by the heart. In his novels he portrays the tragic consequences of the absence of love and conscience, and the dominance in man of reason and logical argumentation. Hoerschelmann similarly asserts that the Fall begins when intellect evicts feeling as the ethical foundation of life.

The problem of death also links Hoerschelmann with the metaphysical world view of Dostoevsky. "Dream, idiocy, insanity, death"—thus begins Hoerschelmann's story "The Crossing,"[11] which in some respects resembles Dostoevsky's "Bobok." Dostoevsky and Hoerschelmann both use the so-called "dream-logic technique" which obscures the boundaries between dreams, hallucinations, and waking life. This technique penetrates the chaotic conflicts of the human soul and portrays frightening mystical revelations, particularly of the spiritual disintegration and moral decrepitude of an atheistic world, as in "Bobok." The development of this theme is carried out against the background of repulsive realistic details—the greenish water near the graves continually scooped up by the grave digger, the uneaten sandwich left carelessly on one grave, the little restaurant where those attending services for the dead make merry. The emphasis is on man in a world that has lost God, man who not only remains indifferent to death, but even after death never thinks of the spiritual nature of the universe and his relationship to it as an integral part.

The thought of death leaves the heroine of "The Crossing" wholly untroubled. Like Dostoevsky's corpses and those in Sartre's *No Exit*, she continues to think and speak of worldly matters: ribbons, fabric, festoons, American films with Greta Garbo, kisses, embraces, and sensual pleasures. And the conditions surrounding her are the most ordinary: a gloomy, rainy day; a bed, blanket and pillow; couch, armchair, porch. But the uncanny story ends with unexpected warmth, a human note: We must learn how to help the deceased cross over peacefully to the other world through understanding and pity. In our godless world the way to the other side, a fathomless well, leads us along wide steps by a cold stone wall covered with grayish-green mold. We must assist the dead on this perilous crossing. (Cf. Egyptian and Tibetan Books of the Dead.) Irony and serious narration, the fantastic and the real, dream and waking, merge into a single perception of the only certain fact of life, impending death. The awareness of this inevitable reality and of the terrible aloneness at death has preoccupied writers like Hugo von Hofmannsthal in the play *Jedermann*, which is a reworking of the English morality play *Everyman*, and Tolstoy in "The Death of Ivan Ilyich." Tolstoy describes the terrible crossing of Ivan Ilyich from one reality to another and his unbearable sense of loneliness and longing for sympathy and pity.

Hoerschelmann, a master of the aesthetics of the grotesque, captures the ever-increasing dangers of the present-day world, with its rejection of religion and its bizarre relationships. He uses the eerie and the ambiguous to present images of a purgation that may ultimately result in illumination. Hoerschelmann's sense of the ridiculous and the fantastic is religious in its intensity. The pathos of the "ridiculous" and the "absurd" is a marked characteristic of several of his stories, and the ambiguous tension between the comic and the tragic is apparent in many of them. Like Dostoevsky, he avails himself of this technique not for the amusement, but to create an atmosphere of loneliness and isolation. His protagonists, afraid of alienation, are unable to transcend their egocentricity and to leave their fantasy world in which they believe they are living a meaningful life.

Hoerschelmann excels in his portrayal of a feverish, oppressive, dreamlike atmosphere which helps to depict the most cherished thoughts of man and the "darkness" of his soul. Death plays an important role in his stories as a strong spiritual experience with its strange, frequently tormenting visions. In Hoerschelmann's eyes, the principal malady of our life is a spiritual torpor and lethargy, and it is to this warped condition that he addresses his art. One of his main themes is the inability of man to communicate with others, so that he becomes isolated, frustrated, and evil-minded toward his fellow men. We have here an intense search for one's own, odd version of redemption. By depicting what is defective, banal, flat, and trivial in the despiritualized society of today, Hoerschelmann strives to transform its monstrosity into a new and fresh realization of what has been lost, to baptize the world, as it were, and to make mankind responsive once more to its spiritual ideals. He creates a fantasy universe with sufficient resemblance to the world as we know to confuse the reader. Like Dostoevsky, Hoerschelmann implies that man without God is ridiculously absurd in his endeavors to come to grips with life on his own terms.

Thus, the grotesque is for Hoerschelmann a kind of religious hyperbole. The haughtiness of intellect, the corruption of ethics, and the rebellion against God—and against this bleak background he portrays, with equally compelling power, the assertion of faith, the necessity of consistency between belief and action. Since he often places his characters into ambiguous situations to highlight their spiritual dilemmas, Hoerschelmann's endings intentionally lend themselves to various interpretations. They misguide the reader and make it difficult for him to accept the possible implications and references to the heroes' solutions to their individual problems. The reader is, however, well aware that there is a struggle going on, the struggle of the heart and mind, in this world of alienation. Through these distortions, the reader can see a life without grace which inevitably results in an endless agonizing search, or a terrible void and frustration in complete isolation and defeat.

Hoerschelmann, however, does not always treat only serious subjects. He excels in humorous miniatures. For example, in "Vstrecha" ("A Meeting"), he presents to us, in an *estranged* fashion, Alexander Pushkin during his exile in Odessa. It is a delightful story about the young poet who meets with Hoerschelmann in the south of Russia, with whom he converses about Odessa high society, Count and Countess Vorontsov, and his love for poetry. The narrative is dazzling in its use of humor and witty characterization of men and women in Odessa.

Another humorous work of Hoerschelmann, "Sovremenny *Domostroy*" (A Contemporary *Domostray*"), which further develops the edification of *Izbornik* of Prince Svyatoslav in 1076, then of Vladimir Monomakh's famous "Pouchenie" ("Sermon") to his children in the beginning of the XII century, and finally of *Domostroy* of the XVI century. "A Contemporary *Domostroy*" is an interesting experiment of Hoerschelmann in the genre of Russian edifying literature, written in a lively, humorous, conversational style. His miniatures "Grekh" ("The Sin"), "Posle pyati chasov vechera" ("After Five O'clock at Night"), and "Ray" ("Paradise") are written in the same ironical tonality, even though their contents are more serious and philosophically rich.

Indeed, Karl Hoerschelmann, with his unique vision of the universe, is an original modernistic writer, in whose works deep philosophical ideas are presented, and profound questions are raised. The warm and sympathetic concern of the writer for the suffering and erring humanity, with its "half-Christianity" and "half-Christ," is evident in his entire literary *oeuvre*.

The well-known critic essayist Pyotr Pil'sky, who left St. Petersburg after the Revolution of 1917 and settled in Revel and then in Riga, had great respect for the philosophical as well as the literary works of Hoerschelmann and praised his originality as a literary critic. Below is an example of Hoerschelmann's essays.

The *Virgin Soil*, No. 6 (1934)

On Contemporary Poetry

In the émigré press pessimistic observations about the state of modern Russian poetry have become more frequent lately. One may reduce them to three statements. First, that there are many poets; second, that there are few readers; third, that the reading public may not be entirely responsible for this state of affairs, for things are not going particularly well in the field of poetry itself.

"The ancient edifice of the poetic art is being undermined and fossilized...superfluities are piled up, there are voids which cannot now be filled, the metric skeleton has become overgrown with a wild profusion of indifferent rhythms and accidental words. Prose is preferred to poetry. The twilight of poetry is setting in." (V. Weidlé, "The Twilight of Poetry," *Vstrechi* [Encounters], No. 3).

"It isn't worth persisting. The soil is exhausted, dried up—nothing can thrive in it now; it should be allowed to lie fallow and recover...Write prose, ladies and gentlemen." (G. Adamovich, "Verses," *The Latest News*, No. 4705).

One cannot wholly disagree with the first two statements. And to a considerable extent the third is also justified. Undoubtedly modern poetry, like all other branches of culture, is expriencing a certain crisis. The only question is how to find a way out. The possibilitites are few, but must this be attributed to poetry as a whole, or only to some aspect of it? In the article cited above, and even more so in his article "Pure Poetry" (*Contemporary Annals*, No. 53), V. Weidlé defines the areas where this improverished soil exists: in the overuse of strophic forms, phonetic forms (meter, rhyme), and stylistic forms (diction, syntax, imagery). In other words, all the formal components of poetry writing are overworked.

It is generally recognized how conditional and vague the terms "form" and "content" are. Here they are considered in their ordinary, narrow sense. There is also no doubt that form is essentially inseparable from content. Form is the embodiment of content. Form must *completely* and *without any excess* reveal the content.

However, the very existence of these terms is an indication of their comparative independence. Their confluence is a rather ideal state. Actually, the predominance of one or the other will always be evident, or at least their divergence to a greater or lesser degree. This can be demonstrated in any individual work of art, as well as in an entire historical period.

Symbolism was to a considerable extent a formal movement. The Symbolists made numorous theoretical discoveries in this area (Bryusov, Bely) and engaged in some purely technical exprimentation as well. In its day Symbolism provided an indispensable reaction against the formal rigidity of the pre-Symbolist period; a professional purity was restored to poetry.

Later movements shared the Symbolist concern with purely formal research. As evidence of the extent to which the creators of numerous "isms" maintained a technical approach to neighboring schools and to their own, it is possible to quote from Bely's introduction to his collection *After Separation,* where the premises of his "melodism" are defined. "Melodism" did not play a significant role, and Bely himself did not attach much importance to it, but the approach is characteristic:

"This little workbook is a search for form...Innovative endeavors were manifested only as a natural division of labor in the refinement of separate elements of verse. Rhythmists and Futurists appeared, stressing the sound of the word; Imagists appeared, concentrating on the importance of images, etc...Now the poem is overloaded with contrivances of image, rhythm, and instrumentation, but all the schools...overlook one essential aspect of the poem—the melody of the whole."

Of course, neither Symbolism, nor Acmeism, nor Futurism, nor any other movement restricted itself to the consideration of purely formalistic objectives. These were often even relegated to the background. But the important fact is that these goals were most often considered apart from ideological problems, or, in isolation and secondarily, as a search for a new and more perfect form—*an und für sich.*

And so, the very idea of the search for form apart from

its relationship to content is an abnormal phenomenon. Experimentation is warranted as an exercise but not as a goal. All "the contrivances of image, rhythm, and instrumentation" are necessary and legitimate, but only as means, and not as ends in themselves. If form is really the emodiment of content ("As if perfect form is not that which embraces the content in its ultimate extension." Weidlé, "The Twilight of Poetry."), then everything that is simply decoration and organically disconnected from the whole poem is essentially superfluous weight and clutter.

The attitude toward form as something self-sufficient is derived from the principle of "art for art's sake," a proclamation which in the 1890s served, perhaps, as the point of departure for this entire process. "Art for art's sake" justified the game for its own purposes: an aesthetic outpouring of jewels from palm to palm. At the time of its declaration this principle was necessary and proper. It counterbalanced the principle of "utilitarian" art of the 1870s, when a sermon on civic virtue and "a university degree in natural history" was expected from the artist, when it was forgotten that art exerts influence in ways that are entirely independent, that the intuitiveness of art, its extra-logical and "musical" structure, place it in a realm which permits no comparison with any other field, especially science. The principle of "art for art's sake" liberated the poet and returned to poetry the right to be regarded as art.

But from a broader point of view it is undoubtedly insufficient. The fate of art is not an endless stewing in its own juices. The objective of art is much wider than merely to serve as pleasant relaxation, no matter how lofty this relaxation is considered (including Schopenhauer's pure contemplation). The goal of art in the final analysis is its influence on life. It must "inflame the warrior for battle," "set fire to the hearts of men with the word." The technique—"the sting of the wise serpent"—is only a means on this path. The content of a work of art is its aspect that transcends the specific features of the given art. Take, for example, the historical, descriptive, philosophical content of poetry: The word, according to the principle of "art for art's sake," is all that was united under the contemptuous name of "literature."

However, the rejection of "literature" leads ultimately to the rejection of form. Absence of content makes the means of its expression superflous; the entire work is destroyed. Form becomes empty, since there is nothing for it to embody. The downfall of the French Parnassians, Mallarmé, Paul Valéry, and others is understandable (see Weidlé, "Pure Poetry"), when the principle of "art for art's sake" brought poetry to self-denial, to a renunciation of the process of creation in general.

If you want to arrive at a certain point, it is necessary to know how to walk. But, once out on the road, you ought to look at the goal and not at your feet. Otherwise you will be wandering around—good for health, but not for arriving quickly at your goal. In order to reveal the content, the attention of the artist must be directed first of all to the content itself. Form will appear as a consequence. One of the best ways to improve form is to forget about it.

The results of the work of the last few decades are substantial. There has been reform in meter (every possible combination), rhythm (alliteration and assonance), and composition (the use of rare stanzaic forms), as well as other essential innovations. But the possibilities in this direction have been exhausted. Well then, a trip may be undertaken for the sake of which the entire work was conducted. Concepts of literature, theme, and content may be rehabilitated, and the creative attention of poetry may be transferred to them.

Not only is this shift of attention desirable; it is already apparent in the most recent émigré poetry. Zinaida Hippius demands "human talent" as well as poetical talent from the poet. Marina Tsvetaeva calls this "the gift of the soul"; she promotes children's and dilettante verses and points out the inadequacy of technique alone for poetry. (See the article by M. Tsvetaeva, "Art in the Light of Conscience," *Contemporary Annals*, No. 50.) These ideas are advanced by Tsvetaeva, a poet who is greatly concerned with form. One of her collections is entitled *Craftsmanship*.

The poetry in the almanac *Numbers* provides an example of this principle in action. *Numbers* clearly reveals a poetic tendency. There is no doubt that the center of attention in *Numbers* is thematic material. This is attributable, possibly, to general considerations of culture and not to poetry itself. The absence of readers and the isolation of the modern poet (especially émigrés) resulted in intimate poetry, poetry of "essential things." A general ideological crisis called for re-examination of all basic cultural, philosophical, and religious values. Hence, the themes of *Numbers* include a basic evaluation of life, personality, and the world, with individual death as the central theme—in general, religious-philosophical themes.

In *Numbers* formal quests are relegated to the background. Poetic culture, of course, is necessary. Each modern poet must in some way pass through the study of the technical achievements of the preceding period, but further involvement is not obligatory. And it is striking that, despite the absence of such involvement, or perhaps because of it, *Numbers* already indicates a new formal direction—a unique "asceticism of form." Its accuracy and purity is a relief from everything extraneous and external.

Asceticism of form is not the only possibility that opens up. Use of all technical achievements is desirable as a means to heighten the expressiveness of meaning in verse. Blok is a good example of the fruitfulness of this approach. Blok's great significance lies in the fact that he used the experience of the early Symbolists in the area of form and for the first time applied it widely and without experimentation. Several Soviet critics, including Zhirmunsky, have already pointed this out. In our time it is Tsvetaeva who follows this path.

The roles of Blok and Tsvetaeva are understandable. But to what degree is the existence of "numerous" second-rate poets justified? We speak, of course, only of those for whom poetry is a cause, a means of self-consciousness and self-revelation. The significance of a poet is defined not by his level of culture, or even his poetic competence, but first of all by the seriousness of his approach. The role of such poets is great. It is not important that their work neither finds readers, nor transcends the bounds of the poetic workshop. The continuity of poetic movements is essential. There must be no letup, the soil on which a great poet of the future can grow must be cultivated, in the event that he appears. Geniuses do not fall from the sky. The purpose of minor poets is to create "an organic medium, a nutritious bouillon necessary for the creativity of a few great poets." (V. Weidlé.) The "uncle theory" proposed by several Soviet Formalists is significant: A great poet learns not from his own great predecessors (his fathers, so to speak), but from his "uncles"—secondary poets of the preceding period. The task of minor poets is to clear the way for the great, "to make the pathway straight for him." Although the depletion of linguistic means (which is referred to in the article by Weidlé) may not permit the development of a Pushkin in émigré conditions, it is still possible to produce a Blok—a poet powerful enough to break through the indifference around modern poetry and once again strike the hearts of the masses "with a hitherto unknown power."

However, the reader's lack of interest cannot be explained entirely by the absence of major poets. The older generation of émigrés are people with a thin skin. They have experienced the destruction of all their ideological foundations and fear even the slightest touch of the open wound. The younger generation, unable to live completely without skin, hastily tries to find a tolerable substitute. All the new ideologies that fascinate youth are similarly *ersatz*—ideologies quickly knocked together, devoid of religious or even firm cultural base, but greedily snatched up, for among the blind the one-eyed is king. In accordance with their own objectives (to give not a profound, but at least a quick answer), new ideologies must evade problems which are too complicated, i.e., those problems which modern poetry so boldly attempts to confront. It is not suprising if for a time poetry must be left to its own resources.

However, sooner or later the necessity for a more solid ideology will be revealed. Sooner or later the masses will pause before the reality of death, which is a major theme in *Numbers*. To regard life in a collective (be it nation, class, or whatever) as justification for individual life is self-deception. A collective is more long-lived, but in the end it is just as mortal as a personality. In all extra-religious ideologies the problem of death is glossed over. Not really solving it, they leave the basic evaluation of life hanging in the air just as it had been even before their appearance. And when this is realized, then the question will be raised, and then *Numbers* will be necessary; *Numbers* will prove to be timely. Till then, poetry must calmly wait and work.

Emigrés have their own experiences which are different from the rest of Russia's writers, and they make use of different possibilities in expressing these experiences. They not only have something to say—they *must* say it. Poetry has turned from experimentation to intimacy, perhaps because too much remains to be said. There is no time for experimentation.

One ought not fear pessimism or pursue false courage. Only one thing is important—that the voice is profound and sincere. Let it even be a naked shout of despair—the deeper the pessimism, the stronger the optimism that grows from it.

Poetry must work out a new form which will provide it with maximum content along with maximum conciseness of form. It is necessary to register what is said, hence the printing of books and magazines unread by anyone. This is the only way to conserve past achievements for a time when it may be needed. If it is not needed, it is not our business.

> I toss these hasty words
> Into the world—like a bottle—into the elements
> Of bottomless human indifference,
> I toss it, like a bottle, into the ocean.

> D. Knut

The first task of the modern poet is to relate the most vital facts in a language similar to the above—briefly, citing exactly the latitude and the longitude of the wreck. The second task is to cork the bottle tightly and trust it to the mercy of fate.

———·———

In "On Contemporary Poetry," the reader sees Hoerschelmann as a perceptive and original critic devoted to furthering the Russian poetic tradition. He deals here with a problem that occupied many Russian émigrés in the 1930s, the direction modern Russian poetry was to take. The development of poetry at this time depended almost entirely on the work of émigré poets, because Socialist Realism in the Soviet Union was not fertile soil for the future of poetry. In addition, the intense work of the preceding decades in the area of form had lost momentum. Hoerschelmann does not deny the importance of formal innovations, but he feels that now poetry must take a new direction. As he puts it, "The fate of art is not an endless stewing in its own juices. . . . The goal of art in the final analysis is its influence on life." He advocates, therefore, a shift of attention from formal consideration to concepts of themes and content. Poetry ought to concern itself with basic themes, themes of spiritual and moral importance. This shift of attention is evident in the most recent émigré poetry; Hoerschelmann cites Zinaida Hippius and Marina Tsvetaeva as outstanding examples. He also praises the almanac *Numbers* for paying attention to "religious-philosophical themes," including "a basic evaluation of life, personality, and the world, with individual death as the central theme." Hoerschelmann speaks highly of the poetry in *Numbers* for its asceticism of form: "Its accuracy and purity is a relief from everything extraneous, external, and unessential." This is the way modern poets should write, he insists, with "maximum saturation of content along with maximum conciseness of form." Beyond that they must simply "trust in the mercy of fate." Hoerschelmann is not concerned that many of the poets are second-rate; they have an important role to play—to cultivate "the soil on which a great poet of the future can grow, in the event that he appears."

Seeing in *Numbers* a liberation from everything accidental, superficial, and nonessential, Hoerschelmann suggests that a similar liberation will point the way for the further development of Russian poetry in exile with perfect harmony of form and content. To achieve this goal, Hoerschelmann insists, it is paramount to sustain the great tradition of Russian poetry, to open the eyes of a new poet to this tradition, and to assist him in absorbing it.

For more information on Karl Hoerschelmann and his works, read Temira Pachmuss' publications: "K. K. Hoerschelmann: A Russian Writer and Artist," *Russian Language Journal*, XXXVI (1982), Nos. 123-124, pp. 205-222, and in *La Pensée Russe* (Paris, 1981), Nos. 3356, 3357, 3379, 3382, and 3399.

NOTES

1. Yu. Ivask, "Memories of Hoerschelmann," *The New Review* (New York, 1952), XXXI, p. 313.
2. *Experiments* (New York, 1955), IV, 76–86.
3. Cf. Zinaida Hippius, "Choice?" *La Renaissance* (Paris, 1970), No. 222, 50–77. Prepared for publication by Temira Pachmuss. Cf. also Yury Terapiano's article on Hoerschelmann, "On the Kingdom of God," in *La Pensée Russe* (Paris), No., 1633, January 21, 1961.
4. *Experiments* (New York, 1953), VI, 23.
5. More about Hoerschelmann's concept of "play" is found in Ivask's poem "Playing Man. *Homo Ludens*," *La Renaissance* (Paris, 1973), Nos. 240–242.
6. *Experiments* (New York, 1958), IX, 68–69.
7. *Ibid.*, 69–73.
8. "On Play," *Experiments* (New York, 1956), VI, 23–24.
9. *La Renaissance* (Paris, 1973), No. 240, 18.
10. "Unpublished Stories of K. K. Hoerschelmann, "Fallen Angel. Extracts from a Diary," *Russian Language Journal*, XXXVII (Fall 1983), No. 128, pp. 165–183. Prepared for publication by Temira Pachmuss.
11. *Ibid.*

ROOS, META AL'FREDOVNA (b. 1904)

Meta Roos was born in Moscow on January 4, 1904. Her father worked as a representative for a large insurance company. She attended a German school associated with the Lutheran Church in Kharkov. The Roos family spent the years of the Civil War in the Crimea, but returned to Kharkov in 1920. When Estonia declared its independence, they travelled to Moscow where they arrived in summer 1921. From there they went through Sosnovy Bor to Tallinn. Both of Roos' parents were born in Estonia, thus her father had no trouble finding a good position in Tallinn. Meta graduated from the Estonian High School in Tallinn and later from the Conservatory, where she had studied piano. She became a music teacher and published, in collaboration with her sister Elizabeth, a literary journal, *Koloko'chik* (The Little Bell). Both sisters contributed to *The Virgin Soil* and to the Russian newspaper *The Russian Voice in Tallinn*. Meta Roos translated opera librettos from Estonian into Russian, adapting her translations to the musical score written by Artur Lemba. In 1935 she married Mikhail Pavlovich Irtel and played an active part in all the meetings of the Estonian "Guild of Poets," which existed until 1938.   After her marriage, she translated Tyutchev's poetry into German.

Roos published a volume of poetry entitled *Martovskoe solntse: stikhi* (The March Sun: Poems; Tallinn: Nov', 1936).   Her poems, picturesque and restrained in style, are similar to Bunin's poetry.   Typical of Meta Roos' poetry is a certain classicial rigor, but she also delights in sounds, color, shapes, feelings, sensations. Among her favorite Russian poets are Bunin (she can "see his poetry, because he is an elaborate painter"), Tyutchev (whose poems have a "strong sound" with the stress on the final syllable, and beautiful images, among them the recurrent "ice"), Anna Akhmatova (whose poetry Meta Roos can recite by heart), and some work by Esenin ("Letter to Mother," "I do not regret, do not call, do not cry").   She dislikes Severyanin because "there is no spirituality in his poetry, only artificiality."   Dostoevsky depresses her, but she likes Tolstoy's novels and short stories, and indulges in English fiction in translation.

In the fall of 1939 the Irtels, fleeing the Red Army, left Estonia and went through West Prussia to Bromberg (Poland). There they lived until 1945, when they moved to Völlmarshausen to work for German farmers.   In 1949 they moved to Göttingen, where Pavel Irtel was appointed a foreign correspondent in a bank. Meta Roos still lives in Göttingen and writes German texts and music for children's songs and plays, for example, *Der Sommerball* and *Frühlingsregen.*

The March Sun

How strange: In rhythmic lines,
You ensconce a particle of your soul,
And look, it flies, like a bird,
Into an alien and far-reaching world.

And maybe it will long be solitary.
It will have to search and pine
Until someone—
            whether close or distant—says:
"I have long awaited you, my bird!"

——————·——————

The city in dove-colored fog.
As if all the bell towers have been severed
By someone's blasphemous hand;
And, pressing to the earth in fright,
Rows of shivering houses
Grow spinelessly rigid.
Strange shadows glide by—
Weightless, gray shadows,
And the dense fog settled on faces
With the tiniest of droplets...

On such a joyless and unhappy day it is good
To recall the cloudless south,
The orchards, which grow faint from the smell
Of golden and tender mimosa...
To recall how, in the pellucid water,
Whitish crabs would crawl out of their shells,
And how curly-haired children with a joyous shout
Gathered them up into their small buckets;
And to remember still how the southern sun,
Gliding my swarthy hands,
Burned ruthlessly...

———————·———————

For you and me, there isn't a thing to talk about,
Only where you've been, and what's new...
And above us an infinite sky,
A nocturnal sky, bluish lilac...

"You know, I went to a sale,
Bought a pair of patent leather shoes"...
Stars carefully watch over
Unknown spellbound worlds.

Glances stretch up to the austere sky,
On the brink of solving the eternal riddle...
"Yesterday I met so-and-so,
He asked me to call Sunday evening."...

———————·———————

Oh, this city of fogs and lengthy autumns,
City of mad winds and gray rains,
City of crooked back streets and ancient towers,
Where the silhouettes of people glide by like shadows...

My youthful years passed without leaving a trace
In narrow side streets, and I can no longer find them.
My sky has been wrapped in a pale shroud,
The northern city has shattered my paths, no longer my
    own...

—————·—————

Beyond the window, burning candles
And flowers, so many flowers.
Beyond the window, in ominous silence,
Someone no longer dreams.

The hyacinths are fragrant,
But he has no need of flowers.
Those shoulders now are resting
From their earthly burden.

In life there were separations and meetings,
But now, separation without meetings...
The candles flicker with a yellow light—
To watch over the new-found peace.

—————·—————

To P. I. B.

Beneath the thick, icy crust
The awakened stream
Laughs so gaily and murmers,
Seethes, overflowing, and mutters
Something incoherent and joyous.

The first have attentively clustered in a circle,
Listening to its babble,
And from the earth, still swollen, black and damp,
Warmed by the vernal sun,
Round leaflets confusedly emerge.

The sun rejoices, like a spring god,
And the air so unusually transparent,
And pure...Here, in festive and flowing tones,
From the distant city floats
The ringing of Easter bells.

————·————

The Virgin Soil, No. 7 (1934)

The Path

Rye sways in the breeze,
Like the fur of an enormous beast,
Fluffy, violet fur...
He writes: The loss is heavy,
He writes: That means everything was only a lie?
He writes: A sin.

*

Through the bright, open field
A road once led.
My soul sang like a bird
In the heavens on high,
Gave thanks to God,
Breathing in His pure morning.

And then, an unknown forest,
With heather, with soft mosses,
Arose like a green wall.
At first it seemed I was home,
Merrily strolling along
Among the tree trunks, alone.

But the thicket gets denser and denser,
In the low ravines it grows dark,
Night has blocked the road
The sky is an enormous cup.
The stars gaze severely.
Where am I to go?

Only pines and firs surround me...
Beneath their dark canopies
Will I ever see light?
No, I won't reach my goal,
I won't get out of the woods.
There is no exit!

It seemed that a flame flared up,
It sparkled brightly amid the trees.
Could it be a friend who has come to help?
No, it was an owl with yellow eyes.
Flying by, it glanced at me,
And again vanished into the night...
. . . .
I walk...The firs have parted—
Fields, open spaces, and wind...
Sunrise is imminent!
The cloudlets are tinted rose,
And someone is walking to meet me
In the pre-dawn light...

*

Rye sways in the breeze,
Like the fur of an enormous beast,
Fluffy, violet fur...
        Someday he will forgive the loss,
        And understand that ignorance is not a lie,
        And love is not a sin.

_____._____

The Virgin Soil, No. 6 (1934)

The same back street and along it the same
Pattern of familiar shadows,
And the same tall dark fence
Cuts off the space in front of me,
As before, cheerless lanterns
Burn modestly all in a row,
And another moonless night drags on,
With no one able to help.

———————·———————

The Virgin Soil, No. 5 (1933)

The Blizzard

The blizzard howls, rages, whirls,
The wind will not let me make headway.
The street lamp, orphan-like, dies out...
But my beloved boy is waiting!

The wind will not let me, but I press on,
Only my heart knows where I am yearning to be.
Let the blizzard howe, rage, whirl.
I want to be with you! Onward, onward!...

———————·———————

The Virgin Soil, No. 8 (1935)

On the Train

"The ball takes flight in the
hands of Nausicaa."
Yu. Terapiano

Strings of telephone wires
Stretch, flow, stream out to meet me.
In flowing speech the sound of the wheels
Lulls me to sleep, like a series of familiar stanzas.

My head droops wearily.
The wind gently strokes my hair...
My memory recalls: Nausicaa,
A ball, and green grass.

In a country resembling a fairy tale I see
A glade illumined by the sun.
This line from Terapiano
Has revealed a forgotten world to me.

I remember: Yes, it was
Long, long ago. I vaguely recall.
I was watching Nausicaa's ball...
Could it be, she and I—are one?...

_____·_____

Prominent motifs in Meta Roos' verse are loneliness and alienation from one's fellow man, and the tawdry, dehumanizing urban existence, which she sees from an aesthetic and philosphical perspective akin to that of Alexander Blok. In many of her poems, the description of nature accentuates the underlying irony. In the poem "For you and me, there isn't a thing to talk about," for example, she achieves a second plane of meaning of juxtaposing the empty conversation with a sharply delineated image of the stars, the planets, and "the bluish lilac nocturnal sky." She also uses elliptical phrases taken from the most mundane and trivial conversations; this may be viewed as a parody of the "Parisian-note" verse with its flat intonations and half-uttered thoughts. By contrasting elements of the celestial with the trite, she achieves a biting and sardonic tone. In "The Path," the pastoral motif functions as an effective symbolic backdrop to the emotional state expressed and constitutes the central narrative of this fine poem. Folkloristic elements, such as losing one's path in "an unknown forest" or the ominous image of an owl, enrich her themes and add subtle colorings to her meditation on love.

In the first stanza of "The city in dove-colored fog," images of fog, with its "rows of shivering houses" and its "weightless, gray shadows," are combined to produce an atmosphere of despair and hopelessness, a sense of urban life where the city causes claustrophobia and anxiety representing hell on earth. In the second stanza, however, the reader moves from the present and actual to the internal world and the poet's idealized vision of the past. Her recollection of the "cloudless south" with its bright warmth, its "pellucid water," and the "joyous shouts" of children stands in stark contrast to the depressed tone of the first stanza. Roos seems to suggest that memory itself can function as a means to conquer the bitter anguish of the present. Thus, the poet's melancholic musings about the past as exemplified in "Oh, this city of fogs and lengthy autumns" achieve almost as tragic an intensity as her grief over the death of a beloved friend. Her torment is again underscored by the gray and dismal visage of the city. As opposed to the preceding poem, the past is now beyond her grasp; memory no longer has regenerative power. The past disappears "without leaving a trace," as it is swallowed up by the indifferent city which offers neither solace nor rest for one who, in losing her past, has also lost her path in life.

"Beyond the window, burning candles" deals with loss resulting from death. As in many of her poems, the anguish of the lyrical "I" is heightened by the proximity of living objects—the fragrance of hyacinths and the light of candles—which form an ironic contrast with the one who "has no need of flowers." In this manner, Roos effectively conveys the depths of grief produced in those left behind.

In the poem "On the Train" Roos again recaptures the mood of a remote dreamlike world. The *persona*, almost lulled to sleep by the monotonous sound and motion of the train, recalls a line from the poet Terapiano, "The ball takes flight in the hands of Nausicaa," and her thoughts turn to another time and place: "In a country resembling a fairy tale I see/A glade illumined by the sun./This line from Terapiano/Has revealed a forgotten world to me." But instead of simply visualizing this other world, the *persona* seems to remember being a part of it herself: "Yes, it was/Long, long ago. I vaguely recall./I was catching Nausicaa's ball..." And in the end, she imagines that she might actually have been Nausicaa.

The regular meter of the poem, trochaic pentameter, imitates the rhythmic cadence of the train wheels. The effect is heightened by such figures of speech as "strings of telephone wires/Stretch, flow, stream out to meet me," or the matter-of-fact, slightly ironical expression "The sound of the wheels/Lulls me to sleep, like a series of familiar strophes."

The Virgin Soil, No. 2 (1929)

A Song

Burning with bright passion
He ran to me,

With poppies, crimson like the dawn,
He covered me.

With a kiss he signed
My lips,

And enthralled my heart
Forever.

_____._____

The poem's simple structure and vocabularly lends grace and delicacy, an ethereal quality difficult to capture in translation. The repetition of the instrumental case in the first line of each of the first three stanzas, and the subjectless verbs which follow in the Russian text, create the symmetry responsible for the poem's refined simplicity. The lines end either in a liquid (verb endings -*al* or -*il*) or in stressed *a/ya*; *a/ya* is a frequent sound throughout and accounts for the open, transparent musical system.

The poem's rhythmic structure is equally noteworthy. The meter is a combination of trochees and anapests; the first line of each stanza is made up of two trochees followed by an anapest and the second line consists of a single anapest. But the first line of the last stanza deviates slightly from the pattern: The accented syllable of the first trochaic foot is omitted, and the reader is induced to make a small pause and to give particular attention to the end of the poem.

_____._____

The Virgin Soil, No. 4 (1932)

To wander together with you through the forest,
And hark to the joyous singing of the birds,
Together with you to explain to the flowers
That our love knows no bounds;
Together with you to live my whole life
In forest depths, where no roads lead,
To love you in those green depths
Where no one could ever find us.

———————·———————

"To wander together with you" is an idyllic love poem in the form of a fantasy wish. The *persona* desires to see her love unfolding and existing outside the realm of time and in isolation from other people. Nature sympathizes and provides a haven for the lovers. Again, the simplicity of the poem is striking both in style and phraseology. Repetition is an important stylistic device. In the original Russian text the prase "together with you" is found at the beginning of three lines. Binary and ternary meters are combined, and the rhyme scheme abab is used in exclusively masculine rhymes.

———————·———————

The Virgin Soil, No. 8 (1935)

Lynx Mountain

I

While travelling, you become accustomed to living without luggage, to the obligatory change in locations and impressions, to occasional meetings and inevitable partings. You become accustomed to it, and reconciled, but all the same there's no way to conquer your feelings of light melancholy and regret when leaving a city where you have spent several exciting days, rich in impressions. The most significant occurrences, some trifle, yet still so vividly perceived, finds such a joyous response, that the mere thought that this joyous sensation must die out and become a memory—this thought, at times, can spoil the romantic nature of your travel impressions.

I remember that there was sorrow even in my feeling of gratitude toward an old friend from Tallinn who greeted me warmly and cordially in Prague and later saw me to the train to Blansko. With him, I wandered the streets of Prague, listening to his stories of the ancient city...

The large, contemporary European Wilson railway station. On the platform, beneath the glass and iron of the gigantic roof, the twilight was soft and gray. There was smell of smoke, grease, train cars...Burdened with suitcases, porters ran by, straining.

I don't like railway stations. There is so much bustle, confused haste, senseless agitation. Everyone cares only about himself, no one has anything to do with anyone else, and so the feelings of loneliness and bewilderment are particularly strong here...Apathetic, curious glances, unfamiliar faces, some beaming with contentment anticipating the delights of the journey, others preoccupied, confused, wistful...

The conductor, in his tight-fitting blue jacket, walked alongside the train with habitual businesslike efficiency, and slammed the doors of the train cars...The high walls of the station flowed backward, the station attendant flashed by, it suddenly became bright, and then multistoried buildings and blocks of houses turned their blank façades to me with intrusive inscriptions of advertisements; courtyards like deep wells opened up, small kitchen balconies...For an instant I peered into someone else's life. And because it lasted only an instant, both people and houses seemed illusory, unreal.

The train, continually accelerating, bent in an arc and once more revealed Prague—already growing smaller in the distance. In the smoke-filled air Gradchany rose majestically. On the hills of Petchin was lightly sketched the delicate "sightseeing" tower, where only yesterday I had admired an overall view of the city...such a strange city, where modernity triumphs over the Middle Ages, where side by side with ancient "gunpowder" towers and gloomy Polish Roman-Catholic churches rise the glass façades of commercial buildings, where in the evening the streets are luxuriantly flooded with the bright, exciting colors of neon signs...

II

In the labyrinth of the low and steep Moravian Mountains densely overgrown with beech and pine trees lay the Blansko railway station. A bus noiselessly glided along the asphalt-covered highway. In seven more kilometers—Matsokha. The famous stalactite caves are there...

It was terrifying to stand on the unsubstantial platform jutting out above the four-hundred-foot-deep precipice of Matsokha; it was frightening to lean against the railing—it seemed so flimsy—and in the distance was a steep, bare cliff, and at the bottom of the gorge, where small shrubbery was growing, lay a tiny dark emerald mirror of water.

I walked down along a small path. A crude door, looking as if it led into a storeroom, was cut into the stone and blended in with the gray mountain mass. In a rather everyday manner, the guide simply went up and opened the door with a key. There was an odor of icy coldness and dampness. The guide walked quickly and occasionally flicked a switch; an electric light would flash on.

I touched the wet, uneven wall with my hand. It was strange to think that I was somewhere "inside," that down the arched, narrow steep steps I was descending somewhere into the very bowels of the earth, to think that overhead and around me was impenetrable thickness of rock through which no shout from here would be heard outside, just as no sound from the outside world would be carried here to disturb the infinite silence of Pluto's kingdom...

I walked, guardedly, with complete unity of soul and mind, as if I were in a temple...From unseen vaults of spacious underground chambers hung pale stalactites, here long and thin like congealed streams of rain; there in wide strips making the shape of a flag falling down over its pole in classical folds, or the shape of the winged shoulders of a guardian angel. Here they reminded one of a fantastic chandelier with a thousand pendants; there a bat, or thin and transparent fabrics, rosy-orange from the electric lights cleverly concealed behind them...

And meeting them halfway—solidified fountains of Bakhchisaray, Indian sepulchres, Catholic altars, lanterns, gnomes, mushrooms...And still another comparison comes to mind: The entire cavern looked as if someone had turned a gigantic cup of thin dough upside down, and here it had stretched out, hung down, and hardened for eternity in enchanting icicles, threads, membranes...

And what antiquity! Older than Egypt and Babylon... Time doesn't exist here. Slowly and aimlessly, creating columns necessary to no one, drop after drop trickles down. A strange museum, where priceless antiquity is under lock and key.

The voice of the guide asking me to get into the boat brought me back to reality (or to a fairy tale?)...It was incredible. We were standing on the shore of an underground river. Dreamy waters without the slightest ripple, as still as glass. The boat glided noiselessly. The river, flowing somewhere in sharp bends, wound into the depths and clefts of the mountain...The guide pointed out places where the depth reached thirty meters. We floated over the precipices. Bright lamps shone beneath the water; the mermaid-green color of the crystalline transparent water, like a facet of a gigantic emerald, bewitched me...And there was no boat cutting through the moisture, no guide; there was only my poetic fantasy leading me into the depths of time, into the world of shadows, where Charon ferries souls of the dead across the river Styx. . . .

VI

In order to complete my final task and climb up Lynx Mountain, I had to reach Popradsky Pool (the lake) by evening. There at the very edge, beneath the cover of dense, dark firs, stood a squat wooden building with a spacious gallery, mezzanine, and service buildings. The mountains rose sharply all around—their base covered with the dark velvet of shale, their crest hidden in the mist and haze of the clouds. Overturned in the mirror of the lake, their dark malachite masses congealed, motionless.

Night was falling as I got up to Popradsky Pool. From neighboring paths, marked by flowery colors, people gathered, singly and in groups— from below, from the valley, like me animated by the picturesqueness of the area, looking with curiosity at the lake and the small building—and from above, from the mountains, tired, gloomy, taciturn, as if having passed through a severe ordeal, which does not dispose them to meaningless light conversation.   Dark, weather-beaten faces, with a kind of glassy luster in their gaze, and all their movements still, deliberate. . . .

It had long since become dark above the lake, but late arriving hikers were still approaching.   Someone lodged for the night beneath the open sky, lying in a fir grove, wrapping himself up in a blanket, and the light of his cigarette glimmered like a garnet firefly.   Some young men untied a boat and took some girls in warm, knitted jackets for a ride.   For a long time, I listened to the lazy splashing of the water beneath the gentle strokes of the oars. . . .

Meanwhile, the sun broke through the clouds, the sky turned blue, the air became fresh, transparent, and it was possible to see far into the mountains.   I conquered the final two hundred meters, and here I was, at the very crest of the pass.   I had a proud feeling in my soul; I had conquered the mountain, and something else besides.   It was as if having overcome the hardships of the path, I had also overcome something in myself. . . .

But it was frightening to stand at the top.   The wind tore wildly, whistled, and howled.   Wisps of dark clouds swept past my feet, catching on the sharp peaks, and streaming down in mists.   For an instant I glanced with frightened curiosity into the precipice, and it took my breath away.   On the side toward Poland the mountain broke off in a bare, steep wall, and far below, edged with an icy rim, glistened Lake Zmrzle.

Menacing giants rose all around, and at the very crest of the Great High Mountain, joined together with a rope, climbed three small figures, now clambering up onto a safety ledge, now hanging above a cleft, striving higher and higher...

A smoke-colored cloud drifted by and hid them from me...

———————·———————

"Lynx Mountain" is a beautifully written prose piece in the genre of the travelog.   Roos conveys a sense of immediacy through her consistent use of the historical present tense (translated here in the past) and through her vivid descriptions that appeal to all the senses: "There was an odor of icy coldness and dampness...I touched the wet, uneven wall with my hand"; "The wind tears wildly, whistles, and howls"; "The mountains rose sharply all around—their base covered with the dark velvet of shale, their crest hidden in the mist and haze of the clouds." Particularly striking are the metaphors and similes used to describe the stalactites: "The empire cavern looked as if someone had turned a gigantic cup of thin dough upside down, and here it had stretched out, hung down, and hardened for eternity in enchanting icicles, threads, membranes..." Roos skillfully creates a sense of times long past in the fairy-tale-like unreality of the underground caverns, and the reader almost feels that he is there with her as she visits this remote world. Blended in with ornate lyrical descriptions are sober matter-of-fact comments like "I don't like railway stations. There is so much bustle, confused haste, senseless agitation." Yet, the overall tone is one of wonder and awe at the strangeness and beauty of Lynx Mountain and the surrounding scenery.

———————·———————

The Virgin Soil, No. 7 (1934)

Sketches

Zhanna had conceived the plan to visit the Pechora area long ago, she had heard so much about it, and her acquaintance kept urging her to go; but the thought of the long road cutting southwest diagonally across all of Estonia frightened her.

Finally she made up her mind to go. The melancholy thought of possible loneliness, idleness, worried her a little... so she bought some Alexandrine paper and replenished her little box of charcoals and pastels.

The town of Pechora turned out to be dusty and boring. Having wandered through the monastery, looked over the grottos and sacristy, and having had her photograph taken in front of the Uspensky Cathedral, Zhanna decided that she had come to know the town well enough and that it would be nice to take advantage of the fine July weather and spend some time in the countryside as well. Pechora wasn't really much of a town, but the cobblestone pavement with the terrible grooves you would not forget for a lifetime. The two-story houses, the market stalls, the posters at the cinema...meant it wasn't a village either.

She followed the advice of some friends and set off for Ulyantsevo, a hamlet of four farms. There, in a new cottage next to a potato field lived some summer residents, a mother and daughter, who gave Zhanna a room. Tiny, simple, and bright, the room pleased Zhanna. Without delay she flung her books and notebook on the table, set up the inkwell, and arranged her toiletries at the hearth: a small tablecloth, a mirror, a compact, and a small sewing box.

Whenever they heated the stove in the kitchen, the toiletries would get warm and the candle would start to melt, and Zhanna, barefooted and book in hand, would leap out of bed.

Zhanna regarded the straw mattress with contempt; the straw rustled at the slightest movement and felt uncomfortable and coarse.

But Zhanna was glad about one thing: She always got up early. She jumped onto the cool floorboards, sponged herself with the icy water which Mashen'ka brought from the little river, tidied up the room, and hurried, for a mug of milk, straight across the garden, over the tall, dewy, and delightfully soft grass, to a prosperous and thrifty woman, the most respected in the village, Antie Natalya.

She greeted Zhanna in the old-fashioned way: "Sit down, young lady. Try a few of our little cakes. They're warm, right out of the oven."

Zhanna would nibble at a sourish, flat cake which stuck to her teeth; get her earthenware pot of milk, the bread, and whatever God provided of eggs, vegetables, or butter, and return home at a leisurely pace.

In the kitchen the sleepy summer resident in a flowery housecoat would say lazily: "At this ungodly hour..."

Turning toward the door, she would call out to her daughter in a shrill voice: "Tanyushka, get up. *Fräulein* Zhanna met some gypsies in the village...Where on earth did you get this cottage cheese?"

. . . .

And all around—fields, wide open spaces. The translucent, moist distance shimmers and dances above the grain. The sweet, fragrant smell of clover is alluring, intoxicating. The rye is forming ears; along the edge of the fields cornflowers, crowding together, sway and flash blue... The blossoming flax is turning azure.

Using a pole to cross the narrow Belka [squirrel] River—such white sand, with the shallow water rippling over it—she would enter the forest. There were oceans of berries, all kinds; all she had to do was bend down and pick them. There weren't any mushrooms yet. Only the heavy ears of grain rising here and there amid the moss and dry grasses.

Early in the morning, with paper, pencils, and pastels in her basket, Zhanna would go off into the forest and wander over the hills, past the alder bushes, along the bends of the Belka. From raspberry bushes taller than she was, she would pick the fragrant thimble-shaped berries and, nibbling on blackberries, would start to draw...

Mashen'ka came to wash the floor and, noticing the sketches, implored: "Young miss, do a sketch of me."

That evening, having taken care of the housework, Mashen'ka appeared with a bright, stiffly-ironed kerchief on her head and cheap blue beads around her sunburned neck. The portrait was finished after two rough drafts. Mashen'ka's face was rather plain and unremarkable; it was difficult to capture a likeness, but the bright kerchief and beads looked brilliantly alive on the paper. Mashen'ka was embarrassed and happy; she disappeared for a whole morning and returned with ripe berries in an empty herring bucket.

"For you, young miss. Raspberries, they're good enough to sell in town, and no worms..."

The next day, when Zhanna was still washing, Mashen'ka's mother-in-law, a tall woman with a beautiful and stern face, appeared: "Do a sketch of me, young miss, and I'll return the favor, with eggs, or something or other..." The woman had dressed for the sitting in holiday attire. Her head was covered with a lilac-colored silk kerchief and heavy earrings hung from her ears. Entering, she modestly placed five large eggs on the hearth and slightly embarrassed, covered them with Zhanna's towel...

Fräulein Zhanna worked with enthusiasm. The peaceful,

sternly wistful face inspired her and aroused her artistic instinct, and so she struck a likeness right away. The old woman sat motionless, as if turned to stone.

"You're tired, grandmother. Walk around the room a bit."

"Why should I be tired? I'm not working, am I..."

The next morning, Auntie Natalya, pouring the milk for Zhanna from an earthenware pot, said: "It's a pity you're leaving, young miss. And we didn't even know that you could draw people. I would have asked you to draw me, too, and my old man, and we would have given you some butter or sour cream...In Pechora, I've heard, they'll snap you and make a picture, but it costs money; while you do it so easily, and in color too..."

—————·—————

This short piece probably reflects experiences of the author herself (Roos also paints). It combines personal feelings with descriptions of nature and country life. Although written in the third person, the story is much like a notebook sketch, evoking a mood with the flow of perceptions.

The story begins with the description of Zhanna's brief visit to the town of Pechora, which she finds totally uninteresting and which stands in sharp contrast with her lively portrayal of life in the surrounding countryside. The sense of touch is especially vivid here; the uncomfortable straw mattress, the cool floorboards, the icy water, the soft dewy grass, all combine to make the reader feel the sensations almost firsthand. Then follows a beautiful description of the open fields and the river, where the interplay of light and color is particularly vivid: "The translucent, moist distance shimmers and dances about the grain . . . cornflowers, crowding together, sway and flash blue . . . such white sand, and the shallow water rippling over it." In the last part of the story Zhanna is sketching some of the country folk. Their simple kindness—they are warm and genuine—as well as the striking peculiarities of their local speech and psychology are eloquently captured.

Roos' style is lucid and transparent, characterized by the constant synaesthetic interaction of sounds, colors, and fragrances. Despite its brevity, the story is complete in mood and atmosphere, and makes delightful reading.

———————·———————

The Virgin Soil, No. 6 (1934)

On Women's Poetry

When you open a Russian émigré journal or a collection of belles-lettres, you can't help being surprised by the large amount of poetic material, and immediately after the acknowledged masters—Georgy Ivanov, Marina Tsvetaeva— you find new names, many of them women—young women émigré poets. Let me say a few words about them.

Complicated problems of existence do not usually concern a woman. She does not meditate on world problems be they political, scientific, or economic. No, more deeply than anything else, it is her own little world that concerns and worries her. It is small, and the woman poet tries to find images for it in her poetic exposition. She finds new, accurate, and expressive words; she captures delicate and harmonious colors. Her natural perception of balance will suggest to her both the composition and the appropriate tone.

And often, in treating simple, unimportant themes, a woman intuitively penetrates to the very essence of things, touches upon their innermost recesses, suddenly making them intimate and understandable. Sometimes these poems are weak from an artistic point of view, but at the same time they rank higher than many good "literary" verses. They are, as Tsvetaeva says, "not yet art, and already more than art."

A woman's creative work contains a great deal that is personal. The presence of the author is so apparent that often, against your own will, you begin to visualize the appearance of the poet; you feel certain features of her character; you mentally draw her portrait.

Ekaterina Bakunina or Lidiya Chervisnkaya in *Numbers* are always intimate and familiar. So what if there is a mistake, so what if the representation is ridiculously unlike the original; what is important is that this representation is organically created and forces one to reread these or other lines.

Bakunina's poetic language is rich in imagery; her themes are serious and profound:

> I gaze with maternal affection
> into the strange eyes.
> I want to tell gently a fairy tale
> to the tormented ones;
>
> About how a tender bosom
> warms a loved one's cheek,
> and how unhappy people
> should join hands.

Bakunina's work is imbued with this feeling of complete understanding and warm, maternal love for all creatures.

Chervinskaya's verse has natural rhythm, light meter, and musicality. How freely her lines flow:

> In May, doubts are silent.
> I know even this is poetry.
> I feel it is spring...
> I believe the sins of those
> Who need pity are forgiven...

Sofiya Pregel' wins our hearts with the simplicity and clarity of her landscapes and scenes from nature. She has written some especially "earthy" verses, saturated with an "earthy" strength:

> Insignificant, timid rain patters;
> A fisherman in oilskins goes by with his fish.
> In the water-soaked house, silence and gloom,
> Forgotten litter and dusty boxes.

The talents of the poets differ and it is possible to regard them in various ways, but all of them have that most valuable essence which one expects from poetry—sincerity. Bakunina, Chervinskaya, and Pregel' all speak their own truths in their own language.

Isn't this why failures exist? When a woman poet

consciously hides herself behind an "objective" image, when
she introduces a complicated structure into an obvious story,
when, in a search for embellishment, she forgets the essence...
The verse then is cold and meager, like a stalactite cave. I
am rereading the works of the women poets of the Prague
"Enclave":

An airy dome curling and drooping with mica,
A farewell flung heavenward with a sling,
Palms flushed crimson, flying in sequence
In front of the sun, as in front of an enormous candle...
(Alla Golovina, "Parting")

Ether beats against the temples. A taut body
Exuded a bluish steam.
A taciturn angel in a white mask
Squeezed the sky into a thin glass...
(Tatyana Rathaus, "Operation")

Fine technique and good taste are undeniably evident,
but one wishes that both A. Golovina and T. Rathaus,
having mastered their craftsmanship, would also find their
own sincerity, spirituality, and femininity.

I consider the poetry of Vera Bulich (Helsinki) to be
authentic creative work. Clear language, exquisite sound, and
that gracefulness with which she leads the reader into the
realm of things lofty, religious, spiritual, and amorous never
fail her.

From the book *The Pendulum*

From God's hand the doves   Doves or angels,
Peck the grains.   Does it matter?
In God's world the doves   We glorify them for that gift
Live long.   Not given to us.

For a wise and simple heart
Wherein paradise dwells,
For that most difficult wisdom:
How not to suffer.

What is there to say generally about the female poets in
Tallinn? They work in literary circles, in the "Poets' Guild,"
participate in the publication of *The Virgin Soil.* From the
material collected in their workbooks and diaries individual
poems have appeared in print. There are lengthy works
collected in cycles, but so far not one book has been
published. I consider it necessary to publish, because it
affirms creativity, fosters self-improvement, and creates that
feeling of responsibility which every kind of art demands.

In connection with publishing arises the question
repeated so often recently: For whom? People don't read
poetry, they treat it almost with hostility, as something
inanimate and superfluous. This is understandable. In order
to like poetry, it is necessary to learn how to understand it
just as with music. One who has never studied music cannot
really appreciate it. But will the time ever come when
people will teach, not how to write poems (this cannot be
taught), but how to understand and love them?...

————·————

This essay by Roos is interesting as a historical piece and as
a poet's perception of the work of other poets. Her attitude
toward women and woman poets as a separate group will seem
antiquated by today's standards. That, as Roos suggests, the
approach of women poets is largely intuitive and the range of their
themes rather limited may be true of some poets, but not all
female poets can be typified in this way, and definitely not Zinaida
Hippius, Anna Akhmatova, Anna Prismanova, or Vera Bulich. It
should be noted that the selections by Alla Golovina and Vera
Bulich contain remarkable sound effects which cannot be
reproduced in the translations. For a fuller appreciation of the
craftsmanship of these poets, the Russian text should be consulted.

Meta Roos published another informative essay in *The Virgin
Soil* (No. 7, 1934) entitled "In Memory of Igor' Shefer (January

18, 1902–July 10, 1934)." It appears below in three excerpts, followed by a brief evaluation.

———————·———————

On July 10, 1934, the life of the young poet Igor' Shefer came to an untimely end. More than once he had read his poems before the Tallinn Literary Circle, and many of them had been published in the local newspapers...but his dream of seeing a collection of his poems in print was not realized.

Before me are several notebooks of verses containing his work from 1922 to 1934. There are collections of poems carefully copied as well as rough drafts with lines crossed out and corrections which afford a glimpse of how the poet worked, searching for the right word or revising an unsuccessful meter.

Igor' Shefer's poems flow easily and freely. One senses that they are neither contrived, nor composed, but written as they flowed from his soul like the song of spring birds. . . .

Nocturne

The drowsy smiles of the sea,
      A patch of moonlight.

Hidden, a pliant reed,
      Swaying, sleeps.

In the heights the clouds are still.
A tiny light on the distant cape
      Barely flickers.

Boundless are the heavens' depths,
Where countless stars have
      Traced their paths.

Still, weary waters,
Dark shore, rocks, and cliffs.

The drowsy smiles of the sea,
A patch of moonlight.
Hidden, a pliant reed,
Swaying, sleeps.

. . . At times the theme of death cuts across the generally cheerful tone of the poems. It seems as if the poet had a premonition of his early end...

Being religious, he often turned to God, seeking in Him the resolution of his doubts. The following lines breathe tranquility and faith:

The lonely stars tremble,
Each with its own prayer,
And, stern in their eternal wisdom,
The heavenly realms are still.

It's as if the whole sky were a road,
A path through both past and future
To the abode of the immortal God,
Where the soul can find rest.

. . .

_____·_____

Igor' Shefer was a promising young Russian poet in Tallinn who won first prize in the poetry competition of the Russian Literary Circle. A contributor to various Russian newspapers in Estonia, he wrote poems, often about love and nature. However, his poems were not always successful.

As the title suggests, the poem "Nocturne" is very musical, both in form and in sound effects. The stanzas form musical phrases of varying length. The nasals "n" and "m," the velar "l," the sonorous long adjectival endings "iy" and "yy" occur throughout the poem, punctuating the phrases and giving them a melodious quality. Written in trochaic meter, rather rare in Russian, the poem consists of four-foot feminine lines alternating with less frequent two-foot masculine lines. In addition, the first four lines are repeated at the end of the poem as a kind of musical coda. The fragile, ethereal nature of the sound elements of the poem is corroborated by the imagery: "A tiny light in a distant cape/Barely flickers," "Hidden, a pliant reed,/Swaying, sleeps," "A patch of moonlight," etc. There are also "Still, weary waters,/Dark shore, rocks, band cliffs," forming an effective contrast with the poet's joyous visions of the moonlit landscape, in the heights as well as on the sea, full of mystery and deception. (Temira Pachmuss)

ROOS-BASILEVSKAYA, ELIZAVETA AL'FREDOVNA
(1902-1951)

Elizabeth Roos studied Slavic philology, German and French languages, and philosophy at the University of Tartu, and wrote her Master's thesis about Anna Akhmatova. Since no critical materials were available in Estonia at that time, Roos developed her own aesthetic theory of Akhmatova's poetry. A great admirer of Anna Andreevna's poetic talent, Roos wrote similar poetry. The two resembled each other, even in appearance, although Roos was blond and had green eyes and Anna Andreevna was dark. Roos was also fond of the poetry of Blok and Gumilyov.

An older sister of Meta Roos, Elizabeth was born in Moscow into a wealthy family of Swedish, German, and Estonian descent. The Roos family left Russia after the Peace of Tartu granted Estonia independence. Upon graduation from the university, Elizabeth taught Russian, French, and German at the high school in Tallinn. After her marriage to Ivan Victorovich Bazilevsky, a forest inspector, she was an instructor in German and handicraft at a school in a small provincial town. Her first poems were published in Irtel's *The Virgin Soil.* They were beautiful, melodious, and lyrical, as well as clear and regular, following the rules of prosody. Two volumes of her poetry, *Khlopya* (Flakes; Tallinn; *Nov'*, 1934), and *Domik u lesa* (A Small House Near the Woods; Tallinn: *Nov'*, 1936), appeared in Estonia. She also translated into Russian the works of Marie Under, the most prominent Estonian female writer, and contributed to *Contemporary Annals* and *The Journal of Concord.*

Prior to the occupation of Estonia by the Red Army in 1940, Roos and her husband left the country, moved to Poland, and later

settled in Germany. She began to suffer depression, especially
when they lived in the small town of Völmarshausen, Germany.
Bored, frustrated, and depressed, she committed suicide in 1951.
She was buried in Göttingen.

The Virgin Soil, No. 4 (1932)

Misty, rosy clouds rush along.
They hurry from afar toward the birch grove.
Pale, soft, water color tones.
In November—an April-fresh, silent spring.
Whoever harbored a bitter grudge in his heart
Forgave everyone and everything at gentle dawn.
In the tranquil morning is born anew,
Fragile and tender, a young girl's love.

————·————

A Small House Near the Woods

A Winter's Day

A white fur coat on the sleeping birch,
    A warm, soft fur coat.
Chopping in the distant woods
    Resounds joyously in the frosty air.

As if of their own accord, skis glide
    Rhythmically forward across the plain.
The sky above us blossoms, azure;
    The snow is silver and blue.

Farther and farther we travel from home
    Into the white wonder—nirvana...
In the evening, languor will envelope the body,
    Our legs will grow blissfully weary.

Then, by the warmly heated stove,
    To dream sweetly of peace
And the hand that thoughtfully covers
    The shoulders with a soft, plaid blanket.

In My Abode

In my abode the fires of sunset
    Have bloomed on the white walls.
The window is open; an aromatic fragrance
    Drifts from afar;

And somewhere there beyond the rosy field
    An unseen singer trills,
And above the transparent birches
    A cloud floats, like a swan...

Openness.   Peace...The barely perceptible
    Whispering of flowers in a half-dream...
The fires of sunset burn on the wall
    In whimsical patches.

———————·———————

From work my hands have grown large and rough
And grief has vanished, completely, imperceptibly.

Everything is so easy and clear: The fields and the meadows,
And the special noise that means the snows are melting...

Soon sultry summer will embrace our house,
Singing, laughing, blushing all around.

The tomatoes, in their small beds, will fill up with scarlet
    juice,
And an intoxicating fragrance will exude from the mint...

This life at home, far from people,
Urban anxieties, and merry escapades;

There where the sky is so near and the forest like a brother,
Where birds and grasses commune with the soul.

I have two worlds: the city and the country,
And although an infinity lies between,
They are joined by the November sky,
Pale, blind—like a hazy desert.

    And beneath this sky everything is intermingled:
    The field, diligently ploughed before the snow,—
    —The snowy lanes of the Vishgorod hill,
    Where the damp fog steams up the street lamps.

Across the meadows, drenched, mud-colored, and thorny,
The wind makes merry like a tipsy lad,
—That same wind boldly weaves across the market,
Twining leaves into a drunken dance.

    And the familiar scent of fresh milk,
    The marvelous smell of rye bread,
    Suddenly, sweetly, waft into the city drawing room,
    Where light, worldly conversation pours forth.

————————·————————

        Legs are tired.
        Arms ache.
    A dull, lifeless gaze.
        The heart is cold.
        The wind sings:
    "Soon winter will come."

Yellow leaves whirl, whirl,
Sweep up in the air, fall into puddles.
        The leaves are cold.
        The wind sings:
    "Soon winter will come."

Soon snowy blizzards will froth and foam,
        The ponds will turn to stone,
And, sinking into inescapable sadness,
        The orchards will freeze in a dream...

The Virgin Soil, No. 7 (1934)

To the memory of A. Yu.

A white, fresh, sunny day.
You were walking, knowing no fear.
Suddenly a huge, black shadow
Grew up alongside the road.

You swayed—your strength ebbed,
Your body grew tired, heavy as lead.
You sat down on the grass, closed your eyes...
So many flowers are left!

The black shadow grows and grows...
It doesn't matter that you are young.
The sun has faded, and night is enveloping you.
Coldness. The final coldness.

———————·———————

The Virgin Soil, No. 8 (1935)

I want novelty! Novelty! To float away
    Like a sunny cloud in the distant azure.
The old is obsolete, it should be discarded,
    The old is a handful of waste.

I'm tired of it all: The same themes and images,
    Used a thousand times,
The sound of my own monotonous voice,
    The same structures and phrases.

Everything repeats itself, this is our curse.
    Novelty—where can it be found?
These same old paths in the October slush
    I see again and again.

———————·———————

A Small House Near the Woods

Night

The same old fly at the window
Buzzes and convulsively beats...
Like the abyss of a black well
    Yawns the haze.

My heart awakens and in the silence
Anxiously, painfully contracts,
While the wind sighs in sorrow
And the rain rustles...

---------·----------

The poems of Elizaveta Bazilevskaya-Roos—she preferred to be called "Bazilevskaya-Ross," for euphony—usually describe two emotional extremes. Some of her verse is a passionate and lyrical outpouring of joy, while other poems approach a tone of despair and longing for a new life. In the former, Bazilevskaya, like her sister Meta Roos and her brother-in-law Irtel von Brenndorff, achieves her aesthetic and thematic aims through the use of impressionistic images derived from nature. But while the beauty and splendor of nature frequently accentuates the desolate, elegiac mood of many of Meta Roos' and von Brenndorff's poems, Bazilevskaya employs the same devices to celebrate the present and the actual. Moreover, this reconciliation with her fate—alien to Meta Roos and von Brenndorff—is enhanced by delightful images of the simple pleasures of hearth and home. This aspect of Elizabeth's verse is most apparent in "A Winter's Day," "In My Abode," and "From work my hands have grown large and rough." The first poem happily recounts a winter outing; the snow is "white fur on the sleeping birch tree." Although far from the "nirvana" which she senses in the distance, the *persona*, away from home, seems content to experience the warmth of the heated stove and "the hand that thoughtfully covers/The shoulders with a downy rug." "In My Abode" achieves a poignant and resonant lyrical tone through the accumulation of sensuous images drawn from the poet's perception of an evening in spring or early summer. Fragrances, the delicate distant trilling, and the "fires of sunset" that "bloomed on the white wall," point to a sense of being and a desire to experience the present as fully as possible.

These lyrics written in the "major key" are complemented by a series of poems written in the "minor key." In "Legs are tired," "I want novelty! Novelty!" and "Night," the *persona* appears no longer satisfied with the pleasures of the moment, which before offered enraptured delight. Instead, a sense of ennui and spiritual restlessness have perturbed her contentment. "Everything repeats itself, this is our curse," she exclaims in despair. She fails to find a way to escape the present; it becomes, at least metaphorically, related to the darkness that yawns "like the abyss of a black well." The tone of these poems approaches the mood expressed in the verse of Meta Roos and von Brenndorff. But in their poems anguish is often accompanied by a tormenting nostalgia for the beautiful past; Bazilevskaya seldom invokes the past and searches instead for the unrealized promise of the future.

Like her sister, who explores the death of a friend in "Beyond the window the burning candles," Bazilevskaya deals with death in the poem "White, fresh, sunny day." The former is imbued with a sense of personal loss and consuming grief. But in the latter poem, this sense of bereavement is almost completely absent. It is replaced by an awareness of the continuity and flux of nature that link life and death. Thus, the friend is gone, but the poet does not feel entirely deprived for she shows that the flowers have remained.

The last two poems reveal Bazilveskaya's increasing sense of boredom and sadness. In "I want novelty! Novelty! To float away" the poet expresses frustration with her own writing: "I'm tired of it all: The same themes and images,/Used a thousand times,/The sound of my own monotonous voice/And the same structures and phrases." She chooses an effective metaphor for the monotony of life: "These same old paths in the October slush." The second poem, "The same old fly at the window," hints at a similar feeling of dissatisfaction, but the poet is more elusive. The reader is aware of a vague sadness and pain of a heart which "Anxiously, painfully contracts," haze that "yawns" "like the abyss of a black well," and wind that "sighs in sorrow." The poem reveals Bazilevskaya's skillful use of sibilants to create an impression of rustling, monotonous autumnal rains, and darkness.

Here is an example of Bazilevskaya's prose:

The Virgin Soil, No. 6 (1934)

Snowflakes

There is a vague sense of mysterious presence...It
floats past very near, brushing the soul with its light
substance. You reach out for it, but already it's gone,
and you don't even know what it was, or even if it
existed at all. Is it joy, or sorrow, mysterious, illusive,
pure...You sit with eyes closed and listen, and suddenly
somewhere within, resounding quietly, images begin to
circle, drift in from afar, fall in soft flakes, and suddenly
whirl in a violent dance... Strange images...

*   *
*

Impetuous torrents in the streets. The hubbub,
the noise, children's laughter. Paper sailboats in the
rushing water. We are powerless to restrain our joy.
Leaving the high school, we join hands and, like a
whirlwind, rush along Sumskaya Street. Flying past the
university students, we hear the joyful "On, on,
cavalry!" It's embarrassing: We are already fifteen
years old. We should be able to control ourselves by
now.
A park turning into a forest. A deep blue lake
surrounded by glades. The April air—so intoxicating.
We pick flowers until we're exhausted. We want more
and more. But already it is evening, and it is getting
damp. Time for us to go home.

*   *
*

A sea so very blue, white sand, orange-red shells
with veins glistening through the water. And the sun.
The sun—you can't even begin to describe it. The soul
drinks in its warmth and grows, spreads out, ripens.

*   *

*

Silver pine trees in an old dense forest. They are
pungent with pitch. How silent and sultry! What
languor in the awakening body! The world is some
where quite close—wonderful, of course, understanding,
expectant. And the world—why, it's everything.

At night the stars shine triumphantly. In the soul
there is a prayer for everyone and everything.

*   *

*

Week...Months...Years...
And there, under the stars, was it the same I?
Was that I?
Night. The windows are shuttered. The stars are
       not visible. Or
maybe there aren't any stars at all.
The world is void. There is no world either.
The circle dance is over. The last flakes are falling.

—————·—————

In this short piece Bazilevskaya attempts to capture her past
hopes, enthusiams, energy, and confidence. She tries to relive the
sensual experiences—perceptions of the sea, the sun, and forests.
All are part of a marvelous world waiting to be discovered by an
eager youngster. The snowflakes represent the attractive,
mysterious, and transitory nature of her youthful views of life. At
the end, snowflakes cease to fall, life and the world cease to be
real.

"Snowflakes" is personal and impressionistic. A series of
images is colored and connected by the author's consciousness.
From an almost imperceptible stirring of the soul, and vague
memories of a distant past in the first section of this prose poem,
the reader moves to a precise image in the second. For a moment
the author is the fifteen-year-old she used to be; she's full of life
and laughter and immersed in the concrete world around her.

Whether light and warm, as in the third section, or dark, cool, and mysterious, as in the fourth, all aspects of life are "wonderful." Reality satisfies the senses as well as the mind: life—"Why, it's everything." But years go by and the author wonders if that ebullient young girl is the same woman who now sits quietly in the dark. With closed shutters barring light from her room and with closed eyelids barring reality, the poet questions everything and doubts the existence of happiness. Her life has come full circle; the last flakes are falling.

The following three unpublished poems were written by Bazilevskaya-Roos in exile. Thoughts of death, loneliness, and an escape into the realm of dreams and recollections of the past dominate the poetic scene. The ideal Arcadia of her youth and of her happy marriage in Estonia stands in sharp contrast to her cheerless and hopeless life in postwar Germany.

In the Country

"I do not regret, do not call, do not weep..."
Esenin.

The stork walks with his mate on the meadow.
The ray of the sun breaks through the fog...
It smells so sweetly of new mown hay.
The brook meanders like a narrow ribbon.

Wild pidgeons coo gently,
Dark pines rock their tops...
Here, one is not sad, one does not call, does not languish
When pensively strolling on the lonely edge of the forest...

Birnbaum
July 7, 1943

———————·———————

On the green meadow, in the silent forest
I pensively stroll completely alone...
Do you remember how two of us watched the fox,
but she proved more cunning than we?

Do you remember how in the spring, on the edge of the forest,
  we waited for a woodcock's languid call?
And now that lovely smell of the awakening woods
  both intoxicated and entranced us?...

Birnbaum
July 8, 1943

————————·————————

You are with me from the dawn to the sunset
and from the sunset to the dawn again...
We have almost nothing to talk about.
Today creeps on again like yesterday.
The hope to see the light
animates my soul with its spark more and more rarely.
I lose heart more and more often
and despair that there is no hope.
Once, a tall gentleman in black
had the nerve to tell me:
"Where do you hurry? What hopes are possible?—
There is only one End, anyhow."

January 1, 1948

BASILEVSKY, IVAN VICTOROVICH (b. 1898)

Ivan Bazilevsky was born into a wealthy family that owned gold mines. His uncle, Prince Suvorov, was a general-aide-de-camp of Emperor Alexander III. The Bazilevsky family had a large summer house in Yamburg, where Bazilevsky's father, Victor, spent almost every day on the mezzanine, writing his memoirs. His sons studied in St. Petersburg at various Cadet Corps, but visited their old father frequently. Ivan Bazilevsky, who graduated from the First Cadet Corps in St. Petersburg in 1916, claimed that his father had been initiated into the mystery of Father Fyodor Kuzmich (Alexander I). Since he had vowed to keep silent about the fate of the Emperor, Victor Bazilevsky took his secret with him to the grave. His memoirs were lost during World War II.

Ivan Bazilevsky participated in World War II as a volunteer, and fought on the Carpathian front. Later he joined the army of Yudenich and retreated with it into Estonia. He worked near Tallinn as a forest inspector and married, in 1930, the Russian poet Elizabeth Roos. His poems were few, but beautifully written. There is something of a wild horsemanship in his verse, which resembles the work of his favorite poet, Nikolay Gumilyov. Like his wife, Bazilevsky was also fond of Alexander Blok. Ivan's artistic technique and masculine lines with their unbridled spirit made him a remarkable poet. He published his verse in *The Virgin Soil* under the pseudonym of I. Varvatsi. Ivan Varvatsi was the name of one famed ancestor, an illustrious corsair who fought the Turks and founded the city of Taganrog where Anton Chekhov was born. As a descendant of Varvatsi, the old Bazilevsky was treated with great respect during his sojourn in Greece.

Bazilevsky's friends in Estonia called him "Gumilyov," and his wife, "Anna Akhmatova." "Here come Gumilyov and Akhmatova," they would say when the Bazilevskys appeared at their literary soirées in Tallinn. In Estonia, shortly before its occupation by the Soviet military forces, Ivan was drafted into the Estonian Legion. He was wounded, evacuated from the battlefield, and placed on a ship which was later bombed by the Soviets. He was one of thirty survivors rescued by a German destroyer.

After the death of his wife in Germany, Bazilevsky left for Sweden. He now lives in Stockholm with his second wife, a poet and portrait painter also from Tallinn, Evgeniya Robertovna von Petsoldi. They married in 1953. His contemporaries, among them N. E. Andreyev, Elizabeth von Hoerschelmann, and Meta Roos, described Bazilevsky as a very kind, pleasant, and cultured man.

The Virgin Soil, No. 4 (1932)

The Nomad

I drive my herd through the rustling feather grass.
I wheel around, waving my lasso,
And the wind, raising the earth-black dust behind me,
Flutters the edges of my cloak.

Across the boundless steppe my cries resound.
My playful horse prances lightly,
And into my face, burnt brick red by the sun,
Lashes his golden mane.

Who, then, wants to pay dowries
And pray to the potbellied god,
If even the steppe winds
Cannot equal in speed this bold horse.

Gaspal, Estonia

———————·———————

An Imitation of Edgar Allan Poe

Outside the window the tempest roared darkly.
The sound of the wind was wistful and hollow.
The sound of the wind was gloomy and hollow.
And in the silence my soul grew dumb.
The fireplace, having burnt down, died out.
The sound of the wind was gloomy and hollow.

The dark gray fingered branches
Kept knocking restlessly on the pane
And the faded leaves flew up,
Now whirling, now disappearing
In the round dance of colorless shadows.
The dark gray fingered branches
Kept knocking restlessly on the pane.

———————·———————

The "I" of "The Nomad" is a spirited and independent
herdsman, who has no need for society's conventions ("Who, then,
wants to pay dowries"). For the nomad nature is the only god
because it is infinitely superior to a potbellied idol. At first
reading, the poem seems straightforward and uncomplicated, but
closer scrutiny reveals the poet's ingenuity and craftsmanship. The
narrative is in the first person. The nomad describes himself, thus
bringing the reader closer to his personality and helping the reader

to feel the pride in the nomad's independence, rough life, and swiftness of his horse. Motion and speed are the poem's heart. Verbs of motion are used frequently and vividly to emphasize the sudden, energetic movements of the nomad ("I wheel around, waving my lasso") and of his playful horse, who "prances lightly" and whose mane lashes into the *persona's* face. The wind, too, is in constant motion, rustling the feather grass, raising up the black dust, and fluttering the edges of the cloak. This image is taken up again in the last stanza, where the speed of the steppe winds is compared to that of a horse. Color is used very effectively. The black earth contrasts sharply with the "burnt brick red" face of the nomad and with the golden mane of the horse. The colorful description of nature contrasts with the conventional "potbellied god." The poem is written in anapests, a meter often used for emotional, romantic poetry. Four-foot and three-foot lines alternate, as do the rhymes (abab). The orchestration of sound is skillful. The hissing consonants are used repeatedly, contributing to the impression of motion, which is central to the poem.

"An Imitation of Edgar Allan Poe" is a delightful poetic joke based on the manipulation of sound, echoes, repetends, and refrains found in Poe's poetry. Poe was a meticulous student of prosaic and poetic devices. Sound was more important to him than meaning and was used to reinforce his effects of melancholy, mystery, and horror. Using the conventional properties of Poe's work—portentous nights, roaring storms, howling winds, bizarre chambers, mysterious knocking or clanking irons—Bazilevsky attains verbal music through repetition of sounds and phrases, and through symbolism. In Poe's poem "The Raven" repetitive phrases demonstrate and amplify the *persona's* increasing anquish. "The Raven," however, is much longer than Bazilevsky's "Imitation." Therefore, the *persona's* anquish is developed slowly and seems the natural result of his insanity. By contrast, in "An Imitation" anguish becomes frenzied and intensity is transformed into parody. In Bazilevsky's rendition, Poe's pathos is subdued by playful irony. The meter and rhyme are controlled without hampering the free flow of verse.

BORMAN, IRINA KONSTANTINOVNA
(literary psudonym Ir-Bor)

Borman, a Russian poet in Estonia, was a physiotherapist at the Tallinn Public Baths. During the summer she always spent time at her father's cottage in Narva-Jõesuu on the Baltic Sea. There she met Igor' Severyanin and they became close friends. She stayed in Estonia during the German occupation and married a former Soviet prisoner of war who had been released by the German army. She was still in Estonia when the Bolsheviks re-occupied Estonia towards the end of the Second World War, but she has not been heard of since.

Borman did not publish a great deal, but all her poems are original, expressive, and musical. Some of them resemble the style and tone of Nadezhda Teffi's verse, with its modernistic, emotional style and colorful imagery. Other poems reflect the precious verse of Severyanin and Nikolay Agnivtsev, with a tendency toward aestheticism and exotic poetry based on erotic motifs. Others are akin to the "decadent" and affected songs of A. N. Vertinsky. However, Borman's treatment of erotic themes, especially her distinctly Eastern eroticism, is always handled in an artistic and tasteful manner.

The Virgin Soil, No. 6 (1934)

> Green moss. Lilac heather.
> A dried-up bog of former swamplands.
> The tranquil north intoxicates me,
> Like the sweet honey of autumn combs.
> The aspens, dropping red leaves at my feet,
> Sound like the tinkling of gold.
> And there is no end to forest chambers,
> There is no beginning to forest paths.
> . . . .
> I wander aimlessly, without a path,
> And I think: You are cruel!
> And my young feet trample
> The wild thorn apple bushes.

*   *

*

Was that love maternal?
Today—yes. And I pitied
The one who had quit the Finnish coast...
Oh, the distance, the silver distance!

————·————

I go wearily into the dark night.
Somewhere beyond the houses a dog is barking.
I have no companions, nor do I encounter anyone—
And no one hears my quiet tears.

Across the sky, keeping pace with me,
A great mysterious star
Moves tirelessly toward God
And keeps repeating: When, when?...

————·————

The Virgin Soil, No. 7 (1934)

The sunset will not be golden,
The sunset will not be violet.
For Neptune in the sea it is golden—
May this summer be stormy!

The white house on the shore awaits
The red-haired queen of the sea.
And for you I still keep
A gull—a sullen bird.

Along a path of belated roses
The queen will pass to the dismal house.
Along a path of autumn dew
You'll come for the white-winged gull.

————·————

The poems of Borman are delicate meditations touching on the traditional themes of love and loss, fulfillment and regret. In the poems presented here, these motifs are refracted through images of the natural world. The pastoral frame of reference is employed both as a framework for her concepts as well as a starting point for her thoughts. Moreover, in "Green moss. Lilac heather," the details of her landscape attain a degree of subjectivity. " . . . there is no end to forest chambers,/There is no beginning to forest paths," she says, implying that these lines serve as a transition from her description of "the tranquil north" to thoughts on the often confused and tangled nature of love. The metaphorical aspect of her walk in the woods is accentuated in the poem's last stanza, for, like the "great, mysterious star" in the sky, the *persona* too "moves tirelessly toward God," Who perhaps is the solution to the aimless wandering.

In addition to other characteristics, Borman uses mythical allusions in "The sunset will not be golden" to achieve a solemn lyrical resonance. Parallel images of "the red-haired sea queen" and "a gull—a sullen bird" are developed in the second and third stanzas. Their juxtaposition accentuates the fading hopes and enduring faithfulness which pervades the entire lyric.

From the album of Elizabeth Bazilevskaya-Roos:

> Every night, the same solitary street.
> Every night, the same lanterns,
> I am a simple girl—
> Do not call me. Do not speak to me.
>
> Sometimes the moon shines,
> But more often—the fog surrounds me.
> I do not know who is reading
> My unfinished romance.
>
> I need happiness, not a miracle.
> So, do not wait and do not call.
> At times it is so hard
> Because of a melancholy which steals upon me...

There is no reason for you to jeer
At my simplicity—
What should I do with myself?
I can only stroll along the solitary street.

April 1934
Tallinn

DIKOY, BORIS (Boris Vil'de; 1908-1942)

The Dikoy family belonged to a group to timber merchants in the Yamburg and Luga regions of the St. Petersburg Province. Boris' father died shortly before the 1917 Revolution and his mother found herself in Estonia as a refugee with two children, Raisa and Boris, and no means of support. Working as an unskilled laborer, she managed to educate her children in the Russian High School of Tartu. Boris was a good-looking adolescent. Adroit, strong, with thick curly hair and cold eyes, he immediately attracted attention. A stutterer, he spoke slowly and with apparent condescension.

After graduation from the High School, Boris entered the Department of Chemistry at Tartu University, but in 1927 he suddenly disappeared. After a few months he returned home, explaining that he had crossed the Soviet border without a passport, was arrested by Soviet frontier guards, and was jailed in the area of Gdov-Pskov. He was repatriated, and the Estonian administration sent him to the oil-shale production region at Kiviili, Kochtlo-Jaarve. There he soon found a suitable position, became friends with Igor' Severyanin, and in a few months disappeared again. This time he was arrested in Lithuania at the German border and sent back to Estonia on a train. Near the Estonian border, he jumped off the moving train and escaped to Germany, where he settled in Berlin and worked in the editorial office of the newspaper *Rul'* (The Rudder). Later he became personal secretary to a German count and lived in his castle near Weimar. All the time, however, he longed to go to China and fight the Japanese occupation. Instead, he proceeded to France to meet André Gide in Nice. The French novelist was charmed by

Boris and later he reminisced about Dikoy's resolute, straight-forward, and uncompromising nature.   Gide recommended his youthful visitor to the School of Foreign Languages in Paris to study Japanese.   Upon graduation from the school, Dikoy became a French citizen and found work in the Musée de l'Homme.   He married the daughter of his professor, a man who was an eminent French scholar of Slavic linguistics and director of the Museum. Although esteemed at the Museum, Boris decided to go to Japan to work as a cultural attaché at the French Embassy in Tokyo. In 1938 he travelled with a group of Russian writers, among them Leonid Zurov, to the the Pechory Monastery in Estonia.   When meeting his former friends, he would proudly say, "We, the French..."

During World War II Dikoy was drafted into the French army, captured by the Germans, and released.   He took part in the Resistance, and was again arrested by the Germans who urged him to renounce his anti-German activities.   He refused and was shot by the Gestapo.   Dikoy, revealing bravery and self-sacrifice during his arrest and execution, was honored posthumously with the Highest Badge of the French Resistance.   General Charles de Gaulle personally signed the order to have his name engraved in gold letters on the Board of Honor at the Musée de l'Homme and the French Pantheon.

As a poet in Estonia, Boris Dikoy-Vil'de used the classical forms elaborated by the Acmeist poets in St. Petersburg.   The other members of the "Guild of Poets" in Tallinn likewise availed themselves of this poetic technique.   Vil'de, however, patterned his verse also on Pasternak, while writing at the same time in the spirit of the "Parisian note."   He contributed to the journals *Field Flowers*, edited by V. Nikiforov-Volgin; *A Russian Shop*, and *The Virgin Soil*.

For more detail, read A. Grinberg's publication "The Biography of Boris Dikoy-Vil'de" in *Opyty* (Experiments), No. 1 (1953), pp. 204-205.   Dikoy translated an anthology of Estonian fiction into French, *Anthologie des Conteurs Estoniens* (Paris: Sagittaire, 1936).

The Virgin Soil, No. 8 (1935)

A little tenderness and patience.
Thank you, my faithful friend.
Oh, how light are the touches
Of transparent and frail hands.

We've become older, simpler, more aloof.
We are equally poor,
And for our secondhand souls
Even half price is enough.

Rare meetings are shorter;
Chance flowers are poorer.
Words are stingier.   Silence is more honest.
The closer you are, the more unnecessary you are.

How little, my friend, is left for us,
And how much more tenderly I treasure
Both the submissive fatigue of hands
And the cold of unresponsive lips.

———————·———————

Boris Dikoy's "A Little Tenderness and Patience" is a very
moving poem, reminiscent of Anatoly Steiger's aphoristic verse.
The poem describes the relationship of two people who are growing
older.   What makes the poem especially gripping is the discrepancy
between the *persona's* appreciation and the little he expects.   In a
way, the relationship has become less intense ("We've become
older, simpler, more aloof"), yet the *persona* is satisfied: "For our
secondhand souls/Even half price is enough."   The tone is
restrained, quiet, and sincere, devoid of all sentimentality.   Dikoy
achieves this effect, in part, by the use of short, impersonal,
abstract statements, as illustrated in the entire third stanza.   The
stanza, seemingly free of emotion, reveals Dikoy's control and the
sense of restraint that permeates the poem.   In contrast, the
increasingly emotional and personal tone of the final stanza is all
the more poignant.
    The form of the poem also deserves comment.   The meter is
iambic tetrameter with the exception of the first line, which

contains an extra foot.   Thus the reader does not pick up the
pattern of the regular meter until several lines later.   This gives
the poem a more conventional tone, creating an impression of
naturalness and sincerity.   It reflects Steiger's laconic, conversational verse, written according to the aesthetics of the "Parisian
note."

Here are two hitherto unpublished autobiographical poems of
Boris Dikoy (from the album of Elizabeth Bazilevskaya-Roos):

Pro domo suo

There are no tender stanzas, nor caressing sonnets,
Nor misty visions in my songs:
It seems that I am a monster in the family of poets,
Or, perhaps, not a poet at all.

The Pushkins, Virgils, Fets
All have in their poems a light, quite and unearthly.
Their stanzas resemble roses, for from among all aesthetes
The poet is indeed the most aesthetical.

The spirit dwells in each of their poems,
But I am different—I do not pray to gods,
And poetry to me is a factory—not a cathedral.

I do not know the delights of inspirations,
My stubborn genius is forged from steel.
I am not a poet. Who am I?—I do not know.

                                            March 30, 1928
                                            Tartu-Yuryev

————————·————————

In Solitary Confinement

It is quiet in cell No. 4.
Day after day without hopes and losses.
Only at times, the square of sky beyond
The iron barred windows reminds me of the world.
It is quiet in cell No. 4.

I grieve for freedom less and less frequently.
Captivity has engulfed and swallowed me up.
The whisper of the gloomy stone walls
Is peacefully disarming and caressingly affectionate.
I grieve for freedom less and less frequently.

The weeks of idleness are so destitute of thought.
I rest from my previous nights,
From the anquish of my lingering hang-over,
From the stain of my useless speeches.
The weeks of idleness are so destitute of thought.

Everything is so simple, easy, and clear.
To live?—to take up deeds and fall again?
—Five steps to the wall and backwards,
And backwards also only five measured steps.

It is quiet in cell No. 4.
The steel of the barred window does not beckon me with
    anguish.
With every day, the peace of a blue insanity
Opens itself deeper to me.
It is quiet in cell No. 4.

Idem.

Dikoy-Vil'de's third unpublished poem from the album of
Bazilevskaya-Roos deserves a special mention because of its
remarkable artistic form.   The letters in Vil'de's handwriting
suggest the motion of the waves that wash away the name of the
poet's beloved which he has written in the sand.   Everything is
constantly changing in the poem—there is neither permanence in
the *persona's* feelings nor in nature as portrayed.   The harmony
between the varying poetic mood, the ever-changing landscape, and
the outlines of the letters stretching themselves viscously along the
lines, is an interesting experiment in connecting visual art, poetic
expression, and the feelings of the poet.   The poem, written in
1921,   was entered in the album in 1929 when Dikoy-Vil'de and
Bazilevskaya-Roos were students at the University of Tartu.

A man in love inscribed the name of his beloved
With his toecap on the sea sand at night.

The night was stormy, and the sea current
Carried the gold sand into the deep.

The foamy wave brought from the deep
New grains of sand onto the moonlit shore.

The blue silk of the sea became quiet toward noon,
And the man in love came again to the shore.

Smiling quietly, he inscribed a different name
With his toecap on the sea sand.

1921
Tartu-Yuryev

NARTSISSOVA, OLGA ANATOLYEVNA

Olga Nartsissova, sister of the poet Boris Nartsissov, still lives
in Tartu, Estonia. She wrote beautiful poems, some of which were
published in *The Virgin Soil*. Here are a few examples of her
poetic work:

The Virgin Soil, No. 5 (1933)

The days pass in tormenting
    anxiety —
You left in silence, without
    saying good-bye
The snow was melting, and the
    gentle radiance of the sun
Was weaving lace from ice
    crystals on the road.

Along the darkened, sodden fields

I wanted to overtake you sooner.

But the mist timidly nested to
    the ground,
And the sky spread into a
    starry fan.

In the lifeless, weathered sedge
I wept, exhausted, inconsolable.
And with a pale strip of light in the east
Morning cautiously dispersed the shadows.

Tartu-Yuryev

———————·———————

The most striking aspect of Olga Nartsissova's poem "The days pass in tormenting anxiety" is the vividness of nature in contrast to the *persona's* "tormenting anxiety." The poem originates in the pain felt at a difficult and unhappy parting, but what the *persona* remembers is the beauty of the scene: "The snow was melting, and the gentle radiance of the sun/Was weaving lace from ice crystals on the road." The original Russian text makes it clear that the "I" in the poem is male and the "you" is female. As the *persona* tries to overtake the one who has left, "The mist timidly nestled to the ground/And the sky spread into a starry fan." With this soft, subtle beauty, the next two lines form a harsh contrast: "In the lifeless weathered sedge/I wept exhausted, inconsolable." But the poem ends on an optimistic note with a delicate description of sunrise, suggesting renewal and promising hope. Thus, the tension between the despair of the *persona* and the beauty surrounding him, which both elevates and intensifies his grief, is released.

The poem is written in trochaic pentameter with every line ending in a feminine rhyme.

The Virgin Soil, No. 1 (1928)

A Dagger

As I gazed at the darkened rusty blade,
Primeval forests arose...
At the water a rock, like a moss-clad mushroom,
And a swath of spreading grass.

And I remember how, peering 'round,
One crept through the monstrous wet sedge,
While another stood motionless, lithe and tall,
Intent on the green moving trail.

He stood in the reeds, and like topaz
His necklace reflected the sun;
The small eyes burned with malevolent rage,
And glowered through narrowed lids.

He raised with might his hairy arm,
And the gleaming dagger flew;
The one in the muddy pelt collapsed,
His face distorted in fear and pain.

He laughed a senseless awful laugh
And sullen, curious, regarded
The shining bloody trail advancing
From the dagger and the torn wolfskin.

———————·———————

The dagger, an object accidentally found, elicits a vision of prehistoric times expressed in eloquent and colorful terms: "Primeval forests arose.../At the water a rock, like a moss-clad mushroom/And a swath of spreading grass." The poem embodies a negative view of man's nature: senseless killing, cruel pleasure from hurting another, and savage anger. All these emotions have existed in man from the beginning of time. The murderer burns with rage and a violent bestial desire to kill: "He stood in the reeds, and like topaz/His necklace reflected the sun;/The small eyes burned with malevolent rage,/And glowered through narrow lids." Like in some of Dostoevsky's novels, there is a feeling of intense heat—the chase and man's primitive anger—symbolizing perverted human ardor.

The rhythmical pattern and the imagery of the poem amplify the impression of a fearsome prehistoric world. The forceful staccato lines echo the beating of tribal drums: "His face distorted in fear and pain. . . . /The shining bloody trail advancing/From the dagger and the torn wolfskin." Color, rhythm, and visual and sensory imagery produce the gamut of destructive human drives.

The Virgin Soil, No. 3 (1932)

You must not cry—we shall leave forever
People and needless cares.
We shall build a palace out of ice
Inaccessible, cold, of pearl.

Growing numb, we shall become perfectly still, and in a
          dream
We shall see, now without trepidation,
How on a translucent wall
Swift shadows will move.

This is life. But it is far away.
You and I will never grow weary.
And blue twilight and silence
Will gently close in around us.

Tartu-Yuryev, Estonia

———————·———————

The central thought in this poem is perhaps as elusive and
inaccessible as the cold, pearly ice palace the poet intends to build.
It is difficult to attach one interpretation to the poem. When
Nartsissova writes "we shall leave forever," the reader cannot be
sure whether she is referring to death or something else, though
the first possibility seems more likely. The images of coldness,
numbness, stillness, silence, and blue twilight suggest death. Life
in the poem is far away; the poet visualizes it as "swift shadows"
moving "on a translucent wall." Death seems at first desirable, a
beautiful ice palace enveloped by blue twilight and silence. Yet
the tone of the poem as a whole is infinitely sad. The
introductory, "You must not cry," hints at grief, and the poet's
desire to escape to another world implies that life has become
unbearable.

In the original Russian text the meter of the poem, anapestic
trimeter, heightens the impact of the *persona's* anguish. The
rhyme scheme is abab with alternating masculine and feminine
rhymes.

KARAMZINA, MARIA VLADIMIROVNA (1900-1942?)

Maria Vladimirovna Karamzina was a spectacularly beautiful blond woman and a talented poet. She was the wife of Professor I. D. Grimm of Tartu University. Ivan Bunin warmly admired Karamzina's poetry. She was the author of a collection of poems, *Kovcheg* (The Ark; Narva, 1938), reviewed by Bunin in a laudatory article published in Paris. In Yury Ivask's opinion, "she wrote excellent poems of full contemporary Classicism," and "stood between Neo-Classicism and Acmeism."

Karamzina, née Maximova, was born in St. Petersburg. After graduating from the University in St. Petersburg she married I. D. Grimm, divorced him in 1929, and then married Vasily Alexandrovich Karamzin. They settled in Kiviili in Estonia. She spoke English, German, French, and several other languages fluently. She was a gifted painter and poet, and the author of short stories and critical articles on literature. When her collection *The Ark* came out, several prominent Russian critics in exile, among them Georgy Adamovich,[1] Pyotr Pil'sky,[2] and Vladislav Khodasevich,[3] joined Bunin in his praise of her verse.

Bunin was Karamzina's favorite writer. In May 1938, he visited her during a trip to the Baltic countries. He valued the friendship of this gifted and original poet, admired her intellect, and urged her to continue writing. Leonid Zurov, who also met Karamzina, remembered her as an unusually attractive woman with mysterious eyes, a beautiful face and figure, and refined feminity. For more detail, read *Literaturnoe nasledstvo. Ivan Bunin. Kniga pervaya.* (Literary Heritage: Ivan Bunin. Book I; Moscow; Nauka, 1973).

Karamzina was arrested by the Soviets during the occupation of Estonia in 1940. Allegedly, she died in a labor camp in 1942.

Bunin was especially impressed by the very first poem in *The Ark*:

The midnight race of luminaries and clouds,
The tramp of streams rushing down.
My soul is a nomadic ark
Tossed by the waves of an amorous flood.

I am waiting for the water to flow down
From the peak of the ancient Ararat—
For I know, I know that then
My song will take wing again.

I shall catch it, quivering,
With a filigree net in the depths of my soul
And I'll send it into the world, reborn,
Behind the first bright olive branch

————————·————————

The images used in the opening lines of the poem convey
transparency; everything is lucid and lighted with joy and
expectation. The sun, the moon, the stars, the clouds, and flowing
water are aptly invoked to portray the *persona's* dreamy state.
The poem expresses the artist's longing for inspiration, which she
knows will come when the time is ripe, just like winter is naturally
followed by the mountain waters of spring. The moment of
poetical inspiration, where the soul takes on wings and soars high,
is likened to melting of glacier ice, which breaks loose and flows
down the mountains in a vigorous, sparkling, unstoppable stream.
The atmosphere is one of confident expectation, far from the
pessimistic or skeptical tone in many twentieth-century Western
European poems dealing with poetic sterility and artistic
inspiration. Karamzina is a poet of considerable spiritual depth as
well literary finish who early in her artistic career found a
distinctly personal and unique poetic voice. Her vision is always
clear and the basic tone of her poetry is sincere, though dreamlike,
and devoid of sentimentality and affectation.

The tresses arranged like garlands,
Underneath them, a frolic of flighty thoughts...
I love the playful smoke of a cigarette,
And the evenings at the yellow lamp.

The narrow parting's inclination
Over an old book or picture—
And an intellectual friendship with a man
Who is in love, but not with me.

————————·————————

Primavera

With its blue eyes
April peers into my confused soul.
I walk along river banks and meadows,
Pressing a reed pipe to my lips.

Mischievous hopes whirl around me,
And, stirring delicate flowers,
The light breezes frolic with the hem of my garment,
Kissing me.

I walk—and am unable to name
The one to whom my song is dedicated,
Into whose embrace the spring is hurrying me,
And what it promises!

———————.———————

In these two poems, Karamzina's imagery is delicate and well chosen to convey the *persona's* impressions and vague expectations. Nature, people, thoughts, and colors appear naturally here, but with Karamzina's usual poetic finish. Her simple, concrete, and transparent images are effective in their emotional appeal, half-hints, and beauty. The poet forms one organic whole with the objects, events, nature, and feelings which appear in her poetic world, and this quality lends her verse its particular freshness. Always sensitive to her surroundings, Karamzina was gifted with keen personal susceptibility and insight. Her poetic universe is tranquil, delicate, elusive, playful, and ambiguous.

NOTES

1.   Georgy Adamovich, *Poslednie novosti* (Paris, 1939), No. 6499 (January 12, 1939).
2.   Pyotr Pil'sky, *Segodnya* (Riga, 1939), January–February.
3.   Vladislav Khodasevich, *Vozrozhdenie* (Paris, 1939), January.

KAYGORODOVA, IRINA DMITRIEVNA

The émigré poet Irina Kaygorodova was the daughter of the famous St. Petersburg painter Dmitry Kaygorodov, who escaped to Estonia after the Revolution of 1917 and opened the School of Art in Tallinn. He was the author of several short stories about the sea, and his father, Professor Kaygorodov at the Forestry Institute in St. Petersburg, had been a writer as well. Irina Kaygorodova published poetry in *The Virgin Soil*, and in her spacious Tallinn apartment she hosted literary soirées called "Near the Red Lamp." She was married to the priest, John Findlow, whom she described in vivid reminiscences published after his death. When N. E. Andreyev moved to Prague to study at the Czech Charles University, Kaygorodova raised the necessary funds. Her poem "Valaamsky monastyr'" (The Valaam Monastery) was so beautifully written that, according to Andreyev, it created a furor in the literary circles of the Baltic countries.

Charismatic Georgy Ivanovich Tarasov was a frequent guest at Kaygorodova's soirées and an intimate and welcome friend. He was an excellent theatre critic, and expert on the history of Russian Freemasonry, a journalist who contributed to several Baltic newspapers and journals (including *The Latest News*), a poet and fiction writer, and, above all, a great aesthete. A former member of the St. Petersburg literary world, Tarasov had a highly developed sense of literature, especially poetry. He appeared regularly at various St. Petersburg literary gatherings and lectured on Russian literature and versification. Andreyev described him as a man "of great St. Petersburg culture and education and very fond of *objets d'art*; he wore around his arm a beautiful amber rosary." Much respected in Estonia, Tarasov was invited to participate in the oldest Russian literary-social organization abroad, the Russian "Literary Circle" in Tallinn. Here he presented lectures on the Russian theatre, Russian literature, and Soviet writers. Through his work with the Library Commission of the association "The Russian School in Estonia," he created a unique Russian library in Tallinn. Tarasov always encouraged young Russian poets and fiction writers in Estonia to improve their knowledge of their native tongue, to broaden their aesthetic education, and to perfect their literary technique. He arranged for the publication of an article in *The Latest News* relating Yury

Ivask's "literary baptism" at a soirée of the Russian literary circle, where Ivask read his first paper, "A Word on Gogol." It was Tarasov who introduced Andreyev to this circle and enabled him to use the Russian library. In 1928 Tarasov returned to the Soviet Union. He published a book about a puppet theatre, and later disappeared.

Tarasov was one of the first critics to point to the beauty of Kaygorodova's poem "The Valaam Monastery."

The Virgin Soil, No. 1 (1928)

The Valaam Monastery

Beneath the yoke of time it is still the same, unscathed,
As centuries ago, and in our sad age
It still looks silently into the heights, protected by lakes...
Beyond the trials of men,
It is the guard of silence, a pledge to the Russia of the past
And the Rus' of the future, immortal and holy.
In their simple habits the venerable monks
Preserve this eternal peace within themselves.
We are enveloped by its unswerving faith,
And when the nocturnal sky resounds
With the melodious chime of bells, and a cupola, austere and
          proud,
Reflects them as it aspires to reach the heavens,
Rises in the distance a summoning, resounding peal
Above the wide Lake Ladoga, and dissolves into silence—
Oh, how profoundly and gently it then wafts over us
The beloved image of Russia, imperial, majestic!
How clear everything becomes! Such faith awakens within us!
We hear the powerful, Russian toll...
There Russia conceals herself
With her pure soul, despite the weight of fetters!

———————·———————

In the original version the poem consists of a single sentence divided into long flowing lines, thus conveying a sense of pealing bells. The resonant "r," the labials "p" and "b," and the long adjectives enhance this tolling sensation, which is further developed through resonance. Deeply religious in mood and contemplative in spirit, "The Valaam Monastery" abounds in details and colors like blue, white, and green.

The poem uses strong visual images, for example, the monks clothed in dark robes, the wide Lake Ladoga, and the poignant image of faraway Russia—the cupola rising up in the nocturnal sky. Most remarkable is the absence of the subject itself, the Valaam Monastery. Yet as a symbol of Holy Russia in all its former glory, the monastery is celebrated in a solemn and majestic manner.

VOINOV, YAROSLAV VLADIMIROVICH

A former officer, Voinov was a talented, handsome, educated man, married to a beautiful Russian woman. He tried his hand at various literary genres, and produced stylized short stories, political feuilletons, and sketches for Russian newspapers in Estonia. One of the principal contributors to *The Latest News*, Voinov was also responsible for its literary section. He published several volumes of short stories, including *Starye gody* (Old Years; Riga: Lit., 1920?) and *Sarkofag odnoy vesny* (The Sarcophagus of One Spring; Tallinn: Kol'tso, 1920), and a book for children, *Goryunova radost': detskaya skazka* (Woeful Joy: A Children's Fairy Tale; Tallinn: Bibliofil, 1922). All were very successful. Eminently representative of St. Petersburg culture, Voinov wrote many sketches about the St. Petersburg world. Toward the end of the 1920s he suddenly left Estonia for Paraguay.

Chimes, No. 23 (1929)

The Annunciation

The Angel is a cloud behind the door,
On his wings are snow and white nights,
And his arms are long, his fingers white,
Beyond him, invisible—the Blessed Trinity.

Bright thawed patches, the new attire
Celebrated spring's timeless garments...
The Divine Mystery's eternal hopes and dreams
Are shielded in the armor of the Archangel's words.

The bed is veiled beneath a canopy, the covers are white,
The windows glow with transcendental light,
And like the morning sky, like the dew,
Beautiful eyes, radiant eyes, shine bright.

The whole day glitters golden, though the Angel hides,
And the silence is so perceptible,
While singing swells in the heart, and the Archangel's
    message
Is as incomprehensible as the mystery of the Trinity.

—————·—————

As the title implies, "The Annunication" describes the Archangel Gabriel's visit to Mary to tell her that she will become the Mother of Jesus. The presentation is similar to the traditional one depicted in icons of the Russian Orthodox Church. In the icons Gabriel stands behind an open door and in the background one can see a blue sky and white clouds. Mary lies inside on a bed of white, and light shines through an open window. In the poem, the figure of Gabriel is inseparable from nature. The Angel has merged with the cloud: "On his wings are snow and white nights,/And his arms are long, his fingers white." The Annunciation is celebrated March 25; the green "thawed patches" of spring's new attire probably symbolize the hope implicit in Gabriel's message. Nature is also used in the description of Mary: Her eyes shine "like the morning sky, like the dew" and the white covers on her bed are reminiscent of snow. In the last stanza Gabriel is no longer visible ("the Angel hides"), but the day is glittering, radiant—like Mary's eyes in the previous stanza. Here, complete silence outside is juxtaposed with the singing that "swells in the heart." The end of the poem stresses the great mystery surrounding the Angel's announcement, a mystery as great as that of the Trinity itself.

BASHKIROVA, IRINA

The Old and the New: A Monthly Journal of Russian Antiquity ed. by N. I. Bagrov, I, No. 1 (Oct. 1931)

The Enchanted Gift

I know a park—its shadow lies
Above the smooth transparent pond,
Where swans majestically glide
And beauty dwells there all around.
    I know a certain pavilion there—
    In the darkness it gleams white
    From time to time a zephyr plays
    High in the branch above.
I saw, arising with the dawn,
The silhouettes of two young sprites—
They stood there, in one embrace,
And fed the swans.

Revel, 1927

———————·———————

The poem depicts a dreamlike landscape in a park, a sort of *locus amoenus* where everything is smooth, pure, transparent, bright, white, and tranquil. In the park is a "certain pavilion," beauty's abode; it is an ideal spot that radiates light, silence, and calm. Swans, symbols of beauty, move and glide majestically and noiselessly; not a sound is heard. The forms perceived by the poet are vague and dimly outlined; this points to the fluid and ephemeral nature of the vision. The zephyr, playing high in the branch, belongs to the realm of the unreal, the imagined, or the dreamed. The silhouettes of two young sprites appear, arising with the dawn, they are in a fleeting, fragile vision of dream and beauty outside the poet's reach. Yet by introducing each first line with "I know," "I know," "I saw," she emphasizes her acquaintance with this enchanted world.   Because she is in the darkness, she is not part of this world of beauty, but she is in contact with it as an observer.   The sprites embrace in the dreamworld of love and harmony, and then feed the swans—nurturing beauty, sustaining it, and keeping it alive.   At the same time, the sprites perpetuate the fleeting aspect of the vision and its ideal beauty, purity, love.   The title of the poem acquires additional meaning in the last stanza—not only is the park enchanted, but the *persona* is endowed with the magical power to conjure up the enchanted, lofty vision.

M. IVANOV

M. Ivanov, one of the younger poets in Estonia, is the author of an unusual poem about the Estonian countryside entitled "Lake Peipus." The poem celebrates the landscape as in a Chinese painting; human life plays a negligible part in the powerful panorama of nature.   There is only a single fishing sail, small as a gull, surrounded by endless depths of forest, by the lake, and by the sky. The landscape is dominated by the spirit of "Old Peipus" and his latent power, his immensity, and his sense of play.

The spectacle of nature is brought to life in the poem through color—the azure foam of a wave, the white of the sail, the deep blue of a pine forest.   The color intensify the vision of spaciousness, depth, and silence.   Nature is also portrayed through sounds heard or implied—waves break, sand crunches, a seagull cries.   A leisurely rhythm mimics the lazy yet powerful movement of the lake.

Ivanov does not dwell on events of historical significance like the Ice Battle of 1242 when the people of Novgorod, led by Prince Alexander Nevsky, defeated the Teutonic knights on the ice of Lake Peipus.   Instead, he has captured the sheer immensity of the natural world, animating it powerfully through various artistic devices.

*The Old and the New: A
Monthly Journal of Russian
Antiquity,* No. 2 (December
1931)

Lake Peipus

Wave after wave gently breaking
Runs up on the crunching sand,
Splashes azure foam at my feet
And recedes in silent impotence.
 Before me, scarcely raising his powerful bosom,
 Old Peipus stretches out lazily,
 While above, pursuing their unknown path,
 Clouds rush into the distance...
And the evening sky has merged with the earth,
Like a seagull is the white fishing sail,
And along the shore in a dense jagged wall
Lies the pine forest, silent, deep blue...
 Half-asleep, mighty Peipus is silent and still,
 And breathes forth a refreshing coolness,
 And reflecting the light of a star in his depths,
 He plays with it, shimmers and sways...

Estonia

IVANOVA, YULIYA

Yulia Ivanova was still a beginning student at the University
of Tartu when she read her own poems and stories at soirées of
the "Guilds" in Tartu and Tallinn.   Here is an example of her
poetry:

The Virgin Soil, No. 8 (1935)

How pleasant it is, with proudly spread wings,
To soar, barely visible, beyond the earth,
And, not suffocating in its pungent dust,
To singe my heart on the nearby sun.

To drown in the cosmos,
Like an incorporeal part of the Being;
To vanish, like a ringing note of the sonorous Muse,
Into the infinite spheres.

How pleasant to sail in an unknown space,
Twinkling like a blue star,
And to justify with an ancient hope
The languor of my eternal wanderings.

How pleasant to indulge in infinity
And, your soul brimming with delight,
To soar up—and never return
To my short, predestined path on the earth.

———————·———————

Airy and uplifting, the poem is in some respects close to symbolist poetry with its ecstatic quality and mysticism. Ivanova selects words for their sound effect; for example, the roaring "r" suggests space and strength. She paints with color; azure denotes infinite and the *persona's* desire to become an organic part of God's creation. The implied gray color of the earth's "pungent dust," on the other hand, symbolizes the poet's boring and restricted existence in the world of finite experience.

RYABUSHKINA, MARIA

Maria Ryabushkina, a Russian poet in Estonia, lived in the countryside, far from the "world" and cultural sophistication. She was inexperienced, a fledgling in literary matters, yet the poetry she contributed to *The Virgin Soil*, portraying the boredom of provincial life, is picturesque and impressive.

The Virgin Soil, No. 4 (1932)

Autumn

Day after day grows darker, drearier...
Rain falls nonstop,

And over the willow near the porch

The wind dances ruthlessly.

Merciless, like an evil force,
The violent wind imperiously
flattens the bushes,
While in the garden the last
flowers tremble
Bowing heavily to the ground.

How many fading laments
In the mournful cry of cranes,
Fleeing the native fields
Against their will.

Syrenets Village, Estonia

———·———

Desolation and dreariness, unceasing rain, and a violent and ruthless wind characterize Ryabushkina's Estonian autumn. On a symbolic level, however, the destructive wind, called "an evil force," may also refer to the Russian revolution. The "last flowers" could represent the fading vestiges of the old regime. This interpretation of the poem finds support in the final stanza, where the "mournful cry of cranes,/Fleeing the native fields/Against their will" evokes the "fading laments" of Russian émigrés. With this in mind, the reader becomes aware, in the first stanza, of the sadness and despair of the poet as she contemplates her fate and that of other Russian exiles.

The formal aspects of the poem reinforce the mood of loneliness and anguish. Alliteration using the letters *t* and *d* in the first two lines, along with the trochaic tetrameter, suggest the monotonous staccato of the rain. Frequently repeated, the hissing sounds *s* and *z* underscore the threat of the "evil force." The rhyme scheme of the poem is abab, and the first and third lines of each stanza end in cheerless, prolonged dactyls which contrast sharply with the dynamic masculine rhymes in the other lines of the poem.

TRANZE, NATALIYA

Nataliya Tranze was a refugee from Russia. In Estonia she
lived with her family in the village of Toila, also the home of Igor'
Severyanin. Tranze and Severyanin were close friends. Nataliya's
father was a Russian naval officer; he died in Toila. She
contributed to the almanacs *The Virgin Soil* and *Staroe i novoe*
(The Old and the New).

The Old and the New, No. 1
(October 1931)

At the End of August

August is beautiful in the loving farewell
Of its last golden days,
In its yellowing foliage, its luxuriant withering,
In the starry shroud of velvet nights.

Its cool, moist mornings,
Bathed in sparkling dew,
With clouds tinted mother-of-pearl
Above the sunset's pale rose glow.

Cobwebs float in the transparent air,
Crickets chirp, the landrails cry;
Amid golden birches, the aspens turn crimson,
The top of a glorious, faraway maple grows red.

Little leaves fall and eddy,
In a lacy rain they drift to the ground,
Whirling round and round like golden butterflies,
And airily swarm chases swarm...

Both a vague sadness and the stillness of silence,
And the embrace of sunbeams no longer bright,
Like the dusky gaze of one's beloved
In the quiet hour of the final meeting.

Narva, 1931

"At the End of August" is about beauty and finality: "August is beautiful in the loving farewell/Of its last golden days." The words "yellowing," "withering," and "shroud" in the first stanza suggest aging and death, but in the next three stanzas the poet concentrates on the beauty of the natural world and only hints at its transitory character. The last stanza reintroduces the themes of finality, parting, and separation. Here "the embrace of sunbeams no longer bright" is likened to "the dusky gaze of one's beloved/In the quiet hour of the final meeting," thus linking the final, beautiful days of August with the termination of an intimate relationship. The muse is solitary, and the mood is pensive and elegiac.

Through an extensive use of color—mother-of-pearl, pale rose, gold, crimson, and red—Tranze recreates the beauty of the sky and the trees. Especially picturesque is her description of the falling leaves: "In a lacy rain" they "drift to the ground," "whirling like golden butterflies." Sound and visual effects play an important role. In the third stanza the reader hears crickets chirping and landrails crying. In the fourth stanza he hears the rustling of leaves, although no sound is mentioned; this is because of the preponderance of sibilants throughout the poem. Several rich rhymes also contribute to the poem's sound orchestration. The rhyme scheme is abab while the iambic metric pattern shows some irregularities. Five-foot lines are combined with six-foot lines; the latter lines are usually broken by a caesura.

NIKIFOROV-VOLGIN, VASILY AKIMOVICH (-1940?)

The son of a shoemaker in Narva, Vasily Nikiforov-Volgin did not receive any formal education. From early childhood he was interested in spiritual matters, in church singing, and in the Russian Orthodox traditions. As a young man he wrote short stories, "sketches from life." Pyotr Pil'sky, a prominent journalist, critic, and a man of erudition and experience, helped him develop his literary competence. Although NIkiforov-Volgin's early work portrays the influence of Boris Zaytsev and Ivan Shmelyov, he soon found his own, stylized, approach to prose. His mode of narration is simple. There are neither unusual themes nor artificiality. Even when he uses church terminology or the Russian "*skaz*" technique (as in "O Mother Wilderness"), his style is transparent. An ardent follower of the Russian Orthodox religion, Nikiforov-Volgin, a "modern Leskov," praised the spiritual and natural beauty of the world and its Creator. He lauded the simplicity of the lives of the Russian saints and their spirituality and devotion to the Russian religious heritage. His short stories are sincere and essentially tragic. They may be referred to as *méditations religieuses*, although on the surface this description seems incongruous.

Nikiforov-Volgin has much in common with Zurov; both write nostalgically of a lost way of life and portray the impact of its spiritual dimension. Nikiforov-Volgin's stories, however, more intensely convey the loss and suffering brought by the Revolution. The beauty of nature and the ancient Russian traditions contrasts with the monumental suffering caused by the Revolution. These themes run parallel in his work. The story "O Mother Wilderness" initially seems concerned with the personal tragedy of Semyon, his love for the land, and his acceptance of death. But behind the story lies the greater tragedy of the peasant's separation from his traditional way of life caused by war and revolution. "The Sealed Altar" conveys the intense emotions stirred by long-established Easter celebrations and describes the perpetuation of religious traditions in the face of persecution.

The imagery used in the stories harmonizes with the religious themes. This is particularly evident in "The Saints' Matins," where the color white predominates, stressing the holiness of the three saints and the purity of nature. Everything, including the saints, is "covered with snow," and whatever is white in the saints' simple dress is given special attention. Nicholas wears a "frost-hardened sheepskin coat"; Sergey, "a skullcap, white with snow"; and Serafim, "a white quilted jacket." And "their white beards flutter in the wind." The whiteness of the snow covered Russian land all around ties in with the main theme of the story: Holy Russia, though "darkened with sins" and "stained with the blood of the Revolution," is really "just a child...the Lord's gentle reverie," and will repent and be saved.

In the short story "Hunger," Nikiforov-Volgin again introduces the theme of human suffering. The description of the starving family is a powerful indictment of the agonies brought on by the Revolution of 1917. It is written in a simple, almost childlike manner and reminds one of Tolstoy's style in "Stories for the People." The imagery, with the use of white and glowing light heightening the sense of spirituality, is typical of Nikiforov-Volgin. The white of the blizzard roves around the house and the moonlike light of the lantern transforms the starving family into ghostly, supernatural figures. The effect is neither weak nor vague. The author is capable of strong, almost brutal images like the one comparing hunger to a wild beast in the dark. The image of the cross appears three times.

"Nikiforov-Volgin was a gentleman, an honest, modest, and pious man, completely devoted to Russian literature and Russian religious culture," said N. E. Andreyev. "Endowed with the power of keen observation, he developed a beautiful manner of narration. He knew in advance that the Red Army would arrest him because of the spiritual content of his stories" and his portrayal of the drunkenness and brutality of soldiers in the Red Army, where the Bible, the icons, and the Russian Orthodox Church had been forgotten.

Nikiforov-Volgin was arrested by the Soviets in 1940. He apparently died in a labor camp.

> *Zemlya imeninnitsa* (The Earth's Nameday; Tallinn: Russkaya kniga, n.d.)

Hunger

We were all hungry. We had not laughed for a long time, but today something was funny. It was little six-year-old Vovka who made us laugh. This is what happened. Vovka who stood by the stove for a long time looking at the yellow, soot-covered bricks, suddenly said in a serious tone: "The bricks look like bread."

When he said these words, the paralyzed father was the first to laugh. His laughter was hoarse and choking, more like sobbing. He was joined by the shy, ringing laughter of the mother. Looking at them, Vovka and I began to laugh too; we rocked with laughter and tears, until we could no longer breathe. It was strange; during the laughter, afraid to look at each other, we tried to close our eyes, like birds when they sing.

But there was a moment when we suddenly glanced at

each other and at once, as if in agreement, we stopped laughing. And for some reason we were ashamed of our laughter.

It became quiet in the room. One could hear the snowflakes as they tapped against the window; the street lantern screeched rustily as it was rocked by the wind.

Vovka's weeping broke the silence.

The weeping of the hungry, like their laughter, is terrible. It resembles a howling beast hungry in the dark, snowy woods under the blue, frosty stars.

The mother bent over Vovka and anxiously asked: "What is the matter, my dear boy?"

Vovka hid his disheveled head in the folds of her dress, and through tears he said: "What are you laughing about?"

"Is it really forbidden to laugh, my little one?" asked the mother, who kept her unblinking eyes on the black cross of the window frame behind which a scraggly rowan tree rocked, as a blizzard began to blow.

"There is no reason to laugh," Vovka answered quietly, lowering his head. "You are so terrible when you laugh!"

By the window the father sat in an old armchair; he looked at the stormy, darkening street and whispered, as if in a drunken delirium: "And what if, instead of snow, flour fell from the sky? But now, instead of flour, snow falls from the sky...and a brick looks like bread...Give me some bread," the father suddenly began to shout.

"There is no bread..." the mother answered in a whisper and folded her arms cross-like on her chest.

"You are lying! You have bread! I smell the bread!"

With the word "bread" Vovka went up to his mother and began to cry: "Mama, I am hungry!"

The mother held her head in her hands and groaned.

"You are crying, dear Mama?" asked Vovka, embracing her knees. "I will not be hungry. I do not want anything. Put me to sleep."

With a terrible cry the mother fell upon Vovka; she began to beat him with her fists and tear at his hair.

"Cursed one," she cried in a frenzy. "You torment me! You crucify me on a cross!"

Vovka was hurt, but he did not cry.

The father did not stir and continued his incoherent,

starving delirium: "Instead of flour, snow falls...Soon the long, long night will come, and we shall fall asleep so peacefully that nobody will even know that we have no bread."

I put my arms around the panic-stricken mother and put her to bed. When she calmed down, she quietly called to Vovka.

He went up to his mother, pressed against her, and she kissed his tear-stained eyes.

Outside the window the wind rocked the lantern, and our whole, gloomy, cold room was filled with tossing shadows. The light of the lantern with its moon-like reflections fell on our faces, which seemed ghostly, transparently delicate, without physical bodies.

In order to lull Vovka, the mother began to sing his favorite song in a quiet, lullaby voice.

"The Christ Child had a garden
and many roses He grew in it.
He watered it three times a day,
in order to weave a wreath later."

It is terrible when the hungry laugh, terrible when the hungry cry, but nothing is more terrible than when a hungry mother sings a lullaby to her hungry child.

———————·———————

(*Chimes*, No. 32, May 1927)

The Sealed Altar

Dedicated to S. V. K.

Bells rang out in the heart of the forest.

It was a clear, flowing sound, like the distant bubbling of a spring.

Like dusk flowing into dawn, it tenderly merged with the April birch forest, the evening mist, the pools of melted snow in the forest, the rustling of spring...

I had lost my way in the dense wood, and now I set out in the direction of the murmuring sound...

Nestled in a white circle of slender birches stood a

shabby, secluded, little monastery. The log church shone golden in the evening sun...

And in the stairwell of the belfry the white-haired bell ringer in his purple skullcap could be seen.

I entered the sacred gates of the cloister.

The doors of the cells barely clung to their rusty hinges. On the roof were bricks from the demolished chimney, and the ruins of the burnt chapel lay in a brown heap.

The birches swayed, and the solemn Easter ringing subsided. Silence.

I sat down to rest on a white stone by the grave of the ascetic monk, Pafnuty, and my thoughts involuntarily turned to the past...

Thus it was, I thought, probably even in the time of Sergy of Radonezh...

The same dense forest, the wooden church, the quiet brook-like ringing, and the humble figure of the monk in the stairwell of the low belfry.

The last peal faded into the sky, the sunset, and the purple twilight...It was an April evening.

And, with the serenity of a quiet evening, the white-haired monk approached me.

He was tranquil and ethereal.

"I am the bell ringer Antony," he said, extending his hand.

"How do you do..."

"Rarely does anyone visit our monastery nowadays. You can see what devastation!"

"Are there many brothers here?"

"Besides myself, there is no one. They left for a land faraway...Some have succumbed to decrepit old age and joined the eternal light, some have gone out into the world, and still others died a martyr's death..."

"A martyr's death!" he repeated as he made the sign of the cross. "The Bolsheviks were here. On the evening of the Feast of the Assumption...They beat us. They desecrated the place. They ran their bayonets through the icons. They went into the sanctuary with their hats on. They set fire to the chapel. That night they shot the ascetic monk Feoktist, the priests Grigory and Makedony, the novice Veniamin, the deacon Sergy...

"Only I remained at the monastery. To the end of my days, I will observe the monastic rites. Just as before, I ring the bells, say the prayers, dig in the kitchen garden, go to the forest for firewood..."

In the old bell ringer's eyes, the setting sun was reflected clearly and peacefully:

"I am not alone here in God's domain...Look at the graves...All their inhabitants are invisibly present in this place...I believe that when I ring the bells, they rise up and quietly walk toward the church, in an invisible throng...

"For five years the gates to the Lord's altar have been sealed, and there is no one to perform the liturgy...But I keep the church open.

"And today as well, my son, whenever you wish we will go into the church. Tomorrow is Easter Monday. I will sing 'The Bridegroom Will Come at Midnight' and 'The Adorned Mansion.'"

We entered the gloomy little log church which smelled of the forest and incense.

Antony lighted a candle in front of the closed altar gates and proceeded to the choir loft.

Stars were already twinkling in the blue dusk outside the small lancet windows.

In the churchyard the birch trees rustled, and the monk Antony sang the Matin of the Great Passion, with a lamenting melody as ancient as the Kitezh and Murom forests:

"The impassable, agitated sea...Glory to the Lord by Whose command the sea had dried up..."

Narva

---·---

The Old and the New, No. 1
(October 1931)

O Mother Wilderness

On a clear blue spring day, along a forest path winding under the green shade of the fragrant birch trees, Red Army soldier Semyon Zavitukhin, with the measured pace of an invalid, walked home to his native Tver' province. He was a country lad, straw-haired and short in stature, with a pale consumptive face and lustreless light blue eyes.

"I am going home to die on my native soil," he told his friends from the same region when he left, "to lay my bones near Volga, my mother, which I haven't seen for ten years, near the rye fields and the forgotten grave of my ancestors, where lights are constantly flickering over the graves, and a gentle consoling melody wafts from the windows of the log church in the cemetery."

Semyon Zavitukhin was very ill. During the Civil War, while lying on the freezing autumn ground, he had caught a cold and started coughing up blood and wasting like a burning candle. They discharged Zavitukhin and let him go where he would.

Semyon walked through the birch forest.

Its blue depths overflowed with the sun, the flowers, the freshness of the blossoming birches, and an ineffable heavenly beauty.

"Ah, how glorious!" thought Zavitukhin, greedily breathing in the fragrant birch wine. In the frenzied succession of revolutionary days when Semyon had been healthy, he hadn't noticed all the beauty so generously scattered throughout the sunny spring earth. Red Army soldier Zavitukhin had no time to think about blue heavens and tender birches and flowers when people were saying the White Army "hydra" was just around the corner and capitalist mercenaries were trying to destroy the achievements of the October Revolution.

When he remembered the years gone by, the Revolution, the oppressive Civil War, the executions of his fellow countrymen, Zavitukhin would curse with a strong, sobbing word and from his agitation start to cough, choking up blood.

Lying down on the fragrant warm earth, he pressed his pale consumptive face to it; he tore off the pungent, stocky little leaves from the birches and, breathing in their intoxicating aroma, reproached himself with bitter anguish.

"What happiness you have missed, Sen'ka Zavitukhin! And what did you get for it?"

Biting anger arose in his soul, and to suppress it he

began thinking about his native village, Korostelovo, on the banks of the Volga, the forgotten joys of peasant toil, and the sunrises over the dewy rye fields. He remembered the native apple trees in their snow-white blossoms, his mother, the age-old songs of the village girls, and everything that brought joy and meaning to all living things, everything that had been so mercilessly destroyed by the Revolution's fire.

Semyon felt like singing the old song about dusk with its many bright stars, its stars without number, but he started to cough and broke off singing.

The closer Zavitukhin came to the Volga and the more keenly he felt the breath of its broad expanse, the more peaceful and reconciled his soul became.

He sensed a purity and a tenderness as at times in his early childhood when, in a white shirt, he had stood in the village church before Christ's golden chalice and waited to receive Holy Communion.

The sun had set beyond the distant hazy forests and a blessed evening stillness had descended upon the twilight Volga and the thatched roofs of the village of Korostelovo. Exhausted and hardly breathing in his excitement, Semyon reached his old hut with its toppled fence and its apple trees all white in bloom.

Not daring to go into the hut immediately, he sat down on a bench under the apple trees and started to cough.

The door of the hut squeaked and a little old peasant woman, dressed in black like a nun, appeared on the porch.

Whether it was her maternal instinct telling her that her lost son was sitting on the bench, or pity for this tired man coughing up blood, or whether he reminded her of her son, she came down the shaky, creaky porch steps and, with the soft tread of an old woman, she sat down beside him. Without a word, she began to stroke the pale, bony hands of the stranger.

Zavitukhin started; seeing the dear face of his mother, he impetuously sank to the ground, lay his head in her lap, and began to weep:

"Mama!..."

He had many beautiful, tender words stored up in his heart for his mother, but all he could say was "Mama!"

Everything was expressed in that one word alone—his

joy and tenderness, his anguish and his weariness.

His mother warmly and firmly embraced his thin neck and softly wept for joy; she too was unable to find words to express her unexpected happiness.

Semyon pressed himself to her mother's bosom and could hear her heart beating.

He started coughing. Blood rushed from his throat. It flowed onto his chin and crept thickly down his green military field shirt like the little scarlet snakes.

His mother took out a handkerchief and began to wipe her son's chin. With infinite anxiety and tenderness, she asked:

"Senichka! My son! What's happened to you, my darling?"

"It's nothing, Mama," her son consoled her, trying to smile. "It will go away. I'll get better. I'll help you...That fence needs mending. The apple trees need to be pruned...see how they've gotten out of hand...Don't you worry about me, Mama. It will go away. I don't cough so much now and I seem to be a little better."

Dropping off to sleep in his own beloved home, for a long time, through the light veil of his slumber, Zavitukhin heard his mother praying before the old icons, and the apple trees in white bloom rustling outside his window.

*

In the morning Zavitukhin woke up with the sunrise. Carefully, so as not to wake his mother, he went out of the hut onto the porch.

The morning was warm and rosy. The white cloudlets floated in soft curls. Dew lay on the white apple blossoms. A transparent mist hung over the distant forests and fields. A coolness wafted from the sky blue Volga. The peasant land was clothed in sunshine and sky blue vestments.

A forgotten peasant response arose in Semyon's soul.

He yearned for work, that beloved peasant work in which an entire generation of Zavitukhin's had found the joy, meaning, and justification for life.

Obsessed by his desire for work, he no longer wanted to think about his mortal illness.

"It's nothing," he comforted himself with a smile. "It will pass. I will breathe the country air and become strong. Everything will be all right, after all."

Semyon strolled about the yard, and with an owner's eye he examined the overgrown apple trees, the toppled fence, the precarious, rotten steps of the porch. Like an owner, in a businesslike, singsong voice, he declared:

"There's a lot to be done! See how it's all gone to pot. Well, God willing, we'll put everything back in order again..."

The prickly gurgle of a cough rose in his chest, but Zavitukhin tried to suppress it, hoping to stifle the thought of his illness.

In the shed he found an axe. He got some nails and was about to mend the broken fence, but he didn't get even one nail in before he felt faint. He sat down on the ground and began to cough in a long wheezing gasp.

When his cough had quieted, he went up to an apple tree, embraced its rough trunk, and began to weep.

He returned to the hut looking very pale, his legs trembling. He lay down on the plank over the stove, gazing in anguish at the golden sun rays shining into the hut and the shadows of the old overgrown flowering apple trees trembling on the wall.

*

Semyon Zavitukhin's last days on this earth passed like the melting twilight or a dwindling wax candle in a lonely church. The final agony of death arrived. He thought no more of the earth or of work...His thoughts more often were fixed on something beyond the earth, beyond the sun and the stars, on the eternal world that blind pilgrims had sung about so sadly once beneath his windows.

He often called for his mother, stroked her wrinkled hands, and kept asking her to tell him something about the old days when forests were thicker and cornfields more fertile, when people were stronger and everything was different.

And his mother, hardly able to suppress her sobbing, told him in ancient verse of days long past.

The lofty, subtle harmony of his thoughts and moods mingled with his mother's ancient lyrics, and a peculiar consolation entered his soul.

*

One golden September day he summoned his mother
and said to her:
"Mama...dearest...Take me to the Nikolin Hermitage.   I
want to pray before I die and cleanse myself with
repentance...I have a lot of sins, Mama...Oh, so many... Some
terrible sins!"
"Won't it be too hard on you, Senichka?   It's about
thirty *versts* to the Nikolin Hermitage, and you'll get
exhausted on the road, my son."
"Don't hinder me, Mama.   Let this road be my one
heroic deed, my chains of penance.   Take me to the
Hermitage..."
"Hermitage...wilderness."[1]   Semyon whispered deliriously.
"Such a pleasant word...a calm, comforting word...You
remember, Mama, how you used to sing about the beautiful
mother wilderness?"
"Mother wilderness, shelter the poor orphan!"
So that her son would not see her grief, Semyon's
mother went out into the hallway and wept.

*

They dressed Semyon in a clean white shirt, wrapped
him in a sheepskin coat, and, supporting him under his arms,
walked him to the cart and put him on the straw.   And so
on that chilly golden September day the mother took her son
to the Nikolin Hermitage.
Semyon lay in the cart and with large eyes made
brighter by his long illness gazed at the deep blue sky.   He
no longer had any desire to remain on earth, but wished to
merge quickly with the infinite expanse of sky, to lie down
under a weathered cross, side by side with his ancestors,
under a canopy of mournful birches, in the cemetery beside
the log church from which gentle, consoling melodies drift.
With bowed head his mother led the horse by the bridle
and softly repeated the Jesus prayer.   They travelled through
the wide Russian fields.   Leaves were falling from the

roadside birches.

Night found them on the road, in the middle of a lonely, deserted field.

Cold and austere, with countless stars, the night enveloped the lonely sufferers.

It was cold and desolate. The mother bent over the face of her sick son, warming him with her own breath; she adjusted his pillow and covered his legs with straw.

The mother sensed her son's suffering and through her tears comforted him with stories about the old days, about the dense forests where the small secluded monasteries of ascetics lay hidden and where wise ascetics dwelt; about his ancestors, strong as oaks, and happy and wise as the earth they cultivated. And she even sang for her son the hymn about the beautiful mother wilderness and about the oak groves of the Lord, strewn with the flowers of paradise.

After Communion in the Nikolin Hermitage former Red Army soldier Semyon Zavitukhin died. He died more quietly than a golden leaf falls from a tree, and even his mother did not hear his last sigh.

With the help of the monks the mother laid her son on the cart. Through those same sad autumn fields, under the same deep blue sky, and accompanied by those same songs of the autumn wind, she carried him, with her head bowed low, back to Korostelovo, to the grave of his fathers, where the old birch trees so caressingly nod over the weathered crosses, where lights are constantly flickering over the graves. Just as before, night found them on the road, and many stars looked down on them.

It was cold and desolate. Withered leaves whirled. Just as before, the mother adjusted her son's pillow, wrapped his legs, and covered his dead body with the sheepskin, as if he were cold in this lonely autumn darkness. As a lament, she quietly sang to him of the beautiful mother wilderness and the oak groves of the Lord, strewn with the flowers of paradise.

Narva

Chimes, No. 10 (January 1926)

The Saints' Matins
(On New Year's Eve)

Covered white with snow, Nicholas the Miracle-Worker, Sergy of Radonezh, and Serafim of Sarov make thier way across the dusky, wide-open fields.

A wind sweeps along the ground and snowdrifts crack in the frost. The blizzard whirls. Frost glazes the desolate, snow-covered ground.

Nicholas the Miracle-Worker is wearing an old sheepskin coat and big felt boots full of holes. On his back is a knapsack; in his hand, a staff.

Sergy of Radonezh is in monastic garb. On his head is a skullcap, white with snow; on his feet, bast shoes.

Serafim of Sarov, in a white quilted jacket and high Russian boots, walks hunched over his stick...

Their white beards flutter in the wind. The snow blinds their eyes. It is cold for the holy elders in the solitary, icy darkness.

"There's a frost for you, a wicked one, there's a sly old devil for you!" Nicholas the Miracle-Worker says cheerfully again and again; and to get warm, he beats his peasant mittens against the frost-hardened sheepskin coat and hurries along with a frisky, old man's gait, his felt boots swishing through the snow.

"This old frost is really laying into us old fellows, and how!...It's so merciless—calm it down, O Lord—it's so merciless!" Serafim laughs and also runs skipping along, not far behind the frisky Nicholas, and his boots ring out against the hard, frosty ground.

"This is nothing!" Sergy smiles quietly, "but in 1347, now there was a frost for you! Grisly..."

"Sure is blizzardy. What if we lose our way in the open field?" Serafim says.

"We won't get lost, fathers!" Nicholas replies cheerfully. "I know all the Russian highways and byways. Soon we'll get to the Kitezh Forest, and in a little church there we'll honor the Lord and celebrate matins. Quicken your pace, fathers!..."

"O frisky miracle-worker!" Sergy says with a quiet smile, holding him back by the sleeve, "So persistent! From foreign lands himself, yet he loves the Russian land above all others. Nicholas, how have you come to love our nation, darkened with sins? Why do you walk along its mournful roads and pray for it tirelessly?"

"How did I come to love it?" Nicholas answers, looking into Sergy's eyes. "She's just a child—Holy Russia!...A meek, fragrant flower... The Lord's gentle reverie...His favorite child...Unreasonable, but beloved. And who will not grow to love a child, who will not be touched by a little flower? Russia is the gentle reverie of the Lord."

"Well have you spoken about Russia, Nicholas," Serafim whispers. "Beloved ones, I feel like kneeling before her and praying, as if to a sacred icon!"

"But, Holy Fathers," Sergy timidly asks, "what about the bloody years of 1917, 1918, and 1919? Why did the Russian nation stain itself with blood?"

"It will repent!" Nicholas the Miracle-Worker answers with conviction.

"It will be saved!" Serafim asserts.

"We will pray for it!" whispers Sergy.

They reach the tiny forest church, covered with snow.

They light the candles before the dark icons and begin to celebrate matins.

Beyond the walls of the church the snowy Kitezh Forest moans. The blizzard sings.

In this desolate forest church, the saints of the Russian land pray for Russia—the beloved of the Savior, the gentle reverie of the Lord.

And after matins, the three intercessors walk out of the church onto the porch and bless on all four sides the snowy land, the blizzard, and the night.

Narva

NOTE

1. In Russian the words have a common root: hermitage (pustyn'), wilderness (pustynya).

NAZAREVSKY, BORIS (b. 1911?)

Nazarevsky, a graduate of the Russian Orthodox Theological Seminary in Pechory, was a teacher in the Province of Prichudye in the Lake Peipus region and was an extremely well-read and pleasant man.   He wrote about the fishermen in his area and contributed various pieces to Russian journals in Estonia. Dramatic collisions and events form the substance of his plots, which occasionally lapse into sentimentalism.   But he was a talented writer and a cultured man. His fate is unknown.

The Virgin Soil, No. 7 (1934)

Epiphany Eve[1] in Obozerye (The Lake Regions)

A Sketch

The red-yellow flame of the sunset blazes above the distant pine forest; the sky burns with a glow, merging higher into a bright yellow and then eastward into a frosty green with pale sparks of faintly flickering stars.   The ice, with its blue-violet shadows from snowdrift islands, reflects red and orange patches of light.

The bells of the little village church by the shore echo audibly in the frozen silence.   Worshippers file out of the church along paths trampled through the snowdrifts.   They carry bottles, jugs, and urns of holy water.

From the lake, in small, dark clusters one after another, come groups of fishermen, returning late, talking and shouting noisily.   The fishermen wear large boots with high tops, and leather aprons wrapped tightly around them and fastened with pieces of rope made from twisted nets; they are all covered with frozen spray...They jump off the sleighs and, clapping their hay-filled leather gloves to warm their hands, run clumsily alongside the horses, and again tumble on the run onto the sleighs.   All their faces are red, chapped from the cold, with white frost-covered eyebrows; icicles hang from their beards and moustaches.   The heavy, ice-encrusted aprons rustle and strike against their knees; they breathe out clouds of steam; the little horses snort tossing their manes, and crunch the ice with their hooves.

The narrow fishing sleighs are piled high with wet nets and weights; ice picks and spades rattle, and the long fishing poles, tied to the sleighs, twist about like white snakes far behind.

Stopping abruptly at the shore, the fisherman gather and loudly, quickly hack the ice with their picks. They cut a big trough in the ice, dump the nets and weights from the sleighs into it, and shove them into the water under the ice so they won't freeze together.

The young people run off to the side and cheerfully and hastily hack a huge "Jordan" cross out of the ice. They pull the cross out of the water and drag it to the assigned place. Little children bring up old Christmas trees on sleds and pile them onto the ice.

The ice cross is zealously smoothed out and polished; in its center a round opening is carefully carved out. They cut a hole in the ice the same size as the cross and insert the cross into it upright. They stick the fir trees into the ice all around it, and—"Jordan is finished!"

Then they run to the sleighs where the leader of the fisherman is dividing the fish by hand with a scoop; holding up their aprons, they advance in turn, get the fish and then, covered with hoarfrost and ice, hurriedly tramp off to their huts.

*

The air is still. In the dark blue sky, stars shine and twinkle and, suddenly breaking away and flashing by almost imperceptibly, fall and vanish in the fathomless darkness. Hoarfrost falls from the sky in flurries and settle silently onto the snow in gentle flakes.

The solemn, frosty silence of Epiphany Eve is broken only by the barking of dogs and the crackling of ice in the frost. Here and there a door slams and hurried footsteps crunch across the snow. Long hissing shots roll across the lake and halt with a hollow moaning echo in the sky over the lake's far reaches.

Dim, yellow lights pierce through the iced-up windows

of the huts, piled high with snow, and cast paths of light on
the snowdrifts.   From the chimneys, blue smoke stretches in
long, thin wisps and rises high into the starry sky.   Supper is
cooking in the village.   On the ice, near the fishing sledges
and ice holes, cats fight and whine...

After supper, the fishermen gather in their huts to
socialize.   Comfortably seated on benches, they talk about
what is new, about fishing and other things...It is hot in the
huts, smoky.   *Makhorka* [a homegrown tobacco] smoke hovers
just below the ceiling in a dense, bluish cloud.

There is an odor of fresh fish, fusty hides, and tar.
Wet fishing clothes and boots hang over the hearth,
splattering heavy drops as they thaw out.

On the village streets there is life, squeals, and
restrained laughter.   Children go about in masks and funny
costumes; they are covered with straw and wearing sheepskin
coats turned inside out...The young girls flock together to tell
fortunes.   They run up to a window and abruptly start
singing loudly and off-key.   Then, breaking off the song, they
run away shrieking and laughing with the boys in pursuit...

The loud, ringing echo of a wedding song is carried
across the frozen silence far onto the lake and merges there
with the crackling of the ice.

The young girls huddle together fearfully around the
dark, ramshackle bathhouse at the foot of the hill and,
gathering courage, jump in together, each one grabbing a
sooty, black rock from the bathhouse stove; shoving one
another they rush headlong away[2]...They crowd together and
with anxiety in their hearts they feel the sooty stones.   Are
they smooth, or rough and angular?...

Covering their eyes, they measure the fence with their
arms and count the stakes.   Odd or even...They run onto the
ice in single file, timidly hold on to one another, bend down,
and gaze with fearful looks into the freezing ice hole.   What
is it they see?...

And then, stealing pine branches from someone's pile,
they hurriedly and secretly stick them in the snow between
the houses where the intended bride and groom live...And
again they sing beneath the window and scatter, shrieking.

Old men, throwing their coats over their shoulders, walk
out onto the porch and gaze a long time at the sky, reading

in the stars what the summer will be like, how the harvest will be, how many mushrooms and berries there will be this summer, and how many fish will come to the shore in the spring...

In the huts people sit around the table after dinner and tell fortunes. Some shriveled old woman suddenly creeps out from behind the stove and, untying the string of keys from her belt and lighting a lamp, walks stiffly into the passage to fumble and rummage for something in an old moth-eaten trunk. From the very bottom she gets out the dried beans that had been buried there wrapped in a rug; rusty and ossified with age, they were passed on to her in legacy. She lays them out on the table and whispers something with her mumbling, toothless mouth...

The old woman tells fortunes and predicts what awaits each person in the coming year...Thin wisps of gray hair fall out from beneath the scarf sitting awry on her head and cling to her wrinkled face; her head and flabby cheeks quiver, her old hands shake, her pale, drawn lips whisper something, and her old eyes intently follow the beans as they scatter across the table...

The boys are bored; they roam the streets in throngs and, having nothing else to do, chase the young girls and push them into snowdrifts. The girls scream and run and hide in the huts.

Then, upon mutual agreement, the boys catch a sleepy rooster from someone's yard, take it inside, and also begin to tell fortunes. They set the rooster on the floor in the center of the hut and sprinkle grain in small heaps around it, one heap for each person. Some on benches, others on the floor, they sit quietly and wait to see whose grain the rooster will peck...Blinded by the light, the sleepy rooster totters to see what is going on around it. For fun and laughs they open its beak and pour vodka down its throat. The rooster sneezes and angrily shakes its head. Then, after standing and thinking awhile, it yawns and begins to talk to itself quietly about something and plucks at itself with an air of importance. The boys sit holding their breath and, stifling their laughter, await the performance.

Scratching its beak with its claw and swaying drunkenly, the rooster suddenly thrusts out its chest, stretches its neck—and screeches. It sings on and on, spreading its wings and angrily ruffling its neck feathers. Sensing the grain on the floor, it scatters it frenziedly with its claws, beckons the hens, sings arrogantly, staggers and, completely drunk, collapses on its side, stretches out its claws, and closes its eyes...

*

At midnight the village quiets down. Lights still burn in only a few of the huts. There, sitting up late, people cast spells and tell fortunes.

In one of the huts a door creaks mysteriously, and a bareheaded and barefooted young woman slips out into the frost with a sieve and a mug of holy water in her hands. She looks around cautiously in all directions and runs around the house at full speed for some reason...Then she glides barefoot across the snow, runs, pours water through the sieve, and keeps repeating something...She is casting an evil spell...

On the way home, out of mischief, as a prank, the boys prop poles up against the doors of the huts on the outside, cover the doors with brushwood, or dig out a snow-covered boat on the shore, drag it uphill, and lean it against a door...

Stealing up to the huts where the windows are still lit and pressing their faces against the frozen glass, they breathe on it and, melting a circle, peer inside to see what is happening...Another young woman, when everyone in the house is fast asleep, undresses completely and with a broom in hand rampages through the house, hissing and chasing someone from corner to corner...She is driving out cockroaches and every kind of evil spirit. Then she sweeps the floor, wraps the debris in a rag, and schemes until the morning bell to bring a neighbor evil...

Soon even the last lights are put out. Sleep and frozen silence descend and reign over the village powdered with snow. And only the roosters in the henhouse, waking at the appointed hour, call out to one another; dogs, alarmed by something, howl, and the restless ice on the lake drones unceasingly, breaking in the frost.

———————·———————

Nazarevsky's description of a holiday eve in a distant northern village is vibrant with life, exciting and colorful. One can almost physically sense the intense cold and the ceaseless motion and excitement. There is nothing personal in this sketch; there is no plot, and the characters remain flat, mere figurines rather than developed individualities. But the straightforward, detailed description of the life-style of these northern Russians is highly fascinating. The piece resembles a panoramic Flemish painting of village life, full of *couleur locale*, movement, and penetratingly distinct sounds and smells.

Epiphany, according to the old Russian tradition, was a time of witchery and prophecy. Not only peasants and common people, but also young girls of the nobility hoped to catch a glimpse of their fate on this night. (In *Eugene Onegin*, Pushkin's heroine Tatyana tries to see her future on Epiphany Eve.) The mighty force of the cold—as ice snaps and cracks and snow covers everything—contrasts with the warmth of intense human activity. The reader is left with the impression of an ancient way of life firmly rooted in nature and in the continuity of a tradition where religious and pagan elements are curiously interlaced. (Cf. In *The Lay of Igor*, written in 1186, supernatural pagan figures appear side by side with the images characteristic of the Russian Orthodox religion.) Nazarevsky's language is vivid and vigorous, abounding in colloquialisms and even substandard Russian expressions, yet the author's moderation is obvious throughout. Through its strangely exotic atmosphere and poetic metaphors, the piece evinces a strong evocative power.

————————·————————

NOTES

1.   Twelfth Night, January 6. In northern Russia this holiday is associated with an elaborate tradition of necromancy and fortunetelling.
2.   The bathhouse was believed to be the abode of evil spirits.

LATVIA

CHINNOV, IGOR' VLADIMIROVICH (b. 1909)

Igor' Chinnov, the son of a lawyer, bibliophile, and polyglot, was born in Riga. He holds a law degree from the University of Riga (1939) and a *licence ès lettres* from the Sorbonne (1947). Having fled Latvia during World War II, Chinnov lived in Paris as an independent *littérateur* until 1952. He then worked for Radio Liberty in Munich (1953-1962), contributing to programs on contemporary French and German literatures and art. Living in the United States since 1962, Chinnov has held successive professorships in Russian literature at the University of Kansas, the University of Pittsburgh, and Vanderbilt University. His first poems and essays appeared in Riga in the Russian literary journal *Mansarda* (The Garret; Riga, 1930, Nos. 1-6) and in *Numbers* (Paris). But he was not acclaimed as a poet until 1950, when his first book of poetry, *Monolog* (The Monologue), appeared in Paris. Sergey Makovsky praised the poems for their "ethereal beauty and glowing reflections." After *The Monologue*, Chinnov published the following collections of verse: *Linii: vtoraya kniga stikhov* (Lines: A Second Book of Poetry; Paris: Rifma, 1960), *Metafory: tretya kniga stikhov* (Metaphors: A Third Book of Poetry; New York: Novy zhurnal, 1968), *Partitura* (A Musical Score; New York: Novy zhurnal, 1970), *Kompozitsiya: pyataya kniga stikhov* (Composition: A Fifth Book of Poetry; Paris: Rifma, 1972), *Pastorali* (Pastorals; Paris: Rifma, 1976), *Antiteza: sed'maya kniga stikhov* (Antithesis: A Seventh Book of Poetry; College Park, MD: Birchbark Press, 1979), *Avtograf: vos'maya kniga stikhov* (The Autograph: An Eighth Book of Poetry, Holyoke, MA: New England Publishing Co., 1984). Chinnov also contributed to various Russian journals and anthologies.

As Victor Terras aptly remarked, Chinnov's concrete imagery encompasses the intellectual, emotional, and aesthetic experiences of a well-travelled and well-read European. He is a skeptic, yet with the true affection for religion; a sober observer of this life, yet eager to catch glimpses of another, mystic reality. His early poems reveal a purely aesthetic *Weltanschauung*. Empirical reality is deceptive; life is a flow of events that bring forth diverse associations connected with the organic whole by the *persona's* contemplative sadness. These verses convey the delicate transfigurations of empirical reality into its shadow, its otherwordly, ephemeral existence. Everything on earth is an illusion, a reflection of some universal, incomprehensible mystery. The enveloping world of material reality teems with dark shadows of an unfathomable cosmic process.[1]

From a formal point of view, Chinnov's early works must be linked with Acmeism and the "Parisian note" poetry.[2] Despite its gnoticism and perpetual striving for contact with a higher reality, the poetry is precise in its imagery and characterized by strict formal control. The verse is very short and often ends abruptly. There is a certain reticence in the thoughts and in the description of emotion. Parenthetical clauses appear between dashes or in brackets. There is a serenity of restrained epithets. An absence of active verbs give a great variety of static, visual images, mainly of inanimate objects. A tendency to conceal the formal polish of the verse, and an occasional hint of irony are also typical. His themes are the "eternally important" (also a characteristic of the "Parisian note"): love, death, human solitude, and beautiful nature. No moral, religious, or philosophical questions are raised. Every sound has its own function in this lyrical variety of emotional sketches. His thought is elusive, expressed in colorful, bright, metallic, and shining fragments of sensations, allusions, and melodies. It is not easy to reconstruct the unity of Chinnov's images or to synthesize his ideas. Despite the concrete outlines of details and the absence of rhetoric, his poems are difficult to paraphrase.

Chinnov's later work is dressed in a decorative "poetic garments," rich in color, graceful in outline, alliteration, and delicate images. *Lines* shows a tendency toward freer rhythms, mysticism, and a slightly more optimistic outlook. Since *A Musical Score*, Chinnov has been manifesting an increasing tendency toward the grotesque and the fantastic, mixing poetic and prosaic language, word games, free verse, and sound symbolism. A poet who had always cultivated the euphonic side of his verse, he now develops sound patterns as genuine "sub-text," and creates surrealistic trains of etymological and acoustic associations. The poet presently smiles sardonically at life's enigmas and mysteries. The world is absurd, life is void of any loftier meaning, the universe is cruel and senseless, and the *persona* can enjoy only sensual perception and purely aesthetic pleasure. Human freedom and an aversion for the

mechanization of man are Chinnov's primary concerns. His former
Neo-Acmeism, with its half tones and crystalline perceptions, has
been supplanted by a new, fantastic, chimeric world, with an
underlying irony and grotesque symbolic, static images.[3]   The
themes in *A Music Score*, *Antithesis*, and *The Autograph* include
hell, death, autumn, apathy, hopelessness, the prodigal son,
childhood, and nostalgia for Russia.   They are treated with irony,
sometimes turning into satire.   But these somber ideas are
contrasted with the poet's visions of beauty and reconciliation with
life.   His new artistic technique is closer to Picasso's.   Responding
to a questionnaire, Chinnov replied that in his poetry he "strives
for 1) melodiousness, 2) sonorous saturation and expressiveness,
3) rich new imagery, 4) transformation of "poeticism" modulated
by irony and prosaic locutions enobled by musicality into a single
poetic whole, 5) reflection of that beauty that exists in life against
a background of its tragic and even disgusting aspects."

Professor N. E. Andreyev and the poet Boris Nartsissov
praised Chinnov's elegiac tone, his rhymes, intentional repetitions in
the middle of the verse, alliteration, word play, Lermontovian irony
changing into anxiety, expressive imagery, and always evident
erudition.   Andreyev stated: "Chinnov is an excellent poet who
understands the power of words, as only Pushkin did before.   He
has his own unmistakable signature in all of his poetry; he has his
own, unique place in the history of Russian poetry."   Georgy
Adamovich, Vladimir Weidlé, and Yury Terapiano also lauded
Chinnov's artistic skill, the originality of his poetic universe.

NOTES

1.   *Columbia Dictionary of Modern European Literature* (2nd edition, 1980).
     Jean-Albert Bédé and William B. Edgerton, General Editors, pp.
     161-162.
2.   Ref. Gleb Struve, *Russkaya literatura v izgnanii*, 2nd ed.   (Paris:
     YMCA-Press, 1984), pp. 368-369.
3.   See more about Chinnov's artistic method in John Glad's article "The
     American Chapter in Russian Poetry," *Russian Language Journal*, Vol.
     30, No. 106 (Spring 1976); Yury Ivask, "Poeziya staroy emigratsii," in
     Russkaya literatura v emigratsii: sbornik statey, pod red. N. Poltoratzkogo
     (University of Pittsburgh Press, 1972), pp. 63-65; *The Modern
     Encyclopedia of Russian and Soviet Literatures* (Academic International
     Press, 1981), IV, 87-90; *Handbook of Russian Literature*, ed. Victor
     Terras (Yale University Press, 1985), pp. 83-84; Dmitry Bobyshev,
     "Memento Mori," *Continent* (1986) Vol. 48, 397-401.

Lines: A Second Book of Poems

The fountain aspires to the moon,
And falls back—like a cypress in a storm,
When the moon is almost alive.

Are those lakes, or islands,
Or clouds, or a flight of birds?
Fountain, fantasy, caprice.

Through moonlit enchantment
My bed flows to wherever I want—
Along the shimmering roof, as if down a stream.

Strips of smoke there, in the distance—
Like snow-swept paths,
And if we are off to stroll along them—

Our words flowed on
Like strange night poetry,
And long the sound echoed,
No longer heard from the earth.

————·————

The distance seems cast in ice.
The wind has bared even the oaks.
Following the last ray of light,
The fields darken gradually.

Those who stroll in autumn groves
Do not pluck branches on the way.
The boughs hang beneath the rain,
Rustling with dead leaves.

Silvery ripples in the pond.
Imagine you see in these flowerless waters
The branches of other trees,
Dropping their unfaded blossoms:

Imagine the branches of another world,
Blossoming in an invisible garden,
And through them flows eternally
A tender, unfading light.

———————·———————

Why not let thinking machines
Replace us? Let's go
Look at the lilies of the valley
In the delicate sun-pierced rain.

Dark cares are not forgotten
In nature's angelic purity.
Two light notes fall like petals
From a white bush.

Birds blossom blue against the sky,
It seems the flowers are audible.
And the deep echo of silence merges
With the song and the flight of the birds.

All is so transparently willful,
So carefree, bantering,
And simple, without the least bit of pain...

(I've fallen into reverie like a child.)

———————·———————

An eternal image: happiness—the wind in the field,
Smoke scattered by rain.
We dwell in anxiety, fear, pain:
"Man is born for tears."

Where can you place your hopes?
In these thunderclouds?
In the dim light of the silent sky?
In its distant rays?

In the brief glimmer above the night road
Along which we'll pass in the dark?
The answer is—silence, and
A short rumble of thunder.

———————·———————

Perhaps all the same—I should say thanks:
For the delicacy of dim pearly light,
For the freshness of the garden stirred up by rain,
For the first signs—already—of fall.

Thanks for the cloud that dissolves and fades
Above the birds flying into the sunset,
And the pink glow approaching the sea...
Well then, here are my thanks. I don't really object...

———————·———————

A Music Score

Already it is getting cool,
and a slender white bird
hovers above the green water
like a remnant of a faded cloud,
or perhaps like a huge snowflake.

The beach is becoming deserted,
but the café above the lilac sand
is still open.
Let's sit down and order
vanilla ice cream,
that looks like
cold white roses.

Would you like to imagine
that these are
two portions of ambrosia
straight from Olympus?

Let's eat them and exclaim,
gazing at the mountains,
—We, too, are immortal.

_____·_____

To Nikolay Otsup

Who released into this gray sky
seven multicolored spheres?
Like seven precious tulips
placed alive in the sky.

Now it is dark, and the spheres
are followed by the lights of an airplane.
It is God decorating with colored globes
the branches of an unseen yule tree.

"It will burst like a soap bubble—and soon—
this sphere on which we dwell."
All the same, perhaps, it won't be so soon.
O, let us pursue the wandering light,
and play for a while with the vaporous light.

_____·_____

Soon sadness will be consumed by flame.
An Alpine wind will scatter
the ashes of sadness.

It might happen then
that you will feel inclined
to write the intensely felt word "sadness"
on the bright summer sand,
on the wing of a dragonfly,
the turbid current of a brook,
on the fine edge of a sunset,
on the muteness of night,
on the invisible Milky Way.

_____·_____

To Anna Prismanova

Name and patronymic are transformed
Into evening flame and cloud,

Date of birth becomes
The reflection of a tree in the lake.

Even one's own profession becomes
A fluttering, a sylph, and a song,

And the remainder of one's old address
Is transformed into a lotus and a stork.

Only imagine—one's surname is now
A pink flamingo—and a lily.

———————·———————

Antithesis: A Seventh
Book of Poems

In the park, near a faceless idol,
There were sitting some charming young men,
And one said: "If our goal is great enough,
Then mercy for the present is a lie."

To my question they replied
That it's senseless to pity the unfortunate,
Since in the coming centuries
All people will be happy—always.

Nearby an old blind man in a wheelchair
Was selling violet lilacs
(And in the azure distance, scarcely visible,
Blue swallows pierced the golden days).

I hoped that he would be healed
And see the light of the sunlit day.
The future happiness of mankind
Aroused me but little.

———————·———————

The wind of life is being stilled, weakened, subdued
in the sagging, torn sail of the body.
On the darkening dunes
sand flows out
of a huge hourglass.
O, broken glass vessel!
The grayish sky,
like a dull pearl-less shell,
expands in the early morning
over the water, drowsing, a darkened fish—
shadow of Charon's boat.

———————·———————

In the desperate prison of Necessity,
In the dungeon of cheerless Inevitability,
In the jail of hopeless Impossibility,

I long for the Lord's wondrous mercy,
I long for the Father's blessed compassion,
I cannot bear this desolation!

I long for the transparency, radiance,
Forgiveness, love, liberation,
Freedom, grace, astonishment
of Thy miracles. Miracles! Transfiguration!

I long for—resurrection from the dead!

———————·———————

A radiant wind sweeps the petals
on the water's sparkling ripple
and flies away.

Clouds hover above the river,
Uncertain landmarks
of fleeting life.

Let these transparent, empty
scraps of shining life
remain.
Or, perhaps,
let these petals of moments
sink, quivering
over the vortex.

Let them pause,
like a swift, dark school
of minnows
in the wan, autumn morning ripple
of a northern stream.

———————·———————

The three collections of Igor' Chinnov's poetry represented by these translations cover about twenty years and exemplify the development and change in the poet's style during this time. The presence of nature is all-pervasive, both in the earlier and later poems. The flight of birds against the blue sky is a recurrent image which he uses as a symbol of the poet's own soaring imagination. Often nature is a point of departure for the flight into the realm of fancy. In "The fountain aspires . . . , " "The distance seems cast in ice . . . , " and in other poems, nature is transformed by the poet's vision when the poet identifies and merges with nature. He aligns himself with nature's subtler vibrations and thus perceives it in a transformed and pure state. This perception of nature allows him to transcend life's difficulties: "Dark cares are forgotten/In nature's angelic purity." However, sometimes nature is distant and unresponsive, and inspires a sense of powerlessness ("An eternal image . . . ").

In the seventh collection, *Antithesis*, nature becomes a reflection, sometimes a metaphor, of human life. Clouds are seen as "uncertain landmarks of fleeting life"; the "petals of moments" sink in the water. The "sail of the body" becomes limp as age progresses. Now the poet feels the passing of time and the approach of death, "the shadow at Charon's boat." In despair he appeals to God ("In the desperate prison. . . ") and longs for the assurance of a higher Reality but without real conviction of its existence.

The use of color is an important element in Chinnov's collections. He favors the pearly shades of twilight—lilac, gray, and rose tones. The use of such colors accounts for the hazy quality in Chinnov's poetry. He writes about the " . . . delicacy of dim, pearly light. . . " and a "tender, unfading light." The lilac sand or the gray sky emphasizes the sadness in many of the poems. The pale shades create a light, vaporous effect so that the poems seem to float.

Yet the mistiness of the poetry does not lesson its impact. The poet has the power to change a simple item, such as ice cream, into a powerful, poetic image: " . . . vanilla ice cream, /that looks like cold white roses." And from nature he is able to evoke a vision charged with feeling, for example, " . . . a swift, dark school/of minnows/in the wan, fall, morning ripple/of a northern stream." Above all Chinnov's imagery is usually delicate and ephemeral; it is sun-pierced rain, soap bubbles, and colored spheres hanging in a dark sky.

Color and imagery merge and complement the soft and reflective tone of the poems. The poems read easily; their language is elegant and transparent. Chinnov has combined these elements to create poetry that expresses the transitory and precious nature of life.

BELOTSVETOV, NIKOLAY NIKOLAEVICH (1892-1950)

Belotsvetov was born is St. Petersburg and died and in Mühlheim, Germany, where he had settled after his escape from Latvia during the Soviet occupation in 1940. Before the annexation, he had wished to live in Tallinn but was refused permission. So, he settled in Riga, and frequently travelled to the neighboring Baltic countries to give poetry readings at various literary soirées. A prominent anthroposophist and a very tall and handsome man, Belotsvetov was also an excellent poet, much esteemed by Yury Ivask. The charm of many of his poems is that they seem to have been written as if in one breath, one continuous musical phase sometimes stretching to twelve lines. His poetry flows freely, and his poetic word is elegant in its simplicity and artistic power. His themes are eternal: God, Love, Death. His imagery is derived from the vocabulary of the Russian Orthodox Church. A deep sense of Christianity motivated his hope for the advent of a new, spiritual humanity. Belotsvetov's father, Nikolay Alexeevich, a wealthy man, likewise devoted to the Russian cultural tradition and historical past, subsidized the Russian journal *Chimes* and the newspaper *Russian World*, both in Riga.

Belotsvetov admired the poetry of Osip Mandel'shtam and knew all of his bewitching lyrical formulas by heart.   In Belotsvetov's own verses one can hear the music of Blok, as is the case with the poetry of Georgy Ivanov.   Each responded individually to Blok's music: Ivanov by parodying it; Belotsvetov by freeing it from everything earthly, from its material content. Anthroposophic meditations mark Belotsvetov's ethereal and incorporeal verse. His poetry is spiritual and pure, belonging to those higher spheres of Being where the poet listens to angels and demons.

As a poet in exile, Belotsvetov often expressed hatred of violence and a nostalgic longing for pre-Soviet Russia.   Even a decade after the Revolution, experiences of destruction and chaos lived on in the exiles' consciousness. There is bitterness because of the excessive, unnecessary suffering, and dismay over the lost cultural continuity of Russia. Like many other works of Russian writers in exile, Belotsvetov's poems at times have a deeply tragic note. For example, in "The Red Flag" the elemental forces set loose by revolution rage uncontrolled for years, until a deadlock is reached: "No way through for man!"   What remains is an anti-Rus', a negation of the eternal values described in Belotsvetov's poem "In the Glory . . . " Here he finds the essence of Russia in her spiritual agonies and artistic creations—the works of her saints and martyrs. They are the values upheld by the spiritual community within and outside Russia after the catastrophe, but they no longer have any physical reality. Thus, Belotsvetov is caught in a paradox of hope and hopelessness. Tied to a spiritual entity that no longer has a physical manifestation, his life, too, tends to "melt, dissolve," to "dissipate like smoke" into the past. In "With its crystal breath . . . , " a similar mood is sustained—one of death, decay, helplessness, and doom.

Belotsvetov uses striking imagery. For example, he compares himself to "a pearl cast into acid, instantly/And forever I melt, dissolving . . . " The poet deplores that important bonds with his culture have been severed. The imagery of decay reappears in "With its crystal breath/The frost has gently shriveled/The last remaining leaves on the tired branches." The red flag and hissing sounds convey the revolutionary fervor—shouting, and chaos in the streets, with a flag red like blood wavering in the air. The fervor is described in short, terse sentences. Yet despite his preoccupation with decay and destruction, Belotsvetov affirms the continuity of Russian culture through the memory of the Russian Orthodox Church. The poem "In the glory . . . " has a hymn-like quality and the gold-domed cupola represents that which is sacred and eternal.

Belotsvetov published the following volumes of poetry: *Diky myod: pervy sbornik stikhov* (Wild Honey: A First Collection of Poems; Berlin: Slovo, 1930), *Shelest: vtoroy sbornik stikhov* (Rustling: A Second Collection of Poems; Riga: Didkovsky, 1936); and *Zhatva: tretya kniga stikhov* (Harvest: A Third Book of Poems; Paris: Rifma, 1953), published posthumously. He also contributed to *Numbers, The Journal of Concord, Russian Annals, The New House,* and others. His poetry appeared in Georgy Adamovich's *The Anchor: An Anthology of Emigré Poetry,* as well as in various Russian collections published in Berlin, where he lived for a while participating in the Berlin Club of Russian poets.

Read about Belotsvetov in Yury Ivask's article "N. N. Belotsvetov," *Novy zhurnal,* XXIV (New York, 1950), pp. 225-227.

Rustling: A Second Collection of Poems

Harvest

Like a pearl cast into acid, instantly
And forever I melt, dissolving
In your expanses, my land unforgotten,
Tormented, luckless Rus'!

Whispering your disparaged name,
I dissipate like smoke in your despair.
O my silenced homeland, teach me
Through your divine forgiveness!...

Wild Honey: Poems

The Red Flag

A red flag in the street, a red flag!
And behind the flag they march and march,
Lusting after vengeance, executions, wealth,
And crying: "Try them, try them!"

A red flag in the street, a red flag!
And behind the flag the somnambulant masses!
The ominous banner flutters and streams,
Banner of uprisings, revolts, and sedition!

The red flag, the red flag howls and shouts
Already for so many years:
"Stop! Wreck ahead! Road closed!
No way through for man!"

―――――·―――――

*The Net: A Third Collection of Berlin
Poets* (Berlin: Word, 1923?)

With its crystal breath
The frost has gently shriveled
The last remaining leaves on the tired birches.
You and I
Will be like them—faded.
We will be like leaves,
And decayed words will drift down in the night
With a dry and terrifying rustle.

―――――·―――――

*Rustling: A Second Collection of
Poems*

In the glory of the ancient
Gold-domed cupola,
In the martyred betrayal
Of righteous men and saints,
In the deeds and prayers

Of the love-giving Dove,
In the miraculous, inexplicable
Mercies of the Mother of God
Rus' lives!

TRETYAKOV, VICTOR VASILYEVICH

Victor Tretyakov, a Russian poet in Latvia, published a collection of verse entitled *Solntseroy* (The Digger of the Sun; Berlin: Petropolis, 1930), and a book, *Latyshskie poety v perevode Victora Tretyakova* (The Latvian Poets Translated by Victor Tretyakov; Riga: Värds, 1931). He also contributed to *Chimes*. Nikolay Otsup, a Russian poet, critic, and scholar in Paris, viewed Tretyakov as an attentive and cultured poet in Nikolay Gumilyov's studio.   Chinnov considers his metric systems unusual but always musical and his verse artistically valuable.   In Russia, Tretyakov published a small journal (four to eight pages per issue) entitled *Osnovy* (Foundations), which he filled with his own writings dealing with subjects like "Nashi lyubimye poetry Pushkin and . . . Zhukovsky" (Our Favorite Poets, Pushkin and . . . Zhukovsky). A Russian nobleman, he held conservative, "right-wing" views.   His fate is unknown.

Chimes, No. 18 (Riga, 1926)

Noontide

The Sun God was motionless in the zenith. A midday dream descended. Flaming threads flow into the boundless, quiet valley.

Between the golden shores the blue Slovutich sleeps,
And the variegated autumn gazes with feline eyes.

Fields along the steep banks sleep...The beast rests in the thicket.
Overpowered by dark intoxication, the peasants now sleep.

And the whole empyrean Kiev knows that in his patterned tower
    chambers
Prince Vladimar Monomakh now rests.

Afterward, shaking off his tenacious sleep, he catches fish,
And his light bay horse is reflected in quiet waters.

With a smile, the sagacious Prince surveys the autumnal expanses,
While above him a ligature of clouds passes by, on the way to a pilgrimage.

———————·———————

"Noontide" is a remarkable, highly stylized poem concerned with Russia's distant past before the country was christened. The god "Khors" was one of the idols thrown into the Dniepr River upon Russia's baptism. The poem is a curious combination of several styles: *solemn* (zenit, zlatye, gorny, pochivat', zret', sniskhodit'), *Old Russian* (lyud, uzornye terema, udolya), *colloquialisms* (otryakhat' tsepky son), and combinations of ordinary and elevated stylistic features (koshachyi ochi). This interlacing of various styles produces a lively picture of the poetic, harmonious existence of the Russian nation during the reign of the wise and kind Prince Vladimir Monomakh, Russia's benevolent ruler. The depiction of Kievan Russia is reminiscent of the English Romantic poets' evocation of a distant, golden past and use of the supernatural (the Sun God, for example). It is a filigree portrayal of a Kiev that never was, similar in flavor to the imagined Xanadu of Coleridge's "Kubla Khan."

The imagery suggests an idyllic picture. From the beginning of the poem with "A midday dream . . . " there is a constant stream of images of golden shores, blue waters, autumn colors, slumbering peasants, and resting beasts, all merging to convey pastoral serenity. A religious preoccupation is hinted at in the last line of the poem: "A ligature of clouds passes by, on the way to a pilgrimage." Piety, peace, well-being, and the beauty of nature all fuse in a picturesque panorama of Kievan Rus'.

Chimes, No. 33 (Riga, 1927)

The rhythmical ramble of a cart
Along the ringing cobblestone road...
A small horse, with her head hanging,
Brought from afar to me in the town.
The fragrance of a field road
So dear to me.
And now I am captive in the gentle paws

Of sweet reverie:

In unknown spaciousness,
In forgotten villages,
The fields are brightly permeated
With the accordion's Russian pain.
And the maidens, rakish and rosy,
Echo them;
There—the moon is light and meek,
There—intoxications are wild.

_____·_____

In its rhythmical pattern, melodiousness, and imagery, Tretyakov's poem, "The rhythmical ramble of a cart," resembles a Russian folk song evoking the merrymaking of young Russian peasants. In the first stanza, the *persona*, remembering his youth spent with nature, becomes captive of "sweet reverie." The rustic theme is underscored by the narrator's mood, presented as holding him in "gentle paws." The second stanza takes the reader back to the spaciousness of the Russian countryside, its green, luscious meadows in moonlit evenings, sonorous songs, beautiful maidens, and the wild intoxication of youth. The mood of nostalgia in the first stanza thus changes into passionate singing and dancing in the second. The imagery corroborates the contrasting attitudes expressed in the two stanzas. In the last two lines, the image of a pale, light, and meek moon contrasting with the wild intoxications described earlier intensifies the reader's sense of the *persona's* pain over a paradise lost in "unkown spaciousness,/In forgotten villages." This is a poignant poetry of a careful craftsman.

ISTOMIN, NIKOLAY

Istomin's various literary activities included publication of a volume of poetry in the Acmeist tradition, *Tsveten'* (The Time of Flowering), and contributions to a cultural journal in Riga, *Our Small Flame.* No detailed information is available about Istomin's life. It is known that he left Latvia for the Soviet Union and settled in Moscow where he lived till the end of his days. Chinnov, who knew him well as a writer, maintains that with the exception of a book on linguistics, Istomin did not publish anything in the Soviet Union.

The Virgin Soil, No. 1
(October 1928)

Russian Day
(Russian Culture Day)

Today is a holiday. Today we can
look one another in the eye.
Let it be—the past will not return,
and the path to it is lost.

O Rus', my homeland, enduring
a decade of fever and fire!
This day foreshadows the joy
Of our impending meeting with you.

We are a people uprooted,
but our souls still sing
the bright beckoning name,
your beloved name...

Enduring the anguish of exile
and beseeching our fate,
we will travel this long road
to come again to you.

And then, divinely enlightened and blessed,
Rus' will shake off the foreign dust,
and we will recall with reverence
this glorious Russian Day.

————·————

Istomin's "Russian Day" opened the first issue of *The Virgin Soil* and served as an eloquent epigraph for the newspaper, an ambitious cultural and literary project undertaken by the Russians living in exile in Estonia. Every year a Day of Russian Culture was organized and celebrated in Finland and the Baltic countries to unite all uprooted Russians with their beloved motherland, to foster pride in the national past, and to suggest the promise of a joyous return to their homeland. The anguish of exile will be superseded by a vigorous renaissance of Russian religion and culture. A divinely enlightened and blessed Russia will shake off the yoke of foreign influences and cleanse itself of foreign dust.

GOFMAN, V.

V. Gofman was one of the younger and relatively unknown Russian poets whose poems were published in *Chimes.* As the following poem illustrates, his verse is remarkable in conception, elaboration, and polish.

The Mermaid

You are a mermaid, a mermaid I knew long ago;
I saw in the depths of your eyes,
In their dark depths, the hidden bottom of the sea
And the surging swell of a wave.
Not in vain did I see how from your dark hair
You picked out bits of grass,
Woven in it were many patterned shells,
Tightly pressed to the curls of your tresses...
That is why everything in you is capricious passion
And why your desires are so free,
That is why your laughter is so melodious and beautiful,
Like the splash of a cloven wave.
You are a mermaid, the cunning daughter of the sea—
Not without reason do I watch over you,
Trembling, scarcely breathing, no longer for the first night
Do I stand guard upon the seashore.
I saw you, splashing, swim between the cliffs,
Glistening with a nocturnal luster,
And the blazing moon trembled in passion,
And you exchanged a smile with it.
I saw how yesterday, quietly swimming up,

You seized a drifting boat
And, smiling, gave it to the fury of the waves,
And the stormy tide shattered it;
You lighted deceitful fires
There, where the abyss is blacker, more frightful,
There ships sailed and were lost
Beneath the lashes of the biting flames,
As you lured seafarers with your pleading eyes,
With the quiver of impetuous shoulders,
Then to entice them away, at the midnight hour,
After you, to the depths of the sea,
There to caress them, there to torment them,
To destroy, to drown, to stifle,
Then at moonlit midnight to swim out once more,
To beckon those passing again...
Do not summon me, do not entice me,
Even without that, I will follow you...
With the lilting laughter triumphantly ring!
Oh, mermaid, mermaid, I am yours!
I will follow you to the depths of the bottomless seas,
I do not fear distant deep-sea realms,
If you wish, slay me with your caresses,
Torment, drown, stifle!
Oh, cunning daughter of the cunning sea!
Oh, mermaid with glistening tresses!
Now I am yours, for this very night
        I will follow, follow you!

———————·———————

Gofman's "Mermaid" is a variation on the theme of the sirens, the mythological temptresses in Homer's *Odyssey* responsible for leading astray many a ship. The theme reappears regularly in Western European literature; a notable example is Heine's "Lorelei." Gofman's treatment of the theme suggests the existence of a real woman, whose deep dark eyes, melodious laughter, and seductive, capricious nature conjure up the image of a mermaid. In the first line of the poem, the poet addresses the lady directly, stating that she is in reality a mermaid and that is why she is so alluring. "That is why everything in you is capricious passion/And why your desires are so free,/That is why your laughter is so melodious and beautiful,/Like the splash of a cloven wave." Then, for the remainder of the poem, the scene shifts to a nocturnal moonlit landscape, reminiscent of the romantic setting in some of Gogol's early stories. The poet stands guard on the seashore, watching the mermaid. Here the imagery is particularly striking and sensuous. The mermaid's body glistened "with a nocturnal luster," while "the blazing moon trembled in passion." As with the Homeric sirens, the mermaid's sensuousness and beauty are associated with death and destruction. She uses her "pleading eyes" and "quiver of impetuous shoulders" to lure men "to the depths of the sea," and "to destroy, to drown, to stifle." The poet begs the mermaid not to entice him, yet "even without that," he is determined to follow her. The last line stresses his determination to submit to his destiny.

In the original, the poem is very melodious. The frequent repetition of the liquid consonants "r" and "l" produces a flowing and mellifluous effect which reinforces the vividness of the mermaid's irresistible charms and the magic ocean world. Similarly, the meter, the anapestic tetrameter, imitates the undulating motion of the waves.

PRINCE KASATKIN-ROSTOVSKY,
Fyodor Nikolaevich (1875-1940)

Here is yet another beautiful, carefully executed poem, published in *Chimes* by the otherwise unknown author Prince Kasatkin-Rostovsky. He published a book entitled *Krestnym putyom k voskreseniyu* (*From Calvary to Resurrection*; Paris, 1948).

Chimes, No. 16 (1926)

The Pealing of Bells

Like a summons or a lament,
From all directions,
      It resounds,
The Lenten ringing
      Of native churches...

The soul's grieving
Rushes with it into the distance,
   Into the fields' expanse,
To forest, hills,
To native snows
   And bygone dreams!...
To the courtyards of estates, to peasant huts,
Into pine wood, or gardens overgrown,
   Into a forgotten home...
Everything there is dear, everything beckoning us,
Both the stillness of graveyards...and the dome of the church,
Where white candles burn,
Where the icons are brightened
   By the brilliance of icon lamps...
In a strange land, raving in the gloom,
We listen greedily as if it were groaning
   To the Lenten ringing.
It calls us far away—
And the heart grieves
   For its native land, its native fields!...
The ringing consoles the aching soul:
"Weep not, grieve not, God be with you,
"Holy Russia is suffering in misfortune's chains.
   "This is the soul's fasting! But it will pass.
   "The full weight of the common Cross
   "You, too, must bear! And once again before your eyes
"The Russian church will rise!"
   The Lenten ringing
   Will transform itself
Into a might summons!
Then the chiming of Easter bells
Will echo in the vault of the heavens,
   The songs's joy shall whirl into the heights:
   "The heavy load of chains has vanished!
   "Holy Russia is risen! Christ is risen!"
Wait, faithful one...Be strong!
           Pray!

_____._____

Like Bal'mont's poem by the same title,[1] Prince Kasatkin-Rostovsky's "The Pealing of Bells" uses meter and rhyme to imitate bells. Each line consists of either two or four iambs with the longer lines broken in the middle by a caesura. Thus the entire poem is based on a pattern of two iambs (-/-/) repeated again and again to create the effect of chimes. Significantly, the only line which departs from this pattern and contains three consecutive iambic feet is "The Russian church will rise!"

Internal rhyme emphasize the caesuras and enhance the ringing effect. Though the rhymes do not follow a set scheme, several rhymes are repeated three or four times and heighten the musicality. Kasatkin-Rostovsky uses an intricate pattern of vowels and consonants to convey the sound of ringing bells: the repetition of "am," "es" (*Khristos voskres!*), and so forth, with the nasal "om" predominating.

The theme here is presented clearly: The Lenten bells of Russian churches summon Russian émigrés to grieve for their native land. The chimes resemble groans, for "Holy Russia is suffering in misfortune's chains." But the bells also bring the Easter hope of resurrection: "The full weight of the common Cross/You, too, must bear! And once again before your eyes/The Russian church will rise!" The poem ends in a passionate admonition to wait, be strong, and pray.

NOTE

1.   Konstantin Dmitrievich Bal'mont (1867–1943), one of the first Russian Symbolists, skillfully played with certain sounds, for example the mellifluous consonants "l," "m," "n," and the sibilants to produce verse of unparalleled richness. Because of his ability to create abundant and ingenious sound effects, Bal'mont became the most admired Russian symbolist poet of his day. Shelley and Poe were among his models. In Russia, he published several volumes of poetry: *Under Northern Skies* (1894), *Buildings on Fire* (1900), and *Let Us Be As The Sun* (1903). He also translated a great deal, especially poetry written in English, including works by Shelley, Whitman, Poe, and Oscar Wilde. Bal'mont often sojourned in Estonia, of which he was very fond. Later, while living in exile in Paris after the Revolution of 1917, he published sonnets, lyrical poetry, and translations in the Russian journals and almanacs of the Baltic countries. Here is Balmont's poem about the pealing of bells at Easter:

Chimes, No. 30 (1927)

The Pealing of Bells

...Ringing of bells at the church...
Prayer book

Hear the pealing—	Hear the pealing—	Hear the pealing—
Heights and slopes,	Temples, ambos,	Green the woodland,
Blue the oceans	Those in distress	In the night of waning
Of the distance.	Hear the voice of God.	An Easter pussywillow.

Hear the pealing—	Hear the pealing—
Children, women,	Into a world of moans,
In the rumble of thunder	With a resounding sweep
Gladness at home.	The miracle's feast.

————————·————————

While listening to the sounds of church bells, the poet's thoughts wander to God, spring, and the miracle of Easter. The poem is highly musical and the form itself suggests ringing. The lines are short, with only one or two stresses each. Every line consists of two trochees or sometimes of a Pyrrhic foot and a trochee, as in the introductory line of each stanza, "Perezvony" ("Hear the pealing"). The rhymes, in the patterns aabb, emphasize the vowel "o" with an occasional "a" or "u," which in Russian brings to mind the ringing of bells. Even the shape of the poem is important. The reader's eyes imitate the motion of a bell clapper as they follow the zigzag arrangement of the stanzas.

Thematically, it seems most appropriate to read the poem horizontally, first the top three stanzas from left to right and then the bottom two. The pealing of bells in the first stanza lifts the poet to great heights and distances. By association he then thinks of God and how the voice of God reaches those in distress, which is the subject of the second stanza (N. B. Ambos were pulpits in early Christian and Eastern churches). The third stanza introduces the theme of spring and Easter. In Russia pussywillows are traditionally associated with Easter, and Easter always occurs during the waning moon. The green woodland also symbolizes spring and rebirth. The theme of spring is contrasted with the image of thunder in the next stanza. Here, "Gladness at home" is perhaps both domestic tranquility and the joy of Easter. The poem reaches its climax in the final stanza, where the bells rejoice that the "world of moans" is transfigured by the Easter miracle. Inherent in the structure of each stanza is a contrasting pair of emotions, attitudes, or objects—distress and consolation, thunder and gladness at home, pealing of the bells and moaning, moaning and a resounding sweep, heights and slopes, the moon and the woodland. These contrasting pairs suggest the movement of the bell's clapper, up and down, with a final sweep up—to the miracle's feast.

SCHMELLING, TAMARA GEORGIEVNA
(née Mezhak, 1916-1982)

The daughter of a high-ranking railway official in Riga, Tamara Schmelling was a member of the Student Circle during her studies at the University of Riga. She wrote sincere and interesting poems which were published in *The Virgin Soil* and *La Renaissance* (Paris). She also participated in meetings of Russian poets in Riga and their various literary activities.

Later she married the poet Yury Ivask and moved to Estonia, and then to Amherst, Massachusetts.

The Virgin Soil, No. 8 (1935)

This feeling, like a white banner,
Is high, high above me.
If it's possible—let spring between us
Always remain spring.

Very early spring—while the soft snow
Is still melting beneath the meadows,
And drifting ice inspires
Celebration and stirring in the drowsy waves.

And while meetings are still festive,
And while lips are still unkissed,
While there is still no way to test
The painful moments of crude truth.

And while there are still buds, not leaves,
And flitting smiles, not laughter—
Only a wave of a hand upraised,
Only—different from everyone else!

If it's possible, let the pointed flame
Be kindled neither by you or by me.
If it's possible—let this feeling be like a white banner
Over my fate and yours!

———·———

In "This feeling, like a white banner," Tamara Schmelling captures both the mood of eager expectation and the latent feelings of fear characteristic of a promising new relationship, when "meetings are still festive,/And while lips are still unkissed." As a metaphor for this feeling she chooses spring, "Very early spring—while . . . drifting ice inspires/Celebration and stirring in the drowsy waves." "If it's possible," she writes, wishing to prolong this early, happy phase of the relationship, "let spring between us/Always remain spring." Through her poetic and original images Schmelling succeeds in conveying excitement and anticipation. Yet the poet doubts that this uplifting sensation can endure forever. The phrase "If it's possible" is repeated three times and hints at a feeling of doubt underlying the whole poem. The meter used in the poem is anapestic trimeter with alternating feminine and masculine rhymes, often used in Russian verse.

PERFILYEV, ALEXANDER MIKHAYLOVICH
(1895-1973; literary pseudonum ALEXANDER LI)

Alexander Perfilyev was a composer, fiction writer, and fashionable and esteemed poet in pre-revolutionary St. Petersburg. Professor Andreyev remembered him as a cultured and talented poet who wrote about the struggle of those loyal to Russia and the country's historical and literary heritage. Perfilyev described Russia in 1917 as "Rushing forward at this meeting time/On a foreign and flaming-red horse..." In his straightforward and frequently bitter lines, the reader finds both the pain and joyous affirmation of a Russian émigré's life. Perfilyev published several volumes of poetry in exile, including *Snezhnaya messa: stikhi 1924-1925* (A Snowy Liturgy: Poems 1924-1925; Riga: Pressa, 1925), *Listopad: vtoraya kniga stikhov* (Falling Leaves: A Second book of Poems; Riga: Salamander, 1929), *Veter s severa: tretya kniga stikhov* (Wind from the North: A Third Book of Poems; Riga: Filin, 1937), and *Odinokaya mat': muzyka i tekst* (The Lonely Mother: Music and Text; Munich, 1967). The following biographical passages are from his wife, Irina Saburova. They were printed in *Literaturnoe nasledie Alexandra Mikhaylovicha Perfilyeva (Alexander Li): stikhi* (Literary Heritage of Alexander Mikhaylovich Perfilyev [Alexander

Li]: Poems; Munich, 1973.

Preface

"My biographer will be very happy.
He'll smile for at least half an hour..."

N. Gumilyov

Besides poetry and musical lyrics, set to his own music or to that of others, Alexander Perfilyev wrote a vast number of witty feuilletons in verse and prose in response to the evils of the day.   These feuilletons are of litte consequence for posterity, but at one time they were considered biting and to the point. . . . He often wrote feuilletons under various pseudonyms, among which the most frequent was "Sherry-Brandy." . . .

Alexander Perfilyev, the second son of General Mikhail Apollonovich Perfilyev, came from an old noble family of Cossack origins from the region beyond Lake Baikal. He was born on October 2, 1895, . . . in Chita, and was registered in the Cossack village of Bokukun. The family could trace itself back to the ataman Perfilyev, a member of the retinue of Ermak.   It was recorded in the family history that Prince Gantimurov, a descendant of Khan Timur, married the daughter of the ataman Perfilyev and was adopted by him. However, the family of the Princes Gantimurov continued to exist independently and died out not long before the First World War.   Perfilyev had intended to add the name Gantimurov to his own, but the war made this impossible.

He attended the Second Cadet Corps in St. Petersburg, but interrupted his studies to join his father on a scientific expedition to Central Asia with the famous expeditionist Kozlov.   Later he graduated from the Orenburg Cossack Military School and joined the First Nerchinsky Regiment, although he also served for a while in the Composite Cossack Household Squadron. During the First World War Perfilyev was seriously wounded several times.   As a cavalryman, he was decorated with the Arms of St. George for capturing the Poeshmen' estate in Western Prussia.   When he was a

Cossack captain, toward the end of the war, he received the
Cross of St. George. . . . After the Revolution Perfilyev was
arrested and spent about a year in solitary confinement.
Upon his release he went into hiding . . . and was sent to
establish ties with the Cossack units of the White Armies in
the south.   Finally, having acquired the appropriate
documents in a most fantastic manner, he "opted" for
Latvian citizenship and at the beginning of the '20s he
departed with his wife for Riga in the then newly formed
Baltic Republic—Latvia.   For a brief time he trained horses
for a Riga factory owner, then began working on the editorial
staff of *The Riga Courier*, and from that time on trod the
path of journalism. . . .

His first book of poems, *A Snowy Liturgy*, appeared in
Riga in 1925.   In the following years Perfilyev worked as
contributor, editor, publisher, and proofreader for the journals
Our Small Light and *The New Field*, the newspaper *The
Word*, the journal *For You*, and the largest Russian
newspaper in emigration *Today*. . . . Apart from his
journalistic work, Perfilyev was always closely involved with
music publishers and artists from various minor theatres,
which at that time were quite numerous in Riga.   He wrote
the lyrics for several revues, sketches, musicals, and numerous
Russian lyrics for the popular fox trots and tangos.   He wrote
lyrics for music of foreign and local composers.   Oskar Strok
was the most famous local composer for whom Perfilyev
wrote.   Indeed, the Russian lyrics for all of Strok's music
were composed by Perfilyev, including the popular song "O,
these dark eyes." Perfilyev considered this occupation "hack
work," but unfortunately he needed the meager wages.
During the first Soviet occupation of Latvia—from
1940-1941—he worked quietly as a night watchman in a
gardening firm.   Under the German occupation, he edited a
Russian newspaper.

In October 1944, Perfilyev escaped to Berlin where he
joined General Krasnov and once again donned a military
uniform.   He was sent to Italy, from there went to Prague
and, after miraculously escaping execution, found himself in
Bavaria where he lived with me in Mühldorf and then in
Munich.   In Munich he worked for the satirical journal
Petrushka, for *Satyricon*, for the monthly journal *Freedom*,

and finally for Radio Liberty.   Now and then he sent his poems, feuilletons, and short stories to the Paris newspaper *Russian Thought*, and the New York newspaper *The New Russian Word*. He died February 26, 1973.

Irina Saburova

—————————·—————————

Alexander Li, one of the numerous pseudonyms of Alexander Mikhaylovich Perfilyev, was in his own words a "Cossack officer, horse breeder, poet, fiction and feuilleton writer, roofer, house painter, river patrolman, broker, firewood loader, mounted policeman, construction worker, shooting victim of the Cheka, newspaper publisher, janitor, refugee, alcoholic, and three times a married man."   The somewhat sardonic tenor of this list indicates Li's pragmatic but also ironic and even cynical view of the world. The variety of experiences embraced in the list finds its reflection in his work, which is often highly realistic and drawn in sharp and concrete details.

Li's conception of the external world and his relationship to it pervades his prose pieces and feuilletons.   By taking a rational idea and drawing it out beyond absurdity, he achieves caustic humor. Ideas, matter-of-fact and rational, are transformed into a pradody of themselves.   For   example,   in   "An   Experiment   in Autobiographical Writing" he claims with mock seriousness that among the famous writers he has known only Anna Grigoryevna, Dostoevsky's wife.   For "indeed, how could I have known a man who died before I was born?   Isn't it enough that I knew his wife?"   Developing   this   line   of   reasoning   further   and   thus amplifying the satire, Li insists that his own love for literature stems from his obstetrician Dr. Sudakov, who "by means of obstetrical forceps transferred his love for the classics to me."   The discrepancy between a tone of high seriousness and trivial or ridiculous underscores Li's basic view of the world as a travesty. This facet of his prose is particularly pronounced in "About Secretaries and a *Combiné*," where Li describes how the secretary of a newspaper is asked by a reader to select and buy some lingerie for the latter's wife.

The satirical approach in "A Fig for the Nations" derives from the poet's bitterness over the discrepancy between the League of Nations' rhetoric—it promises to save the homeless and helpless Russian émigré from a life of continual strife—and the subsequent awareness that such hollow promises only make the refugee's life more difficult. Here the argument is elaborated through a careful manipulation of the fig (*figa*). It not only signifies a piece of fruit, or a crude sign of the hand, but also a pacifier. Moreover, exposing the empty gestures of the League which, "having spread figs throughout the world," "will have to cover itself with a fig leaf," Li adds another layer of symbolic meaning through the Biblical allusion, and thus reinforces both the parody and the grimness of his indictment.

Beneath the bitter parody and satire directed at institutions, the foibles of men, and at times the author himself, one can discern deep despair and uninterrupted emotional torment. The social plights of the refugee, expressed in several of Li's feuilletons, are complemented in his lyric poetry by an existential sense of enstrangement and alienation—not only from Russia, but from his loved ones and himself.

In her introduction to his poetry, Irina Saburova notes, "Almost half of Li's poems are entitled in the original: 'Night. Grief. Loneliness.'" In fact, most of his lyrics are characterized by dark images and moods and a pessimistic tone. This is particularly clear in the poem "I choked with the grief of these fields," where the *persona* mourns his isolation and the sense that he is "useful to no one." He compares himself to a dog who is "old and blind and barks at friends and relatives," thus implying that he is responsible for his estrangement. This sense of despair is relieved for a moment in the line "Thus they slip away gradually," when the poet recognizes that of all the people, places, and feelings which have come and gone in his life, only the one who truly loves him will remain. Yet the inner peace created by this awareness is short-lived and the poem sinks once again into considerations of the void that lies between him and his "true comfort." Such concepts are interwoven with and framed by the *persona's* persistent thoughts of death which imbue the lyrical texture of the poem with an inescapable dread.

In "Autumn slowly walks through the garden," an overriding sense of loss and alienation affects the poet's relationship with nature: "For the first time my heart is not gladdened" by the autumn visage of the garden. Instead, the "multicolored abundance of leaves/That fall onto the dry grass" lead to thoughts of death, in the form of past hopes and dreams.

Viewed as a whole, Perfilyev's verse with its predilection for pessimistic images and dark tones complements the cynical and caustic considerations prevalent in his prose.

Grimasy kisti i pera: sbornik russkikh ymoristov (Grimaces of Brush and Pen: A Collection of Works by Russian Humorist Writers and Artists), prepared by G. Gadalin (Riga: Literatura, (1928?)

An Experiment in Autobiography

Writing one's autobiography is such a boring affair. Praising oneself is somewhat awkward, but criticizing oneself requires courage and experience. A certain measure of professional honesty compels me to leave that to the critics. They're more adept at invectives.

I began to write at the tender age of five. I no longer remember the fate that befell my first humorous story, but I can say that I received, at that time, a far more respectable honorarium than I receive now after fifteen years of work in this field.

The nature of my first experiment was very simple: On a court order, sent to my grandfather, I traced some sort of cabalistic signs and poured ink all over the paper.

Seeing this first product of my free inspiration, Grandfather cried out:

"The boy's got the right idea. They won't get a damn thing from me with this order!"

Now, as for the compensations, they can be divided into two sections—the "idée-fixe" and the honorarium.

My "fix" was that I stood daily in the corner. My honorarium came from Grandmother in the form of a dinner more delicious than usual and a larger saucer of preserves, served to me on the sly in the kitchen, so that Grandfather wouldn't see.

Then Grandmother would shake her head reproachfully and say:

"Oh, you are such a humorist!..."

It was from this time on, apparently, that I became a

humorist.

I should add that at present my writing is considerably more prolific, but not only do I fail to obtain an advance from the cashier (not even on the sly so that the publisher won't see), often I don't even get any dinner at all.

I'll refrain from more detailed information about my childhood, youth, and so forth. The reader will undoubtedly be able to find all of this information in the archives of the late poet and biographer Pyotr Vasilyevich Bykov, the first critic to comment on the appearance of my verse in a journal.

I am pretty sure that, among this venerable elder's works, there will also be an obituary for me, written just in case.

Among famous writers, I know Anna Grigoryevna, Dostoevsky's spouse, and the obstetrician, assistant of Professor Otto, Doctor Ivan Vasilyevich Sudakov.

At this point I might well be accused of being slightly inaccurate. I realize that Dostoevsky's wife is not Fyodor Mikhaylovich himself; but, indeed, how could I have known a man who died before I was born? Isn't it enough that I knew his wife?

I'm including Doctor Sudakov because he was a direct and intimate collaborator at the time of my appearance on God's earth. And since this venerable Aesculapius took great pleasure in Russian classical literature, this circumstance obviously, in a purely intuitive way, influenced my entire life. In short, by means of obstetrical forceps he transferred his love of the classics to me.

The single hidden flaw in my life is that, to this day, I have been unable to define my true profession.

Cossack officer, horse breeder, poet, fiction and feuilleton writer, roofer, house painter, river patrolman, broker, longshoreman, mounted policeman, construction worker, shooting victim of the Cheka, newspaper publisher, janitor, refugee, alcoholic, and three times a married man.

To give you an example, I remember that when I was a Cossack officer it seemed to me I should be a poet and fiction writer.

After the revolution, when I came to live exclusively on my literary earnings, I envied the fate of my next door neighbor, a river patrolman, who would receive a "sea ration," a pound and a half of bread per day.

Now, having experienced all of the above-mentioned professions, I can affirm that they are all good only on one condition—that you get paid (excluding, of course, the following professions: shooting victim, refugee, alcoholic, and thrice-married man).

With respect to passports, it is definitely preferable to be a janitor.

Presently I have come to believe that the very best profession is to be a shooting victim. After all, it's the most peaceful.

Unfortunately, owing to events beyond my control, I did not experience it to the full extent.

But the very worst is to be married three times. This situation, it seems to me, requires no special commentary.

Now, as to personal qualities, I have many in fact, but the most essential ones are, by unanimous opinion of all three of my wives, the following: sloppiness and poverty.

If you ask my friends, they'll say: "Dangerous when drunk—liable to write and declaim lyrical poems."

For my part I'll add this: I have the refugee's peculiar passion for changing pseudonyms. It is convenient with regard to creditors first of all, and, secondly, it helps in receiving an advance.

————·————

About Secretaries and a *Combiné*

> The editorial office of a local newspaper received a letter from a provincial reader, with the request to buy him a lady's *combiné* [lady's slip] for a gift.

All the same, I find that the masses are rather ignorant with respect to the newspaper and its staff. For example, to this day the secretary of the editorial office is looked upon as a sort of boring middleman between visitors and a staff on the one hand, and the editor on the other.

A man sits in the editorial office, looks over letters, receives visitors, reports on them to the editor and staff, counts lines, and oversees the creation of signs such as "Don't disturb without reason," "Silence please."

Being rather ignorant in these matters myself, I have to confess that was my idea too. It turns out, however, that the function of the secretary is much broader than we ever imagined. Indeed, it even embraces a lady's *combiné*! Don't be amazed, reader—I'm serious! At first you might think, what could they possibly have in common: the secretary of a newspaper and a lady's *combiné*. It would be bad form if the secretary brought his family matters to the office. Yet, as it turns out, he must combine this with his other duties; he must consider even a *combiné*.

Recently, for example, the following letter was received in the editorial office:

"Dear Mr. Secretary:

Since I am a provincial person without any acquaintances in Riga ready-to-wear stores who could purchase ladies' underwear for my wife, I, as your reader, am therefore humbly asking you to comply and send to my address one *combiné*, C.O.D. I wish you the same. Herewith receive my most respectful bows. A devoted servant of you and your respected newspaper.

Ilya Skachkov

P.S. My wife is of medium height, but broad in the hips, and in general has an athletic constitution; therefore, please don't muff up the selection. And as for taste, I am counting on you. After all you are the secretary of a respected paper, you must have a feel for such artistic subtleties.

I. S."

Ilya Skachdov, our reader, is a fine one, indeed! That's real class— that's the way the Americans do things! Well, what the hell do we have a secretary for, if all he does is report to the editor or distribute pay checks to the staff? And what if I'm only a reader and don't write any articles, don't get any pay checks, and don't travel to the capital? And if I need, let's say, a model incubator for six hundred pedigree eggs?

Or, for example, I want to enjoy myself in town, but I don't know where to go? This is exactly where the secretary of a newspaper should come in. "If you please, dear reader,

here are some alluring addresses: At this place, they say, you
can get in only before one o'clock; and here, only after one.
Here, for nonpayment, they strike you once between the ribs;
but there, just once on the neck and fill out a police report."
Now this is really wonderful!   Long live our all-purpose
editorial secretaries!

P.S.   Dear readers!   If you need to acquire a cow or
some other all-purpose object with a handle, then appeal
directly to the editorial office.   We can take care of all your
needs.

A Fig for the Nations

Silently, we spread out around the world,
In winter we stroll lightly dressed
And gloomily carry our passports, marked "blacklisted,"
In our jackets, right next to our hearts...
Thanks to Nansen,[1] our "benefactor,"
We're not accepted anywhere...
At every step: "Declared an alien,"
Live where you like, go and live in the water.
And the League of Nations tranquilly
Squints at us through its glasses
And whispers thoughtfully and tenderly:
"Oh, poor émigrés, what a sight you are...
How hard it is for the poor things to live
Bearing their refugee's Cross,
Since there's no Russia, I suppose
It's up to us to save them."
And so, for ten years now they've been "saving"...
But the émigré is as ragged as ever,
And in his refugee's life, thrice-accursed,
He has found peace nowhere.
Summer and winter he goes without work,
If there *is* work, it pays next to nothing...
I swear, in forced labor camps
The daily routine was more pleasant.
And here, amid this fuss and bother,
There's one thing I don't understand:

What has the League of Nations accomplished?
Whom has it saved and from what?
It's possible I'm too naïve
And have a narrow outlook,
With only my starched shirtfront to cover
The shame of my ignorance;
Nevertheless I must admit
It's very hard to grasp!
What's the use of crying and making a fuss
If you're only going to treat the world to figs?
I understand that in the days of bankruptcy,
When progress was swept back,
Fruit growing was very profitable,
But scarcely so many figs are needed now.
And if this fruit for export
Is like our passports,
Who needs it?
Let Nansen eat it himself.
Of course, to feed the suffering
Is a beautiful, noble gesture,
But...I don't think anyone eats
A combination of fingers.
Eventually the League itself
Will be in such a position,
That having spread figs throughout the world,
It will have to cover itself with a fig leaf.

―――――――・―――――――

Literary Heritage

I choked with grief at these fields,
And at night I can no longer sleep.
Is it because my poems, like my cough,
Don't gladden, but rend my chest?

Bedridden with a chill and this fever,
I recall how I wore myself out
Long ago, and am useful to no one,
To neither city, nor fields, nor forests...

It is almost over. What point is there in living without
    a purpose...

Like this dog grown quiet on his chain...
They'll probably shoot him come autumn—
He's old and blind and barks at friends and relatives...

Good old dog, I'm sorry for you, poor thing,
You've been tied to that chain for a long time—thirteen years.
But even without the chain you wouldn't have taken to your
    heels—
Not even in the years when you weren't blind and gray...

And what about me? In the Unknown Settlements,
Will I forget what makes it hard to live here?
What are we seeking along the Heavenly Paths,
If we don't know how to walk on earthly ones?

———————·———————

To Irina

So they all slip away gradually—
Women, and passions, and dreams.
Only you remain immutably with me,
Caressing and near—you.

For a long time we've not loved as we should,
Nor burned with desire for each other,
But you alone are my true comfort,
The rest is mist...

So they slip away in this fog,
Gliding behind the curtains of the past.
And that which was experienced with them
One must neither remember nor forget.

Only those, who are without jealousy,
And to whom dreams are not given,
Will come in the fateful hour
And kiss my sharpened brow.

———————·———————

Autumn walks slowly through the garden,
Tearing leaves off the poplars...
For the first time my heart is not gladdened
By the tender sadness of her beauty.

Through the rusty iron grating
The noise of the city is barely heard.
Yellow beads quietly fall
From autumnal monastic hands.

I loved her quiet step,
The blue of her lifeless face,
And the multicolored abundance of leaves
That fall onto the dry grass.

But I am no longer the same,
And in the faded garden without you
Death strolls in harvest dress,
Destroying all my former hopes.

These soft and ingratiating colors,
These yellow leaves littering the path,
Like your dying caresses,
Cannot deceive me.

And for the first time, perhaps, it weighs on me, heavy,
The rustling of leaves, of fallen hopes...
Where are you, then, never-to-be-forgotten blessing
Of light-winged autumnal hopes?

———————·———————

The Circle of Life

Children romp about the playground,
Shouting, digging in the sand,
And nannies, in sweet reverie,
Sit side by side not far from them.

Knitting needles move drowsily,
And the needlework falls from their hands.
And I doze, again I dream
Of the already closing circle.

It lasts only a short while,
The whole meaning no more than two lines—
The beginning: Sand, a little shovel,
The end: A little shovel and...sand.

1973

NOTE

1.   Nansen was a Norwegian citizen who arranged for special passports to be issued to émigrés in Europe after the October Revolution. While these passports gave the émigrés a legal identity enabling them to reside in Western Europe, they did not grant them citizenship.

ZUROV, LEONID FYODOROVICH (1902-1971)

Zurov was born in Ostrov, near Pskov. At seventeen, he joined the Russian Northwestern Army as a volunteer, served in the regiment of His Serene Highness Prince Lieven, and was wounded twice. After General Yudenich's unsuccessful march to St. Petersburg, Zurov was sent to an internment camp in Estonia where he fell ill with typhus. He graduated from the Russian High School of Mikhail Lomonosov in Riga. Then he spent a few years as a student in the Archeological Department of the University of Prague and several years in Riga, where he worked as a laborer, coach, painter, and secretary of the journal *Chimes*. He also contributed to a Russian newspaper in Riga, *The Word*. From

Riga he often visited Estonia, where in the 1920s he was in charge
of the restoration of the Nikola Ratny Church in the Pskov-
Pechory region. He was a close friend of the Irtels' but was not
on particularly good terms with Yury Ivask. According to the late
Professor Andreyev, Zurov left Latvia for Paris in 1929 primarily in
response to an invitation from Bunin, but also to get away from
the woman he loved, Semyon Irtel's beautiful sister Kira, who was
married and could not obtain a divorce. "Throughout his life in
Riga and France he had suffered much because of his unhappy
love." (Andreyev)

Together with a group of ethnographers commissioned by the
Musée de l'Homme Zurov returned to Estonia in 1935, 1937, and
1938 to record Russian and Estonian folk songs and legends, and to
photograph the Pechory and Izborsk regions. Upon his return to
Paris he wrote two extensive reports. One presented his group's
research on the ancient remnants found in the two areas and the
results of the group's archeological and ethnographical expeditions
of 1935–38. The other described the pre–Christian customs and
religious beliefs of Estonians and the peasants of the Chud' and
Pechory regions. Later on, the Museum sent Zurov to Denmark
and Scotland where he discovered the sepulchre of Lermontov's
ancestors who had lived in St. Andrews between the fourtheenth
and seventeenth centuries. In Paris he contributed to
Contemporary Annals and *The Latest News*. He continued writing
in a narrative style characterized by the use of Pskovian dialect
and tones far removed from the genres and styles practiced by
other Russian writers living in Paris.

Zurov planned to write a monumental novel, *Zimny dvorets*
(The Winter Palace), about the October Revolution of 1917, but he
never finished it. Instead, he published several other works:
Otchina (Fatherland; Riga: Salamander, 1928), *Drevny put'* (The
Ancient Path; Paris: Sovremennye zapiski, 1934), *Pole* (The Field;
Paris: Parizhskoe obyedinenye pisateley, 1938), and two collections
of short stories, *Kadet* (The Cadet; Riga: Salamander, 1928) and
Maryanka (Paris, 1958). Zurov's prose is colorful, expressive, and
precise and concrete in historical details. His picturesque and
graphic language resembles the style of Russian chronicles.

The chaotic nature of primitive human passions always
fascinated Zurov; he had a strong capacity for experiencing nature
and was happy only when on the water or in dense forests.
Endowed with a fine "historical feeling," he loved the simple

Russian folk, who suffered during Russia's national development as a country and state. Apt formulations, simplicity, picturesqueness, pointed literary generalization, and a fresh, innovative, laconic use of Russian vocabulary form the peculiarities of Zurov's literary style. Contrary to what is often said about him, Zurov was not a disciple of Bunin, but rather an original writer. He found the inspiration for his artistic work in Russian antiquity, whereas Bunin was inspired by the present. Zurov was interested in the historical development of the Russian nation, while Bunin was not. Always conscious of his loneliness as a writer and as a human being, Zurov turned to the remote past, which he believed to be allied with the beauty of nature. He wrote about ancient times as if he had known them personally, and he transfigured the old Russian language by giving it a more contemporary appearance. His narrative resembles a personal monologue outside the social and political conditions of any given historical period. Zurov had a sensual vision, an organic sense of "the flesh of life and the world." He felt that the biological principles of life were fused with the powers of nature, with everything ancient, patrimonial, and pagan, and with everything alive in the blood and subconscious of the Russian people. Like Lev Tolstoy, Zurov presented the elemental in life and nature, the stirring of huge masses of people. His protagonists strive to free themselves of their loneliness and attempt to establish contact with other lonely and unhappy people.

Zurov does, however, resemble Bunin in two respects. Like Bunin, Zurov understands, feels, and hears the Russian language and he is a magician of the Russian word. Second, both Bunin and Zurov present nature not merely as a background for their egocentric hero, but as an integral part of life. Since Zurov does not identify with his characters, there is artistic objectivity in his presentations. He was attracted to the ecumenical, which included Russia's spacious green meadows and fields, the country's cultural heritage, and the instinctive confluence with nature which, in Zurov's eyes, characterized every Russian. Hence his preoccupation with psychology in the entanglements of love, hatred, heroism, war, revolution, and death. Zurov once said: "Everything exists within a mysterious, circular motion." This can be seen as the guiding principle in his creations. Zurov's emotions, the way he constructed his sentences, and his portrayals merging with Russian folk songs and chronicles stem from the world view summarized here.

After the Second World War, Zurov was elected Chairman of the Union of Young Writers and Poets in Paris. In Paris he had devoted friends—Madame Vera N. Bunina-Muromtseva, Sergey Zhaba, and Tamara Velichkovskaya. They surrounded Zurov with care, love, and empathy during his illness, when he was suffering from hallucinations and severe delirium. Zurov died of a heart attack in a Swiss sanatorium. His friends remember him as a very good-looking man with the face of an ancient Russian warrior. They said he was an unhappy and lonely person and an excellent storyteller who read his works with emotion, color, and emphasis, delighting his Russian audience at literary *soirées* in Paris.

The Old and the New, No. 1 (1931)

Life in the Provinces

One morning Volodya was studying algebra and looking out an open window. Flies were biting his bare feet under the table. Frowning, he drowsily chased them away and scratched one leg with the other.

It had been sultry since morning. From the bushes beneath the window, the air smelled of languorous foliage. It was hard to look at the clouds; they kept merging and drifting apart. By the river, the black horse stood near the young chestnut filly and scratched her mane with his teeth, while lazily flicking his tail.

Wagon bells jingled. Walking heavily, father came out onto the porch.

"Maybe you'd like to go to town, Voloden'ka?" his mother said from the dining room.

"I'd rather stay home, Mama," Volodya answered in a lazy, plaintive voice.

He imagined with agony how he would have to pull on his high boots, wriggle into the sleeves of the long dust-coat and drag along for fifteen *versts* in the hot wagon, on the sandy road, through fields and pine forest. At the edge of the forest sticky flies would pester them and swarm above the horse as he moved along, and the horse would lash his sweating sides with his tail. Father would give Volodya the reins, adjust his white cap, and have a smoke. The wheels, turning heavily in the deep grooves, would scatter dry sand

along the spokes and sweep heavy dust slowly into the quiet
pine forest which emanates resin and heat. When the horse
emerged onto the highroad, father would urge him on, making
a dusty patch on his rump with the reins, and the horse
would tug and go at a fine trot as far as the outskirts. At
the gray house the rough cobblestone street would begin, and
the wagon would jingle across the stones. They would have
to rattle through the town, past the boring *gymnasium*
building to the post office. Father would then get off, but
Volodya would sit in the sun and, relaxing the reins, would
gaze at the vacant square and low stalls, and would listen to
the din of the carts...

II

His father left. The wagon was already clattering in the
distance, hidden by the rye. Volodya went out into the
garden. The foliage of the apple trees was fluffy and warm,
but the paths were hard, and the earth, turned up by worms,
pricked his heels. Honeybees, indolent and irritable from the
oppressive heat, buzzed over the flowers. Beyond the garden,
on the bank of the river, cattle were grazing; a naked
shepherd boy, Sen'ka, was kneeling down in the water and
digging a hole in the bank with his hands; the hole kept
caving in and filling up from below with muddy water.

"What are you doing?" Volodya shouted.

"I'm chasing the minnows into this little lake."

"Wait, I'll come too," Volodya said and started
undressing.

He felt a light breeze on his body. The moist sand was
cool. In the warm water near the bank, schools of
transparent, shy minnows darted. It was the beginning of
June, and the rye on the opposite bank stood green and
warm, with tender ears. Daisies grew along the edge of the
field, and on the bare spots, where the dry, cracked earth
was visible, were a few blue cornflowers that had not yet
faded. The rye fields rustled gently in the breeze, reflecting
a bluish-gray hue. When the wind died down, the ears
swayed slightly, and again the rye bowed; then waves rippled
across it once more. And above the fields in the intense heat
invisible larks paused in the air, fluttering—they sang, fell,

rose, and sang. Clouds rose out of the distant forest.

The water grew turbid, and Volodya, bored with catching minnows, started splashing Sen'ka. The little shepherd boy, freckled, with black feet, a taut belly and protruding navel, began to defend himself, striking the water with his curved palms and advancing toward Volodya, who had slender arms and blue viens in his shoulders. He chased Volodya into the water up to his waist, and then Volodya swam. In the middle they measured how deep it was. A cold current ran along the bottom. Snorting and laughing, treading water, they shouted to each other and swallowed water from laughing.

Sen'ka jumped out of the water with a distracted expression on his face. He looked at the sky and shook his head. A bluish cloud came out from behind the forest and rumbled intermittently. Sen'ka had stayed in the water too long, his back trembled, his lips were blue, his fingers did not obey, and he hopped on one foot for a long time trying to put on his breeches.

III

A wind gusted in unexpectedly, rustled in the rye, and chased shimmering waves, frequent and rapid, across the field. The entire grain-covered expanse rustled, and the movement of the clouds became noticeable. A shadow ran along the field onto the drooping linden trees. And when the shadow had rolled across the garden, thunder trembled softly above the house and faded away dully; then a heavy thud shook the sky. In the darkening rooms, the women bustled about and shouted, closing the windows and ovens. On the veranda, his feet firmly planted, stood chubby little Vasen'ka, the sharecropper's son, gazing with astonishment into the garden.

From behind the roof of the house a heavy yellowish cloud gathered and grew rapidly, unfolding its dirty edges. A vague rumbling came from the sky. It turned into a rather frightening, dull, persistent roar, as if the sky were starting to boil and heavy stones were being moved. With the approaching roar, in the stillness, an icy coldness wafted from the sky onto the languishing garden where the trees and birds

had fallen silent.   It grew dark.   The earth and trees
continued to resist, still breathing warmth, but in the garden
it was already becoming damp.   Volodya saw how a heavy,
thick, milky sheet fell with a loud rumble on the house.

A large white hailstone struck the leaves of the maple
tree, while two more bounced off the flower bed, and then a
white torrent of heavy hail poured from the sky along with
icy wind and rain.

It crushed the poppies in the flower bed and in a
whirling spray pushed the maple leaves to one side.   A heavy
rumbling filled the house.   The flower bed grew white.
Bringing cold air, the hailstones bounced against the ground.

"Volodya, Volodya!" his mother shouted from the house.

But he stood on the veranda and did not answer.   He
was happy.   The wind carried the rain in gusts, wetting the
dry ground with fans of moisture and blowing a spray of
water into Volodya's face; and when he took a step forward,
the hail would flog him on his hands and face.   He saw a
peasant girl running through the garden beneath the shelter
of the trees, covering her head with her skirt.   The hail beat
against her back.   A foal, beaten by the hail, pushed his way
into the lilac bushes, his whole body trembling.   Laughing,
little Vasen'ka ran along the veranda and gathered handfuls
of hailstones, which bounced off the stairs.

"It's a sin to laugh, little fool.   There'll be no harvest."
A peasant woman dashed onto the porch and, taking her son
by the hand, dragged him into the dining room, where the
women, standing in the darkness before the icons, had already
taken the Holy Thursday candle from behind the icon case
and lighted it.

The hail stopped abruptly; a heavy rain continued to
fall, but the parting cloud revealed a light blue sky, lovely in
its purity and freshness.   Through the thinning clouds the
sun cast a soft light upon the damp garden.   Everything was
in bloom.   The handsome maple tree sparkled gaily, its top
crumpled by the hailstones and wind.   Green leaves, fallen in
the storm, were scattered everywhere.   Water dripped from
the trees, and in the full sunlight which warmed the garden
birds began to sing in the wet foliage.

Along the slippery path, joyful and barefoot, stepping
through the prickly hailstones and feeling the damp ground

under his feet, Volodya ran through the garden, pushing aside
the heavy jasmine bushes. Thunder rang out in the distance.
The lightened cloud, releasing rain, was retreating beyond the
forest. As it lost the rain, the cloud became pale and turned
into gray mist right before one's eyes.

Volodya caught sight of the sharecropper Pyotr. The
old bearded peasant was in a gloomy mood. He was
bareheaded; his shirt was unbelted and wet in the shoulders.

The hail crunched underfoot. The air smelled of a cool
freshness, of poplars and birches, and of all kinds of sap from
the broken foliage.

The field became clearly visible. It sparkled. Blinding
clouds floated across the pure blue sky. With his hat in his
hands, Pyotr walked in his homemade leather shoes along the
clay road, firmly planting his feet. Long stretches of rye had
been beaten flat.

"It has been beaten down, oh Lord, how it has been
beaten down!" Pyotr said. He stopped in front of his field
and, holding his hat in his hands and not noticing Volodya,
he humbly bowed down to someone.

Sen'ka was chasing the cattle from the forest. Volodya
ran toward him through the wet, splashy meadow. His feet
became entangled in the grass. The grass wound between his
toes, and yellow petals and blossoming grass stuck to his wet
trousers. Sen'ka, wet but happy, shouted in a peasant
fashion at the cattle and threatened with a switch. The
animals, their backs wet, slowly emerged from the forest.

The water had risen in the river. Wet sand was in the
crevices. A long-legged stork walked through the flooded
meadow, searched about in the water, and then, lifting his
beak out and tossing it upwards, he shook his head
convulsively, gulping down tiny frogs.

Provence

Chimes, No. 28 (1927)

A Vision of Moscow

The snow grows heavy and starts sliding down the roofs in gentle waves; the roads are yellow from dung; the black boughs in the orchards are damp, and Moscow, shrouded in wet snow, is full of the sounds of the Lenten bazaar.

Low, wide sledges covered with carpets stand at the Kremlin wall. Market gardeners from outlying districts of Moscow begin to summon the people loudly to the wooden stands where sour cabbage, pickled mushrooms, apples in syrup, cranberries, linden honey, and dried boletus mushrooms are on display.

The sounds of the bazaar finally cease; the first crowbar rings out against the ice; hay dropped from peasant carts is swept from the squares where the ice has already melted; the ice breaks up on the Moscow river; the first birch bud bursts open on the Arbat, and blackbirds cry out piercingly and joyously above the fresh, golden cupolas.

Palm Sunday, spattered with wax, fans tranquil Moscow with a warm breeze. Between a maiden's hands Holy Thursday appears rosy.

The night of Good Friday timidly approaches Easter Sunday.

At eleven o'clock, the Kremlin cathedrals are lighted. Reflections flicker on the cupola, gilded by the lights of the octagonal Ivanov bell tower and on the five-domed Uspensky Cathedral.

The murmur of the throng subsides, and the first candles are lighted with trembling flames. At midnight above the old Kremlin the bell of Ivan the Great thunders out. A dense wave of sound flows out into the night, and ringing joyously the bells of Moscow boom in response.

Above the Kremlin, above the wet, green fields of Russia, lie grains of quiescent stars. The sounds of Moscow die down, and again the Kremlin bell ringers set every bell in motion; and against the background of the general ringing, in the swaying candlelight, ancient banners, gold-encrusted crosses, and icons from twelve cathedrals move past the walls illumined from below. The fervent crowd bears thousands of lights, as the people cross themselves and intone: "Angels sing in the Heavens, Christ Savior, of Your Resurrection."

Everywhere—joyous, gentle ringing, young girls' faces, and the spring sky of Moscow.

Above the Zamoskvorechye district and the branches of the Alexandrovksy Garden, fireworks soundlessly cut across the sky. Forming wreaths, they stream down as scarlet and emerald stars, and are reflected in the dark waters of the responsive river.

*

In the morning, the merry singing of copper bells wafts through the open windows.

On the table are *paskha*,[1] Easter cakes, babas, and heaps of eggs amid prickly, fresh green grass. On the sunny decorated streets banners flutter in the breeze.

It's time now to go to the Kremlin to honor the saints' relics—along the paths strewn with sand, past the canons standing behind the cathedral fences—as if for the first time, to hear the thrilling ringing, to see the stone walls and the sky, and to know that a gentle breeze rocks the tassels of the birch trees in the gardens and pussywillows in the fields.

Women in fashionable hats cross themselves, while women in scarves kiss the icons.

Inside the dome of the bell tower it is cool. A damp staircase ascends between the landings where old holy water fonts show gray against the white pigeon droppings; higher up it leads to where the ancient bells ring out and tremble. A fresh wind strikes the face. The bell ringer, propping his feet against the floor and forgetting everything in the world except the booming bell, swings the heavy clapper. When his arms tire, the bell ringer leans agains the railings, and it seems to him that the bell tower is swaying gently and may tip over at any moment.

Now the children of Moscow seize the bell. Under inexperienced, reckless hands, the bells ring unevenly yet boldly the whole day long.

The clear sky is in winged, dove-like captivity.

They're rolling eggs in the outskirts of Moscow. A circular, sandy dip—a wide area—has been smoothed out for this purpose.

One by one, carriages are departing from Maidens' Field. Merchants are taking their sisters, sedately wrapped in heavy winter coats of read plush or green velvet, for a ride.

Steaming horses—sorrels and light bays—trot along briskly.

Their harnesses are of crimson velvet with golden settings.

The young rosy-cheeked daughters of the merchants hide their faces in their light silk shawls.

Somewhere on a side street students are walking and singing. Their overcoats unbuttoned, they stroll at a leisurely pace, sporting a birch leaf in their caps as a cockade. Moscow is fragrant with smells of the earth, grass, and countryside.

Powerful ringing descends from the bell towers. It pounds at your heart. There's no way to describe it—it's simply overwhelming. Clearly it is spring. Clearly the bird cherries have blossomed throughout Russia's glades.

*

The ringing of those days has ceased. The year 1919 came. Many of Moscow's youths fell on their native fields. Never again would they trample the spring grass.

Before, the Iversky Mother of God icon had graced the homes of Moscow families each year, whether in joy or in sorrow or simply to bless their peaceful life.

Moscow had drunk deep of sorrow. The Iversky chapel was closed. Every day distraught women pounded against the locked doors.

Just before Easter they gathered for matins. But gunfire rang out on the dark streets and Red Army patrols barred their approach to the churches.

*

On the way to Saint Sergy's, one feels a certain obligation to drop in at the Khot'kov Monastery to pay one's respects to the saint's parents.

At the Trinity-Saint-Sergy Monastery, Sergy is painted

on the gates. Sometimes he works in the forest, sometimes he carries firewood. Dear, quiet, joyful Sergy lives amid the beautiful green fields and forests.

In 1919 the young monks were taken from Sergy for military service, and the old ones were afraid to perform the liturgy. Nevertheless they decided to celebrate Easter Matins in a secret cell. Amid their quiet prayers, at midnight, the monks heard the ringing of a bell. A Red Army patrol was stationed in the courtyard of the monastery. The commissar jumped out of the sentry quarters and ordered that the bell ringer be removed from the bell tower.

The Red Army soldier did not return. The steady, sad ringing from the bell tower continued. The commissar waited a long time and then sent a second soldier. But that one didn't return either. Then he himself climbed up the bell tower. At the top he saw the two Red Army soldiers, lying unconscious, and a small, white-haired, bent old man, who was ringing the bell.

"What do you think you're doing?" the commissar shouted.

"The time has come, so I'm ringing," he answered quietly. "Look to the right."

Through the murky spring night the commissar saw a sea of white human skulls swaying across the fields; it grew, and its motion was terrifying.

"Ring on," the commissar whispered and collapsed on the wet floor.

Since that time they've stopped billeting in the Sergy Monastery.

That is how the story was told in Moscow in the year 1919, and thus it is told even to this day.

*

In the home of a Russian family living abroad, I saw an Easter egg from the Kremlin matins hanging in a muslin pouch next to the Mother of God icon. It was very light. In its center the dead, dried-out yolk knocked hollowly. Only one sorrowful word was scratched in the scarlet lacquer.

The word was "Moscow."

Zurov writes of the ancient traditions of Russian life as they were respected up until the 1917 revolution. The two pieces in this volume describe vividly scenes that can never be repeated, because those social and religious structures no longer exist. For this reason an intense nostalgia permeates the joyful brightly colored pictures drawn by Zurov. His portrayal is panoramic in "A Vision of Moscow." It encompasses the Easter mood of an entire city and conveys the magnitude of the great holiday as it unites man and nature in joyful celebration. The traditional way of life is threatened by the revolution, but the feeling remains that this way of life is eternal and deep-rooted and cannot be destroyed. These stories were written in the 1920s when the old way of life was still a vivid memory and the vague hope for its revival had not died out.

In the other story, "Life in the Provinces," Zurov conveys a panoramic view of a storm and the close ties that bind man and nature. Especially in the description of the gathering storm his imagery is picturesque and highly effective: "A heavy yellowish cloud gathered and grew rapidly, unfolding its dirty edges"; the thunder sounds "as if the sky were starting to boil and heavy stones were being moved"; and "Volodya saw a heavy, thick, milky sheet fall on the house with a loud rumble." The reader can instantly visualize the scene. The author's portrayal of the storm's aftermath is striking for its beauty and evocative power. The reader gets an almost physical sense of stillness and relief, and of coolness and freshness after the storm. As in "A Vision of Moscow," there is a feeling of joyous anticipation, shown here in the figures of the Volodya and Vasen'ka watching the storm from the veranda. The stories have no real plot; they are more like sketches conveying a mood, a scene, or an eternal relationship with the past.

Zurov's style is simple and clear; it abounds in details and sharply drawn contours which create a sense of immediacy. There is much air and space, fresh winds blowing, rivers and roads meandering in the distance, dark forests looming pensively on the horizon, and other portrayals of the vastness of Russia. Zurov frequently uses caressing diminutives, but the "skaz" technique he uses very sparingly. His narrative mode combines refined craftsmanship and stylistic control with a deeply personal, emotional involvement in the glory of Russia that has vanished and will never return.

NOTE

1.   A special Easter dish made with cream cheese.

PIL'SKY, PYOTR MOISEEVICH
(1878-1941; literary pseudonyms A. Khrushchev,
P. Stogov, Petrony, R. Vel'sky)

Pyotr Pil'sky, an eminent literary critic, also wrote larger works such as *Tayna i krov'* (The Mystery and Blood; Riga: Lit., 1927) and *Zatumanivshiysya mir* (A Misty World; Riga: Gramatu Draugs, 1929), which included sketches about Valery Bryusov, Fyodor Sologub, Vasily Rozanov, and Semyon Yushkevish. He authored *Roman s teatrom* (A Romance with the Theatre; Riga: Shershenevsky, 1929) concerning the ballet dancer Tamara Karsavina, the famous singer N. V. Plevitskaya, Isadora Duncan, Henrik Ibsen, Russian singer A. N. Vertinsky, and other renowned Russian dancers, singers, and actors.   Earlier Pil'sky had contributed to the Russian periodical *Birzhevye vedomosti* (The Stock News; St. Petersburg).   Later he wrote for *The Latest News* (Tallinn), edited by R. S. Lyakhnitsky. M. P. Artsybashev, A. S. Izgoev, Boris Lazarevsky, and V. N. Speransky were among its contibutors.   Pil'sky also wrote for *Our Newspaper* (Riga), edited by P. N. Khudyakov, former editor of the St. Petersburg *Copec Newspaper*.   Professor M. S. Kurchinsky and L. M. Pumpyansky were other regular contributors to *Our Newspaper*.   Pil'sky was devoted to Russian culture and knew how to stir and burn his Russian reader with words.   Later he also published articles in the journals *Numbers* and *Contemporary Annals*, both printed in Paris. A charismatic figure, Pil'sky was a spirited critic of ballet and drama.   In the words of N. E. Andreyev, Pil'sky remained forever a "true knight of Russian liturature."[1]

At the turn of the century Pil'sky wrote critical essays and articles on Zinaida Hippius, D. S. Merezhkovsky, and other modernist writers in the leading Moscow and St. Petersburg journals and newspapers.   Innovative and always sharp and lucid, Pil'sky's views brought him fame and provoked animosity.   In Pil'sky's essays, one can find a host of captivating and stumulating comments on the works of Bely, Bryusov, Blok, Kuzmin, Rozanov, Fyodor Sologub, Gor'ky, Bunin, and Chekhov.   He also expressed opinions concerning significant events in the literary circles of St. Petersburg, Moscow, Riga, and Tallinn.   Moreover, Pil'sky often engaged in spirited debates of current ideas with influential Russian writers and critics.   It is unfortunate that with the exception of one volume, *Kriticheskie statyi* (Critical Articles; St. Petersburg, 1910), his essay have never been collected in their entirety.

After the October Revolution of 1917, Pil'sky left Russia for Tallinn, then went on to Riga where he contributed to the newspaper *Today*.   In No. 205 (1938), he published a complimentary article on Zinaida Hippius' poetry collection *Siyaniya* (Radiances; Paris, 1938).   On pages 245–46 of his *Critical Articles*, he observed that her literary terms were popular with the Russian critics of the day.   "Her excellent observations and remarks," he wrote, "were squandered in the 'literary markets,' . . . in the noisy markets of ignorant literary thieves, . . . and at various critical newspaper auctions.   Unfortunately, the golden observations and thoughts of Hippius have acquired the reputation of having originated with Korney Chukovsky and his kind." Pil'sky often spoke in jest about the St. Petersburg and Moscow "literary markets" with their ridiculous conventions and nihilistic attitudes.

Pyotr Pil'sky is a humorist in much the same vein as Gogol. Not only are certain facets of Pil'sky's style and narrative are reminiscent of Gogol's comic approach, but also his often paradoxical social and religious concerns reflect Gogol.   Pil'sky himself noted that "the sphere of the humorist is the sphere of parody," which appears to indicate that the humorous texture of his own prose, as is the case in Gogol's work, masks profoundly serious questions and concerns.

These features are in the tale "When Leksey Lekseich and I Were at the Elections."   The *skaz* technique employed throughout the body of the narrative, the elaborately constructed speeches of many of the characters, occasionally inflated with needless words and phrases of bureaucratic jargon, the use of hyperbole (for example, "zillions of people" have arrived at the meeting), are characteristic of Pil'sky's literary style, and they recall Gogol's influence.   Furthermore, the narrator's description of the chairman and the secretary of the meeting—"One is a little taller and thinner, the other, just a little shorter but heavier, to make up for it"—is very likely an allusion to Bobchinsky and Dobchinsky, the famous pair of buffoons who appear in Gogol's great play, *The Revizor*.

As in Gogol's work, Pil'sky's stylistic devices suggest a vision of the world where man is subject to an environment of pervasive banality, vulgarity, and *poshlost'* reducing his existence to almost futility. All of the passion and inspiration motivating the narrator at the beginning of the meeting (which in itself may be considered in satiric terms) eventually give rise to the realization that nothing has been done, achieved, or fulfilled by this gathering of Russians who, the narrator thought, were capable of tackling any problem once they assemble for a set purpose. Yet, enmeshed in petty details and preoccupied with respecting the rules of order, these same Russians seem to lose sight of all goals other than the smooth operation of elections and the deliverance of speeches. The narrator's enthusiasm, therefore, is not so much dissipated as diverted by the subsequent discrepancy between the imagined ideal and its inevitable reality. The subtlety and apparent ease with which Pil'sky manipulates his themes, especially his mastery of the *skaz* form, reveals his ability to merge dissimilar elements and modes which, through their juxtaposition, attain humorous, grotesque, but ultimately earnest tone.

"When Leksey Lekseich and I Were at the Elections" will be followed here by a thought-provoking essay about Bunin's art and a perceptive review of the seventh issue of *The Virgin Soil*.

Grimaces of Brush and Pen: A Collection of Works by Russian Humorists Writers and Artists

About Myself

Nobody likes to walk around stark naked in public. Except maybe Adam and some other handsome men.

There's no such thing as a candid autobiography. And frankly, knowing how people are, one should answer their questions in the following manner:

"How old are you?"

"None of your business!"

"How are things?"

"It's of no concern to anyone!"

This isn't rudeness. It's only logical.

But then, what kind of humorist am I?

First, I am not a melancholic (all humorists are melancholics).

Secondly, I do not suffer from an irresistible tendency to have fits of laughter and can't even imagine how one can make people laugh on command. I've succeeded at many things in life, but in one thing I haven't—to this day I have never seen an author of anecdotes. However, undoubtedly such a profession does exist. They too are indisputable humorists. I'd give a lot to see the face of some such professional anecdotist.

They used to praise my memory, but in my opinion that is pure nonsense. It couldn't retain a single anecdote for more than two minutes.

Well, in short, I am not a humorist, and it's too late now to become one. It's not worth ruining your life just for the dubious pleasure of seeing your neighbor howl with laughter. And even if I did occasionally feel the need to elicit a smile, even then it would be unreasonable to hack off your whole hand just because of one hangnail.

The sphere of the humorist is the sphere of parody. And parody is forgery. It is a poor man's imitation of a rich man's signature. Yet it's not very tempting to enter the multitudinous ranks of banal humorists who, like Cossacks, have long been counted in squadrons. They may still think of themselves as writers, but they have no more right to the title than mice who call themselves pets.

To me, the danger in being a humorist lies in the fact that anybody who tells a joke becomes a part of your profession. I would rather the profession were only a part of the man.

Maybe this is just a dream. But other people have stubbornly insisted, and still do, on calling me a romantic. I'm not arguing. It isn't always flattering though. Every overloaded jackass considers himself a romantic, and only the one riding on him understands very clearly that it's not a romantic beneath him, but a jackass.

———————·———————

When Leksey Lekseich[2] and I Were at the Elections
At a Meeting of Russian Exiles

Leksey Lekseich and I got to the meeting first. They said: Be here at five o'clock; and that's when we got there.

On the way upstairs Leksey Lekseich says: "Something's wrong! Either my watch is off or we've turned up in the wrong place."

I get very alarmed. Maybe it really is the wrong place? We look around; nobody there. But we decide to give it a try anyway. So up we go, and there's three people already sitting right at the entrance with a lot of different papers and tickets spread out in front of them.

Leksey Lekseich bows: "I want to go in..." he says, "for the meeting."

And they answer so politely and pleasantly: "Certainly!"

So we pay the required amount, and go right into the hall. Leksey Lekseich coughs ever so quietly behind his hand so as not to disrupt the silence, because it really is quiet—since nobody's there.

We sit a while and wait. Maybe somebody'll come. And in fact a few do begin to slip in. Ten minutes go by like this, and more. Leksey Lekseich shoves his watch right under my nose: "Look," he says, "it's already 5:30. For all I know we may have to sit here till doomsday." We're already beginning to feel pretty uneasy, but there's no point. Just then the crowd begins to gather for real. It's just too much for the mind to grasp, so many people came crawling in.

I'm practically in ecstasy, it's sort of foolish of me: "Holy Moses!" I say, "look, there must be zillions of them here."

And he says: "Zillions? Oh, there's quite a few all right, might even come to a hundred." Well, maybe so. In my haste, I was off a little.

But anyway it doesn't make any difference.

In just the last couple of minutes, they're starting to come in droves. Zillions of people. You just can't breathe; I even get inspired. There you are, I think, when Russians begin to tackle things—hang on! Give us any hall and we'll pack it to the brim, just like French sardines. . . .

We talk in a whisper, but some lady turns to us: "Tell me, if you please, by what right did I not receive any notice, nor did my daughter receive one, nor did my brother; if we have come at all, it's only out of the goodness of our hearts."

At this point Leksey Lekseich rises slightly and replies: "Although this is not our responsibility, nevertheless—excuse us! We weren't notified officially either, and if we are here, it is because we're very curious to see if anything came out of it or not."

And a din of voices is heard around us: "Who? What? How on earth? You, Mar'ya Ivanovna? Is it you I see, Ivan Petrovich? Gracious, well, I never!"

And everybody's asking: "What's gong to happen? Why all the noise?"

And precisely then two guys suddenly walk out onto the stage.

One is a little taller and thinner; the other just a little shorter but heavier, to make up for it. The taller one, of course, is the chairman, and the shorter one, the secretary.

Everybody starts whispering at once. "Ivan Palych Moshkov," they say, "is a very goodhearted man."

And it's true. He gets up and says: "I don't feel like being chairman today. I'll just give you a report."

A compliant person! Easygoing! No burden on anybody!

And he says so politely: "Choose for yourselves," he says, "of your own free will, whomever you'd like as chairman."

They start to call out names. But all those called turn out to be absent, and so much for that! They name one, and everybody will start shouting: "But he is not even here."

They'll name another. "But he's out of town," they'll say.

They begin to look through the audience—who's present?

And do you believe it? They do find, and instantly elect, Mr. Petrov. A very good man, too. Well-mannered.

He steps onto the stage and says: "I bow to you and thank you with all my heart, but I cannot possibly serve without a secretary. Kindly choose someone else from among you as you see fit."

And the same thing happens again. Names are shouted—they're not here; and that's it. This one didn't come, that one's on a trip, this one didn't make it, another one's too busy. Well, what are we going to do? But they find somebody all the same.

"It has to be Vasilyev," we shout, "and nobody but him!"

In the end, to tell you the truth, the meeting is finally opened, and Ivan Palych Moshkov at once begins to talk about how things are going, what we are to do, why we have gathered, and what is in store for us.

It turns out that we opened in the autumn of 1920, in September, but to this day we have done nothing, and with elections just around the corner too. . . .

So right away we get down to the elections, and without any fuss, quietly and peacefully, we elect everyboy we need and don't need, as long as he's a good man.

I was very pleased with the meeting. I love quiet affairs! It's better done at a leisurely pace. We came without haste; we agreed about everything. If you don't offend anybody, nobody'll harm a hair on your head. Sit and hum, but if you do it aloud—well there's plenty of smart people around besides you. That means simply: Don't contradict, just agree.

That's how Leksey Lekseich and I behaved.

"Who's for, raise your hands,"—and we've already got our hands raised. "Who is against?"—and our hands are already in the air. "Who abstains?"—and again our hands are up.

It's better that way, because what would happen if some lowered their hands, others raised them, a third group argued, a fourth didn't agree, and a fifth one even fought for the establishment of a political party? That would be the last straw!

And as we walk out, such a languorous feeling fills our bodies that Leksey Lekseich says:

"Ekh, let's have some pancakes now, like when we were

kids, and then let's flop into bed."
Good job!

Revel, 1923

———————·———————

For You, No. 18 (May 1, 1938)

Ivan Bunin

"He is cold, reserved, inaccessible."
Dreams of the past.   The dead reign supreme.
"What do we know, for the most part?" The
East, Jerusalem, Judea. "My main love."

He is cold, reserved, inaccesible.

Thus they speak of Bunin, thus people judge him,
trusting to first impressions, with little real knowledge of this
writer, this man.   It is true, Bunin said more than once that
neither a scorching fire, nor embers, nor a fever are necessary
in order to create; rather, discipline and aloofness are
important. This is the writer's judgment on writing.

Bunin the man is also marked by restraint.   He is a
man conscious of his own worth.   During his life he saw
much, travelled much, observed much.   Perhaps the thought
that absorbed him most was the notion of inscrutable
eternity, the world of legends and traditions, of ancestral
decrees—the dead reign supreme.

Personality itself can develop, mature, and grow old, but
it cannot change its essence, that uniqueness created by a
whole succession of generations. These dreams of the past,
whispers of antiquity, remain eternal, instilled forever within
us.   The thread of centuries is unbroken, and everything we
create is only the result of these influences, the fulfillment of
someone's age-old plan.   It has been transmitted from one
generation to another, altered a little, enlarged upon or
abridged, as if from century to century it has passed through
the strictest controls and has been reflected upon.

Our ancestors who inspired us, they alone are the great
editors of our works.   This perception is the strongest

impression derived from Bunin's work. All his verses as well as his prose resound with distant voices from the past.

You read them, you listen to them, and suddenly you catch the primary melody—submissiveness. An excellent writer and wonderfully subtle poet, Bunin stands before us in the mystery of his inspiration like the stern executor of someone's orders from long ago, and at these moments his soul appears to have acquired the experience of infinity, enriched by age-old transgressions and insights.

*

A disquieting and vague feeling of universal doom, a feeling that all living creatures are subject to inexorable laws in a world which is ever destroying and renewing, permeates all of Bunin's prose and poetry, which is refracted into the twofold illumination of joy and sorrow, light and darkness.

Death and a sense of the inevitable end, of brevity and joy, of the transience and frailty of all creation—here are the perceptions of life. Sadness and death, love and death—these comprise the principal theme and central motif of all Bunin's reflections, his best poems, and his most valued prose.

How significant is the subtitle of his *Zhizn' Arsenyeva* (The Life of Arsenyev)! It describes the main contents of this book as "The Well of Days."

*

These words are not only a reference to the infantile beginnings of life, but also contain the principle of a general all-encompassing conception. These are not only the wells of a certain life, of a certain man. In a valid and natural extension, these are the wells of all human days in general. They are our connection with the very distant past, the repetition of events, our unceasing transformation, incorporating in themselves indelible echoes of bygone centuries, past existences, accumulated wisdom, inherited traditions, unconscious feelings, and memories, suddenly blazing up and bearing traces of long-extinguished visions.

*

No one today has such firm confidence that the thread of life is unbroken, that each existence is only the result and the sum of the past; no one is as convinced of the inexorable influences of mysterious heredity as was Bunin.

*

His most serious concern is the anguish caused ty the limitation, the insignificance of our knowledge. None of our passions can find expression or be satisfied. All that remains is a bitter awareness of unattainability, of our limited strength and the impossibility of understanding.

"*What do we know, for the most part?*" says Bunin already on the second page of *The Life of Arsenyev.* "For the most part, our knowledge is pitiful and poor." In this instance, Bunin is not only an analyst, but also a mystic. He does not find a solution to the riddle of knowledge in experience or observation, or in conflict or contact with life, but in forebodings and prophesies transmitted by the eternal past. Human wisdom cannot be created by one figure, one century, or one existence, however prolonged or rich with impressions it might be.

The wealth of insight and enlightenment comes as a transmitted gift, handed down from parents to children, from children to grandchildren.

"The knowledge which we acquire during our brief personal lives," says Bunin, "is *too limited. There is other knowledge,* infinitely richer, the knowledge with which we are born."

*

Always, when we read Bunin, we mysteriously and emotionally cross a forbidden border, the vague boundary of distant epochs, unrecognized, yet never quite forgotten. The link with antiquity in Bunin's soul is indestructible. This is clearly evident also in his book "The Shady Side of the Street," and in his stories about the East, Jerusalem, and Judea, those distant kingdoms and realms. Life here is "wild and *primitive,*" "*the phantom of the deceased* in the Byzantine mosaics exudes mystery," the "half-glimpsed visages of *apocalyptic* six-winged Seraphim are eerie," "ancient embrasures" gaze out at you, and the courtyard of the mosque "enchants with its patriarchal mien."

*

Bunin is a *scion*. He is the steadfast custodian of traditions, their enamoured admirer, who acutely feels the breath of vanished centuries. But his keen sense of observation does not retreat even for a moment. He can easily fathom human nature. Always witty in his formulations, he understands others, and himself as well. How does he write? Where does he find his images? They say that *The Life of Arsenyev* is an autobiographical novel. I think that if this is true, then only partially so.

Bunin spoke repeatedly about his creative writing, and he always affirmed the same idea:

"I cannot write the truth. I invent a heroine, let's say. I become involved in her life so completely that I believe in her existence and I fall in love with her. Yes, so much in love...I pick up the pen and weep. Then I begin to dream about her. She appears to me just as I have invented her. One day I wake up thinking: 'Good heavens, this may be the one great love of my life.' And then it turns out that she never even existed."

*

Vstrechi s moimi sovremennikami (Meetings with My Contemporaries) is about Tolstoy, Gor'ky, Chekhov, and Kuprin. I believe the memory of Kuprin left a sad, affectionate mark in Bunin's heart. Bunin had known him a long time, since his stories had come out in the magazine *Mir Bozhy* (The World of God), published by Maria Karlovna Kuprina. They would meet not only in Petersburg, but also in Odessa and Yalta. Bunin loved Odessa. It was there, it seems, that he was married. He used to go to Odessa on vacation, and there he became friends with the writer Alexander Mitrofanovich Fyodorov.

My memory has preserved one of Bunin's amusing

quatrains. Fyodorov had built himself a one-story house on
the very edge of the sea and called this villa by the pleasant,
soothing name "Delight."   Once Bunin dropped in on
Fyodorov but did not find him at home.   On the door he
wrote a teasing verse:

> "You waste all your time with friends,
> In bars, and in restaurants,
> But, brother, don't joke around with Ivan Bunin
> Or I'll pop you in the nose!"

In reality Fyodorov drank almost nothing, so the friendly
joke was even funnier since it accused him of crimes he never
committed.   I remember another amusing story about his
supposed drinking.

Once a visitor from Petersburg dropped in on Fyodorov,
who was sick in bed.   He had the gout although he almost
never drank.

"Hello! What's the matter with you?"

"It's all that drinking you do there in Petersburg, and then
I get the gout—because of you," Fyodrov grumbled.

This was indeed a great injustice of fate.

So there in Odessa they lived almost next door, Kuprin
and Bunin.   Not all writers can live in agreement with one
another and maintain a smooth relationship, but no cloud ever
darkened the friendship between Kuprin and Bunin.   So much
the sadder is it now for Bunin to think of Kuprin, of his
incurable ailment, and of the sad final days of his life.

*

Bunin's visit to the Baltic states had been expected for a
long time. For five years, to be exact. It was suggested that
Bunin should return to Paris after the Stockholm celebrations,[3]
not via Hamburg, but that he should spend some time in Riga,
Tallinn, and Kaunas. Only recently was he able to arrange this
trip.   The first evening he read *Meetings with My
Contemporaries*, and the second evening, *O lyubvi* (About Love).
Everyone is familiar with Bunin's magnificent stories on this
theme, "Ida," "Sunstroke," "Mitya's Love," stories about "the
joy of perceiving the human soul's divine charm."

*

The complicated riddles of the soul are also discussed in the story "Night Sea," which describes two men who had at one time been irreconcilable rivals. One was lucky in love, and the other was the dishonored, abandoned husband. But nothing lasts forever in this world; everything passes, pain grows dull, and hatred dies; only the horror of losses suffered in the past does not fade without leaving a trace. Nonetheless, time and life smooth over and even out the path; and eventually, "after a brief silence, they said to one another, quietly and simply, 'Good night!'"

*

The story "The Son" is about the riddle of a woman's soul, its last passionate outburst of love. It describes tenderness and ardor, fading happiness, love and death, hypnosis and obsession, the exhilaration of delightful last springs when "vivacity and that blissful, gentle intoxication return, that intoxication experienced in the full bloom of spring by those whose youth is behind them." This love encompasses a "sweet fear," a blissful helplessness, as if before dying.

*

Passions now repressed, now raging and unruly, now incurable, rise up in the stories "Ignatius," "By the Road," and "The Grammar of Love"; but the awakening of passions resulting in a youthful tragedy sadly charms us in "Gentle Breathing." The sweet dream of first embraces rushes past like a "Meteor." And no matter how many times one rereads the wonderful story "Ida," or the remarkable "Sunstroke," the impression remains as strong and captivating as before. There is so much beauty, artistic delicacy, brave daring, and profound truth radiating from every page and line, pouring forth in individual words, epithets, similes, and fascinating themes.

*

"In essence," writes Bunin in his story "Unknown Friend," "everything in the world is charming; this need of the human heart is ineradicable; everything in the world is miraculous, incomprehensible." And yet "of each human life one can write at most two or three lines." In the story he states: "Your creativity has the effect of *sad but lofty music*...Someone's hand somewhere wrote something, someone's soul revealed the tiniest part of its innermost life with the faintest allusion...and then, suddenly, space, time, and the disparity of destinies and circumstances all disappear," and all creative people send "their lines to someone unknown somewhere out in space," because "the appeal for sympathy is man's most urgent need."

This is Bunin, his magnetism, his gentle, forceful power, lasting and always beautiful even over the space of years and decades. This strength, this power does not grow dim; it captivates, not only burning but flaring up more and more brightly toward the bright clairvoyant time of wisdom and uplifting inspiration.

———————·———————

Today, No. 5 (January 4, 1935)

The Work of the Russian
"Guild of Poet" in Estonia
(The Virgin Soil, 7th collection, Tallinn, 1934)

Handfuls of stars—Somber words—Diaries and notes—Resurrection from the dead—Utopian fiction—In the Pechory region—Pluses and minuses.

A dark sky and in it a handful of little stars flicker unsteadily: literary circles, cooperatives, unions, and guilds of Russian poets and writers. Even here in Estonia young writers have managed to create their own group, to organize a "Guild of Poets." Last winter they occupied themselves with the critical analysis of works written by the individual members; in the spring of last year they compiled and published the collection *The Virgin Soil* for the Day of Russian Culture. This fall they delivered a series of papers on verse techniques. These young Russians also have translated the works of the Estonian writers: Mälk, Tassa, Roht, Vallak, Metsanurk, Tammsaare, Jakobson, Kivikas, Jaik.

The seventh issue of *The Virgin soil* has just been published in Tallinn under the editorship of P. Irtel.

The main themes of the almanac can be divided into two categories. The first section, including sketches and stories describing the Pechory region, deals with daily life. The other, poetry and prose, reveals the moods, feelings, and anxieties of the young authors. Here are thoughts about death and God, and a fantastic story about a future when death has been conquered and when geniuses, the talented and select few, are favored with artificial resurrection; so far has science advanced. Thus dreams K. Hoerschelmann in his story "The Second Box."

The predominant mood in most of the pieces is sadness—autumn, death, hopelessness, earthly fate—that is, real life, the "insubstantial world." This pessimism (in some places gloomier than in others) is evident in the diction itself in the frequent references to "death," "separation," the hopeless "never," in the images of "coffin" and "the sting of death," in visions of a "corpse"—"how sad, o heart, is thy story of the first death, of the fall." Included is an "Epitaph" and here again "flows the silver light of death." Then, "the road of autumn dew," "sunsets," "dense fog," "pitiful death under the snarling pig (?) of a bus," and the complaint that "not enough light comes through the window," that soon "autumn will greet me."

These mortal anxieties, visions of the inevitable end, also appear in many pages of the fiction. Yury Ivask's article "Provinical Notes" is entirely devoted to them. Its epigraph is "Soaring upwards, to breathe out into death." Next, about God. These meditations are not always valuable and, in referring to God, not everyone is seriously and deeply moved by Him. P. Irtel uses the word "God" several times in his two poems—"Rain from God" and "I whisper to the icon, where Christ's eyes are blue." B. Novosadov writes "Calm gives way to thunder without the trembling of God's lips"; and Irtel's story "The Little Old Man" is devoted in its entirety to the man of God, Ipat. The intellectual will say Ipat is not a typical character. But be that as it may, this does not prevent him from inspiring others with his "idea." A simple woman says of him, "Our Ipat is unique in all the land." He is pious, but no one knows or can guess what he prays for.

In his "Provincial Notes," not so much a provincial diary as religious-philosophical entries, Yury Ivask also speaks about the paths to God. Both externally and internally, the notes somewhat resemble, or try to resemble, Rozanov's fragmentary and significant lines in *Opavshie listya* (Fallen Leaves). There is even direct mention of Rozanov in these pages.

It should be stated that the claim to significance and profundity in this collection is undermined by excessive theorizing and philosophizing. But everything that is clear is easy to understand, while diaries and notes in particular ought not to be difficult. Their lines are supposed to be written for the author himself, who should not need long and complex interpretations and explanations.

Hoerschelmann's story "The Second Box" suffers from this same pretentious profundity. This work of Utopian fantasy transports us into the future, beyond the limitations of ordinary life. And since the author prophesies about the possibility of resurrecting the dead, he naturally mentions the remarkable Russian philosopher Fyodorov.

Hoerschelmann tells about "The Southern Resurrection Company" whose goal is universal resurrection and universal immortality. Death is vanquished. Let the earth grow old and the sun die out, never fear. Refrigerators and heaters will be invented, and life will be transported to another planet, another constellation. If life is valuable, one must do whatever is necessary to make it possible to live. If there is no such thing as immortality, then it must be created. What if it gets boring? No one will force you to continue your existence. Incidentally, after resurrection the lucky man is locked up in a comfortable room where he must spend a month, otherwise the majority of those resurrected will for some reason commit suicide. But after a month, freedom is granted and he may go where he will. It turns out that after the urge to commit suicide has passed—and it persists for an entire month!—the resurrected not only become reconciled to their new life, but want to prolong it by any possible means.

We will not evaluate the fantastic concepts. The majority of them stand, as it were, outside of serious criticism; no one wants to object to an alluring happy dream. But the fantasy in every Utopian novel invariably strives to substantiate itself scientifically, though seldom with success. An all too vivid imagination is detrimental, Utopian fiction flourishes now as never before; the postwar years have opened wide vistas for it. Nevertheless (and this is mandatory), one must not lose a sense of moderation. A grandiose vision easily lapses into an even more grandiose fiasco. It is even possible to formulate a law: The more externally simple the scientific assumptions of the Utopian novel, the more convincing it is. Hoerschelmann's story presents fantasy without inpsiring faith in it.

Besides the verses of E. Bazilevskaya, K. Hoerschelmann, Yu. Ivask, Ir-Bor., P. Irtel, B. Nartsissov, B. Novosadov, and M. Roos, and in addition to the fantastic and religious-philisophical stories, sketches of daily life comprise a large part of this collection. The Pechory region provides the material for all of them: "An Etude" (M. R.), "Epiphany Eve in Obozerye" (B. Nazarevsky), Pyotr Bogdanov's article on the new rural intelligentsia, and two small sketches by B. S., also about peasant life ("Playwright" and "My Friend"). In them one can find successful phrases of folk speech: "If you can make a person repeat it two or three times, you can paint an icon of him as a great martyr..." "The memory, like a bearskin coat, won't let out its warmth."

Finally, a word on the pluses and minuses. It is good that collections are being published, that the "Guild of Poets" continues to work, and that its work is not dismally monotonous; it is good that its *Virgin Soil* comes out regularly. But I repeat that it is necessary for the poets to have their own voices, their own sound, tones, and diversity, and to avoid clichés. In their prose greater simplicity, clarity, and observation, a living connection with real life, as well as fresh and youthful sensitivity, are desirable. In creative writing there is nothing more harmful or terrible than hackneyed words or moods, the absence of distinct outlines, approximations, and inexactitude.

One more positive word should be added: The literacy

of the young participants of the "Guild" is almost irreproachable. Nowadays this is a rarity; there are times when it is considered a miracle if a word simply manages to avoid being inept, and courageous writers do not give birth to monsters.

P. P-y [P. Pil'sky]

NOTES

1. N. E. Andreyev, "Struve, G., *Literature v izgnanii,*" *Grani,* No. 33 (January–March 1957).
2. A folksy way of rendering the first name and patronymic, Alexey Alexeevich.
3. Bunin received the Nobel prize for literature in 1933.

MAXIM, LEV (literary pseudonym of M. MIKHAYLOV)

Lev Maxim was a talented writer of feuilletons and a contributor to the newspaper *Today.* Endowed with a sharp, sensitive eye and a good-natured sense of humor, he wrote feuilletons that were neither aggressive nor offensive. He published a collection of short stories entitled *Kogda v dome rebyonok* (When There is a Child in the House; Riga: Literatura, 1928), introduction by P. Pil'sky.

Grimaces of Brush and Pen: A Collection of Works by Russian Humorist Writers and Artists

Some Words About Myself

Even as a child, I manifested the ability to imitate our very best writers. My first poem, dedicated to the sea, clearly indicated this ability:

Farewell, o element untrammeled,
Before me for the last time
You roll your blue waves, etc.

When I brought these lines to a distinguished daily paper, they were all astonished; it seems that Pushkin himself had written the exact same poem. Indeed, word for word.

There was nothing particularly surprising in this coincidence, by the way; this poem was so charming that of course even Pushkin might have written it. I was eleven then.

At twelve years of age I wrote a story which, it seems, Chekhov had also written in his day. Thus, at this time I easily kept pace with any writer, and my stories occasioned a great deal of amusement.

Then I began to forge ahead of our literature and, as is often the case, my stories began to attract less attention. Later...but I'm not really sure whether I should speak about what followed. Even if I should affirm with all sincerity that each of my new stories—and I am absolutely convinced of this— overshadowed everything before me in world literature, my future biographers and critics would nonetheless express their own views on the subject.

Is sincerity really worth the trouble?

———————•———————

Suicide

Of course, suicide is not a real profession. You can't really say that so-and-so works as a suicide.

But occasionally it can be a fairly good secondary occupation, if you acquire the technique for it.

I knew, for instance, a man who would go to the river precisely on the first of each month, just before he had to pay the rent, and attempt to throw himself into the water. It was all quite in the open and not far from a policeman (invariably near a policeman).

Each time the policeman would grab him from behind by his coattails and save him.

This all became so customary that when they'd ask his wife on the first, "Where is your husband?"—she would answer calmly, fussing with the flowerpots: "He's gone to drown himself!"

Usually the frightened landlord would then postpone the

rent after this incident. The man lived to an advanced age, enjoying great esteem and a certain amount of admiration: "There's a man who couldn't care less if he killed himself or not!"

He even acquired a certain notoriety.

The other case was a new husband, a pleasant and vivacious young man, but a skirt chaser. Every time he deceived his wife and she, discovering his infidelity, threw a hysterical scene, he would run into the living room and throw a rope over a hook in the ceiling. Then, standing on a stool with the noose round his neck, he would call to the maid: "Farewell, Arisha...You did good work...No need to cry, dear..."

Naturally, there was a great deal of confusion in the house; the wife threw herself upon her husband's chest and forgave him everything; Arisha wept, and the suicide was carried in triumph to the sofa and surrounded by the most loving attentions.

In a third instance of a similar nature, the young husband would usually shoot himself with a revolver.

He even had his favorite place in the study where he liked to do it—near the desk, just opposite the portrait of the fabulist Krylov on the wall.

It always happened that the bullet would hit Krylov.

In a rather short period of time the famous fabulist received twenty-six wounds, all of them mortal, while the young husband remained unscathed.

It's a generally known fact that suicides often miss the mark. Even with poison—poison can fall short, too.

A pharmacist once told me that in the course of two months the same woman, who was constantly poisoning herself, came running to him in despair seven times.

And always with the ready phrase: "Give me my antidote!..."

The pharmacist was already used to her. "So, did you gulp down your vinegar concentrate again?" he asked lazily. "And probably, devil knows, it was diluted as usual!"

"Listen, don't be a lout!"

"My dear madam," the pharmacist said to her, in conclusion, with sincere sympathy, "I understand that you want to die but don't know exactly how to manage it.

Look, let me fill this bottle for you with cyanic acid instead
of your vinegar concentrate. Just swallow it once and you'll
be fine and so will I."

The woman was offended and stopped coming.

There are indeed some suicides who never confirm the
hopes placed in them.

I remember one when a friend and I visited the Imatra
Waterfall [Karelia, Finland], a classic spot for suicides, one
might say. It's a gathering point for them.

As it is wont to happen, a personage of sorts
immediately presented himself to us and offered to show us
the famous falls and how millions of buckets of water pour
over its cliffs every minute.

My friend, a practical and rather severe person, listened
glumly for awhile, and finally became angry. "Listen, devil
take it, do you think we are idiots? We didn't come here to
count your buckets—we have sufficient water of our own!
But if you have perchance a decent suicide who is ready to
take on the falls today or tomorrow, then bring him forth!
But don't bother us with foolishness."

"We do indeed!" said the personage. "You came just at
the right time. There is a man upstairs who hasn't paid for
his room in nine days now! That's the usual sign. 'They'
never pay. After all, you have to understand their position.
It's not the smartest thing to pay and then jump right into
the falls. According to our calculations, it should be
tomorrow, and I trust he will afford you a bit of diversion!"

But the next day the personage came to us, a bit
embarrassed. It turned out that the suicide did not wish to
leap into the falls and had no intention of doing so. "Why
should I?" he asked incensed. "I'd rather wait and not pay
for the tenth day!"

On the whole there are only a few among them with
any developed sense of professional honor.

I must say in conclusion that, with the exception of the
usual human failings, suicides are often friendly people and
you can sometimes have a fairly pleasant time with them.

———————·———————

The Thing You Are Looking For

More often than not the thing is right under your nose. But on those days when your guardian angel turns his back on you, there's no way you can find it.

You take all the newspapers and books off the table, shake them all out most carefully, empty all the desk drawers, dig through the basket under the desk, ransack the bookcase, finding in the process dozens of things which you don't need—and finally you throw up your hands in despair.

You're only looking for an old pencil, a stub. In fact, you could easily go and get a new one, you have dozens of them. And if you should find this old pencil stub, you might even toss it out the window. You don't need it at all, really.

The whole problem is that it was here *just now* in your very hand. The pencil is not so important as understanding the incomprehensible: How could it disappear?

The loss begins to nag at you like a toothache that suddenly flares up. There is no peace from it. You can't do any other work. Heaven knows what you wouldn't give now for that miserable pencil!

You feel as if you've been completely abandoned by fate.

Quite unhappy, you call the maid and try to lay the blame on her. "Glasha, didn't you clear my desk today? What did you do with my pencil?"

In a tragic manner, you look at Glasha and, trying to work on her conscience, you describe the old stub in such morose detail that Glasha, touched, gradually agrees that there was indeed such a pencil on your desk. She even saw it today herself.

"Then where is it?"

With a gesture full of restrained grief, you point to the desk from whence the pencil disappeared.

Actually the pencil is lying near the ash tray and there should be no problem whatsoever in seeing it.

But on the day when you are destined not to find it, even Glasha can't see it.

And just as you did, she clears off all the papers and books and shakes them, ransacks the bookcase, digs through the basket under the desk, and even brushes off the top of the Dutch tile stove where you might have laid the pencil only in an extreme attack of delirium.

Still no pencil. But you feel a little better anyhow. You've shared your burden with Glasha, and now she is also interested and impressed by your struggle with the incomprehensible.

"Maybe we should look in the linen closet!" she suggests energetically.

"But how would it get in there?"

"Three days ago I was putting away your linen..."

In the corner of your brain which is not entirely clouded over you admit vaguely that the pencil which you saw *today*, only ten minutes ago, could never have gotten into the linen closet *three days ago*.

Nevertheless you start to dig through the linen closet together with Glasha.

By now your guardian angel, who had turned away, suddenly remembers you, glances toward you with a smile, and at that very moment you see the ash tray, and next to it the pencil. At the same time Glasha sees it too.

"Well, there it is," you say with returning dignity, "and here you are babbling about the closet..."

And sticking the pencil under some newspapers so that you couldn't possibly find it again, you set to work with enthusiasm, pacified and happy.

Exactly fifteen minutes later Glasha takes her revenge. Rattling her keys on a ring round her finger, she comes into the study and inquires with concern: "Sir, didn't I leave some keys in here?"

"What keys?" you ask in a businesslike manner, although you can see the keys on her finger. "The ones you usually carry on your finger?"

"What else? Of course..."

"How could you have lost them?"

For the third time you remove the papers and books and shake them out, ransack everything, dig through anything you can—meanwhile the keys keep on jingling—and finally an idea comes to mind: "Why don't we look in my suitcase, Glasha?"

"But how could they get in your suitcase, sir?"

"Three days ago I opened it to get a flask out..."

And when the suitcase is thoroughly upturned, Glasha's guardian angel in his turn remembers her, she then falls silent with embarrassment and takes the keys off her finger. "What do you know!" she mumbles and goes out smiling.

There is one more peculiarity about things you are looking for. If today you need your notebook, for example, then in all the places it might possibly be you will find the tie clasp or tie that you looked for yesterday. And tomorrow wherever you look for the tie clasp you will find the notebook.

I made note of this strange phenomenon and once when I was searching for my toothbrush, I pretended that I was looking for yesterday's glue. But it didn't work. I found the glue, but not the toothbrush. So I came to the conclusion that you may deceive yourself, but not the thing that you are looking for.

Now when I lose something on the desk, I don't look for it at all. I remain calm—I know that when I no longer need it, it will fall right into my hand.

————·————

With gentle, mocking humor Lev Maxim subtly exposes the ridiculous aspects in human attitudes and behavior. In "Suicide" and "The Thing You Are Looking For," the characters are portrayed as victims of their own befuddled minds and delusions. The potential victims of "Suicide" take great pride in their ability to destroy themselves and, as Maxim comments, they enjoy "great esteem and even a certain admiration . . . a certain notoriety." In all the pieces included here, the semi-serious narrative contrasts with the foolishness of the situations and emphasizes the irrational factors motivating conduct. Man's ludicrous sense of pride and his vanity emerge vividly from these stories. Narrow-mindedness and inflated sense of self-importance are illustrated by the need to impose one's own petty feelings on others. Much of the humorous effect of these pieces lies in the narrator's sharp, though never cruel, mock-serious observations on absurd, yet universally human traits.

GADALIN, V. V. (1892-?;
literary pseudonym of VASILYEV, VASILY VLADIMIROVICH)

V. V. Gadalin was a Russian fiction writer in Riga, Latvia, where he had settled after his escape from Russia following the events of 1917. He wrote the autobiography printed below. He contributed short stories and articles to the journals *Our Little Light* (Riga, 1923-28), of which he was editor, and *Spolokhi* (Northern Lights; Berlin, 1921-23; Nos. 1-21, edited by A. Drozdov). He also wrote the prefaces to L. Leonov's *Barsuki* (The Badgers; Riga: Literatura, 1927), V. Shishkov's *Rokovoy vystrel* (The Fatal Shot; Riga: Literatura, 1927), and M. Zoshchenko's *O tom, chto bylo i chego ne bylo* (About What Had Taken Place and About What Had Not Taken Place; Riga: Literatura, 1927?).

> *Grimaces of Brush and Pen: A Collection of Works by Russian Humorist Writers and Artists*

My Autobiography

It's somehow quite awkward to write about oneself. They'll say I'm advertising myself...

But actually, just what kind of advertisement is this? People know me well enough as it is; indeed, I wouldn't even have thought about writing this if it weren't for some of my friends and pals...

"You," they say, "you inspired the collection *Grimaces of Brush and Pen* and therefore you mustn't besmirch your name, write something about yourself."

Well, okay! I'll try.

I was born on a bright spring morning and, as soon as I appeared on God's earth, the midwife, taking me in her arms, exclaimed:

"Oh, the poor kid's so scrawny and puny! This one won't last long. He's got a head like a teacup!"

Obviously, the midwife thought my head should be at least the size of a good Astrakhan watermelon.

In defiance of her verdict, however, I decided not to

give up and, as you see, have made it to the age of thirty-six.

I became a humorist through the initiative of the secretary of the Kronstadt newspaper . *Kotlin*, Evgeny Evgenyevich Tveritinov, who, upon reading some lyrics I sent to the editorial office, dubbed me a "humorist" and defiled me in *The Mail Box*.

Nevertheless, a short time later my first literary experiments made their appearance in that same *Kotlin*, in *The Kronstadt Messenger*, and in the comic almanac *The Comet*.

Since 1910, I have published in the St. Petersburg journals *World-Wide Panorama*, *The New World-Wide Illustrated*, *Blue Journal*, *Theatre Review*, and in Moscow journals like *The Poor Man's Lot*.

While working in journalism, I went through a whole series of professions of all kinds, starting as a technician on a ship and ending as a miner. If I were to list all the editions I worked on and published as well as all my other professional activities, I'd have to write not an autobiography but a long book along the lines of *The Escapades of Rocambole*.

At present I am the editor of the publication *Literature*.[1] Not long ago I published the humorous calendar "The Joker" and compiled the collection *Grimaces of Brush and Pen*. In Riga, as in many other cities of our boundless Russia, I worked quite a bit in journalism, and I still do.

I have no complaints about my family life. Nor about my life in the publishing business. We have a friendly enough family here at *Literature*. Often we will get together with a whole crowd of colleagues. The room is so filled with tobacco smoke that, really, you could cut it with a knife, especially when the painter Apsit joins us with his pipe. Everyone smokes. Only I myself am, so to speak, a nonsmoker. But I put up with it. Because where there's smoke the work turns out better and the thinking is sharper.

Day after day, month after month, year after year go by in the same way.

I don't know; what else should I say?

Or, maybe this is enough?

———————.———————

The Lessons of Love

Love is a dream, love is a gift of the gods, love is self-deception, love is habit, love is the "instantaneous fire of passion." There are so many possible definitions of love that Irina Pavlovna Kurochkina [little hen], who still had not tasted love although she was already over thirty, understandably got all tangled up in them, and meanwhile arrived at the most naïve definition of all: Love ain't no potato.

It was one of those warm, spring evenings...On a bench along a path by the sea, drowned in soft moonlight, Irina Pavlovna sat and listened to a nightingale...The nightingale trilled, filled the night with warbling, fell silent, and then again poured forth...

"Be my teacher, Nikolay Petrovich," Irina Pavlovna said, turning to the very interesting young man who joined her; it was Zhilin, her neighbor from the summer cottage, who had made such persistent advances to her that she had begun to experience something new and strange, a tickling sensation in her armpits...But it hadn't ever occurred to her that this was love...

"What can I do for you?..."

"Explain to me what love is..."

She glanced at him coquettishly and provocatively...

"Aha...at last!..." Zhilin thought, "We're approaching our aim..."

And so he began to talk...And, how well he spoke!!!

Irina Pavlovna was all ears...But when his throat became dry, he fell silent and looked expectantly at his student...She, it seemed was waiting for him to continue...

"I'll continue tomorrow, Irina Pavlovna..."

And they parted...

*

A year went by...Again it was a warm, spring evening...The nightingale was pouring forth his trills as before...But Irina Pavlovna no longer listened to his song.

She closed the shutters tightly and fingered her pawn tickets. Now she knew what love was, and she dreamed of finding some student to teach him to love, who would buy her textbooks...

_____·_____

At the Summer Cottage

The sun sank beneath the trees, there was a breath of coolness in the air, and a quiet, summery twilight cloaked the earth.

They were sitting and talking in the cozy arbor of a shady garden...They spoke of the eternal beauty of nature, of art so divine, of the theatre...

"When I go on the stage, I'll undoubtedly have to change my name," she said pensively.

He was silent for a few moments and then said in a barely audible voice:

"Lucienne, you can do that without going on the stage!"

Silence sat in again.

Then she whispered very timidly:

"Vova, my dear, talk to Mama..."

_____·_____

Dream and Reality

I had a dream: A sweet young girl
Bends her head toward me;
The little tongue whispers sweet nothings,
Her plump little cheeks burn as if on fire...

The golden silk of her unruly tresses
Softly ripples over my chest...
Suddenly a fleeting, provocative kiss
Seems to scorch my lips...And I awaken.

The maiden has vanished! I stare—by my bedside
My setter is howling away...
Well, old pal, you picked a fine time

To lick my nose!

_____·_____

In his style and humorous intonations, as well as in the underlying view of mankind, V. Gadalin resembles both Chekhov and Nadezhda Teffi.   Like they, Gadalin carefully juxtaposes romantic ideals and dreams with the often devastating consequences of excessive reliance upon such delusions.   This is particularly evident in "The Lessons of Love."   The tale is constructed by means of quick, snapshot-like scenes which, by their very briefness, accentuate the disparity between dream and reality.   Like many of Chekhov's characters, Irina Pavlovna eagerly drinks in the passionate words of Zhilin, which inflame her romantically inclined imagination without, however, achieving the desired result.   In the last scene Irina Pavlovna, who now knows "what love is," holds in her hands the tickets for her pawned belongings, and through this image Gadalin points out with amused irony the lesson she has learned.   Like Chekhov, he leaves his heroine as we found her; she is dreaming again, but no longer of romantic love.

The distinctly Chekhovian quality of Gadalin's prose is enchanced by his gentle humor and by his somewhat detached yet no less genuine sympathy with the foolish tragedies caused by man's foibles.   These motifs and the depressing awareness of the unattainable quality of dreams are deftly interwoven in the playful lyric "Dream and Reality."   The *persona* dreams of a romantic encounter with a beautiful young girl, but the "golden silk of her unruly tresses" flowing over his chest turns out to be the hair of his shaggy setter.   The dream image of a "fleeting, provocative kiss" is correspondingly and satirically lowered when the *persona* realizes that it is his dog who licked his nose.

NOTE

1.   *Literature i zhizn'* (Literature and Life, a monthly; Riga: Literatura, 1928), edited by P. Pil'sky and V. Gadalin.

GALICH, YURY (1877-1940;
literary pseudonym of General Goncharenko, Georgy Ivanovich)

As a novelist and short story writer, Yury Galich excelled in the depiction of military life. A Cuirassier officer himself, he had firsthand knowledge of the Imperial Army and was personally acquainted with several members of the Imperial Family who had held military posts in St. Petersburg and the Russian provinces. After the collapse of the Imperial Army in 1917, Galich retired to his estate in southern Russia. During the Civil War he fled to Latvia where he published his military tales. He was a prolific and fashionable writer, much in demand while in exile during the first years after the revolution.

Galich's works focus on the military spirit and life in the Russian Army before and during the First World War. He writes in relief, carefully observes an artistic distance from his material, and refrains from indulging in the tragedies which often form the essence of his stories. Objectivity in presentation and emotional restraint are distinctive features of Galich's style. In the story "The General-Admiral and Naval Cadet Popandopulo," he assumes an ironic tone appropriate for the portrayal of a young officer's escapades, and it is only in the last sentence that the author reveals the tragic nature of the story.

Galich's control and his successful manipulation of the point of view are even more evident in the other two pieces selected here. "The Would-Be Assassin of the Imperial Family" and "Mikhail Romanov" are concerned with the fate of the Imperial Family at the hands of the Bolsheviks. Galich relates the stories in a colorful yet subdued manner. Particularly picturesque is the description of a New Year's parade on Epiphany in St. Petersburg. Grand Duke Mikhail's farewell to his troops likewise conveys the rich flavor of military life. The story, a sensitive, even intimate portrayal of Mikhail Romanov, ends in an anticlimactic crescendo summarizing the Grand Duke's fate—he was brutally executed by the Bolsheviks. A similar crescendo occurs in "The Would-Be Assassin of the Imperial Family," where two officers of the Imperial Army stationed in Kiev during the revolution bask in the setting sun and reminisce about the old days in St. Petersburg. Then newspaper boys appear spreading the news of the murder of the Imperial Family.

Galich's restrained manner of narration is indeed very effective. Through artistic discipline, the stories assume a heartrending quality. In this respect Galich differs from Ivan Lukash, an émigré writer who first lived in Riga and then in Paris. Lukash portrayed scenes of military life and had a tendency to present the tragic in an emotionally charged tone and occasionally even lapsed into sentimentality.

Among Galich's publications are many novels, short stories, and translated works, for example, a trilogy *Brachny ostrov* (The Conjugal Island; Riga: Didkovsky, 1926), *Imperatorskie fazany* (Imperial Pheasants; Riga: Didkovsky, 1926?); his most famous work *Sinie kirasiry* (Blue Cuirassiers; Riga: Filin, 1936; *Lyogkaya kavaleriya* (Light Cavalry; Riga: Gramatu Draugs, 1928), *Krasny khorovod* (A Red Round Dance; Riga: Didkovsky, 1929); other volumes of short stories, novellas, and fairy tales, and a volume of poetry entitled *Orkhideya: tropicheskie rifmy* (The Orchid: Tropical Rhymes; Riga: Didkovsky, 1927). He also contributed to the Russian periodicals in Riga, *Today* and *Chimes*.

In 1939, during the Soviet occupation of Latvia, Galich committed suicide by taking poison.

Imperial Pheasants

Mikhail Romanov

"His Imperial Highness, Heir Apparent and Grand Duke, Aide-de-camp to the Emperor, the Cornet Mikhail Alexandrovitch, has been appointed Officer of the Day of the Household Guards of His Majesty's Regiment." So read one of the paragraphs in the regimental order of the day. Like so many other things even more valuable and significant, I no longer have it. I have only kept my memories...

Mikhail and I were of the same age.

I began active service at the same time he did, and on the regimental list our names figured next to each other.

The Grand Duke's entrance into the Regiment was discussed at the officers' meeting, for it was the tradition in the old Petrine "Household Regiments" not to make an exception for anyone.

The senior colonel informed the officers of the impending event and asked for their opinions. The meeting was short, since all officers were favorably disposed toward the Duke; after all, the presence of the Grand Duke was an honor for the Regiment. Only the old, singlehearted captain Baron Korff expressed apprehension that this event might eventually break up the regimental family. Nevertheless, the Grand Duke was accepted into the regiment, and he honestly carried out the duties of a junior officer. In the barracks, in the riding school, on the shooting range, and on manoeuvres he was neither worse nor better than most of his fellow officers.

At that time, some forty years ago, he was a stately young man, shy and simple-hearted, with a bright and open gaze. He lived in Gatchina Palace next to the barracks and, in addition to performing his Ducal duties, he participated in the regimental life.

But all the same, there was a certain barrier. The senior officers treated him with a slightly ingratiating and protective sort of attention. Many younger officers could not bring themselves to speak openly or treat him as one of their peers. The main reason for these restrained and delicate relationships was undoubtedly the Grand Duke himself, with his chaste modesty, his palace upbringing, and his fragile nature. Besides, he was placed under the vigilant supervision of hundred-eyed Arguses and was never free from their annoying guardianship.

The Grand Duke had a peaceful, good-natured, and kind disposition. There was little evidence of an excitable temperament; indeed, he was trusting and simple. Though his education had been rather superficial, he spoke several languages fluently. He did not smoke, and at officers' parties he would neither drink wine nor play cards. He was an exceptional horseman and sportsman and devoted most of his leisure time to riding, racing, and hunting.

Ten years younger than the Tsar, the Grand Duke resembled him very little. He exuded health, freshness, and strength, and his beardless face evinced a rosy complexion and an unfailing smile. The tall, slender figure in the tricolored Cuirassier uniform—in white, blue, and gold—on a chestnut thoroughbred horse was undoubtedly one of the most handsome officers in the Regiment. But he had neither a penetrating, fervent mind nor a daring, courageous spirit. The Grand Duke was an ordinary man with average talents, bred in an impractical hothouse atmosphere and, by will of blind fate, elevated to the pedestal of the throne.

After one year the Grand Duke received the summons for the Household Cavalry, and soon thereafter occured an event of a certain dramatic coloring.

*

Among the women in the regiment there was the wife of Lieutenant Wulfert, Natalya Sergeevna, daughter of the lawyer Sheremetyevsky, by her first marriage Mamontova.

She was a stylish young woman with remarkable energy and intelligence.

The Grand Duke was immediately captivated by her.

Neither the awareness of his own high position nor the arguments of his august relatives, even his Mother the Empress, could quell his ardent feelings. The Grand Duke abandoned himself to his feelings with all the passion of untapped youth.

Of course the Grand Duke's infatuation could not remain a secret.

The senior officers were prepared to look at the situation with condescension, but the junior officers could not accept this breach of regimental etiquette. Dissension spread in the friendly regimental family, and the Grand Ducal romance was threatened with serious complications.

Lieutenant Wulfert was forced to leave the regiment, and the same fate soon befell the Grand Duke himself when his ardent passion culminated in a morganatic marriage.

By Imperial order he was given command over the Seventeenth Hussar Chernigovsky Regiment and with his young wife, now called Countess Brasova, he moved to Orel.

He spent three years of his life as a commander of an army regiment and a hospitable Orel landowner. These were also three years of quiet matrimonial happiness far from the St. Petersburg Imperial Court, which the Grand Duke always avoided with a kind of morbid delicacy. The influence of his wife and life in the provincial town left a definite imprint on him.

Soon, with the birth of the Tsar's son, the Grand Duke gave up the title "Heir" and expressed with complete sincerity his satisfaction on this occasion. Then, against his wish, he was summoned to St. Petersburg and appointed commander of a cavalry guards regiment.

Yet a month later he fell into disfavor, lost his Imperial birthrights, and was sent into exile as punishment for a mesalliance sanctioned by the church.

And then came the war.

At the front the Grand Duke commanded a division of the Caucasian Mountaineers, the so-called "savage" division. For his personal courage he was awarded the Cross of St. George and given command over the Second Cavalry Corps.

*

I met him again in the spring of 1916 in the luxurious palace of the Podol'sky landowner Nikitin, where the Corps headquarters were located.

The Grand Duke received me and for two weeks, until our Galitsiysky campaign, I enjoyed his exceptional hospitality.

In intimate surroundings, and in the company of two or three men who were especially close to him, General Jusefovich, General Baron Wrangel, and a personal aide, the young Prince Vyazemsky, we passed the time walking and conversing at the dinner table.

The Grand Duke was still the same simple, trusting, modest man. However, his outward appearance had changed greatly.

He had aged, begun to show wrinkles, his hair had thinned out noticeably, and not a trace was left of the former glowing complexion. Nevertheless, he still reminded me of the handsome youth I had known in the Cuirassier Regiment.

The Grand Duke had a serious gastric disease. He often left the front to go to his estate of Brasovo near Orel, and when in January of 1917 he was appointed General-Inspector of the Cavalry, he left us completely...

*

Near dilapidated Nadvornaya, in the village of Krasna, and against the background of the bluish Carpathians, he made a farewell review.

On a gray Turkman stallion, in a gray Cuirassier coat with a sheepskin hat, the Grand Duke accompanied by a few of his staff galloped around the Cavalry Brigade, which stood in the snowy meadow lit by the bright sun.

"Good day, Arkhangel City Dragoons!   Well done, Irkutsk Hussars!..."

To the sound of the trumpeters we passed by with a ceremonial march, saluted, and answered his greeting according to the rules of the cavalry regulations.

There were multicolored ribbons on the lances, the silver neigh of the horses galloped about, and snowflakes sparkled from under the hooves of the Dragoon and Hussar troops.

In the evening, in the village of Maidan-Gurny, we gave a farewell dinner in honor of the Grand Duke.   Music thundered.   The officers sang, told stories, and recited poetry. It was a simple and happy time, as one can only experience when on leave in a field camp after an exhausting service on a military mountain assignment.

The Grand Duke was pensive.

"You will not believe how sorry I am to leave...It is as if I were leaving forever!"

He had not been deceived.

In July of 1918 he was shot near Perm'...

————————·————————

The Would-Be Assassin of the Imperial Family

This event occured during the January days of 1905, at the unfortunate time of the Russo-Japanese War.

The riflemen of the Imperial Family...who did not know them?   A crimson Russian blouse, a caftan with gold braid, and a gold cross on a lambskin cap.

Present also was Colonel Grigory Davydov or, as he was simple called, Gri-Gri, of the Cavalry Guard Artillery, Commander of a Battery of His Majesty, and future aide-de-camp to the Emperor.

On top of that, there was a New Year's parade on Epiphany with the blessing of the waters of the Jordan...

It was a bright, frosty day.

On the Embankment stood the troops. The breastplates and helmets of the officers of the Household Cavalry and the Regular Cavalry shone brightly in the sunlight. On tall bay and black horses decorated with colorful garlands, a line of shiny, helmeted troops stretched along the Neva. There were multicolored Cuirassier plumes, flags on slender Uhlan lances, and the white plumes of the Tsarskoe Selo Hussars. Unsheathed swords, sabers, and trumpets sparkled brilliantly. Brightly shone the Grenadiers of the Pavlovsk Regiment and the iron bristle of the Infantry.

By the steps of the Jordan stood the Emperor surrounded by a large retinue, the Diplomatic Corps in guilded cocked hats, high officials of the first three ranks, and the clergy in magnificent robes.

Further back stood the crowd, kept at a respectful distance by the mounted and regular police and forced to refrain from a display of patriotic feelings.

The bells of the Isaac Cathedral began to drone. The solemn moment arrived. But...

The Emperor was about to make a speech and suddenly — bang! Gunshots burst forth!

The event was described in rather figurative terms in the next issue of the Myatlevsky pamphlet.

For some reason, one of the guns belonging to the Mounted Battery of His Majesty saluted with the shooting of a battle shell.

Fortunately the gunsight had been placed high, so the bullets damaged only the plaster of the Winter Palace, broke the staff of the standard, and injured several cadets of the Naval Corps.

The Epiphany parade was over.

But Colonel Davydov and the officers of his Battery, Karsev, Kolzakov, and the two Roth brothers, were brought to trial.

The presence of malicious intent was beyond all doubt. But how the battle shell had found its way into the cannon, and who was ultimately responsible for the attack remained unknown.

The officers were pardoned and transferred to the army without losing their rank.

And from this day on Colonel Davydov was designated with the witty nickname of "Would-be Assassin of the Imperial Family."

The incident obliged the Emperor to refrain from attending any St. Petersburg festivities in the future. The traditional May Day Parades at the Mars Field were cancelled, and even on anniversaries and holidays the regiments of the Guards were summoned to Tsarskoe Selo for a parade.

Shortly afterwards I met the "Would-be Assasin of the Imperial Family" in the provinces where he commanded an army division.

He was a very efficient officer.

The unfortunate incident had caused him much harm, but he did not complain about his fate and even considered himself partly responsible for the tragic event. He was a rather decent man.

I remember his ingenious reply to the terrible Commander of the Corps, General Rennenkampf.

At the height of the cavalry manoeuvers, Lieutenant Lebedev ended his life after having shot down the seventeen-year-old Musen'ka, daughter of the Uhlan Colonel Samson von Himmelstern. This sorrowful, romantic story deserves to be told later on.

To the Commander of the Corps' question, how the officers of the division had dared to request a requiem for the funeral of a murderer and suicide, Gri-Gri answered calmly:

"The more a man is a sinner, the more he needs our prayers."

Rennenkampf angrily struck the top of his boot with a whip and ended the manoeuvers.

The last time I met with Gri-Gri was in Kiev, in the Hetman's Ukraine, at the Merchants' Garden filled with cheerful crowds.

We sat on a bench near the steep bank of the Dniepr River, looked into the distance lit by the sunset, listened to the music of the Austrian orchestra, and remembered our old St. Petersburg:

"And how are things there now in the hungry, bloody

Neva capital?..."

Boys burst into the garden with the latest newspapers.

In large, black letters they informed us about the execution of the Imperial Family.

———————·———————

The General-Admiral and Naval Cadet Popandopulo

The General-Admiral Grand Duke Alexey Alexandrovich, whose name in Russian history is closely associated with the name of a French ballet dancer, was essentially not a bad man.

The activities of the fleet interested him little.

To make up for this, he loved art, beautiful women, and bridge parties at the English Club. He had a very sophisticated taste and preferred the aroma of the Parisian boulevards to the smoke of his fatherland.

Romantic and sentimental rumors of all kinds went around about the Grand Duke. People talked about the celebrated Grand Ducal collection of snuff boxes with their indecent shapes. And there was a series of anecdotes, not really reprehensible but rather amusing, all revolving around the most august figure of the General-Admiral.

The lively Naval Cadet Charlie Palmgreen once told me a little joke which clearly testified to my friend's impudent wit...

Charlie Palmgreen was making his way to the Taurice Garden for a rendezvous. He did not walk but glided like a high-speed cruiser along the Neva Embankment filled with the Petersburg spring crowd, the light of a bright day, and the fragrance of the swelling buds of the Summer Garden.

On the corner of Gagarinsky Street a carriage stopped with a coat of arms and golden crown on the lanterns. From the carriage emerged a corpulent officer in naval uniform wearing a service cap in the Prussian style with a slightly elevated crown at the back.

Having good reason to keep himself at a certain distance form the naval officer, the Naval Cadet wanted to slip by the entrance. But, unexpectedly, he was stopped by a heavy arm coming down on his shoulder.

Charlie Palmgreen was shortsighted.

Nonetheless he recognized the General-Admiral at once and realized that the latter was not in good spirits. It is not known what had come over the Grand Duke—for he was indifferent to everything in the world except art, beautiful women, and bridge parties. The General-Admiral asked with a sour expression:

"What is your name, Cadet?"

"Naval Cadet Popandopulo, Your Imperial Highness."

"Naval Cadet Popandopulo, I command you to report immediately to the Corps for failing to salute!"

"Yes, Your Imperial Highness!"

The Grand Duke walked heavily to the entrance of the building. Charlie Palmgreen stood wavering only for a minute. He was not the type for blind obedience and tended toward light-minded criticism and freethinking. So, after a bit of reflection he turned to the right and continued on his way to the Taurice Garden.

In the Garden his troubles soon receded in the background when the young Suzi Bachmetyeva offered him one of the first spring violets and promised him a cotillion.

In the company of his friends, the Naval Cadet dined in a "chambre séparée" at the Millbrett in Kirpichny Lane between the Moyka River and Morskaya Street.

He spent part of the evening in the circus at the Sunday première, and the rest of the evening he passed dancing the promised cotillion. Toward midnight he arrived finally at the Corps.

Three days elapsed peacefully, and the unfortunate incident on Gagarinsky Street began to fade in the memory of Charlie Palmgreen.

On the fourth day, however, the director of the Corps received a telegraphic message:

"What punishment was given to Naval Cadet Popandopulo for failing to salute?

General-Admiral Alexey"

The director of the Corps was an old, experienced wolf. He understood at once what had happened. A Popandopulo had, in fact, been listed on the naval records some time ago, but he was a retired captain of the first rank, a one-legged hero of the Crimean War. From the day of the founding of the fleet there had been no other Popandopulo on the record.

Naval Cadet Popandopulo was an insolent imposter, who of course would not reveal his real name. To appeal to his noble sentiments or to scare him with punishment would serve no purpose. The director would only make himself ridiculous.

This is what the old sea wolf said to himself. He was not pedantic. He thought for a minute, puffed three times on his pipe, and wrote his answer to the Grand Duke:

"Naval Cadet Popandopulo was detained three days ago and put under strict arrest."

And so the story ended.

A year later Naval Cadet Popandopulo, or cheerful Charlie Palmgreen, became a warrant officer and was assigned to a destroyer in the Pacific Ocean.

The following year he was killed at Tsushima.

SABUROVA, IRINA EVGENYEVNA
(1907–1979; Baroness von Rosenberg)

Irina Saburova lived until 1915 in Riga and on her father's estate on the Dniepr River. In 1917-18 she resided in Finland, and then returned to Riga, where she stayed until 1943. During World War II she fled to Berlin and finally settled in Munich where she lived until her death in 1979. She graduated from both a Russian and a German high school and studied at the French Institute in Riga. Her first husband, Alexander Perfilyev, was a poet and journalist; her second husband, Baron von Rosenberg, an officer in the Russian Imperial Navy, died in 1958.

Saburova began writing when she was eight years old and published her first short story at the age of sixteen in the Riga newspaper *Mayak* (The Lighthouse). Until the Soviet occupation of the Baltic states in 1940 she contributed short stories and translations to various Russian periodicals in Riga, including *A New Field, Our Small Flame*, and the newpapers *The Word* and *Today*. From 1933 to 1940 she worked on the weekly journal *For You*. After 1953 Saburova became a regular contributor to the newspapers *The New Russian Word* and *Edinenie* (Unity;

Melbourne). Until 1973 she worked as a translator for Radio Station Liberty in Munich.

Her publications are voluminous. Among the most important are *Ten' sinego marta: sbornik rasskazov* (The Shadow of Blue March: A Collection of Stories; Riga, 1938), *Dama tref: sbornik rasskazov* (The Queen of Clubs: A Collection of Short Stories; Munich, 1946), *Korolevstvo alykh bashen: rozhdestvenskie skazki* (The Kingdom of Crimson Towers: Christmas Fairy Tales; Munich: Posev, 1947), *Razgovor molcha: sbornik stikhov* (A Conversation in Silence: A Collection of Poems; Munich, 1956), *Kopilka vremeni: rasskazy* (The Strongbox of Time: Short Stories; Munich, 1958), *Korabli starogo goroda: istorichesky roman iz zhizni russkoy Baltiki: 1924-1944* (The Ships of the Old City: A Historical Novel about the Life of the Russians in the Baltic Countries 1924-1944; Munich, 1963), *Shchastlivoe zerkalo: rasskazy* (A Happy Mirror: Short Stories; Munich, 1966), *O nas: roman* (About Us: A Novel; Munich, 1972). *The Ships of the Old City* was also published in German under the title *Die Stadt der verlorenen Schiffe* (Heidelberg, 1951), and in Spanish as *La ciudad de los barcos perdidos* (Barcelona, 1958). Some of her poems were set to music by the composers Z. Zubkovich, Avenir de Monfraid, and A. Karpovich, and have been on the repertoire of various Russian and American concert singers.

Among Saburova's favorite writers were the Russians Alexander Grin, Mark Aldanov, and Mikhail Bulgakov, and the Western European and American authors Walter Scott, Victor Hugo, Mark Twain, Hans Christian Andersen, O. Henry, Oscar Wilde, Henrik Ibsen, Erich Maria Remarque, Selma Lagerlöff, and Ortego y Gasset. She particularly enjoyed the short stories and fairy tales of Oscar Wilde and Andersen because of their philosophical contents. In her own fairy tales, Saburova placed princes and witches in an ordinary environment, thus juxtaposing real life with a magical dream world. Her favorite literary devices were the psychological pause and understatement, which she employed to create laconic compressed stories. Saburova read English (John Ruskin, for example), Chinese, and the ancient Greek and Roman authors, some of whose stylistic features she adopted in an attempt to achieve classical transparency. She saw the fairy tale as the aesthetic sublimation of simple incidents and claimed that human life is full of "miraculous" events. But man needs a great deal of experience in order to detect the fairy-tale elements in his own life. A fairy tale, according to Saburova, was a double exposure of the same color negative.

Colors, especially olive green, pale yellow, lilac, orange, and blue—the color of reason and of the Baltic candle of separation —are of crucial importance in Saburova's work. She felt and thought in color tones rather than in images or words. In her fairy tales she used a multiplicity of colors, not details, to create mood and atmosphere. In Saburova's own opinion, "Quiet Night" and "Mr. Smith" were her most successful stories. "Mr. Smith" was the last story she wrote. The inspiration for fairy tales came to her like music or a motif: "You cannot invent or create a fairy tale. It must come to you of its own accord, or it won't come at all. Sometimes only a title may come; sometimes a motif or a poem."

Saburova wrote her first fairy tale, "The Kingdom of Crimson Towers," when she was nineteen years old. Published in *Journal for Every Reader*, the tale proved so successful that she decided to develop her talent in this area further and to continue writing in this genre. In addition to fairy tales, however, she kept writing short stories (thirty-nine in all) and produced several novels. She frequently used the mosaic image or a living image composed of a host of characteristics, experiences, and recollections, all rendered with artistic sensibility. She considered herself a successful writer because of her ability to create these living, mosaic images, and because of her capacity to establish firm compositional patterns, to select eloquent colors, and to individualize her heroes' language. Her plots and the characters' psychological interrelationships and entanglements reveal the author's sense of humor and artistic balance.

Saburova's works as a whole form a curious amalgam of the fantastic and empirical reality. The material is presented with few words and details, with pensive melancholy or gentle humor. It is endowed with a unique emotional tone and aesthetic form. N. E. Andreyev spoke highly about her "rare gift for feeling Romanticism and the Russian element," and about her "excellent grasp of novelistic technique." The poet Irina Odoevtseva, one of Saburova's close friends, wrote about her in *Russian Thought* of April 13, 1978: "The Baltic people, scattered around the world, are proud of their talented writer. In Canada, they even call themselves 'Saburovtsy,' Saburov nationals."

The Shadow of Blue March

The Emerald Ring

On the Eve of St. John it is the custom to search for a
buried treasure or for the flower of a fern which marks the
place where a treasure is buried—and you are quite right,
dear reader, to observe that in our time the number of
buried treasures has increased. Many were buried during the
War and the Revolution...But those are not real treasures,
because there are neither any terrible nor any romantic
stories connected with them. But once I actually did find a
treasure—a real one, mysterious, and with quite a romantic
story attached to to. Since it all belongs to the past now, I
can tell you the story.

It happened several years ago, during a hot and sultry
summer. I didn't have much work to do in the city, and I
felt like running away somewhere without ever looking
back—I was in the midst of an unfortunate love affair; in
short, I loved him, but he didn't love me. With my restless
nature, and having reached a certain point in our
relationship, I decided to just leave it at that and go and
have a good time. After committing more follies in two
months than most people in ten years, however, I finally
realized that things could not go on like this any longer, and
I had to get away. My friends persuaded me to go to the
country and stay at their farm. And so we went. I had
asked them to hold onto me for the first fifty kilometers in
the train, so that I wouldn't get any ideas about turning
back, and indeed, at the seventeenth kilometer I almost broke
away. But then it passed, and everything was all right. I
had not been out in the countryside for a long time, and
here I was eighteen *versts* by horse from the station, and on
such roads! You city people have no idea what it is like!
Oh, how I loved it! The road led through the woods and
fields. The smell of wild strawberries, the rustling of rye—so
splendid!

As we were entering the old pine tree forest—quite a
few trees had been cut down along the edge—I noticed a tall
old tree standing beside the road. Three trunks had grown
out of a single root, but now two of them had been cut

down and only one remained. It was so tall that you had to tilt your head way back to see the top. I said we should absolutely look for treasures near these "three sisters," because I'd stake my life that in a place like this there were some around. It was such a conspicuous pine tree; you wouldn't find another one like it in the whole pine forest. And indeed, in its vicinity and also a little farther off stones were piled up, but not in an ordinary way. No, the huge stones were sunk into the ground and arranged in circles. Apparently they were graves from a long-forgotten time. They say that many ethnographical expeditions and geologists have been here, and when they dug up the earth they found old Pskovian coins, silver articles, and stone hatchets, but nothing remarkable. Almost every peasant has a few of these old coins. After the "three sisters" we still had to travel another twelve *versts.*

At the farm stillness and peace prevailed. It was too still.

Sometimes at night I would stand at the window—mist suspended above the streams, the call of a whooping crane, and everything so still beyond belief—does the city, trolley, or radio still exist anywhere?...Here these things were all unnecessary. The place possessed something else, its own, habitual, ancient quality. Sometimes I would lie like this all night, thinking, and watching the moos cross from one window and another, smoking until I could smoke no more. And later, in the sand by the stream, I would "draw on the glass a cherished monogram"[1]...and wash it away with water...Well, if you have ever been in love, then you, too, will understand how long one must torment oneself to reach a point of indifference...

On St. John's Day according to the old calender (they keep the old ways here), the farmers brewed their own beer. They invited me to be their guest. I walked along the marsh for several *versts* looking for St. John's grass—it grows only there. On St. John's Day, you know, they wave this particular purple-yellow grass over the cattle to ward off the evil eye and to bring good luck...The sound of countless gadflies in that meadow was like a constant moan—they formed an undulating wall—they bit me all over until I was covered with blood. In the middle of the meadow, at the foot of a hill, there was a small well—the wooden framework was low and the water was high enough to reach with your hand. They say that a chapel once stood there but had disappeared underground. Several lucky people have seen the door in the well; and if one were to go down there—well, there are various stories. Some say that only righteous men can descend. Others say that if someone happened to go there and hear the undergound bell tolling, then he would no longer be of this world; or, on the contrary, he would be lucky and successful at everything...We went there together and gorged on wild strawberries; then we were thirsty. I made a little cup out of bark and ladled out some water. I was sprawled on the framework of the well with my head hanging down inside, and I saw reflected in the water—so very clearly—the three sisters, the pine trees; they grew as they had grown before, uncut, with all three of them together...How could this be? I stood up and looked around—no, there was only the meadow and it was half a *verst* to the forest—there were no pine trees at all here, and the "three sisters" were twelve *versts* away. How strange!

I brought my hosts some St. John's grass (they thought me something of a sorceress because I treated people with horse remedies). I recited for them an old charm that I remembered, and we began drinking. We drank a lot, and eventually fell asleep in the hayloft. I lay there and thought about what my friends in the city, proper people, would have said if they had seen me half an hour ago? In a sarafan, in a hut, I had danced a fast Russian dance—I, a proper woman, an artist on whose cherished shelf rested Theophile Gautier and Oscar Wilde in brocade bindings!

But surely he, "my darling, my golden one," would have understood...

Thus I lay, thinking until I fell asleep. I saw the "three sisters" standing as before, uncut; someone took my hand and led me to them, someone—I didn't see who; somehow I felt that it was better not to look around—and he said, "Three steps to the north, seven to the east. Don't take the emerald ring."

I woke up. It was still dark, but it would soon be dawn. I must have slept less than half an hour. And it rang in my ears: "Three steps to the north, seven to the east." Why shouldn't I take it? And immediately it struck me: an emerald ring! "My golden one, my darling"—his favorite stone was an emerald, and I always told him "When I am rich, I will give you an emerald ring of eighteen carats." Exactly eighteen, no more, no less, because in our unsuccessful romance eighteen was a lucky number. I dreamed that maybe some day the money really would fall from heaven—then I would give him...

The "three sisters"—had they really told me, in my dream, where the treasure was hidden? I was trembling and felt that I couldn't wait any longer—I would go! At the very worst I would return worn out and irritable. Near the forest the land belonged to the states, so no one would see me. Everyone was celebrating St. John's Day—they would be drinking for three days.

Quietly I went out of the barn to the tool shed and took a shovel and a bag. I washed near the well. The dogs knew me and didn't bark. I started down the road. I can walk fast; the peasants always used to laugh, saying that I was light on my feet and scarcely touched the ground. And now I really was flying right along. I probably travelled the twelve *versts* in about two hours. A record! Just to get to the "three sisters" there were four *versts* of forest. The old pine forest rustled...I walked along, quite alone. Fog rose up on both sides. The birds had not begun to sing yet.

It was not dark, but it was frightening. It was still St. John's Eve...Perhaps, right here, in this low place the magic glowing fern would flare up? And these mossy twigs reaching out like arms...Brrr! I couldn't help remembering the stories about the brigands who once lived here—nobody could pass through—and this was quite recent, only a few years ago. Though it's true, I wasn't afraid of them, for I had nothing worth stealing, and I always carried a small black pistol under my arm...But what if it were the one in my dream?...I was not walking but running through the forest...What on earth had made me come here?

Finally, the "three sisters." I stopped and caught my breath. The forest behind me rustled in the dawning twilight. Only one of the "three sisters" remained—the other two were cut down and the mossy stones were lying all around. I felt a light tremor going through my entire body.

Three steps to the north, seven to the east...I measured carefully, slowly, so as not to make a mistake. I counted off, crossed myself, outlined a circle, and started to dig. At first it was very difficult because of the grass, roots, and stones...I am not very strong. But gradually my strength increased—something was driving me; and all the time I kept looking around—was someone coming, the one in my dream?...I dug a deep hole. What if there was nothing in it? That could not be. I knew, I felt that a treasure must be hidden there. I sensed it.

And here I was, already standing in the hole so I could dig more easily. Then suddenly—clank! My spade struck something. I almost gnawed the earth with my teeth. I discovered a box, not especially heavy, a small oak chest, bound with copper. By now I had forgotten all my fears. My hands were cut, scratched, chaffed, and covered with dirt, but I managed to drag it out. I dropped it nearby and hastily filled the hole up again with dirt, stones, and twigs. Grabbing the spade and the sack, I headed back to the woods.

I moved further away from the road and sat down. I examined the chest. "Do not take the emerald ring..." Should I take it or not? Perhaps there was nothing in it besides the ring? I started to open it. Of course, it wouldn't have been easy for me to break the lock even with pliers. But in one place the lid was raised just a little. I set the chest against an old stump, slipped the spade under the lid, and tore it off. Then I gasped...

There weren't just Pskovian silver coins! The chest was stuffed to the brim with ancient gold coins, and in the corner, in a separate case, there were precious stones...Have you seen my pearl necklace? That's where I got it. And my favorite amethysts, and some other things...and a large, heavy emerald ring with golden fretwork...Such an emerald I had never seen...I had seen a lot of different stones but never one like this...As I gazed at it, it held me like a magnet. I couldn't tear myself away from its green depths; like the eyes of a snake they hypnotized me...In the forest, in the green thicket, the sun had already risen and was sparkling in the stones...it was just like a fairy tale! "Don't take the emerald ring." As soon as I remembered—perhaps I even heard someone next to me say the words—I jumped up. I thought: I'll go and put it back. There's enough here without it. And I don't care for emeralds anyway. But then I thought—no! It isn't right. Since I was destined to take this treasure—I'll order instead a public church service, a requiem, but I'll keep the emerald...I'll give it to my "golden one." At a glance it seemed to be twenty carats. I knew that I could not surrender the ring to that terrible thing...I could not put it back. It was so beautiful!

Well then, you know what followed. Part of the treasure I left in the chest and hid in the hollow of a tree; I carried the rest home in the bag along with the spade. No one noticed anything. I said that I had gone after ferns and spent the night with a werewolf in the forest...They laughed. The next day I went back for the chest.

A week later, trembling with impatience, I returned home to the city. Passing the "three sisters," I bowed to them and thanked them from the bottom of my heart. And with good reason! I sold the gold not only as gold, but several coins as antiques...A diamond necklace too, and for a good price. But I kept the amethysts and pearls and a few other ornaments, because of their delicate workmanship and exquisite stones.

The jeweler said that the emerald weighed eighteen carats. He offered me a fantastic amount of money for it; he couldn't tear himself away from it. A stone of such rare beauty! However, I didn't sell it. Had I tormented myself only to sell it in the end? Was it only for money that I had found the treasure?

I gave the emerald as a gift. And with the rest of the money—remember I already told you that I had won a large sum in the Red Cross lottery?—I settled all my affairs and bought a small farm...It is called "The Three Sisters" because near my boundary stands that same old pine...I can see it from the windows of my house. I once dreamed of that terrible one...faceless. "Give me the emerald ring." That's all he said. I awoke with fright. Lord, I thought, could he really bring misfortune?...

Everything was going so well. I was already beginning to think I had been mistaken about the mysterious being. I was also mistaken in thinking that my love was unhappy, unrequited. It turned out to be quite the opposite. But precisely herein lay my misfortune...

Why? Oh, it's quite simple. When you love a man from a distance, then he may be "my darling, my golden one." Each rare encounter becomes a moment of magic, but with proximity the charm is lost. The gilt wears off. And rarely does one pass through this ordeal untouched. I married him on the eighteenth, and after one year I divorced him. But I don't regret the divorce—only the lost fairy tale. Can you understand that? What would I give to relive that spring once again—when I felt so miserable! I would pay dearly for this fairy tale—perhaps, perhaps even the emerald ring.

1934

Told with humor and subtle irony, "The Emerald Ring" presents a happy fusion of autobiographical and fantastic elements. It is a Slavic tradition, from before the Christian era, that supernatural events are likely to occur on the feast night of St. John in early spring. The story has all the features of a fairy tale: omens, dreams, a buried treasure, the threat of a curse. On one level they serve to illustrate the vicissitudes of an ordinary relationship; on another, they stimulate interest in the mysterious and magical for their own sake.

The story is told in the first person, and the narrator has a humorous attitude toward herself and her behavior in the relationship as well as toward some of the magical elements in the story. The number "eighteen" reappears with surprising regularity: the "lucky number in our unsuccessful romance," the number of carats of the emerald, and the date of the wedding. It is no doubt significant that at the seventeenth kilometer from the city she almost got off the train to go back but "then it passed, and everything was all right." The narrator also points out that she was "eighteen *versts* by horse from the station," when she first saw the "three sisters."

Considering the coincidences associated with the number and Saburova's slightly ironic tone, the number eighteen seems used here primarily for comic effect. In many of Saburova's other works, however, certain colors or numbers occur as revelations or in association with fateful decisions. This predilection for number symbolism is symptomatic of Russian writers in general. Dostoevsky in *Notes from the Underground* and *Crime and Punishment* uses the Biblical "three" and "seven" to indicate matters of supreme significance, while Zinaida Hippius favors "eight" as a symbol of eternity, and "three" as the divine individuality embodied by the Holy Trinity. Both regarded numerals as links with reality, as symbols of spiritual actuality of divine origin. Like Bal'mont, they believed that "numerals form the essence of the world." (K. Bal'mont, *Poeziya kak volshebstvo*; Poetry as Sorcery, Moscow, 1915, p. 71.) "The Emerald Ring" is based on traditional, folk, and personal associations, on an oscillation between reality and reverie and on a blurring of the distinctions between symbols and concrete reality. Though the story lacks depth intellectually and ethically, it remains an interesting piece of prose.

NOTE

1.   From *Eugene Onegin.*

TSVIK, MIKHAIL
(pseudonym of Mikhail Mironov; 1893–?)

Mikhail Tsvik was a Russian fiction writer. His amusing short stories were published in various local Russian periodicals, including the illustrated weekly *For You.* Tsvik also authored two books: *Pod nebom Parizha* (Under the Sky of Paris; Riga: Logos, 1937) and *V poiskakh shchastya* (In Search of Happiness; Riga: Logos, 1937). His writing was humorous, informative, and humanitarian, and very popular with Russian readers in the Baltic countries.

Tsvik's presentation of comic plots and heroes is somewhat akin to Teffi's manner; her stories emphasize the emptiness of man's existence, man's shallowness, and insensitivity. Tsvik's heroes also seek happiness in vain but, in contrast to Teffi's characters, Tsvik's individuals are not Russian émigrés who attempt to escape a vulgar and uneventful life in exile through beautiful yet false dreams and illusions. While Teffi portrayed the humdrum reality of everyday life in exile, Tsvik painted the human personality in all its manifestations—pitiful, weak, colorless, ridiculous—against the background of an exotic fairy-tale setting.

For You, No. 18 (May 1, 1938)

Fairy Tales for Women: *In vino veritas*

Great Harun al'Rashid was of an exceedingly venerable age when his chief eunuch informed him that some man was in the habit of visiting Harun's favorite wife Ziriab. This daredevil came to her wrapped up like a mummy so that it was quite impossible to recognize him, all the more so since the nights in this happy region were dark, very dark indeed. (If only our nights were so dark...)

"Why haven't you killed him?" Harun asked, filled with indignation.

"What do you mean?" the eunuch justified himself (he didn't stand on ceremony—eunuchs can get away with anything). "How could we kill him when we don't even know how he gets into the harem? He probably has a secret passage."

"Then how is it known to you that my Ziriab receives this man?" The wise Harun was curious.

"The whispering of the lovers and the sound of their kisses reached my ears, but when I broke in on her, he was already gone."

"Hm...the evidence is convincing enough to behead her."

"Behead?" The eunuch was exultant.

"Behead her," Harun decided.

At his age, the head of a beautiful woman gave him as little pleasure as the rest of her. For the wise caliph maintained his harem exclusively to demonstrate to his loyal subjects that he could not live without it. In reality he would have been glad to get rid of this expensive pleasure, if it were not for his concern about prestige: How could he do without a harem? He was no eunuch, no indeed. It did not matter that he walked about all doubled up, and had lived for twenty years on mush. (They didn't know about false teeth then.)

So they led the fair lady to her execution. How she wept, poor thing. The sad procession was met by Harun's chief advisor.

"Where are you going?" he asked.

"She is going to the other world, and we are going to help her get there."

"What's this all about?"

The eunuch dutifully related to the dignitary everything he knew.

"She can go to the other world any old time. This matter needs to be cleared up. Let us go to the wise Harun," the high official ordered.

*

"O wisest of the wise," the dignitary began his speech for the defense, "none of us doubts that in your chest beats a passionate heart, which, like that of any hot-blooded man, rages with jealousy."

The caliph went into indescribable rapture over these words. He had such a fit of coughing that his tongue hung out, and then he couldn't stop sneezing. Finally getting hold of himself, the Great Harun al'Rashid proudly explained to his retinue that all this was the result of a surge of passion.

Catching his breath after the attack and wiping his gray beard with the sleeve of his silk dressing gown, he commanded the official: "Do go on, it's a pleasure to listen to you." The word "passion" evoked in him memories of the far distant past.

"If Ziriab, having such an ardent admirer as our Great Harun al'Rashid, has betrayed you, she is indeed deserving of punishment, and her body should be thrown to the dogs for food," the dignitary continued.

"He speaks eloquently," Harun al'Rashid exclaimed with enthusiasm, for at his age he could think of no better use for a woman's body. The eunuch was in absolute agreement with his master.

"But before we throw Ziriab to the dogs, let her drink of the 'wine of truth,'" the dignity suggested.

"What kind of wine is this?" There was no such wine

in Harun's wine cellars. It was not even required, seeing as there was no truth to be had anywhere in the kingdom.

"This wine," explained the high official, "contains miraculous power. One who has told the truth profits by it, but one who has deceived the great Harun al'Rashid will perish with the very first sip."

"This is remarkable! But where can such wine be found?" Harun asked.

"I have some, o wisest of the wise. Once I bought it from a wandering Bedouin."

"Pour it, let her drink," the impatient Harun ordered, and Ziriab, without trembling or batting an eyelash, drank down the entire goblet right to the bottom. She even licked her lips.

"Oh my sweet little bird, how happy I am that you have been loyal to me," lisped Harun, deeply moved, as he pressed her to his trembling beard. "Let her have the entire goblet full of precious stones for her fidelity," he commanded in his joy.

"Your wisdom knows no limits," his dignitary praised him, and then whispered in the old man's ear: "While you're at it, great Harun, order them to behead the eunuch. You will render me a great service. That'll teach him to slander decent girls!"

"Kindly take care of it for me; one head more or less—it won't make any difference. That's what we're here for—to behead people," Harun agreed, and the eunuch departed this life.

. . . .

And now, my friends and readers, an explanation is called for. The wine, or course, was perfectly ordinary. Lord preserve us from the real "wine of truth." The entire world would turn into a solid graveyard, and I must confess that I, too, would fail to escape the common fate and would be consigned, along with all my fairy tales, to a premature grave. And so, obviously, the wine which they gave Ziriab to drink was the most ordinary wine; but the attentive reader will ask, and understandably so: "But why did the girl drink it without a shudder? She could not know that the wine contained none of the miraculous power ascribed to it." You are mistaken—she knew this perfectly well. Therefore, she

drank it and didn't give a hoot; the principal advisor of the
wise Harun al'Rashid had already revealed to her the secret
that the wine was harmless.

Why did he do this?   A naïve question.   So that he
might pass the nights with her in the harem as before.   It
was for this very reason that he asked Harun to cut off the
eunuch's head, and this was a clever move.   What did he
need witnesses for, especially curious ones, like eunuchs.
Enough of them...

ZADONSKY, ANDREY

Andrey Zadonsky, a young Russian fiction writer in
Riga, published several novels and novellas, including *Stupeni*
(Steps; Riga: Didkovsky, 1929) and *Zoin roman* (Zoya's
Romance; Riga: Didkovsky, 1930).   He also contributed his
works to *Today*, *Our Little Light*, *The Attic*, and *Chimes*.

Chimes, No. 42 (1928)

Grandfather

We knew grandfather had to die the way everything old
and sick has to die, the way our favorite old mare
Kalmychka died last year before Easter on the day when
there was a fire in the village.   But when Kalmychka was
dying, you could see it and it made sense. . . .

One day after dinner, grandpa went to his room and he
did not come out again.   They said he was dying.   But it
wasn't something you could see or hear, and that's why it
was so incomprehensible.   Though he was not among us, we
still vividly remembered everything about him, even his smell,
which we would recognize when grandpa made us sit on his
lap.   The tunic, the epaulets, and his favorite tobacco—it
was the smell of a general!   Grandpa—who remembered
Sebastopol and had served four tsars!   Lavrenty Osipovitch,
our tutor, told us that our grandfather had a stroke, and this
complicated his condition.   What stroke, and who dared to

strike grandpa?...No, it was of course not simply a stroke, but something special. The incomprehensibility of it remained and weighed heavily on us.

That day was the beginning of spring, golden drops of melting snow ran off the roofs, while flocks of robins rose up from the poplars and their cries and the flapping of their wings rang loudly in the air. . . . Lavrenty Osipovitch said we should hurry to our grandmother because an important event was in store for us—on his way to the Crimea, the Emperor was coming from the station to Khatnee to say farewell to our grandfather and to decorate him with a high military order.

I remember how I heard my heart thump, how a chill swept over me making me shiver, and how the warmth and simple joy of the April morning suddenly vanished. . . . God is invisible, like the Tsar, but His abode is the huge, heavenly tent which, so blissful today, is always visible. I remember that my brother Sasha and I sometimes tried to see God. Running up the hill or standing by the wall of the greenhouse where in the summer the sun baked so sharply and luxuriously, we would squint our eyes and shut them with burning eyelids. For a moment we would remain in hot, fiery, golden darkness. Then we would quickly open our eyes and look upwards, directly at the flaming, brocaded sky. Would we see...in heaven amid the clouds, as if shrouded by the burning incense of a church, Savaoth, an old man with a white beard dressed in a silvery chasuble?...But the Tsar you could not see, and his abode was far away, in the fog...And suddenly, he was there, driving up to the porch, where our funny old cannons, no longer able to fire shots, stood...It was simply incomprehensible...

They took us upstairs where they washed and scoured us, and changed our clothes. We were dressed in long black trousers and sailor jackets with deep necklines like grownups wear, but which we usually wore only on Sundays. We were cold and our teeth chattered. We washed our hands, and they turned from their somewhat dirty, red, springtime appearance into something white, cold, and winter-like. When we came down along the spiral stairway and passed the drawing room, we saw through the window a coach standing by the doorway, a bustle of people, and a soldier in

a Cuirassier coat. . . . Grandma was standing in the middle
of the illuminated hall, translucent with trembling rays and
patches of sunlight.   Like the Murillo Madonna on the wall,
she was enveloped in a fragrant, rosy warmth.   We ran up to
her and pressed our faces against the black, rather stiff silk of
her dress out of which the scent of lavender rose. . . . We
looked at the door and waited for the miracle. . . .

A footman flung the half-open door wide open, and our
uncle and a youthful officer entered the hall.   The officer was
wiping his moustache with a handkerchief; I remember that I
looked most of all at that handkerchief.   An imperial
handkerchief!   Was it just like other handkerchiefs? . . . The
officer put the handkerchief in the pocket of his wide trousers
. . . and went to meet grandmother.   I do not remember
what else happened; it seems, there was something slightly
funny and touching when our grandmother bowed deeply
before the Emperor with a low court curtsey.   It seems
something sad was uttered about our grandpa, whom I
suddenly remembered only then.   I distinctly recall how the
Emperor, already in the doorway of the dining room,
suddenly put his hand on my head—so firmly, with all five
fingers—and asked grandmother:

"C'est votre petit-fils cadet?"

And then, when everyone went to see grandpa, Sasha
and I stayed in the hall.   Suddenly, we joined hands and
began to spin around like a top, happy from the experience
and our liberation from something too significant for us to
grasp. . . .

Two days later, again in the morning, we were taken to
see our dead grandfather. . . . On an ottoman in the study
an old man, dressed in a full general's uniform, lay before the
icon case.   Though with the velvet curtains drawn it was
rather dark, we could see that it was grandpa, but not the
one who used to sit us on his lap and sing: *"La petite
marionnette!*...apparently the only song he knew.   This face
was stern, majestic, and portrait-like, the way other
grandfathers looked on the paintings in the blue reception
room.   He was very tall, his legs were stretched out.   Patent
leather shoes were firmly fastened with the foot-straps of his
breeches.   The general's red stripes were taut, not at all in
an elderly fashion, while the long aristocratic hands, as if

carved from ivory tusks, rested firmly and rigidly on his
wide, powerful chest. The face, at which I was at first afraid
to look, was not the least bit frightening—it was beautiful
like the image on a pale, enamel icon. Only a wrinkle by
the large, curved nose suddenly made me think of death and
about the life that had left this body forever. That wrinkle
suddenly frightened me. I looked away and then noticed the
only military decoration which adorned grandpa's chest. It
was a slanting blue cross with Christ crucified on it.

The room began to fill with people. Father Vasily
arrived and began to prepare for the requiem. I tiptoed
quietly to the window, hid behind the velvet curtain, and
suddenly found myself face to face with spring.

The window was open, and in the bushes beneath it the
intoxicating chirp and rustle of restless sparrows could be
heard. The first buds, so resiliently plump with juice,
seemed to grow and breathe fragrantly right before my eyes.
The wind, which jerked at my hair and enveloped my chest
with a glorious cold, was heady and youthful like the day
itself. Flashing whitish-blue, fleecy clouds swam melting in
the sky like incense. And then a terrible and impassioned
pain, a fear for every living thing doomed to die,
overwhelmed me with such strength and torment that,
crossing myself, I sank to my knees by the window.

———————·———————

"Grandfather," Andrey Zadonsky's account of a small boy's
experiences at his grandfather's death, is not merely a beautifully
narrated moment of memory. At the child's first confrontation
with the realities of life and the darker sides of human existence,
shadows fall across the Arcadia of youth, modifying radically and
permanently the way a young mind perceives and experiences
nature, life, and reality. The felicity, peace, and innocence of
youth are forever lost at the child's largely unconscious realization
of the suffering inherent in the human condition.

Before his grandfather's death, the little boy experiences
nature and life directly, sensually, joyfully. He distinctly hears the
flapping wings of the birds, sees and feels the steady golden drip of
the spring thaw, and smells the pungent odor of his grandfather's
tobacoo. And his conception of God, associated with the Tsar who

is equally fantastic and unattainable, is thoroughly naïve. During
the funeral ceremonies, however, the boy is seized by a fear
hitherto unknown to him, the sight of budding nature no longer
provides undivided joy. His idea of the Tsar undergoes a
significant change during his encounter with the real person and,
the author implies, his attitude toward God also will become more
realistic and mature.

    The author's aritistic sensibility is seen not only in his finely
perceived and psychologically convincing rendering of the child's
naïve observations, but also in the poetic descriptions of nature.
He describes warm sunlight "by the wall of the greenhouse, where
in the summer the sun baked so sharply and luxuriously," and
where "we would squint our eyes and shut them with burning
eyelids." At the end, the reader is made poignantly aware that
death triumphs over the joy of awakening nature. The metaphor
of the "fleecy clouds . . . melting in the sky like incense"
underlines the transitory nature of all things. What was theory at
the very beginning of the story, "we knew that grandfather had to
die the way everything old and sick has to die," has become
reality at the end.

SINAISKY, VASILY IVANOVICH (1876-1949)

    Sinaisky was born in 1876 into a family of priests in the
Tambov Province, but most of his life was spent in the Baltic
region. Upon graduation from the Law School of Derpt University
he was asked to stay and prepare for the rank of professor in the
Department of Dogma and History of Roman Law. In 1905 he
went for a year to Belgium, to do research in the libraries of
Brussels. In 1907 Sinaisky attained the rank of *Privat-Dozent*, and
in 1909, after defending his master's thesis, he became an honorary
professor at Derpt University. Four years later he accepted a
position in the Department of Civil Law at St. Vladimir University
in Kiev, where he obtained his doctoral degree in 1913. Between
1922 and 1945 Sinaisky taught as a professor in the Department of
Civil Law at the Latvian University in Riga, where he also founded
the society "Aequitas," edited its journal *Jurist* (in Latvian), and
contributed to *The Latvian Encyclopedia.* He was a member of the

"Société d'histoire de droit" in Paris, "The American Academy of Political and Social Sciences" in Philadelphia, the "Comitato Scientifico della Rivista di Diritto Agrario" in Florence, and the "Istituto di studi legislativi" in Rome.

Although Sinaisky was a law professor and his scholarly research primarily concerned jurisprudence, he was not exclusively interested in questions of law. A number of his works deal with general questions of ancient culture, ancient calender systems, the origins of ancient chronology, and problems of comparative folklore, particularly relating to jurisprudence, which he regarded as a repository of ancient scholarly knowledge. A solid knowledge of ancient languages greatly facilitated his research and he published works in Russian, Latvian, French, and German.

In addition to his professional duties and guest lectures at other universities, Sinaisky took part in Latvian as well as Russian social and cultural life. At Pushkin's jubilee in 1937 he appeared on the Day of Russian Culture with a lecture about "Pushkin and the Law." He gave free consultations at the "Society for Spiritual Aid," and served as president of the "Society of Lovers of Art and of the Antiquity of the Acropolis," founded with his support in 1927. The society organized an exhibition in the Riga State Museum, "Two Hundred Years of Russian Painting," featuring a large number of Russian paintings from local private collections.

At the behest of S. A. Kuzubov, a local patron of the arts, Sinaisky compiled material for an historical essay on the Pskov Cave Monastery and published it in 1929. The monograph was beautifully illustrated with color reproductions of paintings and drawings by S. A. Vinogradov, and was written with the assistance of L. F. Zurov. All profits from the publication were donated to the Monastery.

The Russian authors Sinaisky admired most were Pushkin and Dostoevsky, whose works he often cited in his own writings. Then came Vladimir Nabokov, Ivan Bunin, Ivan Shmelyov, and Boris Zaytsev. He subscribed to *Contemporary Annals*, *The Road*, *The Historian and His Contemporary*, and *The Archives of the Russian Revolution*. At his home in Riga, he entertained many Russian writers in exile, among them the future Archbishop of San Francisco John Shakhovskoy (at that time a priest-monk), Andrey Sedykh, Leonid Zurov, Sergey Mintslov, Pyotr Pil'sky, and Igor' Chinnov. Having studied painting at the School of André Lothe (Figurative Cubism) in Paris and with Sergey A. Vinogradov in

Riga and in Pechory (Estonia), Sinaisky was well versed in the pictorial arts.   He was acquainted with many Russian painters in Riga and Paris, including N. P. Bogdanov-Bel'sky, Konstantin S. Vysotsky, Evgeny E. Klimov, and the son of Dobuzhinsky, V. M. Dobuzhinsky.   Professor Sinaisky exhibited his own works in Riga on several occasions and lectured on Russian literature and art at various cultural gatherings throughout Latvia.   He also wrote poetry, short stories, and plays.   The two as yet unpublished poems below attest to Sinaisky's multifaceted personality, inexhaustible optimism, serenity before death, and awareness of eternal and precious values not always obvious to to the average observer.

———————·———————

Life comes striding,
Bringing joy and grief,
Two equal cups
It hands to you.
One is filled with grief,
Drink it boldly to the dregs!
The other cup, of happiness,
Is almost empty.
Drink whatever is in it,
It is the sweetest of all!
Drink to the dregs, empty the cup,
And, though in grief, sing the song to the end,
Even if it is sad,
For it is given to you by life.

———————·———————

Oh my friends, I beseech you, do not weep over me—
Greatness in life is always beautiful,
Like the blue sky in cold winter,
Like the falling star on a summer night.
Please no speeches over my coffin, no sobbing,
Do not make the great appear ridiculous.
Go quietly into the depth of your memories,
Continue to live, as before, with me alive.
Imagine that your friend has gone afar,

He does not write, but remembers you always.
Years, sustained by warm and lively thoughts,
Will not disappear, fruitless and lonely, in the separation.

———————·———————

The Pskov Cave Monastery:
An Historico-Cultural Essay (Riga, 1929)
The Origins of the Pskov Cave Monastery

In the manuscript at the Solovetsky Monastery there are some interesting facts concerning the founding of the monastery by Jonah and, in conjunction with this event, the creation of a cave by God and its opening. It seems that Jonah had lived in Yuryev for two and a half years before he came to Pskov and left Isidor there in his place. The latter became involved in a religious dispute with the Germans and was thrown into prison with seventy-two other Christians. They refused to recant even in prison and were cast underneath the ice in the Omovzha River on January 8, 1472. In the spring of the same year their bodies were found upriver along the shore. The bodies had been laid in three wooden boxes and were facing the east with Isidor in the center. The legend further relates that Jonah shortly afterward heard about the *appearance of a cave created by God*, felt sorry for Isidor, and became inspired by the love of Christ. Jonah desired to see the cave, which was created by God near the German lands and the Kamenets River and was deep as a moat and flowed towards the east. He came to love the place and built a church on the mountainside to the west of the cave. The manuscript goes on to tell of Jonah's wife Vassa, who was buried in the cave and whose body was thrown out of the earth twice. Accounts tell of the construction of two cells opposite the cave, the difficulties in consecrating the church, and finally *the consecration itself on August 15, 1473*.

This information is truly valuable. 1) The construction of the church began in 1472. If we subtract the two years of Jonah's sojourn in Yuryev, we come to 1470 as the year the monastery was founded. (Cf. *First-class Pskov Cave Monastery*, 1893.) The discrepancy of two years in the dates of Kornily's death—1570 and 1572, or 1572 and 1577 according to Karamzin—is apparently explained by this difference.   2) Thus, the related appearance of the cave created by God should be placed not in 1392, but in 1472, during the lifetime of the public figure Ivan Dementyev. It is the year 6980 after the birth of Christ.   The event is also described in some memoirs, where we read that *the cave was opened during the time of the public figure Ioann Dementyev.* This information is taken from the inscription on a metal tablet above the entrance to the cave; however, the year inscribed there is 6900.   In that case, the cave would have been opened in 1392 (6900-5508).   So we are faced with conflicting information.   It is more likely, though, that the year 6900 was misread since in the very same reference it says: "It is impossible to decipher the words due to the antiquity of the writing," the numeral 8 could easily be read as O, and thus 6900 was recorded rather than the correct date 6980.   This probable mistake, then, was most likely responsible for the statement on page six on the general inventory of monastic property of 1862 that the cave became known in 1392.   In order to reconcile these contradictory pieces of information, it was necessary to refer once more to Ivan Dementyev and place him in the year 1392 under the name of Ioann Dometiev.   However, no matter how the contradictory *facts* of the metal inscription are to be interpreted, and disregarding it altogther, it is clear from the aforementioned reference to the Solovetsky manuscript that the founding of the cave church is connected with *the appearance of the cave created by God*, about which Jonah heard when he was in Pskov in 1472.   In the abbreviated Pskov chronicle the founding of the monastery is not related to *the manifestation of the cave created by God*, but to the appearance in the cave (in that same year) of the *icon* of the Virgin's Assumption called the "*old*" icon, and credited with the healing of a woman in 1473.

   The monastery's founder Jonah was more a hermit than a monk in the sense of the monastic practices. He built only two cells near the cave. A monastic community was founded later on the mountain by a hieromonk named *Misail*, and in this mountaintop monastery a wooden church was built and dedicated to *St. Antony* and *St. Feodosy*, the Kiev Cave

miracle-workers. *Thus,* *with* *the* *founding* *of* *the* *two*
churches, dedicated to the Assumption of the Virgin and to
Antony and Feodosy, there was now a monastery in
northwest Russia similar to the Kiev Cave Monastery in
southwest Russia, where there was also a church of the
Assumption and one dedicated to saints Antony and Feodosy.
But the new cloister built on the edge of forest wilderness
naturally could not develop as quickly as the one at the Kiev
Cave Monastery, located in the capital city of Kiev.
Moreover, the cloister and its two churches—one in the cave
and one on the mountain—were eventually destroyed by
marauders from Livonia. So the first permanent monastery
dates back only to the first decade of the sixteenth century.
According to the Pskov choronicle of 1519, a man named
Misyur' or *Mikhail Grigoryevich Myunekhin*, "began . . . to
dig into the mountain on both sides of the stream and to
construct a large church. He dug still deeper into the
mountain and began to build a monastery in the valley
between the mountains. The stream flowed through the
monastery and they lowered the water into the church of St.
Antony and St. Feodosy, bringing it from the mountain into
the cave, into the new church." The "little monastery on
the mountaintop" became a monastery renowned "as far as
the Varangian Sea." This same Misyur' oversaw the
adornment of the vast Assumption Cave Church with a new
chapel dedicated to Antony and Feodosy of the Kiev Case
Monastery (in 1523), after which the entire ancient monastery
on the hilltop was torn down. From this time on the office
of Father Superior was established in the monastery, along
with daily services and a regular dormitory. This occurred
during the time of Father Superior Gerasim.

And thus the hermitage of the last quarter of the
fifteenth century, devoted to contemplation and prayer, was
transformed at the beginning of the sixteenth century
(1519-1523) into a monastic enterprise, soon taking its
definitive form under the direction of St. Kornily, its most
renowned Father Superior.

*

The Rise of the Pskov Cave Monastery
Under Father Superior Kornily

As in the fate of individuals, so it is in human
endeavors, that what is unknown suddenly becomes eminent
and famous. Thus it happened with the Pskov Cave
Monastery. In 1529 a disciplined monk, unfailingly devoted
to labor and prayer, was elevated to the rank of Father
Superior of the new Cave Monastery. This was St. Kornily.
His administration lasted forty years, and during this long
and significant period in the life of the monastery it
underwent not only further construction, but spiritual
elevation as well. What transpired during this time? What
exactly was the new Father Superior able to accomplish? St.
Kornily, like Feodosy of the Cave Monastery in Kiev, was
endowed with monumental energy, not merely physical, but
spiritual as well. Such lives, therefore, serve as an example
of active love of God and man. Such people are unable to
spend all their time in contemplation or lead an exclusively
ascetic life far from the world, in the wilderness or forest.
Above all they seek opportunities to help others, in particular
to spread the Christian faith (Kornily was an apostle for the
Sets). They aspire to be Christ's warriors and represent the
ideal of monkhood as conceived by Maxim Grek.

It is understandable, then, that the Pskov Cave
Monastery, once it had been brought down from the
mountain and transformed into an active monastery, became
"the city of God" among the local population. They adored
and treasured it as "the home of the Virgin." In Time of
Misfortune men would find their way there and recover their
lost courage. But the ever-alluring city of God on earth
must inspire people with a feeling for the elevated and
beautiful even through its external appearance. For the
acceptance of beauty by man's soul is at the same time the
acceptance of God Himself as the highest beauty. Hence it is
not suprising that Kornily, who understood that the practical
life could not be separated from religion, devoted himself with
his characteristic divine ardor to the creation of a monastery
that would uplift the soul. In place of the wooden church of
the *Forty Martyrs*, which he had constructed beyond the
monastery for the monastery workers, he built in 1541 a

stone cathedral of the Annunciation to emphasize the good news of the renewal of all Creation, Christ's birth.

The city of God not only had to be constructed and adorned—it also had to be protected from enemy forces. Located on the border (at that time) of the Russian state and the German Livonians, the monastery required external fortification and Kornily did not retreat from this monumental task. In 1565 a massive stone slab wall with seven artillery towers ("the stone city") was constructed around the cloister. It was 380 *sazhens* long; in some places the height reached five *sazhens*, and its width was more than two. One only needs to give a cursory glance at the monastery walls to understand how great an undertaking it was.

Plunging down and rising again, the monastery wall seems to urge each person not to fall in spirit. For the strong soul, falling is succeeded by a rising once more to the heights. These powerful dips and rises in the wall signify that the monastery was not designed to be a monastery-fort like the forts of the Livonian Order. It became a fort by necessity. But no matter how threatening the proud and mighty walls were, they were not what saved the cloister. For, under the plan of St. Kornily, still another church was constructed over the gates of the cloister, dedicated to *St. Nicholas the Miracle-Worker*, the steadfast protector of the new cloister. . . .

———————·———————

The essay continues in this manner for the many pages, revealing Professor Sinaisky's remarkable knowledge of both the history of Russia and the history of Russian religion. In both areas, V. I. Sinaisky appears before us as a learned man and a devout member of the Russian Orthodox Church, who always remains in perfect control of the minutest details in his exposition of the cultural history of the Pskov Cave Monastery. His narrative mode is vivid and provokes clear, striking images. All in all, this essay provides the reader not merely with an important historical background of the Russian cultural heritage, but recreates artistically the life of those pious yet nation-conscious Russian monks at this religious center in Moscow state. We also find

interesting and informative references to the sacred Cathedral of
the Holy Trinity in Pskov and to the rule of Pskov's most
prominent, brave and benevolent princes, Vsevolod Mstislavich and
Dovmont.

Sinaisky's interpretation of Pushkin's fiction in the light of
the rules of conduct established and enforced by a legal system
based on divine commandments is equally fascinating in its novel
approach to literature. Sinaisky argues that Pushkin, who had a
profound knowledge of ethical laws, treats the moral problems
confronted by his heroes, such as fidelity, duty, punishment, and
the acceptance of fate, in accordance with the eternal moral laws
which also existed in the Russia of those far-off days.

Pushkin and the Law[1]

I.   Marriage and Love

One could pay no greater honor to a man's memory
than to carry his words perpetually in one's heart with full
understanding of their real meaning. All exterior expression
of esteem is only a shadow offered to his personality. Many
incidental words uttered by Pushkin proceeded from profound
reflections. Some of them are especially close to us; for
example:

> "Love will pass and boredom will come." (from a letter to
> Goncharova of October 4, 1830)
> "I am given to another, and to him I'll be eternally
> faithful."

These phrases are a kind of formula, expressing the
solution to a deep-rooted problem: Love and marriage, a
problem that each person, almost without exception, must
resolve in his own private life.

Pushkin, a connoisseur of hearts, wrote in a letter to
Vyazemskaya in May 1830, just before his marriage, that his
love for Natalya Goncharova was the one-hundred third. We
may give credit to Pushkin in this regard, not only as a man
of genius, but as a man of great experience in matters of love
as well.

In the same letter Pushkin distinguishes two types of

love, remarking that one is always a matter of feeling, while the other is of passion. The first type, sometimes humorous and perhaps even foolish, nonetheless remains delightful to the memory; the second is one of those . grievous errors of the heart. In general, love is our freedom, constrained not even by word of honor (excerpt from "Egyptian Nights"). On the other hand, marriage is a duty which a person takes upon himself and, consequently, it represents a limitation of our freedom in this particular regard. In other words, love and marriage are two aspects of human life—the free and the unfree. Marriage is a legal institution and, consequently, it is here that we directly approach Pushkin's views on the law.

It is understood that marriage is a contract; it is accepted nowadays as a registration of our solemn promise to become the spouse of another person. But for Pushkin this contract stands apart from all others in that it is not only a solemn and public promise, but an oath, something mystical, a sacrament. Thus, marriage without the consecration of the Church is only an ordinary contract and, strictly speaking, not a marriage: "You cannot avoid your destined one, even on horseback." Fate itself is instrumental in marriage. In a number of his stories, particularly in "The Blizzard," Pushkin amplifies this idea. All that we usually explain by chance circumstances in the act of marriage is in reality the decree of fate, unknown to us, uniting people in marriage. Almost any one of us can confirm this concept.

As a consequence of this sacramental predestination, marriage is a union for the entire lifetime of two people who complement one another. If a person should dissolve the marriage union (a frequent phenomenon in our times), then he deprives himself of the greatest gift of fate, takes the wrong path in life, and distorts his life. "I am given to another and to him I'll be eternally faithful," says Pushkin's Tatyana. This oath means the acceptance of the gift of fate, which represents the greatest satisfaction in life for a human being, no matter what form married life takes, joyful or grievous. In *Dubrovsky* Mariya Kirillovna expresses this idea: "I gave my oath, the prince is my husband...Leave us."

The last words, "Leave us," indicate that a person, through the sacrament of marriage, ceases to be "I" which, free before marriage, now merges with another "I" ("Leave us"); it has lost a part of its freedom through uniting itself with another. Serious marital conflicts arise when a spouse preserves his "I," or the same freedom within marriage as before marriage. Therein consists the erroneous concept of marriage as a simple agreement between two contractees: "I" plus "I," but not "we."

The content of marriage—duty in the sense of an accepted mutual responsibility—emerges from its correct concept "we." In *The Captain's Daughter*, Pushkin gives an example of the fulfillment of duty: "To live together and die together," says Vasilisa Egorovna in reply to the commandment of Ivan Kuz'mich, her husband. And she was indeed an example of this attitude. She did not abandon him and accepted a martyr's death along with him. . . .

"Love will pass and boredom will come," but in marriage, even if love should pass, there remains the duty of a mutually shared life and the upbringing of children, and there is no time left for boredom. Love is not eternal; marriage is eternal, forever, and perhaps not only here on earth. Pushkin is outspoken on divorce in particular:

"But I don't agree with you, I cannot condone divorce:
First there is the duty of holy faith, then the law and
nature itself."

(Pushkin to K. G. Rodzyanko, 1825)

. . .

III.   Satisfaction

Pushkin's sharp eye pauses also on the external side of legal institutions. In "The Shot" he shows us that the external institution alone does not attain its immediate goal if it does not take into account its internal goal. In this story he examines the institution of the duel as the right to reestablish one's own dignity. However, killing the offender in a duel does not fully reestablish the essence of one's honor. After his opponent has fired at him for the second time, Silvio replies not with a shot, but with words: "I am satisfied. I saw your confusion, your timidity, I forced you to shoot at me" (for the second time, to which he had no right). "'It is enough. You will remember me. I leave you to your own conscience.' Silvio went out," writes Pushkin, "but paused in the doorway and shot, without aiming, at the same picture which his opponent had hit when he had shot but missed him."

It is characteristic that during the first duel the offensive opponent appeared with cherries, shot at Silvio, missed, and calmly began to eat the cherries. It would have been easy for Silvio, a first-class shot, to kill him. But he kept the shot for later, with the agreement of his opponent, who was indifferent to life at that instant. Silvio would wait for the moment when the latter would value life and would reveal the cowardice and degradation of his personality. When his opponent, the count, had married a beloved woman, Silvio appeared before him to claim his right to the shot. He had attained what he wanted. The count was so humiliated that he even shot a second time. There was no longer any need to take such a person into consideration. Let his conscience, that superior judge, torment him now.

IV.   Punishment and Retribution

In the duel discussed above, the idea of punishment is clear. The punishment consists not in the opponent's humiliation, but in eliciting remorse through recognition of his wrong action. Perhaps the same idea is expressed by Dostoevsky in his novel *Crime and Punishment.* Criminal law must serve to elicit repentance and through it aim at the reformation of the individual. But Pushkin acknowledges direct retribution in those cases when an individual has ultimately lost his human image, when he is deprived of the blessing of punishment. The criminal then receives punishment in the form of his own annihilation. In *Dubrovsky*, the corrupt, false courtroom officials who did not respect the law perish in the fire. Similarly, Arkhip, risking his life to save a cat, "God's creature," from the fire, refuses to save the magistrates—"the cursed ones," as he says—even though Egorovna asks him to do so. He replies to her: "I won't." No punishment will have any effect on a cursed individual. He is simply crossed out of life by fate itself, ceasing to be God's creature. Pushkin points out here that

even punishment is a blessing not meant for everyone,
especially not for those who continually alter the law to suit
their own purposes. Consequently, the conscience of
magistrate and lawyer in particular should stand guard over
the law. . . .

Recognizing *conscience* as the basis of understanding the
law, Pushkin puts these words into the mouth of his hero:

"...Nothing can comfort us amid worldly sorrows.
Nothing, nothing...perhaps only conscience."
And further:
"Indeed, pitiful is the man whose conscience is impure!"

(Boris Godunov)

. . .

VI.   A Superior Law—Fate (*Jus Divinum*)

The human order based on reason (*Jus humanum*) is
subordinate to the higher sacramental order—fate (*Jus
divinum*). In his works Pushkin returns repeatedly to the
idea of fate as a kind of divine law consisting of two
powers—one benign and one malevolent.

Since man possesses freedom of choice, he can protect
himself from the malevolent force by prayer, described, for
example, in "Little House in Kolomna." The concept of faith
as a superior order is founded upon an absolute order—that
of fate. We noted above that human marriage is a reflection
of heavenly marriage in the sense that in human marriage
there is predestination or fate. Rebellion against the divine
order, the manifestation of which is the human order, in the
best situation results in punishment; in the worst, in the loss
of reason ("The Bronze Horseman," the insanity of Evgeny)
and even annihilation (the execution of Pugachev). Grinyov
feels the malevolent power of Pugachev's fate, to which he is
mysteriously bound (*The Captain's Daughter*). He attempts
to avert the malevolent force, but in vain, for Pugachev has
accepted this dark force of fate by his own choice between
the forces of good and evil.

All of this demonstrates that the acceptance of fate in

Pushkin's thinking does not exclude human freedom and that
fate is essentially the superior law of life in two dynamic
manifestations: positive or good force and negative or evil
force.   The first manifestation of fate is beneficent (as in
marriage, for example); the second is harmful to man and
may even destroy him.   The will of fate as a superior law is
directed to the benefit of man.   But it is not absolute, for
then man would be slave of good, deprived of freedom.   The
evil power can be overcome as we have seen; superior
beneficent predestination can only be beneficial, but it is
acceptable only in certain conditions (in marriage, for
example).

In general, rebellion against fate, as the choice of one of
the two powers, should not take place for this very reason
("Mozart and Salieri").   Nonetheless fate is mysterious, a
mysterious order.   Not all of nature (fate in its
manifestations) is accessible to the mind and to the heart;
therefore not everyone can

"Peer into her mysterious bosom as into the heart of a
    friend."

(Pushkin)

"Harmony of mind and heart" is required.   These words
are fully applicable to human law and order as well.   Culture
requires the same harmony for the proper fulfillment of its
law.   Pride stands in the way of this harmony while humility
before the laws of God and man leads with certainty to it
("The Gypsies").

These are the general outlines of Pushkin's thought on
the law.   They comprise a complete legal system, an entity
based on a superior divine law.

V. I. Sinaisky

————·————

There are other interesting pieces of writing on Russian
literature in the archives of Professor Sinaisky, presently in the
custody of his daughter, Natalya Vasilyevna Sinaiski (Bruxelles,
Belgium).

NOTE

1. A lecture read in 1937 in Riga for the "Day of Russian Culture,"
dedicated to the centenary of Pushkin's death. Published in the journal
Law and Court, ed. Jacobi (Riga, 1937), No. 71.

LITHUANIA

RYABININ, ROMAN

Roman Ryabinin was a promising Russian poet in Lithuania.
He contributed to *Russian Annals*.

Russian Annals, No. 12 (Paris, 1938)

Now the fields appear in moonlit patches,
Now a rusty, cast-iron bridge;
Like a taut string,
The poplars do not stir.
A path disappearing in the distance is
Strewn with fiery lime...
I have wanted for a long while to fall asleep,
But the biting wind prevents me.
The rays of headlights
Rush in a flickering arc...
O, moonlight, you are too old
To be the master of my soul.

Lithuania

––––––––––·––––––––––

The poem is a brief poetic travelogue in the traditional iambic
form. It intermittently presents wondrous images of a mysterious,
nocturnal landscape with moonlight, motionless poplars, a path
disappearing in the dark distance and more prosaic objects like a
rusty, cast-iron bridge, fiery lime illuminating the path, automobile
headlights, and a biting wind that keeps the poet from yielding
completely to the moon's magic unreality. The *persona* is
curiously suspended between these two planes of vision, between
reality and dream, new and old. Obviously approving of the
technological acquisitions of modern times, the *persona* addresses
himself ironically to the moonlight—indeed he has long outgrown
the romantic fairy tales and credulity of youth. The poet's
positive attitude toward modern civilization is also suggested by his

description of the landscape—the moon illuminates only patches of the fields and the bridge; compared with the bright headlights of cars, the light of the moon is evidently weak.

Though he seems to have chosen the civilized world of rationality, the poet renders the nocturnal attributes of the night in an expressive sympathetic fashion. And it is the poetic quality of the description that imparts to the *persona's* ironical rejection of the romantic moonlight a certain ambiguity and poignancy.

MINTSLOV, SERGEY RUDOL'FOVICH (1870-1933)

Minstslov was born into the family of a prominent Moscow lawyer and educated at the Cadet Corps in Nizhny Novgorod and later at the Alexandrovsky Military School in Moscow. Various professors from Moscow University, such as I. F. Buslaev who taught Russian literary history, also lectured at the Military Academy. At home, Mintslov's father arranged soirées attended by the well-known professors Veselovsky, Yanzhul, Kareev, and Prince Urusov. Some were active liberals. They held lively debates on new ideas and important issues of the day. After his graduation from the Alexandrovsky Military School, Mintslov joined the Ufimsky Regiment stationed in Vilnius (Lithuania). He was deeply impressed by the natural beauty of the country and developed an interest in Lithuanian folk tales and legends. Mintslov's fascination with Slavic and Lithuanian history and culture lasted a lifetime and made him a zealous collector of rare books and manuscripts. His private library, unique in scope and value, eventually became part of the State library of East Prussia in Königsberg (East Germany). It is because of his lifelong attachment to Lithuania that Mintslov's works appear in this section.

In 1892 Mintslov was transferred to a regiment in the Caucasus. During World War I he found himself in the Kiev Rear Division, but at his own request he was again transferred to the Caucasian Army. In the Caucasus he studied the Trapezond culture and subsequently published a book about it. He also started a Russian newspaper, *Trapezonskaya voennaya gazeta* (The Trapezond Military Newspaper), and was its publisher and editor for some time. In exile after the Bolshevik *coup d'état* of 1917,

Mintslov settled first in Yugoslavia and then in Riga, where he contributed to the Russian newspapers and journals *Russian Thought, Contemporary Annals, Today,* and others.

To characterize the literary output of Sergey Mintslov perhaps the most accurate term is diversity. He wrote novels, short stories, reminiscences, and novellas concerning Russia's past, natural scenery, ways of life, and the Russian provinces. His descriptions are in minute, ethnographic detail. Particularly appealing are the old, often abandoned Russian estates, in their silent and mysterious surroundings. His historical novels on Russian as well as non-Russian themes continue the tradition of Sir Walter Scott, while at the same time they remind readers of Mel'nikov-Pechersky in their portrayal of everyday life in the remote Russian provinces, and of Leskov's works in their skillfull use of anecdote, eccentric narrative technique, and penchant for humor and irony. Mintslov's works are replete with the fragrance of the Russian soil and portray the country's spaciousness and beauty, its flaming sunrises and sunsets, its steppes, distant mountains, and dreamy forests, its luscious gardens and parks, its bright daylight and dark, portentous nights shrouded in mysteries and dangers. In other works, readers travel to distant countries, see ancient and modern cities, meet historical persons, admire the medieval cultures of Italy and Germany, and anticipate the forthcoming collapse and demise of the entire world. Mintslov believes in a mysterious world of silent, unresolved riddles and often populates has universe with vampires, wood-goblins, and house-spirits lurking behind bushes, in ravines, and in abandoned huts, ready to pounce at any moment.

The following two short stories represent Mintslov's varied style and his romantic and psychological portrayals. "The Living Dead," the second story, focuses on the vampire legend of Eastern Europe's mountainous regions. The reader follows the hero, Dushan Prodanovich, through a mysterious, silent, and threatening dark forest. It is not a mere thrilling adventure story, however; it belongs to the realm of serious literature with its memorable descriptions of wild, nocturnal nature and, by contrast, of the sunlit woods with colorful plums, figs, almonds, and vibrant animal life. Remnants of ancient and not so ancient civilizations are left in decay, and the reader is aware of a gradual disintegration, as if greater destruction were impending.

In contrast to the Gothic qualities of "The Living Dead,"

"Two Sergeys" evinces a realistic setting, gentle humor, and psychological veracity. Mintslov's childhood memories are presented without sentimentality. He maintains distance from the material by using the simple language befitting a story about children who find themselves in ludicrous situations and often at the mercy of adults. Mintslov's wit has its roots in the Ukrainian humor tradition of G. F. Kvitka-Osnovyanenko and V. Narezhny, both predecessors of Gogol. "Svistopup" is a nonsensical term with a denigrating ring.

Mintslov also published *Tsar' Berendey* (Tsar Berendey; Berlin: Medny vsadnik, 1923), *Sny zemli* (Dreams of the Earth; Berlin: Sibirskoe Kn-vo, 1925), *Gusarsky monastyr'* (The Hussars' Monastery; Sofia: Zartsy, 1925), *Dalekie dni: vospominaniya* (Distant Days: Reminiscences; Berlin: Sibirskoe Kn-vo, 1925), *Volki: istorichesky roman* (Wolves: A Historical Novel; Riga: Didkovsky, 1927), *Priklyucheniya studentov: istoriko-avantyurny roman* (The Adventures of Students: A Historical Adventure Novel; Riga: Sibirskoe Kn-vo, 1928), *Chernoknizhnik: tainstvennoe* (The Magician: The Mysterious; Riga: Didkovsky, 1928), and *Svistopup: yumoristicheskie i drugie rasskazy* (A Wheezing Potbelly: Humorous and Other Short Stories; Riga: Didkovsky, no date).

A Wheezing Potbelly

Two Sergeys

Old Moscow...

Ostozhenka, an enormous, dove-colored house with heavy white columns, and half-hidden by the surrounding age-old silver poplars. The large grounds behind the house covered almost an entire acre with all sort of farm buildings, and a tall wooden fence separated it from the vast, vacant, neighboring land called "The Monastery." Near the semicircular alley of fragrant poplars a fence cut "The Monastery" in half. From behind the poplars peered "The Assumption on the Tomb," a tiny old golden-rose church. In the distance one could see little wooden huts hidden in the lilac bushes along the back alleys, and behind those a sea of gardens stretching out almost to the Moscow River itself.

In the house with the columns a well-kept, twelve-year-old boy in an elegant brown jacket with a wide, white lace collar stood by the window—it was Sergey Atryganyev, the son of Tambov's wealthiest landowner. While outside, on the thick branch of a poplar tree, sat Quick Feet, a wild Indian in a Russian tunic. God only knows where he really lived—perhaps in the small house at "The Monastery," or in the branches of trees, or even on the flat roofs of the barns where it was so pleasant to stuff oneself with rowan berries and jump down into somebody's mysterious thick woods, called parks by people who don't understand a thing.

This Indian was none other than Sergey Mintslov.

It is only one little step from looking at each other to getting acquainted; the second step leads to the fence, and the third, to indissoluble friendship.

And so it happened with us!

How can I describe the delights we experienced? We were like the martlets and the swallows that hovered over us; we travelled to countries, reaching them by way of our fence; together we climbed mountains—in the form of barns! How many fragrant clusters of bananas, the sourest rowan berries, and apples of the most disgusting type did we not eat! We used to visit the bell tower where its somber sovereign, the snub-nosed sacristan Kuz'ma, allowed us to enjoy the special treat—ringing the huge bell, which was so loud it shook our insides and made it impossible to understand even the shouts of a neighbor.

What space spread before our eyes! How joyful it was to look at the panorama of Moscow, to recognize well-known places!

We had wigwams in the treetops, but our favorite hideout was on the roof of one of the barns, which was shaded, as if with a cap, by an overhanging old rowan tree. Here neither eyes nor rain could reach us. We told each other hundreds of wonderful stories here! Oh, to where did we not fly, lying on our stomachs and dangling our legs! As if in a grotto, we would hang our provisions on branches and leave notes for each other if some secret meeting could not take place.

Sergey Atryganyev was two years older than I, though much shorter and weaker. Since he was the youngest in the family, they took the greatest care of him at home. Why, he even went by carriage to the Katkovsky Lyceum, which really was almost next door.

Once Sergey Atryganyev's mother, an excessively soft-hearted, middle-aged lady of the Georgian type, came out on the porch to get into her carriage. Suddenly she saw her dear Serzhin'ka soaring high in the air next to me, on the tallest poplar tree.

The usual uproar followed. "He will break his neck!...He will fall!" wailed Madame Atryganyeva. "The ladder, quickly!..." screeched the French governess, rushing about..."Servants, quickly!..." Curious passers-by began to stream into the yard...I managed to hurry away while right behind me Atryganyev slid down like a shot. I saw through a clink in the fence how my friend was first clasped to his mother's bosom and how she then, armed with her lorgnette, examined him from head to toe. "You look like I don't know what!" she exclaimed, raising both arms to the sky.

This remark seemed perfectly logical to me as my friend's jacket, because of his quick descent from the tree, resembled a dust rag. The collar was crumpled and turned to one side. The rear of his trousers was completely gone, left hanging on one of the branches.

The next day, smoking a pipe, I waited around the wigwam for my friend until dusk. He did not come. I felt very gloomy, so you can imagine my joy the next day, when the Artyganyevs' footman appeared beneath the windows of the small house in "The Monastery" where I lived. Closely resembling a torchbearer from the undertaker's office, he gave me a letter from my namesake. "Hooray!..." he wrote, "We have won our case! Come soon, Mama will allow us to play together in the house."

Thus I finally entered the stately chambers that I had long known from the outside only.

Apart from Sergey and his mother already described, the family of Atryganyev consisted of a retired Dragoon captain, apparently from the Sumsky Regiment, Alexander Alexand-rovich, and the pretty, but trumpet-voiced, twenty-year-old Lika who was always singing scales and practicing her voice. The captain, on the contrary, was always silent. He walked about the huge rooms dressed in a robe and clinking his spurs. He smoked an ancient pipe decorated with azure blue

beads two *arshins* long and occasionally even whistled some
kind of military march. His face was always serious and
preoccupied, but sparks of laughter shone in his eyes.

Atryganyev, who submitted to me entirely in the yard,
suddenly had a depressing effect on me inside the house.
Since he pretended to know everything in the world, I began
to regard him almost like a supernatural creature. He knew
by heart a great number of poems by different writers and
often recited them to me in a howling voice, which impressed
me as the acme of art.

One lovely evening my friend modestly confessed to me
that he wrote poems and intended to publish them soon as a
collection; he asked me to keep this secret for a while. Then
my idol added that he had decided to establish a literary
society, with the name "Soirées at Ostozhenka." In order to
become a member of this select society, one had to compose
poetry, even if only one verse. Thus, returning home I sat
down at the table. The first two lines were not too bad, but
then I sat motionless over the white sheet of paper, chewing
my pencil in vain. I was unable to continue. I struggled all
evening; I struggled the next evening, but except for two
poor grades received in school, nothing came out of my
endeavors. Finally, after many ardent transports and agonies,
I found a solution to my problem.

I took from the bookshelf a volume of Pushkin and
immediately noticed the poem "The Caucasus is below me, I
am alone on the heights..." etc.

It was in the middle of the book and, therefore, seemed
to me less noticeable and less well-known. I copied it in a
separate notebook, and in my zeal made an enormous ink
blot on the page. At the appointed hour I arrived at the
Atryganyevs' with the notebook in my pocket.

They had been waiting for me—oh horror! Lika, her
mother, and the French governess were sitting in the parlor,
while Alexander Alexandrovich stood by the stove with his
legs crossed, smoking his huge pipe with indifference.

My courage left me.

Seryozha opened the program. He came forward to the
center of the sitting room in a free and easy manner, put his
weight on one leg, and placed one hand under his arm.
Then he began to recite a miraculous poem. It seemed to

me far better than the one in my pocket.

The ladies clapped their hands with excitement. Alexander Alexandrovich waited until their applause died out and shook his head.

"What a swine that Pushkin was!" he said. "Stealing such a beautiful poem from you!"

Seryozha blushed all over. "Not true!" he exclaimed. "What makes you think that it is Pushkin's?"

"Why, from the book you forgot on the table," said the captain. "I was browsing through it!"

"Seryozha!..." said Lika, taking the highest pitch of a reproachful scale "Mi."

"Fi!!" cried the French governess.

"Wait, mesdames!" said Alexander Alexandrovich "Our soirée is not yet over—we have heard only one poet, now it is the turn of the other."

I began to assure them that I had brought nothing, for I had not composed a poem. But in vain. Amid their exclamations and encouragements, my friend, the Judas, searched me and pulled out my ill-fated notebook. The poem was recited festively.

"Drag the entire Pushkin here!!" ordered the captain, "and bring Lermontov, as well!"

The volumes were brought in a jiffy; their contents were checked. My poem was found...

Laughter, uproar, and lively exclamations accompanied this discovery; the captain played a flourish through his fist. Seryozha, forgetting about his own fiasco, rolled on the floor and kicked up his legs...But do I really need to expand? I will only add that in the entire course of fifty years no collection of poetry by Artryganyev has appeared.

And whenever they ask me about my first literary work, I always modestly answer that its author was Pushkin.

———————·———————

The Magician

The Living Dead

From border to border the tall verdant mountains of Macedonia, overgrown with thick green woods, cover the land. Villages are rare here; a little hut here and there with a few gardens. These little houses, saklias, are built from brown limestone, and many of them are in ruins. During the war Turks and Macedonians left their old nests and went to a new fate and a new homeland.

The abandoned gardens are now overgrown and wild; the trees are full of plums, figs, and almonds—a whole acre of them; roses, hollyhock, and all sorts of flowers peep out from the tall grass, but only rarely does someone come and pick the fruit or flowers.

Even the songbirds have abandoned these places; instead there are flocks of partridge, thousands of quail, and even wild boars.

Sometimes in the remote forest thicket, by the gloomy ravine, rises a silent watchtower—a spectre of Roman times—or the ruins of a castle with black holes for windows. One might find remains of a mysterious ancient road leading to the unfamiliar backwoods and the depths of the forests where for centuries no human footprint has been seen...Who built these roads and lived in the towers and castles—it is still a mystery.

Bears, wild boars, and fever now rule these dense forests.

The rare traveler must wander along a muddy rut since the roads are dilapidated. Sometimes he will pause and hide himself in a bush or in the nearest mighty plane tree; the traveler seems to hear voices and the steps of border soldiers or brigands...but no! It is only a row of yellow-black tortoises stepping heavily along toward him on their way to the pond. The largest tortoise leads the procession, while the smallest brings up the rear. There are thousands of them here.

Mountain chains rise up one behind another; they stretch to the south as the last pass opens on the turquoise lake Doyran spreading out in the valley. And in the blue mist, mountains again rise behind it—it is Greece. On this side, along the embankment, meander the streets of the dead city of the same name as the lake.

Most of the roofs of the two-storied houses have collapsed; the narrow alleys and squares are overgrown with tall weeds and bushes while small lights of a bright garnet color burn in the broken windows.

Not a soul appears...only lizards standing still on the walls, playing in the sunshine...there is complete silence...

But raise your eyes upward, almost to the clouds, and you will catch sight of a small black figure on some rocks. It is a shepherd, wandering with a flock of sheep; he stands over the precipice and looks down at the world at his feet.

Here, when twilight begins to fall and creeps along the mountain peaks, a bonfire burns like a bright star, and in the distance the high grass sways as if it were dense breakers. The air is saturated with the heavy smell of mutton.

Somber shepherds with long moustaches sit around the fire and eat their dinner. Like the night itself, they are clothed in black; over their dark trousers, jackets, and little round caps trimmed with braid are draped white felt capes...Near the shepherds, there is a gray ring of huge shaggy dogs waiting for their dinner.

When supper ends, the sky is studded with stars, and people and dogs lie close to the fire, but sleep does not come at once. Leisurely they begin to tell stories...You hear many strange things from the shepherds on such nights.

*

...Dushan Prodanovich, returning from Strumitsy to the village by way of Dzhevdzheli, stayed too long with a friend over a bottle of vodka. It was already dusk as he prepared to leave.

They tried to persuade him to spend the night at the inn, reminding him how frightening the woods are at night. He would meet wild beasts, but that would be only half of the trouble; along the roads, living corpses—vampires —wander in search of passers-by in order to suck their blood. Only a miracle, perhaps, could save him from them!

Dushan had drank too much and now he was in a great

hurry; so he decided there was enough time until dark to move on to the next village and to make up for lost time. He threw his knapsack over his back, took his staff, and started on his way.

He had been walking along for about an hour when he suddenly remembered that the closest road was the other way. All he had to do was turn left, cross the mountain ridge, walk along the ravine, and then the village would be quite close.

Dushan briskly turned left and began to hum a song; for some reason, he felt glad, even happy. He crossed the mountains, coming down along the rocky slope into the ravine. A gray, moist shadow covered the ravine, while higher in the pale sky the rocks shimmered purple and gold.

The woods became thicker; a stream gleamed white and rushed noisily between the huge boulders; the prongs of the mountains were growing dark as the dusk closed in around the age-old trees.

Suddenly Dushan stopped as if before an abyss; he suddenly realized that to his knowledge there was no river in the ravine!...A chill crept between his shoulder blades.

He turned around—and now the woods looked different; instead of the familiar rare oak forest, there were gray-stumped plane trees.

Dushan turned and hurried back. The ravine meandered; the murmuring current did not cease, but there was not a sign of the boulders! Finally, the boulders and the opening appeared. Dushan climbed up through the pass with difficulty and again descended; again the stream was noisy, and again he was surrounded by the plane tree forest...

Dushan's heart sank! Night was coming and he really had to hurry, but where to?

Stars began to come out, but they gave little light; he could not orient himself.

At random Dushan set out along the stream. The moon was rising, a grayish blue light flooded the tips of the mountains and the entire ravine. The stream began to smoke and fog crept among the trees—it seemed as if corpses in shrouds ran from tree trunk to tree trunk, from one black boulder to another...while, in the branches over his head, fiery eyes shone and someone stretched out long arms with bluish green scales.

Stumbling over the rocks, Dushan hurried on. Finally, the woods ended sharply, as if cut off—and a dark field stretched out. The path grew wider and rose up steeply toward the mountains—this meant a village was nearby.

At some point Dushan caught sight of something vast and white and he looked more closely—he saw huts scattered along the slope of the mountain. It was late—one could neither see lights nor hear the barking of dogs. With the last of his strength Dushan hastened to a hut, almost running toward the village.

He reached the first house and rushed at once to the window—he wanted to knock on the frame, but there was only a black hole in the wall. Dushan thrust his head in—he sensed there was nothing alive inside, only rot...There was not even a door. Dushan hurried to another hut standing deserted in the silvery moonlight. All the other huts were exactly the same; the village seemed to have been abandoned a long time ago.

What else should he do? He did not have the strength to go further, and had nowhere else to go. Night had descended over the forest, and there it was even colder, damper, and more frightening!...Looking about, Dushan noticed a house in a little better shape than the others and he looked inside.

As in the other huts, instead of a door and windows there were only holes. Moonlight poured in one window; there was not even a bench or a table in the hut, but the floor had been swept out as if with a broom. A large stove stood in the farthest corner.

Dushan crossed himself, stepped over the threshold, and looked behind a partition—there was another room, only smaller, and also quite empty.

He threw down his knapsack and, while saying a prayer, drew with his knife the outline of a circle between the wall and the stove. He then settled down for the night inside the circle. Although the shelter was open from all sides, it was still more peaceful than in the woods!

Dushan shoved the knapsack under his head as a pillow and laid his staff and knife alongside him. He stretched out on the floor and the exhaustion flowed from his legs into the

ground...Listening, he pressed his ear to the ground...
Everywhere there was unbreakable silence...the yellow moon
shone straight into his face; the window was reflected on the
ground as if on water...And like a stone falling to the
bottom, Dushan fell asleep!

*

As he slept, something troubled Dushan's heart...he
opened his eyes. The room was misty with moonlight, as
before, but by the wall there was something red—it appeared
to be a large piece of meat pierced with a glittering knife...

Dushan blinked his eyes and sat up. "Am I still
asleep?...It was empty when I came in, there was nothing by
the wall."

The minute he realized this, he grew cold all over.
From behind the corner of the stove phosphorous eyes stared
at him...a thick moustache and a wide bluish face appeared.
A smile crept across the stranger's unshaven cheeks as he
looked at Dushan.

"You have awakened, brother?" he uttered hoarsely.
"You slept well. Come on, get up! Welcome! We shall
have supper together!"...And he began to sniff the air, smack
his lips, and then went heavily over to the meat and sat
down.

"Well, come on," he repeated.

Dushan felt relieved—the stranger did not touch him;
he had even invited him to eat—he must be a decent fellow.

Dushan did not feel like eating—every bone in his body
ached from the night chill...he lay down again.

"Thank you...," he answered, "But I am full...I'm dead
tired!"

The man muttered something and began to eat...the
way a horse crunches barley.

Again Dushan was drowned in sleep.

Then he awoke for the second time.

*

It had become darker in the hut—the moon was going
down. Between the wall and the stove, a distance of two

steps, the same fellow squatted with his hands stretched out. As he fumbled about or tried to reach over to Dushan, wolfish eyes illuminated his face—he became quite black and blue.

"Brother, come up here by me...," mumbled the stranger. "I will tell you something important."

Dushan's head fell again on the sack, and he neither heard nor saw anything more...

In the morning he woke up late—the hut had been flooded with sunlight long ago. He rubbed his face with the palms of his hands and at once remembered what had happened.

He looked around—there was nothing, the room was empty as before. He got up and glanced in the next room—no one was there...Lilac thistles peeped in through the broken window. Dushan crossed himself.

"Such a strange dream I had!" he thought.

He went out onto the road and gladness enveloped him because of the warmth, the light, and a general feeling of well-being. Dushan looked about, saw his distant mountains in the blue sky, and began to walk down along the right road toward them.

*

In the evening Dushan sat before a mug of wine at an inn in the village he had hoped to reach the day before. He talked about his recent experiences in the hut. Smoking long cherry pipes, several gray-moustached villagers listened to him.

"You were not dreaming," said one man, pressing the tobacco deeper down in the pipe with his finger. "It was a vampire that appeared to you. You're lucky you drew a sacred circle around yourself, otherwise you would now be a corpse lying in that hut!..."

Paris, 1926

FINLAND

BULICH, VERA SERGEEVNA (1898-1954)

"The poetry of Vera Bulich conveys the impression of a subtle and delicate finish comparable to that of Chinese porcelain," wrote Georgy Adamovich in the daily The Latest News (No. 6255). In La Renaissance (No. 4135), Vladislav Khodasevich expressed the following opinion of the poetry of Vera Sergeevna Bulich: "With respect to taste and refinement, one of the first places in our poetry now belongs to Vera Bulich." In spite of the high evaluation by these two distinguished émigré critics, the work of Vera Bulich has not yet achieved its proper place in the history of Russian literature. The present essay seeks to correct this oversight.

The daughter of an emeritus professor of Petersburg University, Vera Bulich was born and educated in Petersburg. Her father S. K. Bulich, director of the Women's University, was a specialist in Russian linguistics and music history. In the wake of the Revolution Professor Bulich fled from Petersburg in 1920 and settled in Finland on his estate Kuolemajärvi. He was famous not only for his numerous works on history, phonetics, the physiology of sounds, and the morphology of Russian and Slavic languages, but also for his contributions as a theoretician, musicologist, and composer. Almost all of the articles on the questions of music in The Great Encyclopedic Dictionary by Brokgauz and Efron, and most of the articles on linguistics, were written by him. His daughters, Sonya (S. S. Bulich-Stark, later a singer of the classical repertoire in Finland) and Vera, a keen expert in music and a wonderful pianist, inherited their father's musical talent.

In Finland, Vera Bulich worked in the Slavic Department of the Helsinki University Library. In 1947, when the Institute for Soviet Studies and the Finland-Soviet Union Library were founded by the State Council of Finland, she was appointed head librarian of the Institute. Bulich, who loved Russian literature, worked enthusiastically at both insitutions. At the Institute she established a large library of more than 20,000 volumes with a reference department for many areas of Russian and Soviet culture and science. In charge of all important assignments in the Slavic departments of the University Library and the Library of the Institute, Bulich was in constant correspondence with Russian writers and readers in exile and in the Soviet Union. Yury Ivask, A. Ginger, Anna Prismanova, Boris Zaytsev, K. Hoerschlemann, and S. A. Rittenberg were among her most frequent correspondents. She arranged interviews in the Institute's library with Soviet writers who had come to Finland—Ilya Ehrenburg, Tikhonov, Fadeyev, to name a few. Of primary importance to her, however, was émigré literature. She read works of V. Sirin with great admiration, especially his novel *The Gift*, which practically became a reference book for her. Among the Russian painters, she particularly favored Vrubel', Levitan, Rerikh, Somov, Dobuzhinsky, and Lukomsky. In her own words, she loved painting from a poetic—not an artistic—point of view. Russian and Western European graphic design also attracted her attention. Brought up in the best Russian cultural tradition, Bulich was interested in philosophy and was well-versed in foreign literature and painting. The works of Gershenzon, Lao-Tse, Schopenhauer, Victor Hugo, Flaubert, Maeterlinck, Oscar Wilde, S. Frank, Lev Shestov, Berdyaev, and Thomas Mann were among her frequent companions during the lonely evening hours. The theory of poetry, rules of versification, and the objective criteria of literary criticism were among her favorite preoccupations. Her notebooks abound in extracts from the works of V. Zhirmunsky, for example, *Rifma: eyo istoriya i teoriya* (Rhyme: Its History and Theory, 1923); V. Bryusov, *Opyty* (Experiments, 1918); L. Grossman, *Bor'ba za stil'* (A Struggle for Style, 1927); S. Volkonsky, *Obrazy zhizni i sushchestvovaniya* (Modes of Life and Existence, 1924); A. Chebotarevskaya, *Vozniknovenie iskusstva* (The Origins of Art); and K. Mochul'sky, *Alexander Blok* (1948), as well as extracts from articles by Georgy Adamovich and Vladimir Weidlé on poetry and the essence of versification. Her notebooks also contain many citations from the works of D. S. Merezhkovsky, Zinaida Hippius, Anna Akhmatova, A. Blok, F. Sologub, O. Mandel'stam, V. Sirin, A. Ladinsky, L. Chervinskaya, G. Adamovich, Georgy Ivanov, D. Klenovsky, Irina Odoevtseva, Georgy Raevsky, V. Smolensky, Anna Prismanova, Alla Golovina, Vera Inber, and many other writers both outside and in the Soviet Union.

Vera Bulich started writing poetry when she was ten years old. In 1920 her work began to appear in Helsinki newspapers and magazines: *New Life, New Russian News, The Journal of Concord;*

in Berlin: *The Rudder*; in Tallinn: *The Tallinn Russian Voice*
and the collection *The Virgin Soil*; in the literary magazine *Our
Little Light* (Riga); in *Contemporary Annals* (Paris); in the literary
journal *New Home* (New York), and in the anthologies *Anchor*
(Berlin), in *In the West* (New York), and *The Muse of the
Diaspora* (Frankfurt on Main). Her Swedish poetry was published
in *Radiobladet*, and her Finnish poetry, in the newspapers *Vapaa
Sana* and *Helsingen Sanomat*. The short story "Kalme Sararusta"
appeared in the Helsinki magazine *Joulus Sirrka* (1928); the short
story "Princessa Pisara," in the journal *Sirrka* (1929). Bulich's
articles, reviews, and translations were published in such Russian
newspapers and magazines as *New Journal, Borders* (posthumously),
and *The Journal of Concord*. These articles dealt with the work
of Batyushkov, Pushkin, Lermontov, Innokenty Annensky,
Bal'mont, Andrey Bely, Vyacheslav Ivanov, Georgy Ivanov, Marina
Tsvetaeva, A. Ladinsky, Dovid Knut, Lidiya Chervinskaya, Boris
Poplavsky, and other "new poets." Critical surveys and analyses of
the prose of Turgenev, Boris Zaytsev, V. Weidlé, Sérge
Charchoune, and of the collections of *Numbers* comprised the
contents of her other articles. She also wrote comic verse,
epigrams (for example, on Vadim Andreev), études in prose,
compositions on music, scenarios and librettos for ballet (e.g.,
Reflection of a Sunbeam and *Dream of a Poet*), short stories
("Blackcap," "Sunday," "Two Worlds"), tales in verse ("Young
Frog Kva-Kuvak," with illustrations by Vladimir Shchepansky),
tales in prose ("Little Spider—Merrymaker," "Tale of the Spring
Wind"), and lengthy fairy tales ("Tale about the Princess Fairy
Tale," a play for children in two acts and four scenes). The fairy
tale *Snegur Pryanichnoe Serdtse* (Snowman Heart Cake, in two
acts) was successfully staged by the director A. I. Zaytsev in the
Russian Theatre in Finland. Bulich's Swedish fairy tales were
published in Stockholm, as well as in Finland, where she took part
in radio programs on "The Work of Soviet Writers" (Konstantin
Paustovsky, Galina Nikolaeva, Margarita Oliger).

Bulich published two volumes of *Skazki* (Fairy Tales) for
children, one in 1927 in Finland (in Finnish) and another in 1931
in Yugoslavia (in Russian). These fairy tales are written in
poetical and lyrical prose. Original in concept, they appeal to the
reader through their sincerity and soft, water color images. Their
tight composition holds the reader's attention throughout the
narrative, bringing into the foreground the humane ideas of

self-sacrifice, empathy, and love for the lonely and suffering, loyalty in friendship, the defense of the weak, and the struggle against evil. Vivid presentations graphically demonstrate the author's sympathy and, thus, soften the moral admonition of the story. The entire book in Russian is permeated with warm feelings and tender endearment for the young reader.

In 1934, in Helsinki, Vera Bulich published a collection of verse entitled *Mayatnik: pervaya kniga stikhov* (Pendulum: A First Book of Poetry). This edition was followed in 1938 in Tallinn by the collection *Plenny veter* (Captive Wind); in 1947, in Helsinki, *Burelom: tretya kniga stikhov* (Wind-Fallen Wood: A Third Book of Poetry); and in 1954, in Paris, by the collection *Vetvi* (Branches). Love of nature is omnipresent in Bulich's poetry. Nature always played a significant role in her personal life and colored her diary entries. On August 7, 1951, for example, she wrote: "We swam along the rocky shores. The sea was large and glistened with sun scales; there was both so much water and air, and *so* few people, that it was possible to dissolve in nature." On August 15, 1951: "The day is marvelous, soft, lustreless, quiet—not the slightest breeze, tender air, the sun is behind the clouds; sometimes it shines through brightly, and again goes away unnoticeably behind the haze." This profound feeling for nature finds its poetic expression in her verse which, according to her own words, consitutes the main substance of her life, "an unexpected gift" to her from her Muse. She wrote to Vadim Andreev in one of her letters: " . . . I often meditate on the fact that I have scarcely any poems which could have been written on just any occasion; all my poems are more or less accidental. If my life were different—then there would be other poems. There are phenomena, feelings, questions that play an important role in my life, but did not find reflection in my poems, only because the projected ray did not fall on them or did not snatch some detail necessary for the chain of images and sounds to be formed. I plan, but do not accomplish, because my line does not ring true. I wait for the 'God-given' line and yet it does not come. That power alone, which stands beyond me and sends its rays whimsically at its own discretion, is deaf to my entreaties. It autocratically demands obedience. Therefore each new poem is an unexpected gift." Classical music, which Bulich experienced "even more deeply than literature," also finds poetic realization in her verse.

On March 1, 1953, we find an entry particularly indicative of her perception of the world: "The absence of happiness is more painful than the absence of money. Can Socialism remedy this? It cannot say: 'Take happiness from those who have it and divide it among those who have not.' It will be forced to agree with just what Christianity teaches: 'Submit yourself, accept your fate. Forget about yourself, work for the good of others.' Then why was it necessary to reject Christianity?" The poet never abandoned her faith in Christianity, her resignation to fate, and courage in the face of suffering; these attitudes appear throughout her poetry.

Her views on happiness may be found in one of her earlier verses:

The Virgin Soil, No. 8 (1935)

Happiness

In searching, in agonizing pursuit,
Nothing found, nor met, nor overtaken...
So, what remains? To close my eyes,
And plunge headlong into the void?

And when at the last minute
Happiness flung open,
Like a parachute expanding,
A blue dome over my head,

My soul flinched as from a blow:
Must I indeed possess this happiness?
See the radiance of the angelic gift!
So, it was worth the living and the waiting.

A year, a day, an hour...It's easy to let go
When memory is joyous, pleasant.
And—with a steady hand I released
The end of the radiant rope.

———————·———————

This poem expresses the idea that happiness cannot be found or held onto by force. It is a gift from heaven and comes of its own accord in its own time, quite apart from our desires. In this, it is like poetic inspiration (see Bulich's poem "Poetry")—it descends for a time, "a radiant gift," and then departs. What remains is a joyous memory. The paradox is that to have happiness at all, people must first let go of it, as the *persona* does in the last two lines: "And with a steady hand I released/The end of the radiant rope."

The poem reveals the unique poetic diction characteristic of Vera Bulich's work: the thought or image incompletely expressed ("agonizing pursuit"—of happiness? "the radiant rope"—of what?). But the artistic perspective created and the title of the poem enable the reader to grasp the imagery and the pervading mood. A series of forceful negations, "Nothing found, nor met, nor overtaken..." and the compressed sequence of "a year, a day, an hour," along with the visual image of happiness, "like a parachute expanding/A blue dome over my head," all illustrate Bulich's mastery of poetic expression. The meter of the poem is a fairly regular trochaic pentameter, with the exception of one line. The last line of the first stanza, "And plunge headlong into the void?" is cut short at only four feet, appropriately accentuating the abruptness of the thought. Feminine and masculine rhymes alternate in the pattern abab. The frequent use of alliteration also contributes to the poem's sound effects.

There is harmony between form and content in Bulich's verse. Gifted with a sense of lyrical form, she wrote clear-cut, well-executed poems. Her rich and vivid vocabulary, striking epithets (for example, "heavy honey moon" in *Pendulum*) and images, the easy flow of her lines, and the "eternal" themes of poetry—God, nature, love, parting, death—form salient features of her art. Her motifs—sadness, disappointment, loneliness—show a certain resemblance to the poetry of Anna Akhmatova. There is the same narrative intimacy, the same feminine world of love and fear of being abandoned by "him," the same helpless agitation, and almost the same "he." The poet mourns the transient nature of happiness, "his" indifference, unfaithful words, and the necessity of woman's resignation to fate. Bulich's technique, however, is quite different from Akhmatova's. Bulich prefers verbs of motion which create the rapid flow of speech and rhythm, whereas Anna Akhmatova, to express women's emotions, uses mainly nouns which

halt the internal movement of the poem and direct the attention of
the reader to the emotion conveyed.   *Pendulum* is the sincere,
intimate story of a woman; its tone conceals the rigid construction
of the poem and, like Anna Akhmatova's verse, Bulich's poems
display a Pushkin-like gracefulness in her distribution of a sentence
into lines.   There is no monotony in the lyrical narration and in
the repetition of images, but carefully chosen descriptions of a
sunny day (in "Noon," "June," "Spring" and "Impassivity," for
example) convey the *persona's* shifting moods.

Khodasevich, having noticed Vera Bulich's poetic talent and
her refined artistic taste, compared her poetry to that of Alexander
Blok (in *La Renaissance* on September 27, 1934).   A resemblance
to Blok is indeed present in the poems where she bemoans the
instability of everything earthly and the suffering of the human
heart in its striving for the absolute and eternal.   Bulich inherited
from Marina Tsvetaeva the technique of incomplete rhymes, some
new word formations, and aspects of her poetic vocabulary (for
example, "Lullaby").   She sometimes even used bizarre Futurist
imagery (see, for example, "Advertisement of the Sky—A Rosy
Sunset").   Occasionally her poetic expressions are overly emotional,
overly pictorial, and tend to mar the generally restrained style.
Nonetheless, the spontaneous feeling and the lively voice of the
poet invariably shine through the artistic fabric of the verse.

———————·———————

A Recovered Note

Seventy-three years ago.
How pale the ink has become!
Someone's hand...The fragrance has vanished.
Darkness. Oblivion. The grave.

A secret of joy, a secret of tears.
Someone's hand wrote
Briefly, *"Comme je suis malheureuse..."*
Is it really so trifling?

The date: June. Spring, just as now.
White nights are still the same.

The same joy, the same pain of farewells.
But happiness comes less often.

My poor friend. Time doesn't exist.
There's only God's will.
Your grief, after seventy years,
Today became mine.

                                                    1934

———————·———————

The reader can find in this poem all of the attributes that give Vera Bulich her distinct poetic voice. The apparent importance of time in the first line of the poem dissolves in the last stanza through the simple statement: "Time doesn't exist." Grief, joy, and nature remain, changing yet changeless, eternal in the *Weltanschauung* of the *persona*. This sense of timelessness is accentuated in the third stanza by the repetition of the adjective "the same" and by the use of the expression "as now." Through sharp, yet delicate images, the poet impressionistically qualifies and extends this view by showing how the ink has paled and the fragrance dissolved, and by observing that "happiness comes less often." Thus, the poet deals with time and eternity emotionally, seeking, beneath the apparent, a glimpse of the truth that links her to the past. Pain and sorrow persist, as the French phrase, introduced at the proper moment, indicates. With a soul lacerated by the intensity of these feelings, the *persona* echoes the earlier poet of Ecclesiastes, who stated that there is nothing new under the sun.

In his review of *Pendulum*, Yury Mandel'stam paid particular attention to "The Recovered Leaf": "Many could envy these poems! Original, genuine poetry resides in them."[1] He also admired the complete absence of egocentricity in the volume. Indeed, *Pendulum* expresses love and sympathy for others, understanding of their suffering and yearning for the native land. Thus, in her early poems Vera Bulich emerges as an original poet, gifted with a unique lyrical voice and formal and structural craftsmanship.

These same features stand in the foreground of her next collection of poems, *Captive Wind*, where her controlled technique and the precision and accuracy of her images and expressions are evident almost from the first lines of the book. The compositional harmony, the sense of restraint, balance, and artistic taste, accompanied by Bulich's ability to distribute the verbal material carefully and with graceful simplicity, add to the poetic finish of *Captive Wind.* The rhyme, rhythm, syncope, and repetitions are striking and beautiful. There is no attempt here to imitate Anna Akhmatova; on the contrary, the reader is aware of Vera Bulich's own words, her perceptive vision, her sympathy for her fellow man, and a somewhat bitter contemplation of life. Sergey Gorny, a prominent émigré writer and critic, aptly referred to the book as "a profound, subconscious, musical transformation of Akhmatova's poetry."[2]

In *Captive Wind* Bulich develops the theme of the dual forces in human nature—spiritual striving versus empirical reality. Precision and finish in the realm of poetic form are characteristic of the poems about Don Juan, "And Again Holy Friday," "Music-Soul," "Heavenly Delirium," "Spring Pliancy of the Earth," and "Old Film." The musical poem "Departure" and the closing blank verse "About Happiness" also testify to the artistic accomplishment of the work. Bulich's cultivated vocabulary and poetic sensitivity, combined with a spontaneous musicality in all her verse, impart to *Captive Wind* power and expression. Her simple, unexpected comparisons and images ("the wind with large steps," "impetuously, the curtains begin to breathe at the window," "into a frightened grove," "through the foliage, to rock the star"), rhythm, and graceful adjectives impressed Georgy Adamovich, especially in the poem "Will the Distant Music Be Heard Again?"[3]

> Will the distant music be heard again,
> Will the gleam of a heavenly ray be perceived,
> And, feeling again the living weight
> Of a wing, unfurled at the shoulder?
>
> Might one believe that freedom has returned,
> With the warmth of energy unspent,
> And that again they beat against the barred entrance,
> Like a stray butterfly on the pane?
> But fate is cruel, blind, unyielding.
> And still the captive wings flutter...

...Carefully, by hand, I take the butterfly
From the window and release her into the garden.

                                                    1936

_____._____

In twelve graceful lines, the poet moves from a contemplation
of the celestial and abstract to the realm of the personal and
concrete; merging the two through the delightfully executed image
of the "stray butterfly" that is tossed against the barred entrance
much as the *persona*, in her longing once more to feel the (angelic,
perhaps) wing at her shoulder, is tossed by a fate "blind, cruel,
unyielding." The last stanza quickly resolves the *persona's*
dilemma; for by releasing the butterfly "by hand" in order to let
her into the garden, she in turn reaffirms her faith in the
possibility of once again hearing the "distant music" and seeing a
glimpse of this "heavenly ray."

In comparison with Bulich's earlier poems, *Captive Wind*
represents a new mood of longing for freedom and space. As she
writes in her diary in 1937, freedom and space are connected with
the sensation of happiness: "The open space of the sea and
sky—the hope, the freedom of my soul. Freedom gives the feeling
of happiness, and happiness is expressed by the sensation of
freedom." In a letter to Bulich on March 29, 1938, Boris Zaytsev
said of the collection: "These are real poems, and you are a real
poet. I am glad that there is still spiritual culture, freedom, art."

Freedom and fresh diaphanous air fill the book *Wind-Fallen
Wood.* An evening landscape, melancholy, elegiac musicality,
transparent images, an absence of notes in the major key and of
exclamatory tones define the collection. Suddenly war, with all its
destruction and terror, invades the magical world of the poet.
Rhythmical musicality permeates the sad poem about Lermontov's
pine tree cited below. Mournful meditations on human existence
appear in the tender swam song about the tiny dancer. The
volume is divided into three parts: "Leaflets of the Calendar,"
"Wind-Fallen Wood" (the theme of war), and "Loyalty" (of
emigrants, with respect to their native land after the Second World
War). Whereas the first part deals with the central motifs of her
earlier poems, the sections "Wind-Fallen Wood" and "Loyalty"
focus on the theme of war and disclose the originality of the poet's

approach to this theme.   She illuminates war through her own
individual, personal experience and perception, which enhances the
vivid and concrete character of her presentations.   Against the
background of everyday, personal, peaceful life she depicts war with
only two or three strokes.   The universal appears in the
background of the personal, but the individual becomes a symbol of
the universal, its typical example.   Her depiction of the lilacs and
swallows, for instance, is colored by the poet's experiences during
an air raid; a thunderstorm is perceived through a bomb attack;
the general destruction of war, through her father's burning estate
and destroyed grave.   These portrayals are devoid of exclamation
of indignation or expressions of horror; she gives facts and events
amplified with personal observations and experiences, but abstains
from moralizing generalities.   "Wind-Fallen Wood" and "Loyalty"
are a factual, unbiased, and unique poetic record.   As is illustrated
in "The Pine Tree" below, *Wind-Fallen Wood* with its fresh
spontaneity and clarity contains some of the best poems in the
history of Russian poetry.

The Pine Tree

The whisper of skis through the lakeside wilderness,
Whiteness and silence.
On a barren cape, like a dark shadow,
Stands the pine tree of Lermontov.[4]

In the white kingdom, in deep snow slumber,
Does it behold a vision of palms? No,
In severe, lonely contemplation
It regards the even, snowy tracks.

Only in century-old poems
Is the memory of the dream still alive today,
The words about the kindred soul,
The soul, languishing in the desert.

But their sound is a distant echo
In the lonely, impervious silence.

A light snow hovers...I approach and bow
To the lonely northern pine.

1936

---·---

    The continuity and expanded development of the dual theme of time and eternity in Vera Bulich's work, as seen above in "A Recovered Note," is crucial for the understanding of "The Pine Tree."   As in the earlier poem, the *persona* strives to find a spiritual connection with the past—here presented through the image of Lermontov's pine against the "whiteness and silence" of a bleak winter landscape.   The third stanza illuminates the *persona's* motivation to establish such a connection.   In the recognition of a "kindred soul" and in the "memory of the dream still alive" the poet hopes to make sense of the "desert" of the present and of her "impervious silence," while regenerating and extending this dream through poetry.   Unlike the *persona* of "A Recovered Note," however, she is now unable to achieve fully this spiritual and emotional bond with the past.   The dream resounds like "a distant echo," and the reader leaves her empty and yearning, moving toward this longed-for synthesis, but estranged by the horrible reality of the present.   In this respect Bulich's image of the world is somewhat akin to T. S. Eliot's vision in the *Wasteland.*   Russian poets in exile, including Terapiano, Sergey Gorny, and K. Hoerschelmann, as well as Soviet writers, applauded the appearance of *Wind-Fallen Wood.*   In the words of Antonin Ladinsky, a poet who had gone back to Moscow after World War Two,[5] the book was received as a work of the "Pushkin School."

    Branches, Bulich's forth book of poetry, likewise reveals skillful verse, a gift of composition, precision in drawing, and a pensive, reserved tone combined with lyrical expressiveness.   Here, however, the reader perceives an even greater degree of sorrow and perplexity of man facing the mystery of existence.   A sober, almost merciless concentration on the relativity of human convictions and hopes form the subject of the volume.   Even recollections of the past do not distract the poet from the contemplation of the eternal and the absolute.   There are no verbal effects here, only a restrained narrative and polish that mark each poem.   The structure of the verse "Mirror-like Evening" is striking in its use of the image of mirrors to reflect human life in all its varied forms and situations, and the poem "The Bus," written in blank verse, again illustrates the originality of Bulich's craftsmanship. The verse below discloses Bulich's conception of poetry.

———————·———————

Poetry

Not skill, accessible to all
Who join the labor-loving guilds,[6]
Oh no, not skill, nor craftsmanship,
But unexpected sorcery.

When from the heights the swift Muse soars
To the elected one for a brief alliance,
And in this mysterious union of two
One is given hearing, the other a voice.

And the goal is but to listen keenly, to catch
The melody's fragile thread.
I know not why, wherefore, or whence—
I take and pass along the miracle's reflection.

1953

———————·———————

This poem reminds the reader of the poet's letter to Andreev. In both, Bulich alludes to an inaccessible, incomprehensible but sought-after union with the "swift Muse," who imparts to the poet a divine spark, a glimpse of that "unexpected sorcery" that separates mere craftsmanship from the true inspiration found in such abundance in all of Vera Bulich's work. Characteristically, she perceives the role of the poet as passive—that of a receiver—"to listen keenly, to catch/The melody's fragile thread." That melody is heard only imperfectly even by the most skillful of poets, who in turn transmit not the miracle itself, but a vague and imperfect reflection of the miracle.

Even in the face of death Vera Bulich did not lose her love of nature, her stoicism, courage, and loyalty to others. In her poetry, she expressed her firm belief that life on earth continues and will continue, if not for herself, then for many others:

Even if it is not to be granted to me
To gaze out of the window on another spring morning,
Spring will exist for eyes other than mine,
For many, other, living eyes.

By this time already gravely ill, Vera Bulich nevertheless proofread the galleys of her last collection, sent to her from Paris by Alexander Ginger at the request of Sergey Makovsky. Until the very end of her life she courageously, even obstinately, insisted on the right and the necessity of transforming her experiences into art. "Melody" is one of her very last poems, written shortly before her death:

Melody

A single melody sings unceasing,
Like a complaint, or an entreaty.

It sings, it harries and hovers above me,
As it searches for words in the dark of night.

And finding no answer to my sorrow,
It retreats into the dark, lamenting...

―――――・―――――

It is death that is dealt with here while the poet attempts to elucidate the essence of this new song and the subsequent anguish and frustration at her inability to find the poetic garments to cloak the melody. But there is no hint of fear at death's approach, only the attention of the acute sensibilities of a triumphant poet who, at the end, rises above sorrow and weakness in search of the perfect set of words to express the inexpressible sensations of her last living moments.

Vera Bulich died of lung cancer on July 2, 1954, several weeks after the publication of her book *Branches*. Her obituary appeared in all Russian newspapers in Finland and Paris and in all Swedish and Finnish papers. Internment took place in the

Orthodox cemetary Lappviken (Helsinki).

The following essay on Russian émigré poetry will show that Vera Bulich also distinguished herself as an erudite and perceptive critic.   Her views preceded publication of the aforementioned book of G. Struve, *Russian Literature in Exile* in 1956, and publication of other essays concerning Russian émigré literature.

Journal of Concord, No. 6 (1938)

On Emigré Russian Poetry, 1937[7]

Since it is impossible to present an exhaustive survey of all the collections of poetry published during 1937, I will discuss only five authors.

We cannot speak about the appearances of any émigré literary school.   A certain general spirit and a number of tendencies and directions can be observed, but in general each poet answers only for himself, although we encounter people who hold the same views.

Poetry, like every other form of art, has as its task the creative transformation of the world; it conveys a world vision as the artist perceives and interprets it in his consciousness and reflects, in this vision, internal truth.   None of the arts strives to borrow the methods of portrayal from the other arts to the extent that poetry does.   Apart from the purely verbal element in a word, which conveys the nuance of a thought or feeling, apart from the word itself, in its sound and phonetic meanings, various other tendencies are in poetry: painting, music, architecture (in the sense of composition), ornamentation (in the sense of embellishment of the verse through the use of imagery and metaphors), and theatre (the development of intonation, as well as the dynamics of imagery).   In poetry there are emotional, contemplative, and harmonious moments.   The theory of literature defines the artistic word as thinking in images.   But the image itself, which several poets now consciously avoid, may be accepted in its primary sense, that is, in its pictorial and descriptive meaning and in its secondary, metaphorical, allegorical, and symbolical significance.   The combination of these various moments, and the predominance of one or another selection made by the poet, characterize him aptly from a formal point of view.

Sofia Pregel's second book of verse *Solnechny proizvol*
(Tyranny of the Sun), is a characteristic example of painting
in poetry.   When one attempts to characterize her poems,
terms used to describe painting involuntarily spring to mind:
a still life, a lanscape, or a genre.   This results from Pregel's
purely visual perception of the world, which is supported,
moreover, by tactile sensation.

> Again discovering the world through touch,
> Like a child or a blind person.

Here she defines her own relationship to the world.   We
cannot reproach her for blindness; on the contrary, we notice
her intent gaze in every minute earthly detail.   A sketch by
S. Pregel' is vivid.   Every image appearing in her poetry is
not only well drawn, but gives the impression of a distinct,
bold tracing of the contours.   The metaphors are much less
successful than the realistically descriptive images.   Halftones, a certain diffusion of lyrical mood, agitation or
elevation of tone are completely alien to Pregel'; her realm is
the sunlight of daytime.   No "nocturnal thoughts" disturb her
peaceful brush, and this is not surprising since, as the painter
draws from nature during the day, Pregel's poetry, too, is
diurnal.

> I accept the world like grace bestowed,
> I discover you in everything,

she says further on.   And we believe her, in her grateful
visual love of the world.   Pregel' is attracted by the
"life-giving earth," the "solar tyranny," which calls forth from
this earth everything we can see.   She looks at the world
through the eyes of a child or a convalescent for whom all
the primeval charm of things is revealed in its entirety, the
charm of solid things which have weight, color, form, taste,
and fragrance.   We clearly see these elements of her world,
but we don't sense what is behind them, and we do not
come to know the poet herself.   Pregel' does not try to
interpret the vision of the external world she conveys.   She
gives it to us without any commentary, perhaps consciously

tearing it out of her internal world, preferring to dwell on
motifs from her childhood or travels, when the visual
perception of the surrounding world is inwardly justified.

Sofia Pregel' takes her literary origin from Anna
Akhmatova, from that aspect of Akhmatova's work that is
expressed, for example, in her poetry:

> The aroma of flowers and inanimate objects
> Is pleasant in this house.
> Heaps of multicolored vegetables
> Lie on the black earth of the garden.
> There's still a chill breeze,
> But the matting is off the hotbeds, etc.

Pregel' has acquired from Akhmatova the descriptiveness, the
"feel," the palpability of images and epithets, their harmony,
the striving for conciseness and pictorial expressiveness, and
she continues to develop this further, somewhat unilaterally
but originally.

The appearance of a new poet, even if he is not great,
and the appearance of a new book of good poems are always
a true joy for sincere lovers of poetry.

The fresh, genuinely experienced "verses" of Turoverov
arouse a lively response. Not all of his poems are equally
good, and many of them are pallid and long-winded; we
suspect that the author is not yet sufficiently versed in art,
not yet completely independent. So, for example, in the
musical verse "Utpolà in Kalmyk means star," the line
"Utpolà, you are my Utpolà" is an exact reproduction of
Esenin's "Shagane, you are my Shagane," and the image of
the oriental girl emphasizes this borrowing even more. The
influence of Esenin is felt in several other poems as well.
Nevertheless, the book wins one over with the healthy, fresh
current of spiritual wholeness, simplicity, and vitality which
runs through it. This is a quiet story of a courageous poet.
It is about himself and about others and is devoid of posing,
conceit, or any literary artificiality.

The vision of Turoverov is a vision of the heart's
memory. It is directed into the past, and by the past it is
strengthened:

This whole day, such a hot day,
And the sun's unbearable light
I will remember with the greed
Of a child barely eight years old.
I will remember, unaware of it myself,
Remember till the end.
O steppe, blue in the torrid heat,
O profile of my sleeping father.

In poetry Turoverov is partial primarily to painting and the description of everyday life. His theme is defined in the following lines:

In my paradise of memories,
In my tormented paradise,
Carpeted sleighs carry me off
To my native land.

The world, limited by his theme, is idealized by recollections and illumined from within by a sincere feeling of love for his native land, but without any suggestion of fanaticism. It is precisely this restrained intensity of feeling in Turoverov that imparts to his poetry that freshness and vivacity which are absent in many contemporary poems of a literary quality. And it is this same restrained intensity that helps him find the right tone in his poems about Russia.

Lidiya Chervinskaya, in her second book of poetry, *Rassvety* (Dawns), stands in complete contrast to the two poets mentioned above. She does not have the slightest inclination for description in her poetry. Nature and the external world are almost completely absent from her verse. Only here and there a sparsely outlined, unfinished city landscape appears, and only for a moment. Her vision is always directed internally. Personal meditation, twilight moods, and soft words are characteristic of her poetry. She consciously avoids bright images; her material is not paint, but India ink, black and white halftones. She also avoids the musical intensity of verse, directing her attention primarily to conversational tones. With this goal—to impart more vivacity, verisimilitude, and diversity to the tones—she often breaks a four-line stanza, sometimes ending the poem like a sonnet, sometimes introducing an extra line, sometimes ending abruptly in the middle of a word and thus providing an unexpected effect.   In Chervinskaya's poetry one can also observe a tendency toward aphoristic conciseness:

> How cowardly to heed advice:
> Life is wrong, fate always knows right.

> Freedom...how conditional it is.
> Only one path—a very narrow one.

Careful, thoughtful work and great craftsmanship are evident in the poetry of Chervinskaya.   Skillful, sometimes artificial lines, cleverly brought to life by flawless tones, convey the mood of "a city heart." The "dawns" of Lidiya Chervinskaya do not mark a new beginning. Dawn for her is only the merging of dark and light, the end of a sleepless night, and not the beginning of a new day:

> In that life, at last beloved,
> There is no more room.
> In that life we invented,
> Throughout sleepless nights
> We keep watch over the dawn.

What is important for her is just this transmission of semi-shade, semi-light, the vagueness of contour, the diffusion of sensations, the incompleteness of feeling.   Chervinskaya's world is one of shadows, "an invented life."

> —The shadow of grief, like other shadows,
> Does not exist, but will and did.

> —Not love, but only shadow's shadow
> Of that love which is called earthly.

> —...again our shadows
> Crossed for a brief moment.

> —Like an unconvincing shadow
> Dawn rises.

Uncertainty and ambivalence are peculiar to Chervinskaya. The following poems are characteristic of her:

—Autumn is not autumn. Spring is not spring.
Just the noon of winter.

I know without knowing. I love without loving.
I remember without remembering you...

Also characteristic are words like "almost" and "perhaps":

—This almost resembles awareness,
This almost resembles confession.

—Perhaps this is a chance betrayal,
Perhaps a distressing secret joy...

Often she deliberately uses inaccurate, unclear, and at times paradoxical epithets. For example, "unpremeditated happiness," "unembodied weariness," "uncomplicated inaccessibility of the heart," "unforgiving-unforgivable friend." She speaks about a "very inaccurate clarity," or about a "very depraved tenderness." It is characteristic for many of the epithets to begin with the negative particle "not" or "un-". This feature, which appears trivial at first glance, testifies to a certain internal vagueness or constraint (if not force), as if Chervinskaya knows what she must repudiate, but does not know what she must assert.

Not one real word—
It means such a word is unneeded, unattainable.
Everything is said cynically and tenderly.
Very tragically, very carelessly.
It's neither hypocrisy nor indifference,
But only, it seems, a simple decorum.

Chervinskaya's poetry shows irreproachable taste. There is no affectation, declamation, or any other flaws. But it seems that precisely the fear of violating literary decorum, in allowing herself a direct expression of feeling and genuine excitement, compels Chervinskaya to reject the search for a "real word," choosing instead the path of allegory and deliberately limiting her possibilities. Her theme, "Nevertheless, the soul is warmed by the pain arising from itself," often leads her to the extremely personal, notorious "human document." The transformation of the personal into the general, into that which perhaps can be felt and experienced by the reader, is attained only in a few poems. This happens in the best verse in her collection of poems, where the pulsation not merely of the "city" heart, but of the living human heart is heard.

> I remember everything—without memories,
> And in this joy of emptiness,
> Cautious, sad, untimely March,
> You alone support me.
>
> I do not love. But why,
> Not loving, does my heart beat so?
> I read quietly to myself:
> "Onegin, I was younger then,
> I was better, it seems..."
>
>   Hardly,
> Hardly better, but to—sadness,
> To—pride, to—humiliation,
> To—hatred for my own tears...
> To—understanding, to—forgiveness,
> To—fidelity, Onegin, toward you.

If a poet were likened to a radio receiver and his objective defined as the perception of sounds that soar above us but remain inaccessible, and those sounds were transmitted into this life in forms which affect our feelings, then it must be said that in Antonin Ladinsky's poetry one senses an elevated and sensitive antenna, which is directed from the earth into that ether where Lermontov's angel once flew. Ladinsky aspires, as it were, to trace mentally the aerial path of this angel, and having felt the "chill of the ether on the tip of the pen," to finally capture, remember, and transmit that singular and inimitable melody which has the power to transform "the boring songs of the earth."

In reviewing Ladinsky's previous collections in the *Journal of Concord* in 1933, I have already mentioned the theme of Lermontov's angel as fundamental to his poetry. In the collection *Stikhi o Evrope* (Poems About Europe), this theme is developed to its extreme. The poet enters Lermontov's element; he strives to bring down to the earth that remote, heavenly essence which is only barely hinted at in Lermontov's poetry. Like magical incantations the lines ring out about "the white sail on the blue sea" and about the angel who again flies through the "midnight sky." But "it is quite impossible to hold one's breath with one's hands"; "everything slips away."

> The soul will return to God,
> And the music then
> Will subside little by little
> In the blue expanse.

The poems of Ladinsky's last collection are dedicated to the fading away of this wonderful, indistinct music, to the "black twilight" of Europe, and to the vanishing soul of culture.

> With a smile I give my poor lyre
> To the terrible centuries.

Ladinsky is the son of modern culture and he is its bard; in his poetry he sums up this culture. In his poems we often encounter images from mythology, the Bible, and classical works of art. For example, we find the myths of the Abduction of Europe and the Golden Fleece, and images of Nausicaa, Job, the Prodigal Son, Hamlet and Ophelia, Don Quixote and Sancho Panza, Andersen's Swineherd and the Prince, La Fontaine's Oak Tree and the Reed. Personal names do not clutter Ladinsky's poems, as they cluttered the works of several of our Symbolists. They do not clutter the poems because they are not just names, but newly experienced images which are filled with a new content and perceived by us as personages on a stage. Ancient heroes in Ladinsky's poems are born anew, they feel as we feel, live as we live, and endure along with us a common fate. The tendency in Ladinsky's poetry toward the theatre is revealed

not only in his predilection for using stage props, or in his
sense of theatrical atmosphere, but mainly in his theatrical
transformation of the world, in his extremely unique dynamics
of imagery.

The combination of irony and genuine lyrical inspiration,
always with a touch of sadness, the merging of "high and low
styles" (ordinary, everyday nonpoetic words like "digestion,"
"sweater," and "sandwich" with typical poetic words), and
the frequent repetition of a number of his favorite words, like
Rome, soul, muse, snow, winter, bees, farms, oaks, rose,
wheat, and barns characterize Ladinsky's poetry. All of this
creates a special, distinctive, closed world, subordinate to his
theatrical laws. Ladinsky seldom presents the image in its
primary pictorial and descriptive aspect. More often one
meets the secondary aspect of an image which is transformed
into a symbolic image, then somehow connected with a
preconceived notion, for example, Rome and Muse.
"Farmers" personify the everyday, worldly concern for daily
bread, which is inevitably present in their conversations.
These agricultural concepts of diligence and earthly blessings
are joined with the images of bees, wheat, and barns. The
"rose" is Ladinsky's image of fascinating but useless beauty.
For example, the comparison of the soul with a rose:

> In this agricultural world,
> You are as strange as a rose in a barn.

"Winter" is a reminder of a "very cold drama," which the
world experiences. The "snow" has a decorative meaning; an
"oak tree" embodies heroism. Short and light lines with, at
times, syncopic meters convey the impression of "fading
music." In general, Ladinsky's poetry gravitates toward
music, toward the musical transmission of thought, toward
musical suggestion by means of one and the same reappearing
melody.

Ladinsky's interlacing of the theme of Lermontov's angel
with the theme of the destruction of Europe is not accidental.
One flows from the other. The tragic fate of the soul,
thrown into the "coarse and real" world and preserving in its
memory the "sky of midnight." On the one hand, there is
"important business and trifles"; on the other, a vague and

music" which breaks through the word combinations and thus justifies them; sometimes it is the musicality of a *romance* or love song, which evokes fairly concrete associations. Apparently some of Ivanov's poems are simply connected with music that he has heard. Consciously or unconsciously, he introduces words of well-known *romances*, sometimes leaving them unchanged, and sometimes paraphrasing them. Such are the beginning lines: "It is the ring of bells from afar" (a gypsy *romance*), "Snowdrifts, happiness, have buried you" (serious music lovers will find it hard to accept the adaptation from "Snowdrifts have buried you, o Russia"), "How sad, but still I want so to live. And the air smells of spring" (from a *romance* by Rachmaninoff to the words of G. Galin: "How painful it is to me, how I want to live! How fresh and fragrant is the spring!"). These lines evoked by *romances* imperceptibly merge with his own, and influence our hearing and arouse musical memories. Georgy Ivanov pays great attention to the instrumentation of his verse, to its purely external musicality. Ivanov's depiction is subtle, refined, subjective. He brings all the qualities of his spiritual state into his portrayal of the external world, thus giving us a twofold picture, a living reflection of the world as it appears to him, a world transformed by his emotional experience, and therefore unique.

> The sky began to change,
> Slowly the moon sailed by,
> As if it had no strength
> To rise more quickly.
>
> And rose-hued stars
> In the roseate distance
> Could not shine any brighter
> Through the fast chilling air.
>
> And I dared not extinguish them,
> And I could not help them,
> Only the night moved uneasily
> Through the black branches.

In this poem several characteristics of Ivanov's poetry are

futile longing for the otherworldly exists.

The tragic fate of a culture no longer enriched
inspired by spiritual life, but stagnated in lifeless beat
doomed to a slow disintegration—a culture that "eve
will abandon in sorrow."

The soul finds consolation only in creative illusior
in the theatrical transformation of the world, in this "f
charm." But this consolation is not salvation.
nonspiritual nature of our entire life, the stifling of spi
inquiries by the problems of everyday life, the unres
discord between the earth and the heavens, "the coldne
empty hearts," the gradual fatigue, the extinction of the
("We ourselves are not strong enough to withstand
pressures")—all this leads to the destruction of culture:

> Neither kaffir grass, nor the terrible whisper
> Of palm trees and oaks, nor fear,
> Nor night, nor the barbarian footfall
> On the Elysian fields.
> More terrible: the soul, its doubts
> And anguish, the yearning for death,
> The feeble singing of the Muses,
> The hand grown tired of ruling.

Much has already been written about Georgy Ivar
anthology, *Otplytie na Ostrov Tsiteru* (Departure for
Island of Cythera). But in considering poetry collection
1937, one is forced again to recognize this book a
remarkable example of an exceptionally close link betv
poetry and music. Not one of the modern poets convey;
his poetry such a powerful musical effect—comprising
setting of a poem and revealing two planes within it-
clearly and convincingly as does Georgy Ivanov. The
Poplavsky also possessed this ability to a high degree. '
twofold plane of poetry—a series of images and a lead
melody—appear more sharply in Poplavsky's poetry, owing
his unique and unexpected images, and, at times, to
divergence of the two planes.

In Ivanov's poetry, the two planes—the visible and
audible—are more closely harmonized. The musicality of
poetry is different from Poplavsky's. At times it is "p

revealed with subtle strokes—exhaustion, impotence, fatique, helpless melancholy, and in the end the uneasy music of the night, music which comprises the essence and core of his entire work.

Ivanov's poetry is deeply pessimistic. Here is his point of departure:

> —It serves one right—to go to sleep forever.
> Nothing more is necessary.

> —It is good that there is no one,
> It is good that there is nothing.

> —He who dies is blissful,
> He who is doomed is blissful.

Here we find his assertion of nonexistence, void, fatality. "It serves one right," Ivanov says, "it is good," and finally the highest glorification: "He is blissful." But at the same time he makes a vague promise:

> —When everything is lost to him,
> At that moment everything is gained.

These lines are the key. The awareness of death calls forth the most intense feelings, which makes the "immortal music" of the world audible and works a miracle by transforming darkness and despair into "celestial radiance."

> The world gutters like a candle,
> The flame burns one's fingers.
> Ringing with immortal music,
> It spreads out and dies.
> And darkness is no longer darkness but light.

It is no accident that one of Ivanov's most favorite and frequently used words is "only." The word has the meaning of limitation (I have only this), or indicates a choice or preference (I retain only this), as well as the possibility of an exception from the rule (only this I do not reject). The concepts which are connected with the word "only," in

essence, are Ivanov's only real assertion that something
actually exists.

What does Georgy Ivanov affirm?

> —Only a yellow dawn,
> Only icy stars,
> Only millions of years.
> —Only the stars above an empty garden,
> Only the blue light of your soul.
> —Music. It alone
> Will not deceive.

From the void that surrounds him, Ivanov isolates and
affirms the concepts of a universe that is indifferent to man,
of the soul with its own special light, and of music.

Music is essential to his perception of the world—the
all-transforming force, which translates dissonance into
harmony, and alone can justify the world with its
unforgivable evil. There is the opposition:

> Everything is forgiven. Nothing can be forgiven.
> Music. Darkness.

Darkness, transformed by music, becomes light and radiance:

> —And darkness is no longer darkness, but light.

> —This gloom is beautiful.
> It is almost like radiance.

Music and light—they are always present in Ivanov's poetry.
Music is a theme and a means of expressing ideas, not to
mention the technical musical aspect of his poetry. Light is
a theme and a constant feature of his landscape; words
referring to the source of perception of light—dawn, dusk,
rose-colored sky, stars, moon, radiance—are especially
preferred by Ivanov.

But music and radiance do not yet constitute happiness.
"There is no happiness in this world"; it has been "buried in
snowdrifts." Music is not an active life force, but sorcery
("everything else is only music, a reflection, sorcery"); music

music" which breaks through the word combinations and thus justifies them; sometimes it is the musicality of a *romance* or love song, which evokes fairly concrete associations. Apparently some of Ivanov's poems are simply connected with music that he has heard. Consciously or unconsciously, he introduces words of well-known *romances*, sometimes leaving them unchanged, and sometimes paraphrasing them. Such are the beginning lines: "It is the ring of bells from afar" (a gypsy *romance*), "Snowdrifts, happiness, have buried you" (serious music lovers will find it hard to accept the adaptation from "Snowdrifts have buried you, o Russia"), "How sad, but still I want so to live. And the air smells of spring" (from a *romance* by Rachmaninoff to the words of G. Galin: "How painful it is to me, how I want to live! How fresh and fragrant is the spring!"). These lines evoked by *romances* imperceptibly merge with his own, and influence our hearing and arouse musical memories. Georgy Ivanov pays great attention to the instrumentation of his verse, to its purely external musicality. Ivanov's depiction is subtle, refined, subjective. He brings all the qualities of his spiritual state into his portrayal of the external world, thus giving us a twofold picture, a living reflection of the world as it appears to him, a world transformed by his emotional experience, and therefore unique.

> The sky began to change,
> Slowly the moon sailed by,
> As if it had no strength
> To rise more quickly.
>
> And rose-hued stars
> In the roseate distance
> Could not shine any brighter
> Through the fast chilling air.
>
> And I dared not extinguish them,
> And I could not help them,
> Only the night moved uneasily
> Through the black branches.

In this poem several characteristics of Ivanov's poetry are

futile longing for the otherworldly exists.

The tragic fate of a culture no longer enriched and inspired by spiritual life, but stagnated in lifeless beauty is doomed to a slow disintegration—a culture that "everyone will abandon in sorrow."

The soul finds consolation only in creative illusion and in the theatrical transformation of the world, in this "fragile charm." But this consolation is not salvation. The nonspiritual nature of our entire life, the stifling of spiritual inquiries by the problems of everyday life, the unresolved discord between the earth and the heavens, "the coldness of empty hearts," the gradual fatigue, the extinction of the spirit ("We ourselves are not strong enough to withstand these pressures")—all this leads to the destruction of culture:

> Neither kaffir grass, nor the terrible whisper
> Of palm trees and oaks, nor fear,
> Nor night, nor the barbarian footfall
> On the Elysian fields.
> More terrible: the soul, its doubts
> And anguish, the yearning for death,
> The feeble singing of the Muses,
> The hand grown tired of ruling.

Much has already been written about Georgy Ivanov's anthology, *Otplytie na Ostrov Tsiteru* (Departure for the Island of Cythera). But in considering poetry collections of 1937, one is forced again to recognize this book as a remarkable example of an exceptionally close link between poetry and music. Not one of the modern poets conveys in his poetry such a powerful musical effect—comprising the setting of a poem and revealing two planes within it—so clearly and convincingly as does Georgy Ivanov. The late Poplavsky also possessed this ability to a high degree. The twofold plane of poetry—a series of images and a leading melody—appear more sharply in Poplavsky's poetry, owing to his unique and unexpected images, and, at times, to a divergence of the two planes.

In Ivanov's poetry, the two planes—the visible and the audible—are more closely harmonized. The musicality of his poetry is different from Poplavsky's. At times it is "pure revealed with subtle strokes—exhaustion, impotence, fatique, helpless melancholy, and in the end the uneasy music of the night, music which comprises the essence and core of his entire work.

Ivanov's poetry is deeply pessimistic. Here is his point of departure:

> —It serves one right—to go to sleep forever.
> Nothing more is necessary.
>
> —It is good that there is no one,
> It is good that there is nothing.
>
> —He who dies is blissful,
> He who is doomed is blissful.

Here we find his assertion of nonexistence, void, fatality. "It serves one right," Ivanov says, "it is good," and finally the highest glorification: "He is blissful." But at the same time he makes a vague promise:

> —When everything is lost to him,
> At that moment everything is gained.

These lines are the key. The awareness of death calls forth the most intense feelings, which makes the "immortal music" of the world audible and works a miracle by transforming darkness and despair into "celestial radiance."

> The world gutters like a candle,
> The flame burns one's fingers.
> Ringing with immortal music,
> It spreads out and dies.
> And darkness is no longer darkness but light.

It is no accident that one of Ivanov's most favorite and frequently used words is "only." The word has the meaning of limitation (I have only this), or indicates a choice or preference (I retain only this), as well as the possibility of an exception from the rule (only this I do not reject). The concepts which are connected with the word "only," in essence, are Ivanov's only real assertion that something actually exists.

What does Georgy Ivanov affirm?

>—Only a yellow dawn,
>Only icy stars,
>Only millions of years.
>—Only the stars above an empty garden,
>Only the blue light of your soul.
>—Music. It alone
>Will not deceive.

From the void that surrounds him, Ivanov isolates and affirms the concepts of a universe that is indifferent to man, of the soul with its own special light, and of music.

Music is essential to his perception of the world—the all-transforming force, which translates dissonance into harmony, and alone can justify the world with its unforgivable evil. There is the opposition:

>Everything is forgiven. Nothing can be forgiven.
>Music. Darkness.

Darkness, transformed by music, becomes light and radiance:

>—And darkness is no longer darkness, but light.

>—This gloom is beautiful.
>It is almost like radiance.

Music and light—they are always present in Ivanov's poetry. Music is a theme and a means of expressing ideas, not to mention the technical musical aspect of his poetry. Light is a theme and a constant feature of his landscape; words referring to the source of perception of light—dawn, dusk, rose-colored sky, stars, moon, radiance—are especially preferred by Ivanov.

But music and radiance do not yet constitute happiness. "There is no happiness in this world"; it has been "buried in snowdrifts." Music is not an active life force, but sorcery ("everything else is only music, a reflection, sorcery"); music can't change anything in real life.

> It cannot change anything.
> Nor can it help anything,
> That which only weeps and trills,
> And grows dim and fades into the night.

And in another poem:

> In this world everything remains the same,
> The moon rises as before.
> Pushkin mortgaged his estate
> Or was jealous of his wife.
> And nothing has been amended,
> Nothing compensated
> By the vague, wonderful music,
> Heard by him alone.

The nocturnal poetry of Georgy Ivanov envisions a terrible world, the ice-cold infinity of the universe, the doom, the inconsolable loneliness of man. There is no happiness on earth. And therefore, although admitting that music is only sorcery and cannot change anything in reality, Georgy Ivanov confirms it as the sole guiding force. It alone uplifts to heights from which he can see "beyond time and space, above the poor earth, an unearthly radiance." It is only thanks to music that, despite spiritual bankruptcy, creation is still possible.

> One can sing with full voice,
> When there is nothing left to sing of.

And Georgy Ivanov abandons himself completely to music:

> As Byron went to Greece, without regret,
> Through stars and roses and darkness,
> Toward the voice of singing, sweet beyond reason...

There is, however, in the sweet voice of Ivanov's muse a subtle poison, and this voice is sometimes reminiscent of the seductive voice of the Siren that entices one into the abyss.

Is this not why, for certain young poets not possessing a strong creative will, the influence of Georgy Ivanov's poetry, precisely because of its power of fascination, turns out to be far from beneficial?

———————.———————

The Journal of Concord also contains Vera Bulich's illuminating essays on the poetry of Vyacheslav Ivanov, Vladimir Smolensky, Dovid Knut, and other Russian writers in exile, 1920–1940.

NOTES

1. "Vera Bulich. *Pendulum.* (Poems), publ. Libris, Helsinki, 1934," *Numbers* (Paris, 1934), No. 10, pp. 289–290.
2. *The Russian Word* (Warsaw–Vilno), February 24, 1938.
3. See his article on the poetry of Bulich in *The Latest News* (No. 6255), dated May 12, 1938.
4. A reference to Lermontov's poem "The Pine Tree."
5. "Precision, clarity, and simplicity are salient characteristics of her book." *Soviet Patriot*, No. 158, dated October 31, 1947.
6. An obvious reference to the First and Second Workshops of Poets in Petersburg during the 1920s, as well as to the "Guild of Poets" in Estonia in the 1930s.
7. A lecture presented by V. S. Bulich, January 21, 1937, in Helsingfors at the literary–art society "Svetlitsa" (Tower Chamber).

The archival materials of Vera Bulich were made available to me through the courtesy of the Library of Helsinki.

SAVOLAINEN, JUHANI
(literary psuedonym Ivan Savin; 1899–1927)

"He was," according to Yu. Ivask, "a poet of white dreams." Ivan Savin, born in a distant rural town in the Poltava province of the Ukraine, was the son of a notary.   Ivan joined General Denikin's army as a volunteer in 1919 and served in the Twelfth Uhlan Belgorod Regiment.   His elder brothers, Mikhail and Pavel, and the younger ones, Nikolay and Boris, also joined the White Army as volunteers.   Mikhail and Pavel were killed in a battle; Nikolay and Boris were shot by the Bolsheviks. Sick with typhus, Ivan was taken prisoner of war by the Red Army in the Crimea.

But toward the end of 1921 he managed, with great difficulty, to reach St. Petersburg. From there, in 1922, he escaped and joined his parents in Finland. In Finland he worked as a laborer, but he also wrote and contributed to many Russian émigré newspapers and journals, such as *Today, Field Flowers, Chimes, Russia Illustrated,* and *The Journal of Concord.* He also published, at his own expense, a Russian literary journal *Parus* (The Sail) and was its sole editor. It was not until 1923 that he began to write serious works; these were about Russia, his love for the country, and the catastrophe of 1917. As a consequence of his war injuries and tuberculosis, Savin spent many months in a hospital until he died in Finland at a very young age.

Like many of his contemporaries, Savin had witnessed the destruction and violence of the revolution in Russia before he left for exile in the West. His story "Drôle," though couched in humor, reveals the anguish over the loss of human values and the traditions of the past. The same is true of his poem, "A canary bird, geraniums . . . , " where a painful nostalgic longing for the simple things of old Russian life haunts the poet who fled to Finland. But the images are of violence. The years of what could have been Russia's future have been cut down like a forest, leaving only the undergrowth of a few outer forms. The writer, who lived through the period of arbitrary shooting, describes his own soul as "executed," dead, although his physical form continues to live. "Jealousy," on the other hand, is a delightful poetic joke—a conversation between a miller-dreamer and a little jealous girl in love with him.

Savin was an excellent stylist, musician, painter, and actor. He glorified the White Army's desperate military opposition against the Bolsheviks. Both his fiction and his poetry were highly valued in his new homeland and in the Baltic countries densely populated with Russian nationals forced into exile by the unsettling events in their own country. His poetry lacks all patriotic clamor and sentimentality, for Savin is not concerned with political acts and facts *per se.* Instead, he presents his themes in the form of a spiritual pilgrimage, a portrayal of the soldiers and officers of the White Army in moments of heightened spiritual awareness as they fight Bolshevism with its political despotism and physical violence. Savin's lyrics are rich in images, yet he remains economical in his descriptions. Wtih a few strokes and subtle nuances he creates expressive, meaningful pictures. An ardent admirer of Pushkin, he

planned to write a novel about Pushkin's epoch. He also hoped to
visit Egypt and India to study the local history and mythology in
order to integrate this knowledge into his poetry, music, and
painting.

   Savin's poetry was published shortly before his death in
Ladonka: stikhi (Amulet: Poems; Belgrade: Izd. Glavnoe Pravlenie
Gallipoliyskogo ob-va, 1926). A second edition appeared in 1958
(New York: Izd. Pereklichka). For a further discussion of Savin,
see Xenia Denikin's article "Ivan Savin," *The New Russian Word*
(New York, July 12, 1957). Ivan Bunin commended the
originality, poignancy of feeling, beauty, and tragic power of Savin's
poetry, especially the lines written in the solemn Old Church Slavic
vocabulary:

> "Remember all the murdered ones, Russia,
> When Thou reachest Thy kingdom..."

---·---

Amulet (1926)

A canary bird, geraniums,
Pink calico in the window,
A creaky sofa in oil cloth,
On the wall *The Isle of the Dead*.

Affected laughter, the rosy
Priest's daughter in a blue dress,
The copper sheen of a samovar.
And last year's issue of *The Fields*.

The thunderous music of winter Sundays,
A beribboned chestnut braid,
Waltzing *pas de trois* to the "Autumn Dream,"
And card games on Monpassier—
All of this age-old undergrowth
Of madly felled years,
With every thought I kiss
This trampled trace of Russia.

Like the blooming of a distant childhood,
Like dew from the Lord's garden,
Like a mother's blessing
I carry this in my executed soul.

And the more repulsive, the more deceptive
The present day, the more I treasure
The dead truth of geraniums,
And the shimmer of felled years.

———————·———————

Jealousy

The little girl asked softly:
"O miller, what makes you so sad?"
Outside the door lay fields of grain
And heavy, heavy silence.

Her eyes quivered and flashed blue
Above the closed book.
"I dream of a beautiful fairy,
The queen of the mountain lakes."

The dulcet call of a nightingale,
Dew falling from the leaves,
"What is she like, this royal lady?
And does she have long braids?"

"The queen has most illustrious eyes—
Which captivate you in a single glance.
Her long braids are of pure gold,
A golden billow to her knees."

And the child said, tugging
At her own little black braid:
"In love with a redheaded fairy—
Isn't that just great!"

———————·———————

Experiments, No. 1 (1953)

"Ivan Savin began writing at the age of twenty-two. 'Drôle' was one of his first stories. Although it was written thirty-one years ago, the story has neither faded nor aged. When reading it, one has the impression that the action takes place not after the First World War, but during the Second.

Savin died at a young age, before he was twenty-eight. His biography is simple and tragic. He was born in September 1899 in the city of Akhtyrka. He graduated from the *gymnasium* during the Revolution and immediately joined the Volunteer Army. He was taken prisoner by the Bolsheviks and sentenced to be shot. With the aid of a soldier he managed to escape, and in 1921 he came to Finland. He spent his first year of freedom in a hospital, and it is during this period that his short literary career began. In the course of five years, Savin contributed to Russian émigré newspapers, wrote the long narrative 'Captivity,' 'Essays on [the concentration camp] Solovki' for the Archives of the Russian Revolution ('Solovki' was translated into Polish, Finnish, and English), three plays and several books of poetry. Shortly before his death in 1927, he began work on a major novel about Pushkin.

Savin thought and wrote only of Russia. It is difficult to predict what his creative contributions might have been had he lived longer. Would he have become a great writer? In any case, he had a genuine talent.

T. T."[1]

———————·———————

Drôle

(From a Book of the Past)

He was incredibly fat and so nearsighted that when he bumped into a kiosk plastered with posters or into a telegraph pole, he would take off his hat and mutter apologies. Once, when riding his bicycle, he ran into a herd of cows ambling along the street. Rubbing his injured knee, he said in embarrassment, "For God's sake, excuse me, gentlemen. Believe me, I really did not mean to."

He waddled from side to side, like a duck. He spoke in a ridiculous tenor—it always seemed as if a loosely-stretched string was buzzing in an empty keg.

In the evenings, at the Department of Public Education where he was in charge of some section or other and where he lived in a dark storeroom—while the crowd of young ladies in their twice-altered dresses were dispersing for home—he would sit a long time at the rickety piano, picking out melancholy melodies to the verses of Hoffmann, which he knew by heart.

This blatant incongruity—the bald head on the fat and flabby and, to all appearances, drowsy body, and the fragile, delicately ringing lines of the court poet—made the Department of Public Education clerks in their thrice-altered service jackets laugh until they cried. The registrar Kuvshinkin, the town wit, would even say that Hoffmann had sent a telegram from the other world, begging that his memory be spared posthumous mockery.

His surname was the most ordinary—Prokopenko. Such prematurely obese, clumsy, bashfully good-natured people inhabit our sunny land in great numbers.

His given name and patronymic Sergey Grigoryevich were also undistinguished. But once the wife of the prominent contractor Nagorny, a vivacious music-hall singer from Lyon who had known Sergey Grigoryevich in the days when he was a member of the circuit court, said within everyone's hearing, clasping her hands artlessly:

"*Mais comme il est drôle, cet homme-là!*

From that time on, whether because he truly was comical, or because of the provincial weakness for the French "dialect," the nickname Drôle firmly attached itself to Prokopenko. Even the street urchins, having learned the meaning of a new word with the gracious assistance of that same Kuvshinnikov, sang out from every crossroad:

Drôle, Drôle, drolly Drôle
Potbellied bean...

Besides his bald pate and his bashful inclination to play music, Drôle also had an enormous, overly impetuous heart. One might imagine that in this heart, this foolish heart, little pieces of wax were stuck together, not with wax but with an old tangy wine; too easily intoxicated, his heart melted,

covering his rotund cheeks with a very young, passionate
blush.

Drôle had been in love sixteen times. Sixteen times he
had picked out a melancholy melody to Hoffmann's "Infanta."
Sixteen women had laughed at him, each passing on to the
next, as a sort of inheritance, the beautiful heart of the
bald-headed Drôle. The indefatigable Kuvshinnikov had told
sixteen anecdotes to the young ladies from the Department of
Public Education in their twice-altered dresses.

For the seventeenth and final time, this dear, funny,
nearsighted Drôle flung his nearsighted heart at the feet of
Elena Den.

Many charming faces were seen in the land now lost;
many were dreamed about in the fragrant darkness of our
native gardens. But such monumental beauty, so intoxicating
a smile on crimson lips, such incredibly radiant eyes have
never yet been seen, neither in waking, nor in delirium.
Whenever Elena Den, artfully draping her shoulders with her
hair the color of ancient gold, would burst into laughter like
a melodious reed pipe, for some reason one felt like crying
long and silently, to flood this unbearable beauty with large
tears. To make it fade, this too alluring beauty, one felt like
carrying it far, far away, like veiling it, hiding this starry gift
God gave to the dark earth...

Is it any wonder that Drôle flung himself completely at
this seventeenth and final love?

Elena Den was surrounded by a noisy retinue of young
people—former officers, former students, all kinds of "former"
people—clerks, registrars, and office workers from seven
institutions.

According to the established etiquette, created in jest
yet strictly adhered to, someone from the retinue, by
appointment of Her Highness, was daily in attendance upon
the "Queen." The one on duty was dispatched to
innumerable queues, scrubbed floors in the Red Army
barracks for the "Queen," announced new decrees, safeguarded
the apartment form "densification" by new occupants, and
listened to the wistful little songs of Vertinsky which she sang
superbly.

Somehow it turned out that Drôle served the beautiful
Elena more often than all the others. With equal joy,

almost with ecstasy, he shovelled the snow in front of her apartment, applauded Vertinsky's aching melancholy, and stood for hours in Shop No. 7 where Elena received her ration.

To his face she called him "my faithful page"; behind his back—"that bald-headed fool." The bald-headed fool served his seventeenth and final love probably better than the most ideal, medieval knight. He served, knowing that he was throwing away his aging tenderness to get absolutely nothing in return. The only time he was not boring was when he used his youthful ardent fingers to play Scriabin, Rachmaninoff, and Medtner on Elena's great-grandmother's piano, which had miraculously escaped nationalization. He played with compelling intensity, in no amateur fashion rendering all the nuances and peculiarities of the modern music. Beyond this, he was insignificant, uncommunicative, and perhaps even pathetic.

They made fun of Drôle in town. Elena would respond to every joke, often coarse, coming from her court with an inviting laugh, thus augmenting the hidden suffering of her faithful page.

"Drôle, kiss my hand!" she'd say capriciously, the astonishing blue seas of her eyes sparkling.

Drôle would jump up impetuously, but the shapely hand would hide itself in Elena's Turkish shawl.

"How funny you are, Drôle...First cry a little, and then you may kiss..."

His face twitched for a long time, his eyes blinked absurdly, but there were no tears.

"I can't. Ask me to do anything but cry. I've tried..."

Affecting great sympathy, one of her attendants slapped him on the shoulder and advised him to go on stage:

"You know, they'll teach you how to cry in a jiffy there...then you'll be kssing the queen's hands all the time..."

And Elena, putting her golden head on her small palm, would laugh, such an unbearably beautiful laugh, that one wanted to cry. Not because of the hands, but just because...One wanted to cry out of impotent and pointless tenderness...

When shells began to whine above the frightened city, when every place was pelted with rapid machine gun fire,

Drôle, of course, was in Den's small apartment, crammed with furniture. Standing at the window, he would report to Elena:

"This morning there was an intelligence officer of theirs...of the Germans...a Ukrainian Cossack, with a forelock on his shaven head...He said that they would enter the town tonight for sure. There's panic among the Bolsheviks..."

Vishnyakov, a former captain and now an engineer in the Finance Department, raised his meticulously groomed head and asked sarcastically:

"Aren't you afraid, Drôle?"

"Of what?"

"Of getting shot. You know, it's scary. They might even kill you, eh? You'd better come away from the window. You're much too visible a target."

Drôle opened the window and leaned out, resting his elbow in the window sill.

Elena raised her eyebrows coquettishly.

"Drôle, please take a stroll to the cathedral and back and calculate for me the approximate frequency of the German artillery fire."

Vishnyakov shouted after him:

"Hurry and do it! You'll get the St. George medal..."

The sky seethed like an enormous cauldron, stirred up by the rumbling of the guns. Every minute the pavement shuddered. Somewhere very near, beyond the muddy river, rifles cracked, emitting, along with the whistling bullets, a thousand-voiced echo. The smoke drifted low. The street was deserted and quiet, as if it were four in the morning. Now and then Red Army soldiers sped past on exhausted horses—their headquarters had already been evacuated two days before—and a dog with a broken paw limped along behind them.

Drôle, hatless, his teeth tightly clenched, turned the corner toward the cathedral, which shone white in the distance. A shell landed dully near the bakery with its bobbing pretzel sign.

It didn't explode immediatley, seemingly thinking—is it worth making so much noise for the sake of a lousy pretzel? Then it burst with a metallic ringing and hurled into the air a part of the wooden sidewalk, a corner of a house, rocks, and fragments of the pretzel sign. A dog dashed out of the way with a yelp, past Drôle, who was covered with a fine dust.

A distraught woman appeared in the window of a neighboring house. She motioned with her head and shouted through the window:

"Sergey Grigoryevich, are you out of your mind?!"

"I am..." Drôle answered confusedly, making his way toward the cathedral.

On the walk back the artillery fire was less intense, but the hurricane of machine gun fire lashed the air with extraordinary force. Apparently, the forces of the invaders were drawing toward the center. A stream of bullets poured down the street, wailing thinly.

Only by chance could one avoid this rain, and Drôle wandered aimlessly, tucking his head into the collar of his jacket remade from a uniform.

In the yawning gap, where the bakery had been, stood a mounted Red Army soldier. He looked Drôle over curiously and stopped him.

"You fed up with life or something, wandering around here like this? Take off your boots! Got a watch?"

Drôle sat down on the splintered edge of the sidewalk and lifted up his foot. His nearsighted eyes gleamed with a strange, flickering joy. His left hand was removing his boot; his right stroked the crumbled pieces of brick.

"Well, it's plain to see you're a 'holy fool'...Go home, brother, or else they'll kill you for sure," the horseman said and, crouching over the saddle, he galloped uphill.

Elena met Drôle with a smile of amazement. Did it only seem so, or was there really fear in the corners of her incomparable eyes when she asked standing at the door:

"Are you alive? I was so worried...You poor thing..."

Drôle went up to her, embarrassed.

"Twenty-nine shots...in ten minutes...They must be six-inch guns."

He sat down in the arm chair and began to smoke, clenching and unclending the fingers of his left hand.

He had never had this habit before, this feverish movement of his short, crackling fingers. On that same day former captain Vishnyakov informed Elena's retinue of the old fool's ridiculous habit, of how he played frantic melodies on his jacket remade from a uniform while Elena was talking to him.

A week later Elena was galloping in a man's saddle alongside an unnaturally well-built German lieutenant. With unblinking eyes, Drôle followed the delicate whip in the delicate hand, the rye-colored lock beneath the blue veil. The gold and blue patches flowed together into an iridescent circle, and the fingers of Drôle's left hand wanted to convey something important to the moist glass on which he was playing out his melody.

When the red-haired colonel in yellow leggings and with an Iron Cross haughtily sticking out on his chest, who knew only one phrase in Russian—"Whip him!"—waltzed with Elena at the club, and when her tiny feet would gracefully glide to the rumbling music of the Bavarian orchestra, Drôle, tormented, would sigh heavily in the next room, peering nearsightedly through the open door. And the fingers of his left hand tapped just as feverishly against the tattered cloth of the billiard table...

In early spring, right after the withdrawal of the German troops and the Hetman's regiment, Elena was arrested for collaboration with German counterintelligence and for military espionage.

The charges were nonsense from beginning to end. But could "her faithful knight" leave any stone unturned in the Special Department,[2] pleading for clemency, even if a deserved punishment should befall the girl with the unforgettable eyes? Or could he, having achieved nothing, refrain from writing to the Revolutionary Tribunal that he, Drôle, was an agent of German counterintelligence and a spy, that he had persuaded Elena to take the blame upon herself, thinking that they would spare her, a woman...

Foolish, affectionate Drôle, unable to speak German and fearing like death any kind of political game; Drôle, in love with his queen and with Hoffmann...

During Shrovetide, on a dark, stormy night, Elena Den was shot. Drôle was also shot, for complicity and for repenting too late.

In prison, he surrounded Elena with such anguished attention, such anxious love, that former captain Vishnyakov, a witness in the Den case and likewise sentenced to be shot, talked to him in their bullet-scarred prison cell. Opening his mouth with difficulty, for it had been smashed during his interrogation, Vishnyakov said:

"Drôle, you have a magnanimous soul...You have the heart of a hero, Drôle... Maybe it is only my delirium...my head aches so...can it be that you are a saint? And we laughed at you...we...it is an honor for me to know you, Drôle..."

Nine others were led out along with them on that dark night. On each one's shoulder there was a shovel; in each one's eyes there flashed the glazed look of horror...barefooted, their heads uncovered...

Drôle carried two shovels, his own and Elena's, and he dug a grave for two. Her face distorted, Elena squeezed his throat with both hands, making it hard for him to dig the frozen earth. Drôle swayed a little and whispered, singing a lullaby in his ridiculous tenor—for the last time the string buzzed in the empty barrel:

"How can you really be afraid, my little girl?...Is it really necessary!... I love you... I am here, with you..."

Four bullets cut into Drôle with a short thump. He was able to balance himself above the grave, shielding the panic-stricken Elena. The fifth bullet toppled him into the pit. The sixth bullet shattered Elena's elbow, the seventh—her head...

The echo reverberated in the empty distance. The Red Army soldier standing nearest lifted his rifle and with all his might hurled the butt agains the rye-colored hair.

"Go on and croak! Howl, will you..."

And, turning his head away, he asked angrily:

"Is that it?..."

———————·———————

Savin writes in a straightforward manner, avoiding stylistic embellishments. If his style seems weak at times, it is the result, no doubt, of the author's youth and inexperience. Savin wrote the story when he was only twenty-two or twenty-three.

Drôle is initially presented in the manner of a caricature, as the incarnation of inadequacy: fat, nearsighted, clumsy, foolish (he apologizes to telegraph poles and cows). With a ridiculous voice and a waddle like a duck, he seems to be a ludicrous character indeed. But then the representative function of the portrait becomes clear when the reader is told that "Such prematurely obese, clumsy, bashfully good-natured people inhabit our sunny land in great numbers." Gradually the reader is led to feel more sympathy and respect for Drôle until he becomes the tragic hero of a story and no longer comical. Even Elena, his ideal of beauty and perfection—her name is not accidental—who always laughs at him and initially is the stronger of the two, is presented as weak and dependent at the end. The leitmotif characterizing Drôle throughout the story is his "enormous, overly impetuous heart." The change in the description of his heart between the beginning and the end of the story determines the change in one's attitude toward Drôle. At the beginning Savin writes humorously, "One might imagine that in the heart, this foolish heart, little pieces of wax were stuck together, not with wax but with an old, tangy wine; too easily intoxicated, his heart melted, covering his rotund cheeks with a very young, passionate blush." By the end of the story, Vishnyakov, who had previously laughed at Drôle, tells him that he has "the heart of a hero" and wonders "can it be that you are a saint?"

Thus, what begins as the burlesque story of a pathetic man changes into a dramatic tale of strength and courage. The earlier knightly metaphors no longer seem ridiculous, as the reader perceives that Drôle is indeed a man of unusual qualities and not just a fool desperately in love with an unattainable woman. The turning point comes when the soldier finds Drôle walking unarmed through a hail of bullets and calls him a "holy fool." The image of the cathedral, "which shone white in the distance," serves to heighten the effect of saintliness. Drôle must be either a fool or a saint, and the moment of his death ultimately reveals which. Significantly, the execution takes place during Shrovetide, and the narrator remarks that, in addition to Drôle and Elena, nine other people were shot, a total of eleven. Eleven, of course, is the fool's number traditionally associated with Shrovetide celebrations, and the author's ironic intentions are obvious. At carnival time people are allowed, for a short time, to act out their true natures, fools become sages and sages behave like fools, and at the masquerade at the end of the novella the executioners are clearly to be seen as the criminals, whereas the condemned civilians, especially Drôle, triumph as morally superior to the judges.

The pronounced irony and humor in the narration initially distract the reader; the story's essentially tragic nature is not immediately perceived. There is humor in the diction ("the French dialect," instead of "language"; the "young ladies in their twice-altered dresses," the clerks "in their thrice-altered service jackets"), and in the absurdity of some situations. There is even a subtle joke in the narrator's seeming confusion over the name of the town wit first referred to as "Kuvshinkin" and later as "that same Kuvshinnikov" (meaning "waterlily" and "ewer," respectively). The author creates an ironic distance between himself and his characters through the use of courtly images and exaggerated romantic clichés and epithets. This is particularly evident in his description of Elena's incomparable and "unbearable" beauty—"the rye-colored hair," "so intoxicating a smile on crimson lips," her "laughter like a melodious reed pipe." But by the end the realities of war and death have overcome the ironic narrative style, and the story is perceived finally as a deeply serious and moving account.

One could argue that Drôle is in fact an ironic symbol for the Russian people as a whole, representing their naïveté, romantic sentimentality, ineffectualness, and suffering, but also their fidelity, love, and moral courage. Elena may be interpreted as a symbolic personification of Russia the beautiful.

Like her classical namesake, Elena is coveted by various parties. As consequence of her flirtations with enemy officers, her lightheartedness, and disloyalty, and because she is primarily interested in gratifying her own wishes and vanity, she loses out in the end, and old Russia dies with her. But Drôle's unfailing solidarity with his ideal lends a note of tragic dignity and moral optimism.

NOTES

1. Identity unknown.
2. The Cheka, or secret police.

VADIM GARDNER (1880-1956)

Vadim Gardner was one of those few poets who could write verse in two languages—in his case, in Russian and in English.

His father, Daniel Thomas Gardner, was an American engineer; his mother, Ekaterina Ivanovna Dykhova, was a Russian fiction writer and a businesswoman in St. Petersburg. Vadim Gardner was born in Viipuri, Finland, and educated in St. Petersburg. He descended from a very unusual family. His father was the son of Daniel Pereira Gardner, author of books on chemistry and medicine. Vadim's grandfather, the court physician of Brazilian Emperor Don Pedro I, married into the celebrated de Paiva Pereira family of Portugal. Vadim's mother, the daughter of General Dykhov, after completion of her education at the Kazan' Institute for Noble Girls, went in 1871 to St. Petersburg to meet Emperor Alexander II personally to seek his permission to study medicine at the Medical Academy of St. Petersburg. The Emperor, who spent one and a half hours with her, kindly advised her that a university would shortly be established for Russian women and that she would be its first candidate. Not wishing to wait, the young Dykhova went by herself (an unheard-of thing in Russia at the time!) to the United States to study medicine. There, still a student, she met her future husband, married him, and brought him with her to St. Petersburg. Back in Russia, she wrote novels—which were very popular at that time—and articles, which she contributed to A. K. Sheller-Mikhaylov's journal *Delo* (The Enterprise) and to the Brockhaus-Efron Encyclopedia, did translations, and, together with Anna Pavlovna Filosofova,[1] championed equal rights for women, such as admission to Russian universities and participation in the political and social activities of the nation. She attended various international conferences and congresses concerning equal rights for women.

Mrs. Gardner described her lengthy meeting with Alexander II in the St. Petersburg Summer Garden in the journals *Istorichesky Vestnik* (The Historical Herald) and *Rukssky Arkhiv* (The Russian Archives).[2]

The Gardner family in St. Petersburg was related to the talented Russian novelist, Maria V. Krestovskaya-Kartavtseva, the daughter of the fiction writer Vsevolod V. Krestovsky, who authored the famous Russian novel *Petersburgskie trushchoby* (St. Petersburg Slums, 1867).

Vadim studied law at St. Petersburg University, but was unable to complete his studies due to his expulsion from the University as a result of his involvement in the 1905 uprising. He was imprisoned for two months, then released and allowed to study at the University in Tartu. During World War I, in 1916, Gardner applied for Russian citizenship, and was sent for two years to London to work under General Gedrojc on the Committee for Supplying Arms to the Allied Forces. In the Spring of 1918, together with the poet Nikolay Gumilyov, Gardner returned to St. Petersburg on a military transport. In 1921, he fled from the Bolsheviks to Finland, where his mother owned a small estate in Vammelsuu on the Carelian Isthmus. After the Soviet-Finnish War of 1939, Gardner moved to Helsinki where he died in 1956.

Vadim Gardner's volume *Stikhotvoreniya: sbornik pervy* (Poems: A First Collection, St. Petersburg: Braude & Co., 1908) opened to him the doors of several literary salons, among them the famous "Tower" of Vyacheslav Ivanov. After Gardner's book of verse, *Ot zhizni k zhizni* (From Life to Life; Moscow: Al'tsion, 1912) came out, he became a member of the Acmeist "Tsekh Poetov" (The Workshop of Poets) in St. Petersburg. He published a few poems in the journal *Hyperboreus*,[3] and some others in *Russkaya Mysl'* (Russian Thought).[4] *From Life to Life* was reviewed by the poets Mikhail Lozinsky[5] and Sergey Gorodetsky.[6] Nikolay Gumilyov mentioned it in *Apollon* (Apollo),[7] and Alexander Blok discussed it briefly in another literary journal.[8]

Gardner's third volume of poems, *Pod dalyokimi zvyozdami: stikhotvoreniya* (Under the Distant Stars: Poems),[9] reveals his continuing devotion to the ideals of Beauty and Harmony and his constant nostalgia. His poems are written in a cultured, restrained, transparent, poetic language.

Vadim Gardner also contributed to *Yakor': antologiya zarubezhnoy poezii* (The Anchor: An Anthology of Poetry in Exile)[10] and *Rossija: Anthologie* (Russia: An Anthology),[11] the latter appearing in the German language.

Vadim Gardner knew the French, English, German, Greek, and Latin languages, and was an expert in Greek mythology and Slavic philology. He was brought up in the best Russian, West European, American, Roman, and Greek cultural traditions. Well versed in music, he was able to use it for his varied rhythmical patterns in versification.   His poetry is mystical, romantic, and religious in its essence.   His imagery often contains whimsical combinations, like the *saraband* of apparitions, similar to those fantasies of Hieronymus Bosch, or abstract currents in the universe, far away from the world of finite experience.   Romantic reveries and resplendent hopes and aspirations also appear in his verse.   He wrote sonnets, ballads, poems in *terza rima*, long poems, chain strophes, Sapphic strophes, rondels, and so forth.

The formal characteristics of Gardner's poetry include collision of images, unexpected turns of thought, expressive, novel epithets, and a free play of poetic imagination.   The main force of his work lies in its bright coloring, impetuosity of inner movement, and ecstatic religious transports.   Concrete, visual details are organically fused with lively fantasy.   The simplicity and lucidity of his style harmonize with solemn, Hellenic, or even ecclesiastical elements.

Gardner availed himself of varied forms of versification. Among octaves, which he often used for portraying elegiac experiences and a philosophical, contemplative vision of the world in all of its poetic manifestations, his favorite was *Ciciliana*, an old Italian octave originating, as its name suggests, in Sicily.   Its marked characteristic is the presence of two rhymes (in pure octave, there are three), alternating throughout the verse.   One of them is feminine; the other, masculine.   Gardner also used *Ciciliana* with feminine rhymes only.   In his poetry, we also find the so-called Spenser strophe, invented by the English poet Edmund Spenser (1553-1599), which has three rhymes, in eight lines of iambic pentameter, and is followed by one rhyme in the ninth, Alexandrian verse (iambic hexameter), with compulsory crossing in the middle.

The technique of *trochaic gloss* was employed by Vadim Gardner in those of his poems where he used Lermontov's or Pushkin's strophes as an underlying idea and a rhythmical basis for his own poem (see, for example, Lermontov's "On the ethereal ocean..." and Gardner's "Do you remember the foam and the surf?").   The concluding lines of Gardner's four *decimas* form the four trochaic initial lines from Lermontov, taken by Gardner as the gloss.   Each line in Lermontov's strophe, in exact sequence, forms the last line of Gardner's *decima*.   In each *decima* the final rhyme coincides with the ending of the last strophe in the poem.

Gardner also excelled in the poetic form of *rondeau*, in both its simple and complex forms (iambic pentameter and hexameter), in which the final line of each strophe repeats, one by one, the lines of the initial quatrain.   There are two rhymes: feminine and masculine.   All strophes have the same number of lines and are equal in their "crossing" arrangement of rhymes.   Often, the *refrain*, taken from the first line of the initial strophe, appears at the end of the final verse.

Vadim Gardner was a careful and skilled technician in versification, as were all the poets of the St. Petersburg school during the Silver Age of Russian poetry.   He translated into English four chapters of Pushkin's novel in verse, *Eugene Onegin*, remaining close to the rhythmical structure and poetic imagery of the original language.   With the same poetic expressiveness and precision, he translated several poems of Lermontov into English. Wishing to enrich English poetry, he strove to acquaint the English-speaking reader with the spirit of the Russian poetic creations.

Examples of Gardner's poetry follow.

Solitude

Here, in this seclusion,
I see with sadness that
There is no single soul responding to mine...
A lonely poet, here I create.
Of what concern am I to all these people?
My sorrows, my flame,
My aspirations upward—what are they to them?
All that is left to me is—to rise to the stars!
I am encircled all around
By icy indifference.
A lonely poet, I create, but
There is no response to my heart.[12]

December 12, 1925

A later sonnet also reveals the *persona*'s loneliness and his awareness of futility and impotence.

Oh haughty Helsinki, a favorite of winds,
Remote you are to me.
I roam about your streets and squares.
But you, with your two languages,
Are alien to me: these separate us like a wall.
Your cold beauty does not attract me.
I feel I am an uninvited and useless eccentric here,
With thoughts and feelings so irrelevant to yours.
Although in the past your granite captivated me,
When in the capital [St. Petersburg], it no longer lures,
After my heart has felt the spiteful cold
Of your race, inimical to us of Russia.
The cruel silence of your rocks
Does not engender sympathy in my heart,
Symbol of your soul. Closed to us, you repulse me.

Helsinki, 1942

Don't Sting Me, Oh Wasp!

Don't sting me, oh wasp!
I have been stung by life, without you,
I regret too many things,
I have known of too much grief,
Of pain, illness, and chains,
While quarreling with our impoverished century
Within the depths of my soul.
It is time that the sky pleases me
And enlivens my reserves.
But some demon malevolently
Muddles my spring of inspiration.
I was born at the tumultuous time
Of revolts and changes,
Into this godless and violent century
Whose seal is death and corruption—
Into this age of conceit and vulgarity,
Into this age of pretentiousness,
Into this age of cruel tyranny and crucified Beauty.

But the spaciousness of the Spirit is eternal,
And neither the chaos,
Nor the triumph of falsity,
Will affect my awareness of the All.

Helsinki, 1943

Ciciliana

Dull autumn, you plunge me
Into the harmonious rhythm of my Cicilianas.
When the leaves fall onto the earth,
When the mist hovers around,
When the clouds are grey,
My drowsy reveries are melancholy;
And when some indistinct chimeras confuse my mind,
A Muse of beauty
Commands me to observe the laws of graceful moderation.

1942

Triolet

I passionately love the fragrance
Of your flowers, mignonette.
A delicate dream,
Your flowers' aroma.
It entices and bewitches me.
The enchantments of my past are always in your bouquet.
I passionately love the fragrance
Of your flowers, mignonette.

1942

From the Cycle, the Diary of a Poet

With my shovel, I slice
My way through the snow
And sit down to rest beneath some old windfallen trees.
Draped in snow, the forest around me slumbers.
It stands in drowsing, enveloped by a dream of crystal.
See the white-mustached grove of fir,
Enchanting, like a Christmas fairy tale, it dozes.
Everything around is covered with winter's silver mask.
It begins to snow. I catch a flake.
The snow rustles. No wind. The winter darkness
Shows blue. How beautiful it is in the forest!
How pure the air! Christmas has come.

                              Metsäkylä, Finland, 1929

Of the Soil and of the Sun...

A man
Of the soil, of the sun, and of the moon
I reveal our age
With my many-stringed lyre.
The heart of the soil
Can be felt in my poetry,
The sap of the trees
Can be perceived in the rhythm of my metre.
The luminous verse
Absorbs in its words
The radiance of the bright luminary
And warms.
The ruby of the silent moon,
Silver, gold,
And wisdom are displayed in my strophes.
I, man of the soil, of the sun, and of the stars,
Sing,
Glorify the sapphire abysses of
My native land.

                              Metsäkylä, Finland, 1929

The following poems are from a collection of Vadim Gardner's early poetry, written in English.

I am in Russia

I am in Russia. For Russia, I mourn
And I love Her, for here was I born.

Full of grief is Her changeable fate;
For Her sufferings I love her, the Great.

Oh! This drunk, martyred land of my birth;
Yet, in the future, the Eden on earth.

And with Her whom I love and condole
Am I sharing the sparks of my soul.

Thee, o Russia, I thank for Thy bread,
For, half Russian, in Thee was I bred.

Thou hast taught me to pray and to woe,
Lays of love for Thee, o Mother, I owe.

How they pain me, Thy church bells that toll,
Yet at daybreak they gladden the soul.

Things ineffable, church bells that ring,
All that trembles on Easter in spring—

I do tenderly love. I was born
Here in Russia. For Russia, I mourn.

St. Petersburg, 1918

I wait and wait for Thee, o my Salvation,
And for Love's tidings from the source of Lights.
What's life to me without regeneration,
Without new strength from spiritual heights?

The source of time, like any other motion,
The might of silence and the soul's repose—
All this is vain without the heart's devotion
To God, whose guidance I forever chose.

Metsäkylä, Finland, 1921

Distichs

Many moments have passed miraculous, beautiful, charming,
Many tears have I shed, many times have I loved.

Bypass the hours, they flee. Who knows what may happen
    tomorrow?
Onward the river of Time, secretly, restlessly flows.

Often so near to me seem the limits of Truth and Perfection.
And of the scintillant stars luminous tokens on high.

Often at night, the moon floats in azure and light
    snow-white, flaky
Clouds meet the silvery horns of the pale Huntress divine.

Finland, 1921

See! The sun of September is glowing,
And the leaves of the maples are red,
And within me a gladness is growing.
There is no trace of the tears that I shed.
And so joyful my heart is that surely
There's no brighter, no loftier mirth.
So profoundly I love and so purely
All that's lovable, sacred on earth.
And it seems that I have penetrated
The most secret recesses of the soul,
The great mysteries God hath created,
That all sufferers I now can console.

And it seems all within and all round us
Hath been built by the Master All-Wise,
That His love to the Cosmos hath bound us,
That all winds with the Spirit advise.

Metsäkylä, Finland, 1921

The charm of thine autumnal eyes
I love like clouds in the skies.
To me their wandering fancy seems
A chain of vague reflected dreams.
In their blue mist I've often caught
The bitterness of mournful thought.
I love thy dark thick eyebrows' wing,
Thy noble longing sad and calm.
Of thy red lips I love the spring
And thy trustworthy tender arm,
Thy feelings gentle and humane,
Expressed in all thy features sweet.
Thou hast endured grief, suffering, pain,
Thy kindness deep my feelings greet.
Though hardened in life's heavy fight,
Thy soul conceals soft beams of light.
With thee, my Love, with thee alone,
The fullness of the world I own,
The stars' celestial bliss and sights.
The charm of thine autumnal eyes
I love like clouds in the skies.

Mesäkylä, Finland, 1920

Devoted to ideals of Truth, Christian Goodness, and Beauty, Gardner wished to appear in his poetry as an apostle of Faith and human dignity, as one having hope in a spiritually rich future for mankind, and as one possessing that love which should bind all people together into one harmonious and intellectual whole. Disappointed, however, because these ideals could not be attained, he withdrew from his fellow man into himself, his poetic imagination, and the colorful and fragrant beauties of nature. Like

other profoundly cultured Russian poets of the Silver Age, he fled
from the everyday hubbub and trivia of his time. Until his death
in Helsinki in 1956, he was absorbed in his visionary conceptions of
the world, which he described as "fairy tales of Otherworldliness."

All of these materials, published and unpublished, were
graciously offered to me by the poet's widow, Mme Maria Gardner
of Helsinki, Finland. I wish to express here my deep gratitude to
her for her courtesy, as well as to Mr. Ben Hellman, who kindly
introduced me to the poetry of Vadim Gardner in the summer of
1987 in Helsinki.

NOTES

1. A. P. Filosofova (née Dyagileva, 1837–1912), a well-known social figure,
    stood at the head of the feminist movement in Russia in the nineteenth
    century. She carried on a personal correspondence with Turgenev and
    Dostoevsky, and both visited her in her St. Petersburg salon. She was
    Chairwoman of the Committee for the Creation of a Private Women's
    University in St. Petersburg. Courses were begun on January 30, 1872.
    The school was called Vladimirsky Women's University. Filosofova also
    started a medical unit and a savings association in her district. At the
    end of the 1870s the Russian government banished Filosofova to
    Germany, where she lived until February 1881. On her return to
    Russia she resumed her activities for women's equality. In 1899, in
    London, she was elected Vice-President of the International Women's
    Council. She went in 1903 to a women's conference in Geneva, and in
    April 1904, a celebration was held in St. Petersburg, marking her forty
    years of social work.

2. From a letter of Mrs. Ekaterina Gardner:
    ...In the Spring of 1871, I prevailed on the Emperor to meet
    with me to obtain from Him His personal permission to study at
    the Medical Academy. . . . I was admitted to entrance exam-
    inations at the Univerity of Moscow. With impatience I waited
    for the Sovereign's reply to my petition, submitted to Him
    personally one day after our meeting, concerning the admittance
    of women to medical education in Russia. At that time I was
    living in St. Petersburg and frequented the Sheller-Mykhaylovs.
    The Enterprise accepted my novel *On a New Road* (Na novom
    puti) for publication, and I passed my entrance examinations at
    the University. Toward the end of August, I received a letter
    from the Head of the Academy, Mr. Chistovich, that the question
    of medical courses for women would be considered shortly and
    that I would be the first candidate on the list of those who
    would be admitted. . . . His indefinite response I found
    unsatisfactory, and, in my eagerness to study, I immediately
    packed my suitcases and left for the United States. Upon my
    departure for America, I was asked to contribute to *Golos* (The
    Voice) and to *Delo* (The Enterprise), which I later did, writing

for these publications a column called "Letters from America about the Women's Movement in the United States."

My first letter from Philadelphia for *The Enterprise* was written of my impressions of the historic artifacts, dating from the time of the Revolution. I wrote, among other things, of the building where the Declaration of Independence was signed and proclaimed, and of the Liberty Bell (already cracked, but sometime ago loudly calling the people to unite in their struggle for independence). My letter also described the Second Congress of Women, which overwhelmed me with delight, as I became aware of that active propaganda which the women of the New World were engaged in. . . .

I bowed to Mr. Sheller–Mykhaylov at his grave site, with our deep Russian bow, bidding him my last "Farewell," for his unchangeable devotion to the women's cause, and for his profound, active sympathy with all the hungry and poor.

Ekaturna Ivanovna Gardner,
née Dykhova

3. No. 6 (1913).
4. Nos. 2 and 10 (1913).
5. *Hyperboreus*, No. 6 (1913).
6. *Rech'*, No. 48 (February 18, 1913).
7. No. 3 (1913).
8. Ref. R. D. Timenchik, "Zametki of Akmeizme" (Notes on Acmeism), *Russian Literature*, Nos. 7/8 (1974).
9. Paris: Concorde, 1929.
10. Berlin, 1936.
11. Berlin: Verlag E. Strache, 1920.
12. Vadim Gardner, *Pod dalyokmi zvyozdami: stikhotovoreniya* (Paris: Concorde, 1929).